BRINGING DOWN THE MOB

BRINGING DOWN THE
MOB

THE WAR AGAINST
THE AMERICAN MAFIA

Thomas A. Reppetto

A JOHN MACRAE / HOLT PAPERBACK
Henry Holt and Company   New York

Holt Paperbacks
Henry Holt and Company, LLC
Publishers since 1866
175 Fifth Avenue
New York, New York 10010
www.henryholt.com

Library of Congress Cataloging-in-Publication Data

Reppetto, Thomas A.
    Bringing down the mob : the war against the American Mafia / Thomas A. Reppetto.
        p.   cm.
    Includes bibliographical references and index.
    ISBN-13: 978-0-8050-8659-1
    ISBN-10: 0-8050-8659-5
        1. Mafia—United States.   2. Organized crime—United States.   3. Organized crime
investigation—United States.   I. Title.
    HV6446.R473 2006
    364.106'0973—dc22   2006043704

Originally published in hardcover in 2006 by
John Macrae / Henry Holt and Company

First Holt Paperbacks Edition 2009

Designed by Kelly Too

Printed in the United States of America

5   7   9   10   8   6   4

CONTENTS

. . . .

BRINGING DOWN THE MOB

INTRODUCTION:
THE AMERICAN MAFIA

Longtime business associates Allen Dorfman and Irwin Weiner frequently lunched together. On a day in January 1983, they emerged from Dorfman's Cadillac onto the icy parking lot of a suburban Chicago restaurant, ten minutes late for their one o'clock reservation. According to Weiner, they were walking between parked cars when two men ran up behind them and yelled, "This is a robbery." One of the men fired a .22 automatic at least half a dozen times. Only Dorfman was hit. He fell to the ground in a large pool of blood that quickly froze into red ice. When the paramedics arrived, he showed no signs of life.

At fifty-nine, Dorfman was a nationally known figure, and his death would be reported across the country. His murder was news, but it was not a surprise. He had been a key figure in the world of organized crime for more than thirty years. Beginning with Jimmy Hoffa, successive presidents of the International Brotherhood of Teamsters (IBT) had allowed him to use his position as head of the pension fund to provide sweetheart loans to mob figures, money that bankrolled the Mafia's control of several Las Vegas casinos. The union itself, which had access to top business leaders and politicians right up to the White House, was run as a virtual subsidiary of the American Mafia. A month before his murder, Dorfman, Teamsters president Roy Williams, and a top Chicago mob figure, Joe Lombardo, had been convicted of attempting to bribe U.S. senator Howard Cannon of Nevada. After his conviction in December 1982, Dorfman was released on $5 million bail pending sentencing. He stood to receive as much as fifty-five years in prison.

In addition to the bribery case, the government was also conducting an investigation of money skimming in mob-backed Vegas casinos. Dorfman knew the secrets of both the Teamsters and Vegas. If he decided to cut a deal with prosecutors, talking in return for a more lenient sentence, many gangsters—and supposedly legitimate businessmen and officials—would end up in prison. The head of the Chicago Crime Commission told *The New York Times*, "There's no doubt in my mind that Mr. Dorfman was killed to keep him quiet . . . if he ever coughed up to investigators . . . this country would be shaking for a month." Someone with access to the crime scene apparently decided to ensure that at least some of Dorfman's secrets did not die with him. He made a photocopy of the dead man's memo book and sent it to the Chicago Crime Commission.

Though he was only an associate member, Allen Dorfman's life provided a window into the world of the American Mafia at its highest levels. Beginning in 1949, it took him just five years to rise from physical education instructor to millionaire, thanks to Hoffa's largess and the connections of his racketeer stepfather, "Red" Dorfman. At the time of his death he headed a financial empire that included insurance companies, condominium developments, resorts, and other projects, and he maintained homes in four states. He was a major contributor to various charities and was frequently honored by civic associations. Yet over his career he had been denounced by congressional committees and constantly pursued by federal law enforcement officers. He was indicted on several occasions, though he usually managed to win acquittals. In 1972 he was convicted of conspiring to facilitate a loan from the Teamsters Pension Fund in return for a kickback of $55,000, but he served only nine months in jail.

After his latest conviction, Dorfman should have been wary of his former associates. He might have known that the bosses of the Chicago mob would be worried that a man long accustomed to the affluent life might not be able to face spending the rest of his days in prison. True, Dorfman had not rolled over following any of his previous arrests. But in the Mafia world that was irrelevant. Chicago mob bosses Joey Aiuppa and Jackie Cerone, who were also caught up in the Vegas skim, had followed very different paths from Dorfman's. Their rise to the top had been slow, prefaced by years spent doing the dirty work with guns and blackjacks. Unlike Dorfman, they could not pose as businessmen and civic benefactors. Instead, they lived by a hard code that mandated that all doubts must be resolved in favor of the organization. They could not take the chance that someone who had so much potential to hurt them would stay silent.[1] Since it was standard mob procedure to eliminate witnesses, Weiner's survival and his tale of attempted robbery caused some investigators to speculate that he had set Dorfman up.

The fact that Dorfman was not Italian had prevented him from becoming a "made" member of the Mafia. Still, he was well aware of its rules, though perhaps he did not think they applied to a big shot like him. The same lack of understanding had undoubtedly cost his old boss Jimmy Hoffa his life eight years earlier. Then again, a lot of people on both sides of the law had always found it hard to comprehend the culture of the American Mafia.

Books about mob life often end up on the true-crime shelves of bookstores, alongside biographies of serial killers and accounts of last year's "heist of the century." In some respects it is the appropriate place for the colorful criminals of the American Mafia. Each generation has brought forth an Al Capone, Lucky Luciano, Frank Costello, Sam Giancana, or John Gotti, all of whom have fascinated the public, as have their big and small screen counterparts: *Scarface, The Godfather,* and *The Sopranos.*

Yet the American Mafia is more than just another group of criminals. Since the 1920s it has been the heart and soul of American organized crime. As such it has exercised significant influence on the political and economic life of the country. In *American Mafia: A History of Its Rise to Power,* I told the story of the organization up to the early 1950s. I described how the Mafia managed to acquire all the trappings of an independent state, flouting the authority of the United States government. It promulgated its own laws, not infrequently imposing the death penalty; it even

1 At the time of his death, Dorfman had not made a deal with the government, but some people with knowledge of the case believe he was considering it.

maintained diplomatic relations with foreign countries, such as Cuba. And perhaps most critically, in both politics and business it managed to link the underworld to the upper world. That an organization that never had more than five thousand full-fledged members could exercise such immense power is one of the most phenomenal accomplishments in the history of the United States. It was not, however, a lasting achievement. The present work, an account of events from the 1950s into the twenty-first century, is the story of a declining power. Essentially it is a domestic military history, in that it describes the fifty-year war that law enforcement has waged on the American Mafia.

Words like "organized crime" or "Mafia" lack precision. Attorney General Robert Kennedy, who crusaded against the organization, told his subordinates, "Don't define it, do something about it." Over the years, "Mafia" has come to be used as a shorthand for the leading element of American organized crime. Like "Hollywood" as a synonym for the movie industry, or "Wall Street" for high finance, it has become so embedded in the national consciousness that it is impossible to avoid using it. Attempts by official bodies to define the Mafia often fell short, or were misleading. In 1950–51 a U.S. Senate committee chaired by Estes Kefauver of Tennessee exposed the face of organized crime in a score of American cities. In its final report the committee declared that a Mafia, descended from the Sicilian original, controlled the most lucrative rackets in many major cities and tied together criminal groups throughout the country. A 1967 presidential commission described organized crime as "underworld groups that are sufficiently sophisticated that they regularly employ techniques of violence and corruption to achieve their other criminal ends." They explained that

> the core group of organized crime in the United States consist[s] of 24 groups operating as criminal cartels in large cities across the nation. Their membership is exclusively Italian, they are in frequent communication with each other, and their smooth functioning is insured by a national body of overseers.

In fact the Mafia in the United States was not an offshoot of the Sicilian version. While only men of Italian lineage could be "made" full-fledged members, the organization was not entirely Italian. Nor was the national "commission," as its body of top overseers was called, ever as clearly defined or powerful as it was sometimes portrayed.

In the nineteenth century, some people blamed the newly immigrated Italians for the prevalence of vice and crime in urban areas. But organized crime was well established in the New World long before Italian Americans arrived. Gamblers, saloon keepers, brothel madams, and other criminals paid off the police, who in turn funneled a large share of the take to their political masters. A few immigrants who came to the United States had been members of Old World criminal bands, such as the Neapolitan Camorra and Sicilian Mafia. It is clear, though, that the Italians who would turn to crime in this country (a tiny fraction of the whole) simply took advantage of what they found when they arrived. Even after Mussolini's crackdown on the Mafia in the 1920s propelled some genuine Sicilian mafiosi to the United States, the forms of organized crime they adopted were essentially American.

The Mafia in America produced bosses like Calabrians Frank Costello and Albert Anastasia, as well as Neapolitans Al Capone and Vito Genovese. For practical purposes it also included Jews such as Meyer Lansky and Benjamin "Bugsy" Siegel of New York, Abner "Longy" Zwillman of Newark, and Morris "Moe" Dalitz of Cleveland, and these men often exercised power equivalent to that of the Italian bosses. Lansky (né Maier Suchowljansky) was generally ranked among the top three or four mobsters in the country. His success was the result of his financial skills and his ability to forge alliances with key leaders such as Lucky Luciano and Frank Costello. For similar reasons, Moe Dalitz would become a major figure in Ohio, Kentucky, and Nevada. Irish Owney Madden, though confined to the resort town of Hot Springs, Arkansas, after his exile from New York City, managed to reinvent himself as an elder statesman of the American Mafia. Welshman Murray "the Camel" Humphreys (né Humpreys) was always near the top of the Chicago mob hierarchy, as were Jake Guzik and Gus Alex, who were Jewish and Greek, respectively. To emphasize the organization's American origins and its frequently multiethnic makeup, I refer to it as "the American Mafia," though to avoid constant repetition of the term, I will usually refer to it simply as "the Mafia," sometimes only "the mob(s)," or in individual cities by its local equivalent, such as "the Chicago Outfit" or the name of a particular New York family.

One clear indicator that the American Mafia was homegrown was its organizational structure. The American gangs replicated the political machines in the areas where they operated. Chicago, for example, was dominated by the Democratic county organization, though certain ward bosses were given considerable latitude. The Chicago mob controlled the metropolitan area but allowed some of its leading figures to operate with a high degree of autonomy. New York was too large to be ruled by one political organization. Tammany controlled Manhattan, but Brooklyn, the Bronx, and Queens had their own machines. The New York Mafia's five-family structure dispersed mob power similarly across the five boroughs. In Tammany days, a "commission" made up of a powerful politician from Manhattan, another from Brooklyn, a boss gambler, and a representative of the NYPD regulated organized crime. After 1931, a local Mafia commission composed of the heads of the five families performed the same function. At the same time, a national "syndicate" also developed, directed by a commission that included the New York families and representatives from other cities. The national commission reflected prevailing political practices as well. The Republican and Democratic national committees were dominated by big states, such as New York, Illinois, Pennsylvania, Ohio, and Michigan. In the national syndicate, the New York, Chicago, Philadelphia, Cleveland, and Detroit mobs called the shots (sometimes literally).

The internal arrangements of the families (*borgatta*s or simply gangs) also resembled that of the political machines. The Tammany and Cook County party chairmen and the Mafia family heads were all called "boss."[2] Both Tammany and the Chicago organization often had number two men; in the Mafia they were called underbosses. Tammany had leaders over every assembly district, while Chicago had a party committeeman in charge of each ward, and the Mafia had its middle managers too. In the post-Apalachin period, law enforcement began referring to mob sub-bosses by terms such as "capo" (head). While neat on paper, it did not always conform to local practice. In Chicago, instead of being called capos,

2 Not "don," a general term of respect in some Latin countries, or "godfather," though a few bosses liked the honorific title or styled themselves as fathers of their mob family.

sub-leaders were usually referred to by the territory they controlled: boss of the Loop, the Near North Side, the Far South Side, etc. In other places they might be known as captains or crew chiefs. The Tammany wise men were called sachems; the Mafia families' equivalent was *consigliere*, or counselor, though the job began as a sort of ombudsman to whom aggrieved gang members could appeal. Since "Tammany" was an Indian name, its rank and file were accordingly known as braves. On law enforcement charts, the lowest ranked members of the Mafia were called soldiers, a term that might also encompass crew members who were not "made." While it is sometimes claimed that any Italian made man outranked any non-Italian, this was not the case. A mob soldier, even a crew chief, had to be very respectful around "Bugsy" Siegel or "Shotgun" Alex, men whose nicknames alone indicated their temperament and propensities.

Even the boss title could sometimes be misleading. Some who bore it were no more than titular leaders. Gaetano Gagliano was formally boss of what became the Lucchese family from 1931 until his death in 1951, when he was succeeded by his underboss, Gaetano "Tommy" Lucchese.[3] Yet during the period when Gagliano was supposedly in charge, there was virtually no mention of him, while Lucchese was well known, just as European kings and presidents have often been overshadowed by their prime ministers. Sometimes it was unclear who was actually running a particular Mafia gang. In the 1980s the federal government prosecuted "Fat Tony" Salerno as head of New York's Genovese family even though he was actually the number two man.

The key to the American Mafia's success was its ability to buy or neutralize public officials. Until the 1920s, organizations such as Tammany Hall or Chicago's First Ward had the final say over organized crime. Then Prohibition-rich gangsters turned the tables and began to act as the partners or, in some instances, controllers of the politicians. As one criminal justice official told historian Arthur Sloane, "The mobsters have always been wedded to the political system. That's how they survive. Without that wedding they would be terrorists and we'd get rid of them." The decline of

---

3 Who, because of a childhood injury to his hand, acquired the nickname "Three Finger Brown," after the famous Chicago Cub pitcher Mordecai Brown.

the Mafia began after the 1950s, when the mobs could not muster the political influence to protect themselves from the law enforcement assault led by the federal government.

In the present work I have adopted a broad approach, as opposed to a more narrow focus on a particular mob family or individual leader. Sometimes police or journalists have labeled gangs such as New York's Gambinos or the Chicago Outfit the premier mob families in America. Such assessments are like rankings of college football teams. The view of one expert is not always shared by another or borne out on the playing field. A similar practice is to designate an individual gangster such as Vito Genovese or Carlo Gambino "Boss of Bosses." For a long time, law enforcement followed the same narrow approach in its war on the Mafia: Go after an individual Mr. Big. The turning point in the war came in the 1980s, when the federal government broadened its targets and took down most of the leadership of all five New York families in one fell swoop.

It is also my belief that the story of the Mafia cannot be told by concentrating on just its principal bastions, New York and Chicago, much less one of them alone. Having a considerable acquaintance with both cities, I can affirm that the mob culture is different in each. By the same token, an account of organized crime in the second half of the twentieth century that neglected events in places like Cleveland, Kansas City, Detroit, Las Vegas, New Orleans, Florida, or Cuba would provide a very incomplete picture. The story of the American Mafia is much too broad and complex to be told in the life of a single family, boss, or city. It has been a national, not a local, phenomenon.

While my focus has been on the big picture, I have kept in mind a comment made about a four-volume history of British intelligence in World War II, that "it assumed the war was won by committees in Whitehall." While some presidential commissions and congressional committees or Justice Department officials made significant contributions, the war against the American Mafia was carried on through the efforts of thousands of human beings in the field, employing successful strategies and tactics against thousands of other human beings. Therefore, I frequently highlight some of the individuals on both sides of the law who actually fought in the trenches during the great Mafia war.

As the twenty-first century opens, many observers judge that the American Mafia has reached its final stage. Some analysts have characterized the mob families as "melting icebergs," regressing from sophisticated criminal cartels back to street gangs. The report of the Mafia's demise may be premature. If the federal government were to accept the view that organized crime is no longer worthy of major concern, the mobs might come back with such force that the gains of the past twenty years would be erased.

Another real possibility is that a new, more powerful type of Mafia may emerge. In the current world order, multinational syndicates operating from secure foreign enclaves might penetrate target countries like the United States through respectable fronts. At the operating level, they would assign tasks such as bribery and murder to skilled specialists. In such an arrangement, the American Mafia might become subcontractors to an international syndicate or syndicates. In some instances there might be links to terrorist groups. It took the federal government from 1957 to the beginning of the 1980s to develop means of administering crushing defeats to the American Mafia. To combat a more powerful future Mafia, law enforcement will have to adapt to the new threat far more rapidly than it did to the old one.

CHAPTER 1

THE ROAD TO APALACHIN:
WAR IS DECLARED ON THE AMERICAN MAFIA

I t was a typical scene from American middle-class life. More than sixty men were gathered at a large rural estate in the southern tier of New York, near the Pennsylvania border. The weather was warm for November, and after an early morning drizzle the sun began to shine. The only off note was the guests, who wore silk suits, white-on-white shirts, and polished soft leather shoes—hardly standard attire for a country cookout. By 12:40 P.M. the affair was well under way, with one group congregated around a barbecue pit grilling steaks while others conversed over Scotch and wine in the main residence or the nearby summerhouse. The parked Cadillacs, Chryslers, and Lincolns bespoke the guests' affluence. Suddenly, some of them noticed that a car had pulled into the parking lot behind the garage, and that the four men in it were taking down license numbers. Though they were wearing civilian clothes, it was obvious that they were police. The host's wife shouted, "It's the state troopers." Her husband, Joe Barbara, assured the guests there was nothing to worry about. It was just a bit of the occasional hassling that he was subjected to by nosy cops. As if to confirm his statement, the intruders began backing their car down the driveway and soon disappeared from view. The men resumed eating and drinking until 1:15 P.M., when a deliveryman who had just dropped off a load of fish came racing back to the estate, shouting that the cops had set up a roadblock down at the bottom of a hill where the dirt road from the estate intersected with a state highway. This announcement prompted some of the guests to head for their cars.

Watching through binoculars, Detective Sergeant Edgar Croswell of the New York State Police began laughing. Up until then he had no legal grounds to question anyone, since the men were on private property. Once they hit the state road, however, cops could demand licenses, search cars, and ticket or arrest anyone they found in violation. When he set up his roadblock Croswell had radioed for reinforcements, and from barracks across the region, men in gray uniforms and Western-style Stetsons piled into patrol cars and raced toward the intersection of old Route 17 and McFall Road, in the little hamlet of Apalachin (pop. 350). The name of the village (locally pronounced "apple-aykin") and the date—November 14, 1957—would henceforth be a part of American history.

Commonly considered an urban entity, the Mafia was also alive and well in rural New York. Barbara was proof of that. In 1921, at the age of sixteen, he had left his home in Sicily with an older brother and eventually ended up working at a shoe factory in Endicott, New York. By the 1930s, "Joe the Barber" was a small-time bootlegger and gambler in nearby northeastern Pennsylvania. He was also the suspected gunman in several murder cases arising out of intramural disputes among gangsters. No charges could be made to stick, but the Pennsylvania cops made things so hot for him that he eventually returned to Endicott. There he became a successful businessman and posed as a respectable citizen, while functioning as head of the Mafia group that flourished along the Pennsylvania–New York border.

The story of the Apalachin raid has often been presented as a case of some hick cops stumbling on a mob conclave. The facts are a bit different. Founded in 1917, the New York State Police was a spit-and-polish outfit with the ethos of a cavalry regiment (hence "troopers").[1] Forty-four-year-old Detective Sergeant Edgar DeWitt Croswell, a burly man with a lined face, had joined the force in 1941. Like all rookies, he was initially assigned

1 In some accounts Croswell's troopers are referred to as his "deputies," as though he were an elected county sheriff. Descriptions of the Apalachin raid tend to disagree on various details. I have relied on the evidence presented in the federal case that arose from it. (See Notes, chapter 1.)

to cleaning out the horse stables. His first encounter with Barbara came in 1944 when, as a plainclothes trooper, he caught one of the employees at Barbara's soft drink bottling plant stealing two cans of gasoline from a company truck. It was wartime and gas was a precious commodity, so Croswell assumed the man's boss would appreciate the collar. Instead, when the short, squat Barbara was called to the police station, he refused to sign a complaint and began berating Croswell for making the arrest. Noting a bulge under Barbara's coat, Croswell asked him if he was carrying a gun—illegal under New York law without authorization. "Sure, gotta permit," he snapped, and produced a license signed by a judge. After that Croswell kept an eye on Mr. Barbara: A federal appeals judge would later observe that for thirteen years, "As a modern Inspector Javert, Trooper Croswell pursued Barbara in all ways possible." He even went so far as to photograph Barbara's estate, and was caught in the act by Mrs. Barbara and several unfriendly boxer dogs (he explained that he was a photographer taking pictures of beautiful homes for possible inclusion in a magazine). On wiretaps of Barbara's phone, Croswell sometimes heard guarded remarks such as "That matter we talked about, we'll fix," but nothing incriminating.

In 1956, a New York state trooper stopped three men in a speeding car. When the driver produced a license that was not his, the trooper took him into custody and ordered the other men to follow him to the station, where the case was turned over to Detective Sergeant Croswell. The driver turned out to be Carmine Galante, who would later rise to the top of New York City's Bonanno family. The false license charge, though minor, carried a jail sentence, so Galante tried to bully his way out of it, hinting that he had powerful political connections. Unimpressed, Croswell ordered him booked. An investigation determined that Galante and the others had been at a meeting in a Binghamton hotel with family heads Joe Bonanno and Joe Barbara. While Galante was out on bail awaiting trial, politicians from New York and New Jersey did indeed begin putting in good words for him. A ranking officer from another law enforcement agency visited Croswell and implied that it would be worth a thousand dollars to him to drop the case. Croswell ordered him out of the station, and Galante ended up serving thirty days in jail. The incident undoubtedly confirmed Croswell's belief that Barbara was an important mob figure.

The usual reason cited for the Apalachin raid was that Croswell's suspicions had been aroused the day before, when he and his partner, Trooper Vincent Vasisko, were investigating a bad check case at a motel. Barbara's son Joe Junior came in, causing the troopers to step quickly out of sight. As they listened, young Barbara engaged three rooms for two nights, explaining that the guests would be attending a business meeting. Asked for their names, he declined to give them and departed with the keys. Their curiosity piqued, the cops drove past Barbara's home, where they noted several parked cars with out-of-state license plates. Later that night the motel owner informed Croswell that the guests had refused to sign the register at check-in. The surly attitudes of the men did not seem consistent with the behavior of soft drink salesmen.

It is possible, though, that the motel incident was not what first aroused Croswell's suspicions: A federal appeals court judge later wrote that Croswell likely "got wind of the meeting, if not its purpose, via wiretapping." Barbara had previously been suspected of violating federal liquor laws, so Croswell notified some friends at the local office of the Treasury Department's Alcohol and Tobacco Tax unit. The next day he and Trooper Vasisko, accompanied by Treasury agents Art Ruston and Ken Brown, headed out to the Barbara estate to check out the doings. He wisely alerted his supervisors that he might be needing reinforcements. This did not present a problem for the troopers, since there were always reserves on duty in the barracks.

A virtual congress of the leading elements of American organized crime was about to convene, and the only police agency on the case was a rural patrol force assisted by a couple of federal revenue agents. Where was the FBI? In fact, like most Americans of that time, it knew very little about organized crime. Since then, the Mafia has been extensively probed by the government and become a staple of the entertainment world, though it is still not fully understood. Anyone who claims to have knowledge of the Mafia is usually asked whether the characters and events portrayed in *The Godfather* or *The Sopranos* or any of their screen counterparts reflect the reality of mob life. The answer is no—and yes. Cinematic depictions of cops stress the dramatic aspects of their occupation, making unusual events such as murders and gun battles seem like a typical day's work, whereas in real life, few police officers work homicide or ever fire their guns. Yet the higher-quality shows do tend to capture the ethos of the cop world. It is the same with portrayals of gangsters.

Life in the mobs tends to follow a standard pattern. Over the years, most mafiosi have come from neighborhoods where organized crime was strong: Manhattan's East Harlem or Lower East Side, Brooklyn's Bensonhurst, Chicago's Taylor Street district, Boston's North End, South Philadelphia. As boys, they were in street gangs where they developed criminal skills as burglars, robbers, and hijackers and honed their reputations as tough guys. Early on they were marked as potential members of the local mob. A New York police official described the attraction of mob life for young men in Bath Beach, a Bensonhurst neighborhood:

> They meet the young toughs, the mob enforcers. They hear the tales of glory recounted—who robbed what, who worked over whom, which showgirl shared which gangster's bed, who got hit by whom, the techniques of the rackets and how easy it all is, how the money rolls in. . . . With a little luck and guts, they feel even they may someday belong to that splendid high-living band, the mob.

Social scientists have sought to explain such choices. One common view is that they are a rational means of achieving success in communities where more legitimate avenues to advancement are not available. The problem with various theories is that they can never explain why one boy becomes a gangster and his buddy (or even his brother) does not. Hollywood has portrayed this dilemma many times. In the final scene of some gangster movies, three childhood friends—a murderer, a cop, and a priest—are reunited while walking the last mile to the electric chair. The condemned man jokes, the cop weeps, and the priest prays. The audience is left to wonder why one of them ended up as he did.[2]

In some places becoming a made man was akin to enrolling in a fraternal

2 Corny as such movies are, I could personally cite families I knew in which one brother became a priest, another a cop, and a third a criminal (though none of the last category went to the electric chair).

organization. An aspirant required a sponsor and often had to go through some type of ritual such as swearing an oath on a holy picture, with a gun and knife alongside, and the ceremonial drawing of his blood. In southern cities and in Chicago, initiation into the mob might require nothing more than answering a few questions and receiving a pat on the back or a handshake. Sometimes membership rules required that the candidate commit a murder, or at least serve as an accomplice, but the notion that one could become a made man only through homicide was not universally correct.

A made man introducing another one to a third would say, "He is a friend of ours." If a man was not in the fraternity, he would be introduced as "a friend of mine." It would then be understood that mob affairs could not be discussed in his presence. Sometimes a mob member would be identified by a local slang term such as "goodfella" or "wiseguy."[3]

The requirement for entry that both parents be of Italian descent (generally southern Italian, and in later years amended in some places to one parent) was meant to ensure that recruits possessed the right values. The Mafia believed that young men from Italian immigrant families, bred to place blood ties above all other considerations, would show equal loyalty to the mob. To be accepted into a Mafia family, as into any other kin group, meant that one could count on the support of the other members. The reverse was that you were expected to help the family even if it meant possible death or imprisonment. Like many other enterprises, getting in was easier if one had a relation in the top ranks of the organization—though many mob bosses preferred that their children pursue careers outside the world of organized crime.

The organizational rules to which members subscribed were fairly simple. A made man could not threaten another member, or fool around with his wife or girlfriend. The latter rule was intended more to avoid bloodshed than to uphold morality. If a member was in prison, his wife was definitely off limits to other mobsters, or anybody else for that matter: A jealous convict might be tempted to become an informer. When cops found a dead

---

3 Mafia rituals are not unique in America. Many noncriminals belong to fraternal organizations such as the Elks, Moose, Masons, Knights of Columbus, or Yale's Skull and Bones Society. These too induct members via exotic ceremonies, swear them to secrecy and mutual support, and have phrases or signs by which they can identify each other. Similarly, the police avoid talking shop in front of people who are not "on the job."

man who had been shot in the genital area, it was generally assumed that he had violated the Mafia's moral code. In some places, being involved with drugs or prostitution was forbidden, though it was a rule that was frequently ignored. Anyone who violated the code of silence, known as *omerta*, by disclosing organizational secrets was subject to the death penalty. In practice, the most important rule in the Mafia was never to cheat your superiors out of their share of your earnings.

Mob membership conferred status. A soldier could expect a great deal of deference from people in general. A barroom tough guy who was not a made man would always lose if he got into a fight with someone who was. Even if the tough won the first round, he was sure to lose the second, since no gang would ever allow one of its members to be beaten up without retaliating. Even to insult the wife or girlfriend of a made man was a dangerous thing to do. If a mob entrepreneur was competing for a million-dollar contract with a nonmob guy, the latter would be expected to withdraw his bid.

Mob soldiers did not usually receive a salary. Instead, they were permitted to run activities like gambling, loan sharking, and hijacking, and they were expected to pass on a large percentage of the proceeds to the bosses. In return, they were protected by them from the law or other gangsters. Protocol dictated that before a mobster moved in on a territory, he would check to make sure that he was not poaching on some other mobster's operation, which could lead to serious trouble. In New York, where there were five separate families, it was especially difficult to determine whether someone was connected.

Within the families there was a division between the gangsters and the racketeers. Gangsters were the ones who did the shooting and slugging, while racketeers ran the moneymaking operations. In many instances racketeers were men who had started out as gangsters and could still wield a gun, but, as befitted their higher status, they distanced themselves from everyday violence. Some bosses even came to believe that they were just businessmen, or even better, sportsmen. Sitting in his box at the racetrack, New York mob boss Frank Costello fancied himself as much a gentleman as the blue bloods who sat around him.

Many mafiosi had old-fashioned views. Most put their mothers and wives on a pedestal and kept their mistresses out of sight. In some places the rule was you could go out with your mistress on Friday, but Saturday night was for the wife. Many mob guys also respected clergymen (especially priests), the military, and, surprisingly, cops. *The Godfather* contains a scene set the day after Pearl Harbor, when Michael Corleone stuns his family by announcing he has joined the Marine Corps because, unlike them, he believes it is right to fight for your country. In real life the Chicago mob's overseer in Hollywood, Johnny Roselli, volunteered for the Army though he was in his late thirties and sickly. He even maneuvered to remain with an armored division slated for overseas combat. His desire to be a hero was not fulfilled: After his indictment for attempting to extort Hollywood studios, he was stripped of his uniform. New York mob boss Paul Castellano once startled his soldiers by declaring, "You know who the true tough guys are? The cops. They go on these domestic disputes and things and they never know what they're up against."

Around the time of the Apalachin raid, it was estimated that the Mafia comprised twenty-four families, with approximately four or five thousand members and ten times that number of associates.[4] The Mafia were thickest on the ground in the Northeast. The heaviest concentration was in New York City, with about 40 percent of the membership. There Tommy Lucchese, Joe Bonanno, and Joe Profaci headed families that bore their names. (In the 1960s, as a result of family conflict, the Profacis would become known as the Colombos.) Albert Anastasia ran the family that had been headed by Vince Mangano, while Frank Costello was boss of Lucky Luciano's old family, and until recently held sway as the "Prime Minister" of mobdom. All had seats on the national commission that coordinated the loosely organized national confederation or syndicate of mob families.

Joe Ida headed the Philadelphia family. Simone "Sam the Plumber" De-Cavalcante led a group under his name in New Jersey. In the early '50s, Raymond Patriarca of Providence succeeded to the leadership of the New England Mafia, known as "the Office." Steve Magaddino was the boss of

---

4 The exact number of families depended upon how the count was taken. A city like Youngstown, Ohio, which was under the supervision of both Cleveland and Pittsburgh, might be listed as a separate family.

the Buffalo-area Mafia, locally referred to as "the Arm." Magaddino, Ida, and the five New York family heads all held seats on the national commission, and Patriarca would soon acquire one. Joe Barbara ran the group that was based on the Pennsylvania–New York border, while another small family operated out of Pittsburgh.

Chicago was the midwestern stronghold of the Mafia. The Chicago Mafia was still called the "Capone Gang" for years after Al Capone's 1931 imprisonment. Later, it was referred to as "the Syndicate" and, in the late twentieth century, "the Outfit." Tony Accardo was boss, sharing his throne with Paul "The Waiter" Ricca (né Felice DeLucia). Ricca had been one of the Chicago leaders sent to jail in 1944 for shaking down Hollywood. He probably could have claimed the top job when he was paroled three years later, but he preferred the role of elder statesman. Either man was allowed to represent the family on the national commission.[5] Cleveland's boss, John Scalish, was also a member of the national commission. His family, sometimes called "the Mayfield Road Gang" for the neighborhood of its origin, coexisted amicably with "the Jewish boys" headed by Moe Dalitz. The old Jewish Purple Gang of Detroit had ceased to exist by the 1930s, but in popular parlance its name was transferred to the Italian organized crime family, led by Joe Vitale and later by Joe Zerilli, who had a seat on the national commission. Kansas City, St. Louis, and Milwaukee had strong families but no commission seats.

In New Orleans the boss was Carlos Marcello, whose domain extended to Dallas. Marcello had the distinction of heading the oldest Mafia family in America and held at least de facto membership on the national commission. In 1954, Santo Trafficante, Jr., succeeded his father as top man in Tampa, Florida, also inheriting his extensive holdings in Cuba. In 1957, Frank DeSimone succeeded to the head of the Los Angeles family after the (natural) death of Jack Dragna, but he did not have a seat on the national commission. San Francisco, San Jose, and San Diego had small Mafia families, as did Denver.

By the mid-twentieth century the mobs were strongly entrenched in

5 Not surprisingly, Chicago's dual leadership mirrored the political situation in that city in the 1930s and '40s, when power was shared by the Democratic county chairman and the mayor.

many legitimate enterprises. The fields it found most fertile were those with a shaky financial base, such as the garment industry, nightclubs, and restaurants, or ones with an oversupply of labor, like the docks, construction, or trucking. Vending machines were favorite mob cash cows. Despite their power, most mafiosi usually did not seek total control of an enterprise. Ownership might have required more skill than they possessed. Therefore they contented themselves with a large share. Mob influence in a particular field allowed them to fix prices, designate territories, and ignore antitrust laws. Many legitimate businessmen preferred these arrangements to the uncertainties of competition. Within a family, the top boss got a piece of every substantial enterprise. As a result, all were millionaires. The captains were chosen not only for their toughness but for their ability to earn dollars for the family. Some of them were wealthy in their own right. Soldiers who were very active could sometimes make more money than a relatively inactive capo. In economic terms, a typical mob family was like a large law firm in which senior partners make a very good living off the work of the juniors and associates.

Another "industry" the mob extracted tribute from was professional crime and vice. In many cities independent robbers, burglars, hijackers, and bookmakers (i.e. those not affiliated with the Mafia or politically protected) were expected to pay a "street tax" to the local family. In this practice the Mafia was acting as an alternative government: pursuing those they termed "outlaws"; requiring them to obtain "licenses" to operate; and collecting taxes on their earnings. Those who did not pay might end up in the trunk of a car. In Chicago parlance, they would become "trunk music." Street criminals avoided operating in Mafia-controlled neighborhoods. A robber caught mugging an old lady in Manhattan's Little Italy or Boston's North End was dealt with summarily, not turned over to the police. In such places mob guys presented themselves as defenders of the community. And in turn, the residents of some areas were so loyal to the Mafia that they would instantly raise the alarm if they spotted an outsider who they thought might be a G-man or a cop.[6]

The Mafia could never have achieved the wealth or power that it did

---

6 Though both Little Italy and the North End were always hospitable to the throngs of tourists who frequented them.

without the help of thousands of associates, the individuals who were connected to the mob but not full-fledged members. Some worked in crews or managed mob businesses ranging from nightclubs to labor unions. Others were lawyers and accountants who provided services that went far beyond the ethical rules of their professions. Certain lawyers functioned as house counsel for the mob: When assigned to defend a member, their job was to protect the organization, not the client. If the defendant showed any inclination to cut a deal with the prosecution, the mob lawyer was required to report it to the bosses, though he knew full well that he was signing his client's death warrant. In some instances skilled associates wielded more power than some of the captains. Attorney Sid Korshak, the Chicago mob's liaison with the entertainment world, had the respectful ear of mob bosses and Fortune 500 executives alike. The latter justified using him by rationalizing that he had never been convicted of a crime. Another important group were mob "protectors": crooked cops, prosecutors, judges, and politicians.

Gangster films usually stress the violent aspects of the mob world. It is undeniable that violence was an important and not infrequently employed weapon of the Mafia. Mob sanctions, even against their own soldiers who had muffed an assignment, could be very harsh. In 1957 a Chicago hit man killed a banker but neglected to remove a receipt from the body that revealed that the dead man was owed $100,000 by a mob boss. As punishment, the careless killer was taken for a ride the hard way, tied to the back bumper of a car that sped down a suburban dirt road at sixty miles an hour. Afterward he was shot and his body left in a trunk. The only item found on his person was a comb. The message to his kind was clear: When you hit a guy, comb him for anything that might embarrass your employer. When a victim had incurred no personal rancor, his death might be a smooth one—a mob family member whose removal was deemed necessary for one reason or another would be spared torture or terror. In such cases the usual procedure was to administer a shot in the back of the head that the victim never saw coming.

The amount of violence a particular mob engaged in usually reflected the personality of its boss. Albert Anastasia, lord high executioner of the Brooklyn waterfront and later family boss, had a fierce temper, ordering hits left and right. When an ordinary citizen recognized bank robber Willie Sutton and informed the police, Anastasia became so angry that he had the man murdered even though Sutton was not a mafioso. Tony Accardo of Chicago was much more businesslike, authorizing bloodshed only when necessary. Angelo Bruno, who took over Philadelphia at the end of the 1950s, went out of his way to avoid violence.

In the 1930s the national syndicate adopted a rule against killing cops or journalists. Adherence was not a hundred percent: In 1949, the gunmen of Los Angeles boss Jack Dragna deliberately shot and wounded a detective working for the California attorney general's office. In 1956 a Lucchese capo had a journalist blinded. In the 1970s a member of New York's Colombo family put out a contract on a federal prosecutor who he thought had disrespected him (the hit man killed the intended victim's father, a judge, who had the same name). In the 1980s the Bonanno family offered half a million dollars for the murder of an FBI agent who had infiltrated their ranks.

Individual families had their own style of operation. The Cleveland mob did not hesitate to use bombs, while New York stuck to bullets and Chicago employed both. In the 1920s, Chicago introduced the Thompson submachine gun into mob warfare, but by the 1950s that was considered a bit over the top. By then only some detective squads rode around with "Tommy guns." Chicago loan sharks were notorious for applying baseball bats and ice picks to borrowers who missed a payment. In other cities, if the debtor was trying to repay the loan, the lenders were usually more patient.

In 1950 and '51, the televised U.S. Senate hearings on the Mafia, chaired by Estes Kefauver of Tennessee, had brought mobsters into the average American living room and created a furor. But the public outcry was short-lived, and from 1951 until 1957 things ran smoothly for the mob families. Then Vito Genovese upset the comfortable world of the American Mafia. Extradited from Italy in 1945 to stand trial for an old murder, he was acquitted after the chief witness against him died in a Brooklyn jail, having ingested "enough poison to kill ten horses." If Vito had not been forced to flee the country in 1936 to avoid a murder charge, he would have become Luciano's successor instead of Frank Costello. Now he wanted the job, and Costello was vulnerable. In testifying before the Kefauver committee, Frank had made a fool of himself on camera. In the aftermath, with the Feds pursuing him for contempt of Congress and on tax charges, his stock had gone down among his peers and he was no longer regarded as the New York family's prime minister. It was an ideal situation for a boardroom coup, mob style. Still, many people did not want the rash Genovese to take over. In 1943, the world-famous anarchist (and outspoken anti-Fascist) Carlo Tresca had been murdered in New York; it was rumored that the orders came from Genovese in Italy, attempting to curry favor with Mussolini. Killing a prominent person in New York City on behalf of a Fascist dictator—during the middle of World War II, no less—was plain stupid. Years later, Lucky Luciano still could not get over it, telling a writer, "Goddamn if Vito don't put out a contract from Italy on Tresca." Such recklessness had become Genovese's signature.[7]

One night in May 1957, as Costello was walking into his deluxe Central Park West apartment building, a burly man approached him, yelled, "Frank, this is for you," and shot him in the head.[8] The wound was superficial, but the message was penetrating: Costello was finished as boss. The family that Genovese took over bears his name to this day.

Frank's closest ally, Albert Anastasia, was the next target. Underboss Carlo Gambino was as ambitious to become head of Anastasia's family as Vito was to take over from Costello. So Carlo and Vito arranged to work together. Anastasia, too, was in disfavor—he had angered other bosses by unilaterally opening up the membership rolls and selling admission to the Mafia to undeserving people. After the attempt on Costello, Albert began to keep a low profile, sheltering behind the walls of his New Jersey house. In October he made one of his regular visits to the barbershop in midtown Manhattan's Park Sheraton Hotel. No sooner had he settled into the chair than two men walked up and pumped five bullets into him, killing him instantly. Though the shop was crowded, no witnesses were forthcoming.

7 Though the account of Genovese's role is accepted by most Mafia experts, there are equally compelling alternative explanations for Tresca's murder.
8 The assailant was Vincenzo "Chin" Gigante, who many years later would become boss of the family.

Anastasia's bodyguard had somehow wandered off. With Carlo as boss, the family would eventually become known as the Gambinos.

Costello and Anastasia were national commission members, and any hits on them should have required its approval. Some bosses wondered if, in exile, Genovese had acquired the idea of becoming Il Duce of the American Mafia. The unilateral killings were not Genovese's only offense against the mob's etiquette—he was also pursuing the drug trade at full throttle. Many bosses, like Chicago's Accardo, thought this was a bad idea. For one thing, it made politicians reluctant to deal with the mob. And Congress had recently tightened up drug laws—a conviction followed by a long sentence could encourage defendants to talk, *omerta* or no. With so much to discuss, a sit-down was in order. A preliminary session of the 1957 gathering was held on November 10 in Livingston, New Jersey, at the palatial home of a capo in Vito Genovese's family. It adjourned with the next session set for four days later at Barbara's estate. The Chicago mob had offered to play host to the meeting, but it was Buffalo's Steve Magaddino, a charter member of the national commission and its regional overseer in upstate New York, who reportedly selected the site.

When the flight began at Apalachin, the first car to drive into the state police roadblock was stopped by Sergeant Croswell personally. It contained five men. At the wheel was Russell Bufalino of Pittston, Pennsylvania, Barbara's underboss. Alongside him was the big man himself: Vito Genovese. Also in the car was Joe Ida, boss of the Philadelphia family. With neither the cops nor mobsters certain of what cards the others were holding, both were polite—but wary. Genovese produced identification and submitted to a frisk. Croswell asked him why so many people were visiting the Barbara estate, and Genovese replied that Joe had heart trouble (which was true) and that his friends had come by to cheer him up. As an afterthought he opined that he did not think that he was obliged to answer that question. The license plates of the guests' cars had been radioed to headquarters to see if there were any wanted notices on them, but the information would not be back for hours. Since he could bring no immediate charges, Croswell might have waved Genovese and company through and had his troopers repeat the same procedure with the others. If one of the plates checked out to a wanted criminal, however, he would be subject to criticism. It was a difficult position for a mere sergeant, but Croswell rose to the occasion. He commanded his troopers to begin searching the cars. When Treasury Agent Ruston reported seeing men running through the woods, Croswell sent other troopers to pursue them.

Among those running was a distinguished-looking gentleman in a camel hair coat. His elegant attire proved to be his undoing: The coat got snagged on a barbed wire fence and its owner had to be helped free by a trooper. The dapper sixty-four-year-old John Montana had been in the United States since he was fourteen without acquiring a criminal record. Indeed, he had many legitimate accomplishments to his credit. He was the owner of the largest fleet of taxicabs in Buffalo, New York, where he had served on the City Council and had been a delegate to a state constitutional convention. In 1956 a civic group had named him Man of the Year. Of the sixty-three men captured or identified as being at Apalachin, it was Montana whose presence caused the most head-shaking in law enforcement circles. He had managed to conceal his Mafia membership for many years, despite the fact that for a time he had been underboss to Steve Magaddino. Over the next hour and a half, questioning continued at the roadblock. More men would be arrested—in the woods, hitchhiking on the highway, or standing near a house a mile away. Around 2:30 P.M. it began to rain, so Croswell ordered the suspects to be taken to the state police post at Vestal, New York, where interrogations went on until midnight.

The notables apprehended included New York leaders Profaci, Bonanno, Galante, and Gambino. Later it was established that Magaddino, Lucchese, and Detroit's Joe Zerilli had been among the estimated thirty or forty men who escaped the scene, arrived in the area after the raid, or were clever enough to remain in Barbara's house (which the police had no authority to search). Of the men who could be proven to have attended, more than two-thirds were from the East; eight were from the Midwest, three from beyond the Rockies, and four more from the South or Cuba, plus a visitor from Italy. They ranged in age from forty-three to sixty-six. Clearly the gathering was too large to be a meeting of the national commission. Yet it must have been about something very important to have drawn so many men from such widely scattered areas. When questioned, many echoed Genovese's line that they had been there to see their poor

sick friend. Others said that they had simply turned out to enjoy a barbecue or discuss legitimate business. Those caught away from the grounds of
the estate denied they had been there at all. John Montana could not bring
himself to admit that he socialized with gangsters, so he claimed that he
had been driving his Cadillac along a nearby highway when it developed
engine trouble. Realizing that his casual business acquaintance Barbara
lived nearby, he headed for the estate, hoping that he could obtain the services of Barbara's plant mechanics to help him with his vehicle. According
to Montana, no sooner had he arrived than some sort of ruckus broke out.
As a good citizen, he decided to remove himself from the scene by going
for a walk in the woods.

When the state police inquiries finally came back, none of the men were
wanted, aside from one New Jerseyite who had broken his parole by leaving the state. Nor was anyone carrying a firearm—back in 1928, when a big
mob conference in Cleveland had been raided by cops, arrests on weapons
charges had caused considerable embarrassment. (In addition, the notori-
ously short tempers of some of the bosses made their colleagues uncomfortable with weapons in the room.) With over $300,000 among them on
their persons, the prisoners could hardly be charged with vagrancy. So
they were fingerprinted, photographed, and released.

Rumors about the real reason for the Apalachin raid circulated for years.
One held that a dissident Mafia faction had tipped off the police in revenge
for the attacks on Costello and Anastasia. The absence from the gathering
of Costello and his close ally Carlos Marcello of New Orleans has been
cited as evidence for this theory. Other accounts have pointed to Meyer
Lansky as the tipster. But anyone familiar with law enforcement would recognize that if there had been advance warning, a raid of such import
would not have been carried out in an ad hoc fashion under the direction
of a noncommissioned officer.

Regardless of the mechanics of the bust, the law enforcers and journalists who had been warning about the Mafia in the wake of Kefauver
were delighted. Skeptics—FBI director J. Edgar Hoover among them—
who had denied that there was a national syndicate would now be hard-
pressed to explain what all those gentlemen were doing in a remote
corner of New York State. A number of the Apalachin visitors went through

long legal hassles with their local and state authorities, or were subjected to journalistic inquiry when they got back to their own towns. The Feds undertook to deport some of the guests who had been born in Italy, including bosses like Profaci and Gambino. The host, Joe Barbara, was hit with income tax charges.

The real question was what crime the Apalachin guests had committed by attending the conference. There were no laws on the books forbidding membership in the Mafia. There were statutes that made it a crime for individuals with criminal records to gather in a public place, or to plot offenses, but Barbara's estate was not public and the cops never determined in a legal sense what the meeting was about. J. Edgar Hoover, who had been as surprised by the meeting as anyone else, could offer no helpful advice. Others in the Department of Justice thought there might be a legal way of getting to the bottom of the gathering. In April 1958, New York lawyer Milton Wessel was named special assistant to the attorney general of the United States and assigned to investigate Apalachin. In May 1959 he convened a federal grand jury in New York City, which returned indictments charging conspiracy to obstruct justice against twenty-seven of the men who had attended the Apalachin meeting. Thirty-six others were listed as co-conspirators. The rationale for the prosecution was that the defendants conspired to give perjured testimony to the grand jury. In December 1959, twenty defendants were found guilty, and the following month Federal Judge Irving R. Kaufman imposed sentences of three to five years. Joe Barbara was not one of those convicted; his bad heart had given out earlier in the year.

On appeal the outcome was different. In 1960 a three-judge panel of the U.S. Court of Appeals for the Second Circuit, which included such strong champions of law enforcement as J. Edward Lumbard and Henry Friendly, reversed the conviction. The court held that there was no evidence that the defendants had conspired to give false testimony. It observed that

Doubtless many of Barbara's visitors are bad people, and it is surely a matter of public concern that more is not known of their activities. But bad as many of these alleged conspirators may be, their conviction for a crime which the government could not prove, on inferences no more valid than others, equally supported by reason and experience, and on evidence which a jury could not properly assess, cannot be permitted to stand.

It was the only decision the court could have arrived at, given the state of the law at the time. But the reversal of the convictions did not matter: What was more important was the galvanizing effect the raid had on the federal government. It would stimulate a revival of congressional interest in organized crime and rouse the FBI. Too many people were joking that the Edgar who had accomplished the most against organized crime was Croswell, not Hoover, and nothing prompted the FBI head to action faster than personal criticism. He ordered his troops to start making cases against the various mobs. From Apalachin on, the United States government was at war with the Mafia. But victory was far from assured—foot-dragging, bureaucratic rivalries, and inept leadership would stretch the government's assault out over nearly half a century, and even then the Mafia's defeat would not be total.

Historians have not been able to determine who started the American Revolution at Lexington by firing "the shot heard 'round the world." In the Apalachin story there is no uncertainty. Though he did not discharge his weapon, in the symbolic sense, Detective Sergeant Edgar Croswell fired the first shot in the war against the Mafia, on a back road in upstate New York.

CHAPTER 2

TOP HOODLUMS:
THE FBI PLAYS CATCH-UP

C hicago's North Michigan Avenue—known as "the Magnificent Mile"—
is a street of expensive stores, deluxe hotels, and high-rent commercial buildings. It is also a frequent target for professional burglars. In the
spring of 1959 they had become exceptionally troublesome, so the Chicago
police were staking out the area at night, putting officers with rifles on
rooftops. Their presence did not go unnoticed. One night a shadowy figure
spotted them as he was casing the area, preparing to make an unlawful entry into one of the buildings. The observer was not a burglar, though he
could easily have been mistaken for one. He was an FBI agent named Bill
Roemer, who, with his partner Ralph Hill, was planning what the Bureau
called "a black bag job"—a surreptitious entry to gather information. In
this instance he was looking to plant a concealed microphone, or "bug," in
a second-story tailor shop that served as a meeting place for the leaders of
the Chicago Outfit.

Electronic eavesdropping, wiretapping, and microphones—or in FBI
jargon, elsurs (electronic surveillances)—was a controversial subject. Wiretapping of phones had been outlawed by the 1934 Telecommunications
Act. Planting a bug usually required trespassing onto private property, and
the U.S. Supreme Court had declared that unlawful. However, the FBI had

been permitted, in certain circumstances, to do both.[1] Still it was a tricky business. Thus the fruits of such efforts had to be kept in-house and could not be used as courtroom evidence. Agents conducting black bag jobs on the mob were ordered not to carry credentials. They were forbidden to tell anyone, including the police, that they were FBI; if they got caught, the Bureau would disavow them. They were also open to prosecution under state law, and could even be shot as burglars.

The FBI had been wiretapping the phones of individual mob figures for several years, but thus far, the results had been disappointing. Gangsters knew to be discreet in their conversations or to use public phone booths. Even when they did slip and say something revealing, it was of limited use. What was needed was a bug in the mob equivalent of a corporate boardroom. Then the Bureau got a break.

Agents on field surveillances (fisurs) frequently trailed organized crime figures to the corner of Rush and Ontario, the heart of Chicago's glamor district. Closer observation revealed they were entering a nearby building, but a canvass of the premises did not turn up a rendezvous point. Then one day Roemer observed Murray "The Camel" Humphreys using a service entrance to a corridor that led to an adjacent building that fronted on Michigan Avenue. In this second building, mob leaders were meeting inside a custom tailor shop where they bought their expensive suits. The owner, grateful for their business, had made his plush private office available to them. The Chicago FBI office received permission from headquarters to plant a bug in the tailor shop.

Roemer got confirmation from police sources that the men on the roof were cops. He couldn't risk asking for them to be pulled out of the area; such requests never stayed secret for long. The surveillance meant that the shop could not be penetrated at night. So Roemer's team of agents began work on Sunday mornings, after the cops had left the rooftops and the area was deserted of shoppers and business people. Even the restaurant on the

1 Just before World War II, the U.S. attorney general had ruled that the FBI could wiretap in national security cases. In 1946, an attorney general's memo was interpreted by FBI director J. Edgar Hoover as also permitting wiretapping in major criminal investigations. In 1954, another attorney general memo authorized bugging of subversive groups, such as the Communist Party, under the provisions of national security laws. Hoover supposedly interpreted this memo too as applying to major criminal investigations.

first floor below the tailor's was shut up—which was a good thing, because during the operation an agent fell through a hole in the floor and landed in it. Working over six consecutive Sundays, they completed the task and got the bug up and running. Named "Little Al"—a nod to "Big Al" Capone—it soon began spouting reams of high-grade information, which Roemer and other agents listened to in a special room at the local FBI field office a couple of miles away. J. Edgar Hoover was so pleased that he awarded Roemer a commendation and a merit pay increase. Little Al, the first of its kind, was soon followed by other FBI bugs, planted in places like a vending machine company in Providence, Rhode Island; a plumbing shop in Kenilworth, New Jersey; a travel bureau in New York City; and casinos in Las Vegas. Perhaps the oddest location was a Niagara Falls funeral home where Buffalo boss Steve Magaddino and his family held their meetings. It took a while for the Mafia to figure out that they were being bugged. When G-men came around asking questions about topics that hitherto had been secret, it was assumed that some made men were informing. One New York capo was heard on a bug urging that informers be hunted down and hung from a flagpole with their severed genitals exposed, as a warning to others.

Hoover had reason to relish the successful elsurs. Apalachin had hit him and his FBI like a bombshell. In fear of his wrath, both the Buffalo and Albany field offices had produced maps showing that Joe Barbara's estate was in the other's jurisdiction.

For several decades, Hoover had firmly and repeatedly denied the existence of a national syndicate. But despite his protestations, he knew better. FBI investigations of interstate thefts often caused them to focus on mobsters. Post-Kefauver, the Bureau had instituted a "Top Hoodlum Program" (THP) in which agents compiled reports on major organized crime figures who were sometimes referred to as "Mafia members."[2] A 1954 report from the San Francisco FBI office, which was circulated to offices across the country, identified "presumed heads of the Mafia" in sixteen American cities. The problem was not that Hoover was unaware of the Mafia, but that

2 For example, a 1953 report uses the term in describing Angelo Bruno, future boss of the Philadelphia family, and Russ Bufalino, Joe Barbara's underboss.

he did not want to do battle with it. Some critics ascribe Hoover's reluctance to bribery, others to fear of blackmail. Thirty-four years after his death, such accusations are still unsubstantiated. During his career, Hoover acquired many enemies, all alert for any hint of indiscretion. The Los Angeles and New York City police departments were frequently on bad terms with him; his close association with *Daily Mirror* columnist Walter Winchell did not endear him to rival columnists like Ed Sullivan of the *Daily News*. In Washington, too, Hoover had his share of political and journalistic foes. There was no shortage of people who would dearly have loved to see him brought down by scandal. The fact that their fervent hopes were not realized suggests that there was no real substance during his life to the accusations made after his death.[3]

The more likely explanation for Hoover's reluctance to take on organized crime lies in his managerial style. The Bureau was just that: a classic bureaucracy, with detailed procedures for everything and rigid lines of authority. FBI SACs (special agents in charge of field offices) frequently punctuated their remarks with "Bureau regulations require" or "Bureau regulations do not allow." The FBI maintained field offices from Hawaii to Puerto Rico and attachés in nineteen foreign countries, but decision making was centralized in the Washington headquarters, known as seat of government (SOG). For practical purposes, that meant Hoover's desk. Agents were thoroughly regimented. On duty they were required to wear conservative suits with white handkerchiefs in the breast pocket, white shirts and subdued ties, and to keep their hair neatly trimmed and their shoes polished. At graduation, each new agent class was paraded through Hoover's office for his personal inspection. Those who did not measure up, in appearance or demeanor, never reached the field. According to Bureau lore, men were fired for offering the director a sweaty hand to shake: Hoover thought it was a sign of weak character (and red ties a mark of insincerity). In the field, strict discipline and surprise inspections were the rules. Officially, agents were not allowed to drink coffee while on duty—in practice, this meant they did it in out-of-the-way spots. Unlike other federal law

---

3 Of course Hoover, like many another bureaucrat, was prone to using his subordinates to improve the fixtures in his home or office.

enforcement agencies, Hoover's G-men (he allowed no women) were not covered by civil service laws. Essentially, they served at his pleasure. Despite the working conditions, the Bureau had no trouble obtaining recruits. Salaries were higher than those of other federal investigators and many government attorneys. An agent in good standing who resigned after a few years would receive a letter of thanks from Hoover and access to a network of contacts that guaranteed a well-paying job.

In a classic bureaucracy, the most important task is to maintain and enhance the organization. Since Hoover *was* the FBI, that meant maintaining and enhancing him. Appointed director in 1924, Hoover had witnessed the disastrous attempts of the Prohibition Bureau to enforce the dry laws, an undertaking that came to be characterized by widespread bribery of their agents, disgrace for the administrators, and a general lessening of respect for law enforcement. His own agency had come into existence in 1908, when the U.S. Secret Service had been stripped of some of its authority in retaliation for bringing a case that led to the conviction of a U.S. senator. Unable to use Secret Service men to conduct its investigations, the Department of Justice obtained authorization from President Theodore Roosevelt to create its own investigative bureau. (In 1935 it was given the prefix "Federal.") Attacking organized crime could expose Hoover's agency to similar problems, and himself to retaliation from the Mafia's political friends. Far better, he reasoned, to continue to pursue garden-variety crooks, and the highly unpopular American Communists.

Despite the huge TV ratings garnered by the Kefauver Committee hearings, Hoover did not jump on the bandwagon. Instead, he was largely uncooperative, publicly disagreeing with the committee's assertions about the Mafia and its national scope. The only federal law enforcement agency that targeted the Mafia was the Treasury's Federal Bureau of Narcotics (FBN). Its commissioner, Harry Anslinger, had gone so far as to open offices in Europe, where he detailed agents to keep an eye on narcotics traffickers like Lucky Luciano. In direct contrast to Hoover, who never let his own men work undercover lest they become too comfortable with criminals, FBN agents were assigned to infiltrate drug gangs. The FBN had amassed much more information on American mobsters than the FBI had, but Hoover was not about to humble himself and ask Anslinger for help. And if he had, he would not have gotten it—Anslinger too was an imperious bureaucrat, unwilling to share his turf.[4]

Hoover had been caught napping, and now he had some serious catch-up to do. And in typical Hoover fashion, he wanted to get as much credit for his efforts as possible. He had ridden to glory in the 1930s by pursuing individuals designated "public enemies" like John Dillinger, "Pretty Boy" Floyd, "Machine Gun" Kelly, and Ma Barker and her boys. More recently, the Bureau had begun publishing lists of the ten Most Wanted Fugitives—the '50s version of public enemies. Each time one was caught, it was good for a national story. Now he expanded his Top Hoodlum Program. Whereas previously the Bureau had just been collecting information, in cities where there was a suspected Mafia presence the FBI field office was ordered to identify the leading local figures and to assign agents to make cases against them.

Under the rudimentary post-Kefauver THP, the Bureau had received most of its information from local police.[5] Cops knew the players in their local mob world, though they had never been particularly successful in combating them. The Kefauver Committee had exposed organized crime's corruption of local law enforcement in Miami, New Orleans, Philadelphia, Chicago, and Los Angeles as well as in smaller jurisdictions. At the time of its New York hearings, a massive police corruption scandal had decimated the top command of the NYPD and driven Mayor William O'Dwyer from office. It was the usual equation: Police were linked to politics, and in many places politics were strongly influenced by organized crime.

If gangsters were daring men with little concern for tomorrow, most cops were just the opposite. By definition, people who worked in the civil service had a fairly lengthy time horizon. They looked forward to periodic raises, promotions, and a pension. Cops of the 1950s had either joined up during the Depression or lived through it as children. During the 1930s, in

---

4 Even if he had been willing to share information with Hoover, Anslinger's understanding was less than perfect. No one did more to popularize "the menace of the Mafia" than Anslinger, but his focus on narcotics had led him to overestimate the connections between the American and Italian groups, as well as the overall importance of drugs to the financial health of the American Mafia.

5 In the previously mentioned 1954 San Francisco office report, though their names are redacted, the source of the information is clearly two San Francisco detectives, Frank Ahern and Tom Cahill, who had served as investigators for the Kefauver Committee.

many big-city neighborhoods the only people who had steady employment were policemen and firemen. In those days, to lose one's job was a catastrophe. Incurring the enmity of a politician by bothering his friends in organized crime was not conducive to a long and successful police career. If the bosses at City Hall wanted to do business with the Mafia, or simply were not willing to take it on, the cops would follow suit.

At the same time, police departments valued stability as much as any organization, and crooked politics were a threat to that. The scandals that swept over municipal government usually resulted in a housecleaning at police headquarters, followed by a long period of organizational tension and uncertainty. Thus, means had to be found to lessen the consequences of such periodic eruptions. Honest police administrators—and there were many—recognized that the eradication of gambling, prostitution, and other vices was impossible. Even during periods when reform administrations were in power, it didn't happen. In New York under Mayor La Guardia and Police Commissioner Valentine, both vigorous leaders noted for their personal integrity, a 1939 *Fortune* magazine survey found plenty of gambling and prostitution. Drawn from the urban blue-collar milieu, cops believed that *some* sin was a natural and even necessary part of life. And many honest politicians saw organized crime as just another bloc that had to be accommodated, in the same way as business, labor, religious, or ethnic groups.

There were also elements of law enforcement culture that militated against large-scale investigations of organized crime. The police-prosecutorial world was geared to the quick resolution of individual cases. "Cops expect an arrest within 24 hours" was a familiar newspaper cliché. Making cases against organized crime would have required a huge investment of resources, including the use of specialized personnel such as accountants who were rarely found in D.A.'s offices and never in police departments. Instead, the most common police strategy was one of containment, not suppression. Special squads were designated to make enough raids to keep the gamblers and madams off balance; others within the department were detailed to weed out or neutralize rogue cops. The experience of America's three largest cities illustrates how local police dealt with the mobs in the pre-Apalachin era.

In New York, Mayor Vincent Impelliteri, who in 1950 succeeded the disgraced O'Dwyer, was friendly with Tommy Lucchese. Not so coincidentally, the man he appointed as police commissioner was also acquainted with Lucchese. In 1953 "Impy" was defeated by Robert Wagner, who, though a quality candidate, owed his election to Tammany boss Carmine DeSapio. Many people hailed DeSapio as a new type of Tammany leader, one who supported good government. In fact he was beholden to Frank Costello. In the 1950 mayoral election he had led the fight for Costello's candidate against Impelliteri, but despite help from mob gunmen, DeSapio's man lost.

In 1957, DeSapio alighted from a taxicab leaving $11,200 in crumpled bills behind in an envelope. In an era when the average income was less than $4,000 a year, it was a substantial sum. The cabdriver turned the money over to the police and the passenger was identified from trip logs. When contacted, DeSapio denied ownership of the bills. Though embarrassed, he did not suffer any consequences as a result of the incident. Carmine's associations were well known at police headquarters, and a few years later, when he and a Lucchese family capo were jailed by the Feds for extortion, detectives were not surprised.

In the mid-'50s, the principal NYPD unit dealing with organized crime was the Central Investigation Bureau (CIB), commanded by Deputy Chief John Shanley. Fearful of corruption hazards, Shanley preferred not to have his men approach mobsters directly. CIB was composed of three main elements: surveillance, electronics, and investigation. The surveillance unit was made up of officers who did not look like cops—short, thin, un-Irish-looking men—who tailed mob figures, identifying their haunts. Next, electronics would move in and tap telephone wires, which was legal under New York law with a court order. Then detectives from the investigating section would listen in on the tap from a nearby location, such as a public school. From surveillances, taps, and general street knowledge, the CIB developed a rough picture of how the mob families were organized and operated. Some detectives, like Ralph Salerno, were particularly knowledgeable. Despite an unfavorable political climate, Salerno made it his personal mission to combat the mob. When the FBI began the Top Hoodlum Program, he shared his information with agents.

Alongside the NYPD was the New York County District Attorney's Office, a uniquely powerful entity. Though officially the office served only Manhattan, since Tom Dewey took it over in the mid-1930s it had assumed a status well beyond that of any local prosecutor in New York or most other places. Dewey's successor, Frank Hogan, held the post for more than thirty years, and under his leadership New York County and its hand-picked attorneys and detectives made some solid cases against organized crime.

In Chicago, both Mayor Martin Kennelly and Police Commissioner Timothy O'Connor were acknowledged to be totally honest men—with little power. Kennelly was a millionaire businessman whose previous public service had been along the lines of heading Red Cross drives. The ward bosses put him up for election in 1947, after it became apparent that longtime mayor Ed Kelly was so unpopular with the voters that he could not win another term. Kelly had somehow managed to become quite wealthy on modest public sector salaries, but his replacement had made his fortune honestly in the moving business, causing some people to quip that the office was being given to a man skilled at filling space.

The situation in Chicago proved that organized crime did not have to own the mayor or police commissioner to flourish—there were other ways to influence local law enforcement. In a reflection of city politics, the police department was a collection of baronies over which the commissioner had little control. Most district police captains took their orders from the ward boss, not O'Connor. His only weapon against organized crime was Scotland Yard, the local name for the secretive commissioner's office squad that spied on cops, among other tasks. After the Kefauver hearings, O'Connor appointed a gangster-hating Marine veteran, Lt. Joe Morris, to head a special antimob detail within Scotland Yard. Operating out of an abandoned West Side police station, it began surveilling Outfit members. The methods were often inventive, as when the squad's star detective, Bill Duffy, disguised himself as a Good Humor man and pedaled his ice cream cart onto the grounds of a suburban home where a gala mob party was in progress (when unmasked, he had to beat a hasty retreat). The squad was sometimes accused of employing electronic eavesdropping—illegal under Illinois law—and of roughing up hoodlums. On occasion, civil suits were brought against its members, and in one instance the local state's attorney

charged some of them with assaulting a mob enforcer. When word was relayed to Morris that all complaints would be dropped if he took it a little
easier, he refused to back down. As a young Marine, Morris had been stationed in China in the '20s; when World War II broke out he immediately
rejoined, despite being overage with a family and professional responsibil-
ities. He was not a man to back down from the hoodlums or politicians.

In 1955, Richard J. Daley defeated Kennelly in the Democratic primary
and went on to win the general election for mayor. Because Daley was the
party boss, it was expected that he would fire O'Connor and throw the
town wide open. He did neither. However, Morris's squad was abolished.
According to rumor, during the campaign they had tapped Daley's phone.
The truth was that the offices of both the Democratic Party headquarters
and a gambling center were located in the Morrison Hotel. Scotland Yard
tapped the bookie's line, but not the one running into Democratic Party
headquarters. Daley obviously held no grudge, because in the 1960s, Morris and Duffy would be given high positions in the Police Department.

The Los Angeles police operated very differently from other big-city departments. Its cops were essentially independent of City Hall, because the
chief held civil service tenure. From 1950 on, L.A.'s top cop was William
Parker, an iron-willed man in the Hoover mold (naturally, the two were bitter enemies). One of Parker's first acts was to establish an intelligence
squad under Captain James Hamilton, which monitored organized crime
by employing informants and electronic eavesdropping. It soon began to
acquire extensive dossiers that, under a legal ruling, were deemed Parker's
personal papers, not public records subject to subpoena. The secrets contained within those files were thought to have helped him fend off critics
and thereby remain chief until his death in 1966. During the Kefauver
hearings he shared much of his information with the committee.

Hamilton and his squad were always a threat to organized crime,
sometimes a very direct one. A special detail was stationed at the airport
to spot incoming East Coast gangsters, who would then be unceremoni-
ously rerouted onto the next plane back home. The squad's handling of a
1951 mob hit was typical of its vigorous approach to fighting organized
crime. Two freelance robbers held up a bookmaking joint and shortly afterward were themselves murdered, on orders of Los Angeles boss Jack

Dragna. Intelligence detectives received a tip that one of the hit men was Aldena "Jimmy the Weasel" Fratianno. He was arrested and taken to the Ambassador Hotel, where the intelligence squad maintained a suite of rooms, to be interrogated by Chief Parker and Captain Hamilton for the next five days. But Fratianno refused to confess, and finally had to be released. From then on Hamilton was constantly on his tail, and three years later the squad made an extortion case against him that resulted in Fratianno's receiving a one-to-ten-year sentence in the state penitentiary.[6]

When the Top Hoodlum Program was expanded, Hoover specified that all agents assigned should be volunteers. Since fighting organized crime could lead to failure, with a long-lasting negative impact on careers, in some FBI offices the volunteers had to be obtained the Army way—"You, you, and you are volunteering." In Chicago, one such "volunteer" was thirty-two-year-old Bill Roemer. He had been an agent for seven years, working a succession of East Coast field offices before coming to Chicago in 1955. There he was assigned to Security Squad 1, running down members of CAPUSA (Bureau-speak for Communist Party USA) who had gone underground during the McCarthy-era crackdown. CAPUSA and the Mafia were both secret organizations, so when Hoover was forced to target the latter, he did not initially call upon his crime section chiefs; instead, he assigned the task of compiling information about the Mafia to his assistant director in charge of foreign counterintelligence. One researcher, after consulting a hundred years' worth of news clippings and two hundred books, produced a two-volume report.

With CAPUSA greatly reduced in membership—in some cells, Bureau informants outnumbered the party faithful—Roemer's services were no longer necessary. Another factor in his selection was that the ex-Marine was a former heavyweight boxing champion of Notre Dame who still sparred regularly at local gymnasiums. When the FBI had been assigned to

6 The 1996 movie *Mulholland Falls*, in which Nick Nolte plays an LAPD detective lieutenant of the 1950s, portrays some of the legends of that era. The title comes from a scene in which he and his squad throw a Chicago hoodlum off a cliff along Mulholland Drive. They then warn him that the same thing will happen every time he returns to Los Angeles.

pursue robbers like Dillinger and Floyd a generation earlier, it had learned a hard lesson: Most of its agents lacked the training and experience to go up against armed desperadoes. Raids were botched, bystanders shot, and G-men killed. Not until it augmented its ranks with sharpshooting lawmen from Texas and Oklahoma did the Bureau come out on top in gun battles. The Chicago mob was known to play rough, so it was probably a good idea to police them with agents who could handle themselves. In Roemer's case there was one hitch: He had made up his mind to leave the Bureau and practice law with his brothers in South Bend, Indiana. To that end, he had been taking long lunches in the Chicago Public Library preparing for the Indiana bar exam. But in his new assignment he would be part of the office's Criminal Squad 1, the major case unit that handled high-profile assignments like bank robbery, kidnapping, and extortion, and that was a challenge he couldn't pass up. The fact that the job had been given to C-1 indicated that it was one of Hoover's major priorities.

The plan was to assign one agent to each of the top ten members of the Chicago mob—but who were they? Roemer has described how the agents huddled with Morris, Duffy, and the other members of the defunct Scotland Yard unit, who identified Tony Accardo as boss. In fact the mob bosses' names were not totally secret. Since the early 1950s, lists of them had appeared in Chicago newspapers, Jack Lait and Lee Mortimer's *Chicago Confidential* book, the report of the Kefauver Committee, and a Federal Bureau of Narcotics list of eight hundred top mobsters (which it allowed some journalists to see), though the rankings tended to differ from list to list. The eager Roemer expressed a preference for an assignment as Accardo's case agent. But an earlier recruit to the squad had already claimed him. What the lawmen didn't know was that Accardo was no longer boss. Early in 1957 he had voluntarily stepped aside in favor of Momo Salvatore "Sam" Giancana. The reasons are mysterious: Accardo was only fifty, in good health, and most of the crew chiefs did not like the idea. Accardo had been an ideal boss: tough, strong, and fair. He listened carefully to all sides before making a decision, but then he could act ruthlessly. Within the organization he was called Joe Batters, a name Capone had given him for slugging a man with a baseball bat. When outfit treasurer Jake Guzik withheld some money, Tony had him kidnapped and held until Jake's arithmetic improved.

Some bosses would have killed Guzik, but Accardo restored him to his role as financial brain of the outfit (his sudden death from a heart attack in 1956 was a blow to the mob). Tony was also discreet in his personal life, a family man not given to frequenting nightspots with a blonde on each arm. The media, which loved to hang nicknames on mobsters, was largely unaware of the "Batters" moniker—all that they could come up with for Accardo was "Big Tuna," because he had once had his picture taken holding the prize catch in a fishing contest.[7]

Giancana, unstable and a man about town, was Accardo's opposite. He liked to boast that during World War II, when the draft board asked him what kind of work he did, "I told them I steal for a living, [so] they thought I was crazy." A product of the Near West Side, one of the mob's traditional recruiting grounds, Sam had been a member of a famous street gang, "the 42s," with a reputation as a top getaway driver. Working his way up the mob ladder, he distinguished himself by leading a bullet-punctuated takeover of Chicago's black-owned policy (numbers) wheels. During one kidnapping of a policy kingpin, a police officer who happened on the scene was shot. In a similar attempt, a mob heavy was killed by a target's bodyguards, who were off-duty police officers. Both incidents brought a lot of bad publicity to the Outfit. Shoot-outs with cops had been common back in the days when Giancana was in the 42 gang. But the success of the American Mafia was based on the ability of its leaders to rise above their street-tough ways and behave like corporate execs when the occasion required it. Some crew chiefs worried that Giancana might not be up to the job. To calm their fears, Accardo agreed to remain as a sort of counselor (the term *consigliere* was not in local usage) along with Paul Ricca, and it was felt that between them they could surely keep Giancana out of trouble. As it would turn out, Accardo was only on leave—and perhaps that's the way he had planned it all along. Throughout his career he displayed a great facility for adapting to the times. He may well have sensed that with a man like Vito Genovese replacing

7 I have tried to use nicknames and terminology common to the particular time and place, e.g., I refer to Accardo as "Tony" or "Tuna," the nickname hung on him by Chicago reporters, not "Joe Batters." I have made a concession to revisionist history and called Giancana "Sam," although during the time under discussion, he was known to the police by his boyhood nickname, "Mooney" (as in spacey). By the same token, I will call the Chicago mob "the Outfit," although in the '50s and early '60s it was referred to as "the Syndicate" (a term that might cause it to be confused with the national body).

Costello, and the Apalachin raid, the Mafia was headed for a rough patch. Historically, number one was a vulnerable spot, and Tony was no fool: He died in bed at the age of eighty-six never having been shot or having spent a night in jail, a rarity among mob leadership. Regardless of his motives in stepping down, it would have been better if had he issued a press release. As it was, he went on the Top Hoodlum list as target number one.

Others who made the roll were Giancana, Ricca, labor racketeer and political fixer Murray "The Camel"[8] Humphreys, and Capone's cousin Rocco Fiaschetti. The top ten also included territorial overseers such as James "Monk" Allegretti, boss of the Near North Side nightlife district, and Lenny Patrick, overseer of the Jewish gambling groups then in the process of relocating from the Far West Side to the Far North Side. Roemer drew as his target Gussie "Shotgun" Alex, boss of the Loop. Notable for their omission were Giancana's close associate Marshall Caifano, who had a hand in many enterprises; Felix "Milwaukee Phil" Alderisio, a much-feared enforcer; and Frank "Strongy" Ferraro, who had just been named underboss. As the G-men began to learn more about the mob, these three replaced Fiaschetti, Allegretti, and Patrick on the list. The agents also managed to plant a bug in the Amory Lounge, a suburban bar used as a headquarters by Sam Giancana. Since at the time he was known as "Mooney," they named the bug "Mo."

It was a stretch to think that just ten G-men were going to break up a forty-year-old organization with three hundred made members, thousands of associates, and powerful connections. Even if the Bureau had assigned fifty agents to THP, it would still have been at a disadvantage. G-men were not yet as streetwise as big-city detectives. In a place like Chicago, most cops had grown up in the same environment as the mob guys and were aware of the Outfit. As cops they could not avoid knowing about it, especially those who worked in districts where the mob was active, or investigated crimes it was involved in, such as vice, gambling, burglary, and hijacking. The usual characterization of the '50s FBI as a bunch of small-town hicks with the street smarts of Boy Scouts, however, is inaccurate. A fair share of the agents came from big cities, or from police families, or had been cops themselves. Those assigned to squads such as

8 The "camel" nickname was thought to be a play on "Hump," though he was also known to favor camel hair coats.

cartage knew of Mafia involvement in hijacking. However, they were not encouraged to come to grips with the mob. FBI agents also had certain advantages over the municipals. They were thoroughly conversant with the laws regarding such complex topics as criminal conspiracy. Years of trailing spies had made some of them experts at conducting surveillances. And they were part of a national agency insulated from local politics; they had access to generally incorruptible federal courts, and a rich uncle to finance them. The ideal arrangement would have been a joint task force composed of G-men and selected city cops like Morris and Duffy, but that would be years in coming. Instead, the agencies had to get by with informal liaisons.

During the FBI war on the Mafia it was necessary to formulate rules of engagement on both sides. Over the years the Mafia had maintained its own codes of conduct. For the most part it rejected violence against law enforcement officers. One reason was that they recognized that cops were simply doing their jobs—and if one of them were killed, another would take his place. Even more compelling, the police were very likely to retaliate if a colleague got hurt.[9] However, there were certain lines that the Mafia did not wish law enforcement to cross. One of the most important was the sanctity of family, which could have a very broad definition. Normally, mob guys' wives and children were sheltered from their business dealings. Since they were innocent civilians, the cops were willing to leave them alone. But sometimes situations arose in which police duty was at odds with deference to noncombatants. When a mob hit took place, it was common to pick up the bosses for questioning. Realizing that the press demanded this charade, the bosses played along, even though they were not about to talk and would soon be sprung on a writ of habeas corpus. What they did not want was to be arrested at home. As they would tell detectives who violated the protocol, "All you had to do was call me and I would have met you anyplace you wanted me to. Don't embarrass my kids." (Of course,

9 In the 1980s, after a Bonanno family associate murdered a federal drug agent, law enforcement officers mounted an all-out manhunt to find the killer. The five New York families immediately ordered their troops not to shelter him. One member of the Lucchese family disobeyed the order and hid the wanted man. When his bosses found out, he was told to kill the fugitive at once. He refused, so the Luccheses set the cop-killer up for a hit by the Bonannos. They then killed their own man for failing to obey orders. The affair was a reminder that in the Mafia world, protocol and family welfare were more important than personal friendships.

if a wiretap had picked up such a conversation, the detective might have been back in uniform the next day.)

Weddings and funerals were also off limits. Often these were state occasions for the Mafia, and everyone in mobdom was expected to attend—a tempting opportunity to update file photos or ID some new face. Because mafiosi were sensitive about having their daughter's wedding or their father's funeral spied on by strangers, a cop sent to do it was wise to keep a low profile and have a backup team nearby in case trouble developed. One trick was to place an obvious police surveillance van near the door, causing guests to turn their faces away as they entered. When they did so, they would be photographed by a hidden camera strategically deployed in a nearby apartment building. Even simple dinner parties could provide valuable intelligence. At mob affairs, seating arrangements and the amount of bowing and scraping a guest was accorded were strict reflections of rank.

These rules went only so far, and between the FBI and the Mafia there was a learning curve. In New York City in the early 1960s, an agent observing the funeral of a mob elder statesman was set upon by a Mafioso, beaten, kicked into unconsciousness, and relieved of his service revolver. The assailant was jailed, and some agents called on members of the mob and forcefully emphasized the Bureau's displeasure. In Philadelphia a young FBI agent on a routine investigation entered a poultry shop, unaware that it was owned by a mob underboss; he was seized by four goons and thrown out into the street. A few hours later a squad of veteran agents returned to the shop and administered an etiquette lesson to the goons. Incidents like these soon convinced the mob that FBI Boy Scouts could quickly turn into Marines. In Chicago, Bill Roemer became known as "the G's muscle guy"—a reputation not without its downside. Outfit hoods began casing his house and making threatening phone calls to his wife. Eventually Roemer negotiated a pact with Murray Humphreys in which both sides agreed not to get too personal.

As FBI agents started to get acquainted with the Mafia, they became aware of something that most people did not suspect: Mob life was dull. Most of the soldiers and their associates sat around eating, drinking, and playing cards, occasionally making the rounds of their various hangouts.

New York mobsters liked to congregate in their own social clubs. Chicago Outfit guys preferred getting together at bars and restaurants that they or their associates ran. Mob soldiers also spent a lot of time talking about possible big scores, most of which never came off. Across the country, agents listening to wiretaps or bugs soon learned that mob guys spoke in cryptic fashion and employed slang or Italian phrases that made it hard to follow the discussion. Nobody seemed to have a last name, only nicknames like "South Side Joe" or "Fat Louie." The South Side of most towns had a number of guys named Joe, and since mobsters spent a lot of time eating, many Louies were overweight. Some hoodlums might spend twenty minutes talking about "Butch" running around at night and getting into trouble before the Feds grasped that Butch was a pet dog.

In the past, a few gangsters had occasionally brushed up against the FBI. They knew that federal cases were always well prepared and tough to beat. As was commonly said in the underworld, "When the Feds get you, they got you." But traditionally the FBI had been only an occasional presence. Now Uncle Sam was seen a lot more often. When the mob bosses consulted their wise men and political friends, they were told that the federal heat was probably a temporary drive that would soon be called off. Possibly J. Edgar Hoover felt the same way. In 1958 the headquarters team that had compiled the two-volume report that said there was a Mafia circulated copies to key government officials. When Hoover learned about it, he ordered all twenty-five numbered copies recalled.

The Federal Bureau of Narcotics had its own version of the Top Hoodlum Program. At midcentury, Vito Genovese topped the list. In 1957 a New York drug dealer named Nelson Cantellops was sent to prison as a result of a case brought by FBN agents. The Puerto Rican Cantellops was an associate, not a made member, and he suspected that this was why he hadn't been furnished with a high-priced lawyer who might have beaten the rap. So he contacted the narcs and began to tell tales. According to Cantellops, for two years he had functioned as a courier, carrying heroin between New York and other cities. He claimed this brought him into face-to-face contact with some top figures, including Genovese. Cantellops related that on one occasion he had even accompanied Genovese to a meeting in the Bronx where allotments of territory were being discussed.

If Cantellops was telling the truth, Genovese's organization had been incredibly careless. In 1958 Vito and twenty-three of his gang were indicted. Many observers thought the case, which relied on a single informant, would never hold up. But Cantellops sat in the witness chair for four weeks being worked over by teams of skilled lawyers without changing his story. To everyone's surprise, the defendants were found guilty, and Genovese was sentenced to fifteen years in prison. In 1969, NYPD detective Ralph Salerno described the evidence against Genovese as "questionable," noting that "to anyone who understands the protocol and insulation procedures of Cosa Nostra this testimony is almost unbelievable."

An alternative explanation is that Cantellops was primed by Tommy Lucchese and Carlo Gambino in order to get rid of Genovese, who they suspected might be thinking of getting rid of them in a more violent fashion. Despite his conviction, Genovese continued to run his family from a cell in the Atlanta penitentiary until his death in 1969. Cantellops, who won his freedom by testifying, was killed in a brawl a few years later.

In Chicago, Richard Ogilvie, who had taken leave from a partnership in a major law firm to head the Midwest office of the Department of Justice anti-organized-crime operation, was preparing a tax case against Tony Accardo. Big Tuna had reported an income of $60,000 a year—a substantial sum in 1959—from a job as a beer salesman. It was assumed that he was selling beer the old-fashioned way, by telling saloon keepers, "Take my brand, or else." FBI agents were dispatched to interview them and build an extortion case. The problem was that most of the customers had never met Mr. Accardo or any of his boys. The beer they purchased was their regular supply. Seemingly, the brewer had retained Accardo as a goodwill ambassador, and on some occasions, without using any coercion, Tony urged his friends to buy the product. The real purpose of the arrangement was to give Accardo a way to account for his illegitimate income if the IRS went after him on what was called a net worth case. If Treasury agents could show that the gangster had a level of expenditure that required an income higher than he reported, he could be prosecuted. In this instance he had paid taxes on his $60,000 and, like a regular salesman, had taken a $3,000 deduction for the use of his car. It was the deduction that provided the basis for a charge. Accardo was not making the rounds of customers, therefore the deduction was not legitimate, and he was indicted for filing a false tax report.

The relatively minor charges against Accardo illustrated another problem in targeting top hoodlums: It was counter to general principles of American criminal justice. The usual practice, investigating a known crime in order to apprehend unknown culprits, was reversed. Now the government was investigating a known criminal to find crimes he might be charged with. It was the philosophy that had been used to get Capone thirty years earlier on tax charges, but many lawyers did not like the idea, fearing that someday the government might decide to target other people it deemed undesirable.

In situations like the Accardo indictment, the Outfit usually relied on Jake Guzik or Murray Humphreys. Though neither was a lawyer, both were skilled at obtaining acquittals for their mob friends—they had a number of acquaintances on the bench. Jake's fatal heart attack had not only removed him from the scene, it had also given an opportunity for Humphreys to demonstrate how clever he was: Guzik was stricken while dining at a posh Loop chophouse frequented by top lawyers and judges, and Humphreys knew the association wouldn't be good. He had the body removed to Guzik's house, where he told Mrs. Guzik to announce that her husband had died at home.

In the Accardo case, the judge assigned was unreachable. So Humphreys got a list of the jury panel and identified a couple of them as having union ties. One was a truck driver, and a call was made to Jimmy Hoffa to determine if he was a Teamster. He was, so if he were selected, his union leaders would be sure to tell him what a good fellow Tony Accardo was. A mob soldier was instructed to strike up a friendship with a gas station attendant whose name was on the list, with a view toward bribing him if the man was seated on the jury. Humphreys outlined his strategy to his boardroom colleagues, and it was heard on Little Al. The FBI immediately alerted Ogilvie, and the judge agreed to switch jury panels with a colleague, a tactic that had also been employed during the Capone trial. Accardo was tried in front of an unfixed jury, convicted, and sentenced to six years in prison, though he remained free while he appealed the verdict.

It was not the only setback for the usually cautious Accardo. In 1959, he and his wife went on a European vacation with another couple who were old family friends. The man also happened to be a Chicago police lieutenant. When news stories about the travelers began to appear, it caused a furor, and the lieutenant, a thirty-seven-year veteran of the force, was fired. The cop was a gentlemanly person, just shy of retirement age. He did not hold a position where he was privy to confidential information about organized crime, but his ill-advised trip was the kind of thing that made the Feds reluctant to share intelligence with the local police.

The U.S. Court of Appeals ordered a new trial for Accardo. By that time, Ogilvie had left the Department of Justice and embarked on a political career that would eventually lead him to the governorship. At the second trial, Accardo was acquitted. Even if he had been sent to prison, it would not have made much of a difference; in 1944, when most of the top echelon of the Chicago mob had been jailed in the Hollywood extortion case, the Outfit had hardly missed a beat. The Top Hoodlum Program may have been a useful way to obtain information, but it would never break the Mafia. Back in the 1930s when Dillinger and the other gunmen were being killed or imprisoned, taking out the leader and a few lieutenants had been an effective tactic. Unlike the robbers and kidnappers, the American Mafia was not a partnership or a small business. It was a corporation, and like the more conventional ones, it had a life beyond its top leadership.

In the end, the government's initial post-Apalachin efforts against the Mafia in New York, Chicago, and elsewhere amounted to little more than intelligence gathering and occasional prosecutions. By 1960, the Top Hoodlum squads in New York and Chicago actually had fewer agents assigned than when they were started, and Hoover's suppression of his Bureau's report on the Mafia did not bode well for the prospect of a sustained federal assault.

CHAPTER 3

WHEELING AND DEALING WITH MOBSTERS:
THE FRIENDS OF JIMMY HOFFA

From the Civil War through World War II, railroads had been America's principal freight carriers. During that period, railroad strikes had twice so paralyzed the nation that the federal government had used troops to break them. Now the dominant mode of transport was trucks, and the potential disruptive power of the trucking union was immense. The International Brotherhood of Teamsters, Chauffeurs, Warehousemen, Stablemen and Helpers of America (IBT), with one and a half million members, was the largest and richest union in the country. Whereas the railroads were run by a few giant corporations, which possessed great political influence, the trucking industry was made up of thousands of smaller firms. It was the union that swung the weight. And during the 1950s, some people began to suspect that the Mafia might be swinging the union.

In 1957 a Select Committee of the United States Senate launched a probe of labor racketeering. Among its targets was the IBT, some of whose legal services were provided by the firm of the rising superstar attorney Edward Bennett Williams. On a snowy night in February, one of Williams's partners, Edwin Cheyfitz, a PR man turned lawyer, invited two guests to his home for an intimate get-acquainted meeting. The first was a Teamsters vice president, forty-four-year-old James Hoffa. Though a key figure in the all-important transportation sector, as yet he was little known to the public. But if he became the next head of the union—and this seemed likely—he would be a household name. The second guest was Robert Kennedy, chief counsel for the Senate Investigating Committee. Only thirty-one years of age, he too was someone to be reckoned with. He was a member of a rich and powerful family, and had managed his brother Jack's successful 1952 campaign for the U.S. Senate. Everyone in politics knew it was only a matter of time until Jack Kennedy, a member of the investigating committee, made a run for the White House.

In arranging the meeting, Cheyfitz, an ex-Communist who was acquainted with both Robert Kennedy and Jimmy Hoffa, was engaging in the classic Washington lawyer-lobbyist gambit: Provide your client with access to the powerful, and in so doing, demonstrate to both sides how well connected you are. Except that Cheyfitz was trying to pull off a triple play. Ostensibly he represented the union and its president, Dave Beck. But at Hoffa's behest, he had been passing derogatory information about Beck to Kennedy as a means of hastening Jimmy's ascension to the top job. At the same time, he was pitching Hoffa as a man whose potential for reform outweighed his earlier transgressions: Therefore Kennedy should destroy Beck and embrace Hoffa. For Hoffa's part, this supposedly good bad man had set a scheme of his own in motion. Knowing that he would be a target of Kennedy's investigation, Hoffa had hired New York lawyer John Cye Cheasty to infiltrate the Senate committee by obtaining a job as one of its investigators. Cheasty, who had served in both the U.S. Secret Service and the IRS, informed Kennedy of the scheme and agreed to act as a double agent.

Most people involved in such byzantine maneuvers would not have thought it prudent to sit down to dinner with their adversary. But Kennedy and Hoffa both placed a high premium on toughness, and they wanted to measure each other face to face. Hoffa, though only five feet five and a half inches tall, was often described as being "built like a truck." Kennedy, of medium height and weight, had played end on the Harvard football team. When they shook hands, Kennedy commented on Hoffa's firm grip. Jimmy thought to himself that Kennedy's handshake was a limp, perfunctory gesture, showing a lack of respect. During the meal, Hoffa bragged at length about how he could get the best of anyone who gave him trouble; Kennedy thought that a real tough guy would not be so boastful. At 9:30 Mrs. Kennedy called and asked to speak to her husband. In an attempt to be humorous, Kennedy said within Hoffa's earshot, " I'm still alive, dear, but if you hear a loud explosion I probably won't be." Hoffa, unfamiliar with Harvard-style witticisms, was not amused. He asked Kennedy to tell his wife that he was not as bad as people thought, but by now Kennedy thought that he was worse. Mrs. Kennedy had called to report that there had been an automobile accident in front of their house and the hysterical driver was sitting in their living room, and that provided an excuse for Bob to depart. The dinner party had not been a success.

James Riddle Hoffa was not a criminal in the conventional sense. He had worked hard all his life, and his only convictions arose from union battles. At age fourteen he had left school to help support his widowed mother. As a teenager he unloaded boxcars for thirty-two cents an hour, became involved in a strike, and was later hired as a Teamsters organizer. The union's name came from the days when members drove teams of horses pulling delivery wagons, a job that took considerable physical strength. In the nineteenth century, police chiefs sometimes obtained recruits by going down to the local freight terminal to watch teamsters battling for places at the head of the line. The bruiser who emerged victorious would be offered a patrolman's badge. Hoffa, a freight handler, did not learn to drive a rig until the 1950s. Still, he had the Teamsters spirit and was frequently involved in violence. During one strike he was arrested eighteen times in twenty-four hours, being bailed out repeatedly in order to return to the picket line.

In 1935, the twenty-two-year-old Hoffa was made a business agent for Detroit Local 299. Two years later as part of his training he was sent to work with a Trotskyite-run local in Minneapolis. He admired the vigorous way they conducted organizing drives but was not attracted to their socialist philosophy. Even the presence in Detroit of labor statesman Walter Reuther of the United Auto Workers did not prompt Hoffa to look beyond immediate union concerns. Power, not theory, attracted him, and he was a keen student of union politics. Up to this point Teamster locals consisted largely of short-haul delivery truck drivers. It was the Trotskyites who had the idea to organize long-haul interstate freight drivers; signing up the "over the road" truckers would allow locals to expand their jurisdiction to distant areas. When the Trotskyite leaders tried to secede from the IBT and join the CIO, Hoffa was part of a team dispatched by the International's president, Dan Tobin, to block the move. Tobin was a key member of FDR's New Deal coalition and had direct access to the president, which has often been cited as the reason why the Department of Justice indicted the Minneapolis Teamster leaders for violation of the Sedition Laws in 1941. Their conviction and imprisonment helped pave the way for Hoffa's rise. Hoffa also benefited from a draft deferment: Though he was only in his twenties and classified 1-A, his work as a union officer was deemed essential to the war effort.

It was probably inevitable that an empire builder like Hoffa would hook up with the Mafia. The upper Midwest of his time was also the spawning ground of powerful organized crime groups. When Hoffa became a Teamster official, Detroit, Chicago, and Cleveland were strong Mafia towns. As Jimmy used to tell his lieutenants, "They were here before we were." Like so many other people in public life, he saw them as a power bloc that had to be accommodated. In the 1930s it was common for Detroit employers like the Ford Motor Company to employ Mafia goons to break strikes. Yet when Teamsters Local 299 conducted bloody organizing drives in the late 1930s, the Detroit mob remained neutral. And in the early 1940s, support from the gangsters enabled 299 to win a violent struggle against a rival CIO union. Some accounts credit Hoffa with securing mob backing. One avenue of access to the gangsters was a former girlfriend with close ties to several Detroit gangsters.[1]

In 1945 Hoffa became president of Local 299. Using the wide-area approach pioneered in Minnesota, he began expanding throughout the Midwest. By 1949 he was head of the Central States Teamsters. He always fought hard for his members but never neglected to take care of his own welfare with under-the-table deals. He continued to do business with the mob in Detroit and elsewhere, usually operating on a quid pro quo basis. In Detroit, when gangsters assisted the union in organizing drives, the Teamsters

1 In later years, Sylvia Pagano and her son lived with Jimmy Hoffa and his wife and children. Her son, Charles "Chuckie" O'Brien, and one of her boyfriends, Detroit capo Tony Giacalone, would figure prominently in the investigation of Hoffa's disappearance in 1975.

in return provided tips on where valuable merchandise was stored. They might also leave trucks unattended, giving thieves a chance to loot the cargo.

In 1949, Jimmy met Paul "Red" Dorfman of Chicago. Red had been a small-time featherweight prizefighter in the 1920s, then began doing strong-arm work for the mob, winning the favor of Murray "The Camel" Humphreys. In 1940, the head of a Chicago waste haulers' union was murdered. The only other official of the local was a man named Jack Ruby, who was not selected to take over (he later relocated to Dallas, where in 1963 he murdered Lee Harvey Oswald on national television). Instead, Red Dorfman—who had never worked in the field—walked into a union meeting, plunked down his membership dues, and was promptly elected secretary-treasurer. Humphreys had used his influence to persuade the members to support him, and in his new job Dorfman operated according to Humphreys's principles. An employer who did not meet his demands could expect Red to walk into his office, drop two bullets on the desk, and announce, "The next one is going into your head." Dorfman and Joey Glimco, the mob's overseer of both the Fulton poultry market and the city taxi drivers union, obtained the support of the Chicago mob bosses for the Teamsters organizing drives in return for Hoffa allowing the gangsters to loot the Local's funds or go easy on employers who paid them off. In 1950 Hoffa awarded the Central States Teamsters' health and benefit insurance account to Red Dorfman's twenty-six-year-old stepson, Allen Dorfman, who had recently gone into the business, despite having neither a license nor an office.

Hoffa was the top man in the Midwest and was making inroads in the South, and Dave Beck of Seattle was head of the IBT in the eleven western states. One of the two would be Dan Tobin's successor. Hoffa perceived that the key to dominance of the union was in the eastern states, particularly the New York metropolitan area. In the East, there was no powerful regional leader, only a collection of fiefdoms—many of them controlled by organized crime figures. One of Hoffa's first moves in his campaign for the top seat was to take control of New York's 125,000-member Joint Council 16. He prevailed on Red Dorfman to enlist the support of Anthony "Tony Ducks" Corallo and Johnny DioGuardi, capos in the Lucchese crime family. The unions under

their control were made up of blacks and Hispanics, who worked for minimum wages, received no benefits, and knew better than to complain.
Corallo and DioGuardi were ex–street toughs who had been schooled in the
garment center: The New York Mafia's equivalent of the Harvard Business
School, it was a place where many hoods learned the effective—if legally
dubious—management skills that enabled them to run various mob enterprises. When Hoffa met the two, they were already millionaires.

Corallo acquired his nickname from his ability to dodge or "duck" criminal charges. In addition to being a labor racketeer, he was also involved in
bookmaking, loan sharking, drug dealing, and an occasional murder; he
would eventually become the family boss. In 1935, twenty-two years old
and fresh from serving a six-month wrist-slap sentence for drug dealing,
Corallo had been given his big break by Tommy Lucchese: an assignment
collecting debts from garment center employers. In a business as uncertain
as the fashion industry, it was almost impossible for a manufacturer to get a
bank loan to finance his operations, particularly during the Depression.
The mob filled the void, making loans at high interest rates. If a borrower's
line sold well, both parties made out fine. If not, the manufacturer might be
unable to make his payment, and that's when Ducks would drop by to remind him of his obligation. Corallo, with his burly build, piercing dark eyes,
and fierce stare, did not have to do much more than look the debtor in the
eye to get results. In some instances, the cash-strapped manufacturer could
meet his payments only by handing over a piece of his business to the mob.
This wasn't necessarily to his detriment—a gangster-dominated union
might enter into a sweetheart contract with the manufacturer, enabling
him to cut his labor costs. If this upset the workforce, Corallo or some other
mob heavy would suddenly appear on the shop floor and look around.
Their mere presence was usually enough to stifle any protest.

DioGuardi, known in the mob world as "Johnny Dio," was an alum of
Sing Sing. After serving his apprenticeship as a slugger in the garment district he moved up to being a full-fledged labor racketeer. By the 1950s he
was raking in $100,000 per week. He dined out six nights a week with
friends, always picking up the checks; at Christmas he would give his wife
a shoe box with $50,000 in cash and tell her, "Go buy yourself some nice
clothes, honey." This generous man was more vicious than Corallo. In

1956, he shocked the Mafia by breaking the long-standing mob rule against assaulting cops or journalists. Victor Riesel of the *New York Mirror* was a prominent New York newsman whose syndicated column appeared in 193 newspapers across the country. Labor racketeering was one of the subjects he frequently wrote about, and at the time, he was sharing his information with a federal grand jury targeting Johnny Dio. One night in April, Riesel appeared on a late-night radio show, discussing union corruption. After the show he went for a meal at Lindy's, the famous Broadway rendezvous for highfliers of all stripes, including mobsters. Leaving the restaurant at 3 A.M., he had gone only a few steps when a man appeared out of the shadows and hurled sulfuric acid in his face. He was blinded for life. The assailant was a twenty-two-year-old Lower East Side thug named Abe Telvi, who is generally believed to have been paid $1,175 by Johnny Dio to carry out the attack.

When Dutch Schultz had proposed killing prosecutor Tom Dewey in 1935, Lucky Luciano warned him off, saying it would "bring the whole world down around our ears." According to legend, Luciano ensured that the reckless Schultz did not carry out his threat by having him murdered. Riesel's blinding created a furor. In every era there are journalists of the Damon Runyon school for whom gangsters make cute copy; this incident reminded them that they were not immune from mob violence. Runyon himself was dead, but his great friend Walter Winchell—also a *New York Mirror* columnist and one who was on friendly terms with the likes of Frank Costello—was among those crying for retribution. Fearful for his life, Dio swore to his fellow mobsters that he was not involved in the attack. For his part, Telvi only discovered how prominent his victim was when he read the papers. Asking Johnny for an additional payoff, he got it—in lead. In the end, although Dio and six other men were indicted for obstructing justice, he was not one of the three convicted.

Corallo and DioGuardi's experience in the garment center had provided them with business acumen of a certain kind, as demonstrated by their expansion of operations to the airport. The waterfront was dying—in part because the mob had made it too expensive for shippers to use. So the gangsters began moving in on the new freight bonanza provided by air cargo. In addition to the money that could be extorted from union members and employers, the $60 billion a year in freight that would eventually pass through Idlewild (later Kennedy) Airport became an inviting target for burglars and robbers who had access to Teamster information. Some of New York's top hijackers of the next generation would learn their trade and practice it frequently at JFK. By transferring their members around and loading the rolls with gangsters who did no work, Corallo and Dio created additional "paper locals." Since it was the votes of locals rather than individuals that decided Teamster elections, this made their support even more valuable to Jimmy and his allies. In return for their services, Hoffa gave them a free hand in running their unions as adjuncts of the Mafia.

Across the river on the Jersey side of New York Harbor, another one of Hoffa's new allies was Tony Provenzano, a brawny, tough-talking capo in what became Vito Genovese's family. "Tony Pro," as he was known, had been installed by the mob as head of Teamsters Local 560. An ex-boxer, Provenzano owed his success to muscle. Union members who questioned his orders were liable to a beating, and in some cases murder. Once a fellow 560 officer running on Provenzano's slate got more votes than he did. Tony worried that someone that popular might get ideas, so one night the man disappeared. Making someone vanish was an old Mafia trick. Not only did the absence of a body frustrate investigators, but the uncertainty caused fear and anguish among the victim's family and friends. On a more practical level, it prevented anyone from collecting life insurance—a person was not presumed dead until seven years after his disappearance. When Hoffa later became president of the IBT, he quickly promoted Tony Pro to be head of a Joint Council and vice president of the International.

Tobin finally stepped down in 1952, but the time was not right for Hoffa to claim the top job. He had risen too quickly and had too many rough edges. In contrast, Dave Beck was highly regarded in western business and civic circles: Though a school dropout, he had been a member of the University of Washington's Board of Trustees. He appeared much more suited for a job in the national spotlight. Jimmy Hoffa threw his support to him; in return he was given the title of vice president and the right to run his own domain without interference. Tobin had maintained union headquarters in Indianapolis, Indiana; Beck moved it to a "marble palace" in Washington, D.C. He also moved the union away from its traditional Democratic support and toward the Republicans who, under President Eisenhower, took over the White House and Congress. Hoffa wasn't worried. He knew a few things about the real Dave Beck, and he was confident that the top job would be open again before long.

Robert Francis Kennedy inhabited a different world from that of Jimmy Hoffa, Red Dorfman, Ducks Corallo, Johnny Dio, or Tony Pro; his father had seen to that. Joseph Kennedy, Sr., made part of his fortune in the liquor business, and during Prohibition he reportedly dealt with mob figures like Frank Costello. But he kept his family sheltered from that part of his life. The sons of FDR's ambassador to the Court of St. James were educated at elite schools, and their ambitions were directed toward high public office. Of the four boys, it was Bob who most possessed a Boston Irish politician's talent for making both warm friends and fierce enemies. And always he strove to do what his father had taught him was most important—win. After he managed Jack's successful campaign for the Senate, he went to work as an assistant counsel for Joe McCarthy, then chairman of the Senate Permanent Subcommittee on Investigations. That stint was brief, because he was unable to get along with chief counsel Roy Cohn. He returned as chief counsel in 1955, when the Democrats had regained control of the Senate and the subcommittee was chaired by John McClellan of Arkansas.

The 1950s were a time of high-profile investigations. Senator Kefauver pursued the Mafia. The House Committee on Un-American Activities and McCarthy's Senate committee chased Reds. Then the Senate went after McCarthy for interfering with the U.S. Army. The 1954 Oscar-winning movie *On the Waterfront* caught the national mood. Marlon Brando plays a young longshoreman who informs on gangsters (including his own brother) running a corrupt union on the New York waterfront. The film was the work of a writer and a director who had named names at hearings of the Committee on Un-American Activities. Meant to portray informers as men of high morality—a Catholic priest played by Karl Malden constantly assures Brando that in giving up his friends he is doing God's work—it neatly switched villains from the Reds to the Mafia. It was a wise decision: Anti-Communist movies, even with superstars like John Wayne in the lead, were proving to be box office bombs, while the Kefauver hearings had restored gangbuster films to popularity.

McClellan wanted to probe labor racketeering, but it was not within his jurisdiction. So a select committee was formed, composed of four senators drawn from Investigations and four from the union-friendly Labor Committee, with McClellan as chairman. Jack Kennedy was one of those selected from the Labor Committee, but it was Bobby who formed the heart and soul of the investigation.[2] A tireless worker, he infused his energy and zeal into a staff of one hundred that included lawyers, investigators, accountants, and support personnel. He also received information from a network of law enforcement officers such as Captain Hamilton of the LAPD intelligence squad and federal narcotics agents.

In some respects the Kennedys were going against type. Northern Democrats were generally strong supporters of labor. Because Dave Beck had made the Teamsters one of the few unions that backed the Republican Party, it was the GOP members of the committee, such as Karl Mundt of South Dakota and Barry Goldwater of Arizona, who tended to favor them. During an earlier probe of the IBT led by a Kansas Republican congressman, Hoffa had retained the services of former Kansas Republican governor Payne Ratner. Shortly afterward the investigation was quietly dropped.

This time around, Hoffa thought his safety was John Cheasty. In March, before the committee hearings got underway, Cheasty met Hoffa in Washington's Dupont Circle and gave him a folder containing committee documents. In return Hoffa handed Cheasty two thousand dollars in crumpled bills. FBI cameras filmed the action. The next night Cheasty passed more documents to Hoffa, though without receiving any money. Hoffa walked into the lobby of a nearby hotel and was arrested by the FBI while still in possession of the papers. At midnight he was arraigned at the District of Columbia courthouse. As he was led in, he noticed Bobby Kennedy waiting, and the two men glared at each other for a few minutes. Then, during a brief discussion, they began arguing about who could do the most push-ups. The young chief counsel, a lawyer who had never tried a case, rashly

2 "Bobby" was the name by which the press generally referred to Kennedy, though only his family were allowed to do so to his face. Friends called him Bob, while Jimmy Hoffa referred to him as Booby.

promised that if the jury failed to convict Hoffa, he would personally jump off the Capitol dome.

Hoffa's trial commenced in June. Edward Bennett Williams was his defense attorney, and an African-American female lawyer was among his co-counsels, possibly selected with an eye toward the eight black jurors. During the trial, an African-American community newspaper printed a special edition extolling Hoffa and his lawyers, and delivered copies to all the jurors' homes. On the day that Hoffa took the stand, former heavyweight champion Joe Louis dropped by to put his arms around his "good friend Jimmy" in full view of the jurors. Despite what appeared to be solid evidence, Hoffa was acquitted. Edward Bennett Williams immediately announced that he was going to buy a parachute for Bobby Kennedy to use when he jumped off the Capitol. Although Williams's legal skills and the plug from Joe Louis were given the credit, one racketeer in the courtroom was heard to say, "Let the lawyers think they did it." If there was any funny business, it would not have been the only time a Hoffa jury was tampered with.

A shaken Kennedy simply told the staff that they now had a lot of work to do. He was so obsessed with the investigation that one night, as he and a friend were driving home at 11 P.M., he noticed lights still burning in Hoffa's office and immediately went back to his own office to work for several more hours. When Hoffa heard of the incident, he supposedly ordered that the lights be left on every night.

Dave Beck was not as fortunate as Hoffa. Reports that Kennedy received from committee investigators (and sub rosa from Hoffa) showed that Beck had used Teamster money to build his home, complete with a swimming pool. He had also gotten kickbacks on contracts and had failed to pay taxes on some of his earnings. When he was called before the committee he invoked the Fifth Amendment 117 times. With his troubles mounting, Beck announced that he would not run for reelection as president of the IBT at the 1957 convention. Later he would be sentenced to prison.

In August it was Hoffa's turn to face the committee. He did not take the Fifth, but his testimony was nevertheless evasive. Republican senators lobbed him softballs that enabled him to launch into long, rambling, irrelevant statements. When addressing the chief counsel, Hoffa would usually preface his remarks with phrases like "Well, you see now, Bobby." Other times he would fix Kennedy with a fierce stare of the type he used on employers. When speaking to reporters, he was openly contemptuous of Kennedy, characterizing him as a rich man's son who had never done a day's work in his life. It was typical of the intimidation that was employed in union negotiations—put the other side on the defensive with personal attacks. It was also a serious miscalculation. Kennedy was not some small-time trucking company executive, but the chief adviser to a man who might someday be president.

Hoffa would return to the witness stand several more times. During the course of the investigation, many of his allies were also called to testify. In a later hearing, Kennedy played wiretaps legally obtained by the office of Manhattan district attorney Frank Hogan. In them, Corallo and DioGuardi were heard discussing the arrangements they had made with Hoffa that would allow them to loot the union. When Ducks Corallo appeared before the committee, Senator McClellan declared him "one of the scariest and worst gangsters we ever dealt with." Another witness was a 300-pound ex-prizefighter and New York waterfront slugger named Barney Baker who worked as a Teamster enforcer. When Kennedy questioned Baker about waterfront activities, the witness mentioned a certain Mr. John "Cockeye" Dunn. Kennedy immediately pounced, asking, "Where is he now?"

"He has met his maker," Baker replied.

"How did he do that?" asked Kennedy.

"I believe through electrocution in the city of New York," Baker meekly answered. Kennedy then asked about another of Baker's chums, one Andy "Squint" Sheridan. Catching on to the game, Baker volunteered, "He has also met his maker." Kennedy smilingly asked, "He was electrocuted?" "Yes, sir," Baker answered.

This style of questioning captivated the TV audience. When a bordello operator from Porter County, Indiana, admitted he was not a citizen, Senator McClellan broke in to thunder, "What is this man doing here [in the United States]?" In his high-pitched, Boston-accented voice, the chief counsel deadpanned, "I believe he is running a house of prostitution in Porter County, Indiana." The spectators were convulsed with laughter.

Another witness was the Teamster insurance broker Allen Dorfman. Prior to his abrupt entry into the business, Dorfman was a physical education instructor with an annual income of $5,900 a year. Since then he had earned millions in fees from the Teamsters and had acquired fourteen different insurance agencies and ten other businesses. College-educated and a war hero, with a Silver Star and Purple Heart earned as a Marine on Iwo Jima, the energetic, quick-thinking Dorfman might well have succeeded in other walks of life. Described as a look-alike for movie star Ben Gazzara, he could sometimes be gracious and charming. The next moment he would come over as a mob heavy. His New York State license had recently been revoked for failing to cooperate with an investigation, and when he appeared before the committee he took the Fifth, refusing to answer questions. Years later, in an interview with journalist Steve Brill, he gave his version of the committee's operations:

> It was all bullshit. All those hearings. You know why they were held, don't you? I mean, what the fuck else generated all the publicity that made the Kennedys? The Kennedys ran it.

It was an assessment that did not do justice to the committee chairman. Unlike Kefauver (or Jack Kennedy), John Little McClellan was a member of the Senate's inner circle, which gave him real power. Without his backing, Robert Kennedy would have been reined in—on more than one occasion, Republicans like Goldwater urged the chairman to do just that. Hoffa's own view of the investigation was that the Kennedys were playing up to the conservative, anti-union southern Senators in order to secure delegate votes at the 1960 Democratic convention. Republicans accused them of hypocrisy, claiming they ignored the misconduct of Democrat-friendly unions such as Walter Reuther's United Auto Workers, which had been known to employ strong-arm tactics in labor disputes. Still, Reuther had fought Detroit gangsters and in 1948 had been wounded by a mob gunman. In contrast, Hoffa's attitude toward organized crime was made clear when Robert Kennedy asked him if the fact that many of his associates were mobsters troubled him. Hoffa's answer was, "It doesn't disturb me one iota."

As a sop to the committee, Hoffa appointed a three-member antiracketeering panel headed by former Republican senator George Bender of Ohio. A few years earlier, as a congressman, Bender had conducted an investigation into the IBT. He had started out blasting the Teamsters, but when they agreed to support him in his (successful) race to fill a Senate vacancy, he shut down the hearing. After Hoffa placed him on the IBT payroll at $5,000 a month (in 1958 dollars), Bender sent form letters to every local asking if they had a corruption problem. Not surprisingly, none replied in the affirmative. When later questioned by his former Senate colleagues, he admitted he had not uncovered a single instance of racketeering.

Hoffa had not come over well at the hearings, though he managed to avoid any criminal charges. At the Teamster convention he was elected president despite threats from the AFL-CIO leadership to expel the union if it did so. When the convention ignored the ultimatum, the Teamsters were ousted from the larger body. The defiant Hoffa began moving to form an alliance with the International Longshoremen's Association (ILA). It was fitting, since the West Coast branch of the ILA had been expelled from the AFL-CIO for Communist influence, and the East Coast branch for alliances with racketeers. Hoffa also began to organize airline employees, aiming at building a coalition of transport workers. To top it off, he defiantly announced he would organize police unions, starting with the NYPD.

The McClellan hearings began what came to be called the Kennedy-Hoffa Feud. Some have attributed Kennedy's hostility toward Hoffa to personal animosity, but the Senate investigation was an eye-opener for him. He was genuinely shocked to encounter men who would have a journalist blinded, or murder their own union members. Later, as attorney general of the United States, he would listen to recordings from the Chicago FBI bugs in which mobsters described with relish how they had tortured or killed people. In one instance, a loan shark known as "Action Jackson" had been hung on a meat hook while his captors used an electric cattle prod on his genitals. Chicago detectives knew Jackson to be a slobbering 350-pound torturer himself. When a debtor was slow paying his loan back, Jackson would break into the man's home while he was away and rape his wife as a warning to pay up. Cops might take a philosophical approach to his fate, saying "He finally got his" and not shedding too many tears. Kennedy recognized that the murder of anyone diminished everyone.

The Apalachin raid provided Kennedy with the blueprint for how dangerous a Teamsters-organized crime connection was. On November 13, 1957, a Narcotics Bureau supervisor testifying before the McClellan Committee mentioned that one of the Teamster leaders in New York belonged to the Mafia. Kennedy challenged the statement, asking, "Is there any organization such as the Mafia, or is that just a name given to the hierarchy in the Italian underworld?" The federal agent hedged a bit, but he finally said, "We believe that there does exist today in the United States a society loosely organized with the specific purpose of smuggling narcotics and committing other crimes." The next day the raid took place. The alliance between the crime syndicate and a union that could cripple the economy by calling a national strike was for Kennedy as threatening to the United States as Communist subversion. A few years later he summarized his thoughts in a book that he entitled *The Enemy Within*, writing:

> The Teamsters Union is the most powerful institution in this country—aside from the United States government. . . . The life of every person . . . is in the hands of Hoffa and his Teamsters.

Not long after the hearings ended, Robert Kennedy received a personal reminder of the extent of Hoffa's economic power. The makers of *On the Waterfront* planned a similar film about Kennedy's racket investigation. Since *Little Caesar* and *Scarface* in the 1930s, movies about mob bosses and the men who fought them had been a Hollywood staple. Not this time. After preliminary meetings went nowhere, it became clear that no Hollywood studio would dare risk Teamster retaliation by making a film critical of Jimmy Hoffa. Not even having the hero's brother in the White House made the project attractive.

For the Kennedys, the McClellan hearings were ultimately more than just exposés of union racketeering and a chance to achieve favorable publicity. They were part of the transition in American politics that Jack and Bobby would lead. In the early postwar years, foreign policy and defense were the key national issues. Urban problems, including organized crime, were largely ignored. The same was true of racial discrimination. Even before the McClellan racketeering investigation, Kennedy began riding around at night with NYPD detectives and federal narcotics agents, observing real life in places like Harlem. The Kennedys were among the first, and certainly the most important, national figures to recognize that the deterioration of cities and the mistreatment of blacks would require the attention of the national government.[3]

The McClellan Committee hearings were also a decisive moment for Jimmy Hoffa. He inspired great affection from his members, who recognized that at heart he was one of them. Some labor leaders, like Dave Beck, sought to emulate the lifestyle of a corporate CEO. Others wanted to attend Harvard seminars where they could sip sherry and pretend to be intellectuals. Jimmy was an ordinary guy who liked John Wayne movies, country music, and shooting the breeze with the boys. Some union heads dined regularly on French cuisine at four-star restaurants; Jimmy's preference in food ran to well-done steaks, served in a blue-collar setting. Walter Reuther shared confidences with cabinet members and presidents; Hoffa would take a phone call from any Teamster who had a problem. Rank-and-file Teamsters supported Hoffa in part *because* he defied the establishment. In postwar America, blue-collar workers like truckers were looked down on. Kids were warned by their parents that if they didn't go to college they would "end up driving a truck." It had not always been that way. In the 1930s, Hollywood had portrayed truck drivers as knights of the road. In truth, it took more skill to pilot a tractor-trailer over mountain roads than it did to perform many white-collar jobs. Jimmy's ability to best the Harvard bright boys fit the idealized image of a trucker—a two-fisted guy who did not back down from a challenge.

Yet his combativeness ultimately proved his undoing. If Hoffa had cooperated with the government's efforts to purge the IBT of organized crime, or at least not obstructed them, he might have become the most important labor leader in America. Instead, he made two huge mistakes. He entered into a personal feud with the Kennedys, and he allowed his union to become linked with the mobs. In both instances, Jimmy's confidence in his own toughness betrayed him: He honestly believed that he could get the best of both the United States government and the Mafia.

3 By the 1968 presidential election, in which Robert Kennedy was a leading candidate until his murder, crime and racial justice would be major issues.

The first mistake would result in the loss of his job and his freedom. The second would cost him his life.

The man who would become a vital bridge between Hoffa and organized crime was Allen Dorfman. Hitherto Jimmy had won support from the mobsters by allowing them to steal Teamster funds and to extort payoffs from employers by threatening to call strikes or agreeing to sign sweetheart contracts. Now he would provide the Mafia with a vital resource: its own bank. He put Dorfman in charge of the Central States Teamsters' pension fund, where he began making loans under unusual terms. Mob-connected individuals could secure generous financing without sufficient collateral, or at below-market rates. One such beneficiary was Moe Dalitz. With money from his Mayfield Road Gang allies in Cleveland and Dorfman's Central States Pension Fund, Dalitz opened the Desert Inn in Las Vegas. Soon the pension fund was giving money to other mob families to acquire interests in casinos. While most pension funds kept less than five percent of their portfolio in risky ventures like real estate, by 1963 Central States had over sixty percent of its funds invested in property. Dave Beck had turned his West Coast pension fund over to the professional management of a large insurance company; in that way, members' money was not only wisely invested, but there was no treasure chest to attract mob pirates. Giving the mobs access to the Central States fund was a move that ensured they would vigorously resist any attempt to curtail their influence in the IBT.

The irony was that after he became Teamster head, Hoffa no longer needed the Mafia. With a membership that eventually grew to more than two million members, he could have had a close relationship with whoever was president of the United States. Dan Tobin, with fewer resources, had mastered the game of becoming a White House favorite. Dave Beck was starting to do the same when corruption brought him down. Official Washington tended to judge individuals by the present, not the past. If Jimmy had behaved himself, his previous delinquencies would have been forgiven. His inability to grasp this indicates that in the final analysis, Hoffa rose higher than his ability warranted. He certainly wasn't the first to do so—many people managed to survive in similar situations by listening to competent advisers. But Jimmy was never one to take advice, preferring instead to dictate to his lawyers and financial advisers. Most mob bosses were smart enough not to do that.

At the end of the 1950s, the American Mafia was still riding high. Kefauver, McClellan, and Robert Kennedy had not been able to damage it significantly. Though Congress passed the Landrum-Griffin Act, which made it a crime to misuse union funds, Teamster dollars were flowing to the mob. Besides the IBT and ILA, the Mafia also had a strong presence in the Laborers International Union of North America (LIUNA) and the Hotel and Restaurant Employees International. The real story of the decade was a shift in public opinion. The Kefauver investigation had shown the face of organized crime on the living room TV set. Apalachin had revealed its national scope. The McClellan-Kennedy hearings had demonstrated its potential to cripple the national economy. By 1960 the American public was conditioned for a real all-out war on the Mafia and its allies. All that was needed was the election of the right sort of president, and the Kennedy brothers believed they knew who would fit the bill. In 1960, the television networks that had made Kefauver a household name, made Robert Kennedy a hero and Jimmy Hoffa a villain, and destroyed Joe McCarthy, would help make a president.

CHAPTER 4

"DO SOMETHING ABOUT IT":
BOBBY KENNEDY'S ATTACK ON THE MOBS

Carlos Marcello, the Mafia boss of New Orleans, was born Calogero Minacore in Tunisia in 1910. His Sicilian parents brought him to America as a baby, but Marcello never bothered to become a United States citizen. The only document that purportedly authorized him to be in the country was a false Guatemalan passport. Beginning his career with convictions for such crimes as armed robbery and drug dealing, he managed to rise to the top of the longest-established Mafia family in America before he was forty, becoming a national figure through his partnership with Frank Costello in Louisiana gambling and nightclubs. Speaking ungrammatical English with a Cajun accent, he was an important power broker in the traditionally corrupt world of New Orleans politics. In 1961, the head of the local crime commission told the McClellan Committee, "His wishes are considered orders by numerous persons in public office." At that point the United States government had been trying to deport him for eight years; his political clout had repeatedly stymied their efforts.

On April 4 of that same year, Marcello made his required quarterly visit to the local office of the U.S. Immigration Service—a drill that had become as routine as a periodic dental checkup, and far less painful. In Louisiana, even federal officials bent over backward to avoid inconveniencing a Mafia boss. This time it would be different: Without warning, Marcello was arrested, handcuffed, and taken to a waiting vehicle. Sirens screaming, it conveyed him to the airport, where he was placed on a border patrol plane. As he later described it, "You would have thought it was the president coming in instead of me going out." Marcello was flown to Guatemala, his purported homeland, and dropped off without ceremony. It was only the beginning of his troubles. Local officials took him to a village just over the border in El Salvador, where he was arrested by soldiers. After five days in custody he was released—still clad in a silk suit and alligator shoes—in a remote mountain area of Honduras. It was seventeen miles to the nearest village, and during his journey he fell several times and broke two ribs. He would later claim that he also had to elude some locals who he feared might rob and kill him. According to Marcello, he managed to get a commercial flight to Miami and from there to New Orleans. Upon arrival he was indicted for illegal entry and presented with an $835,000 tax lien. Government investigators would later learn that he was actually flown to Miami in a military plane provided by Rafael Trujillo. The Dominican dictator owed the Mafia for several favors, including kidnapping one of his prominent opponents off the streets of New York.

The treatment of Marcello served notice on the Mafia that there was a new sheriff in town. Ten weeks earlier, Robert Kennedy had been appointed by his brother to be attorney general of the United States. When Marcello had appeared before the McClellan Committee in the '50s, Bobby had described him as "the head of the underworld in the southeastern United States." Now Kennedy was in a position to do more than talk. The mob bosses did not have to call their clever lawyers to find out what was going on; it was clear that the new administration had them in its sights. Some of them felt that this was a double cross.

Even supporters of President John F. Kennedy were shocked when he nominated his younger brother Robert to be the attorney general. A thirty-five-year-old man, only ten years out of law school, hardly seemed the right choice to head the world's largest law firm. A *New York Times* editorial observed, "His experience . . . is surely insufficient to warrant his present appointment." In previous administrations the attorney general's post had generally been given to a distinguished member of the bar. For some it was a stepping-stone to the U.S. Supreme Court. Even the occasional attorney general appointed for straight-out political reasons had at least tried cases. Young Kennedy had not. The White House rationale was that the president required someone who would not be afraid to tell him when he was wrong. Since Bobby hardly needed a cabinet post to obtain access to his brother, the explanation did not wash. Falling back on his disarming sense of humor, Jack quipped, "I just wanted to give him a little legal practice before he becomes a lawyer."

Given the driving energy Robert Kennedy had shown as counsel to the McClellan Committee and the leverage provided by his relationship to the president, it was clear that the new attorney general was going to shake up the Justice Department as it had not been shaken in a long time. The last major overhaul had been in 1924, when President Coolidge named Columbia Law School dean Harlan Fiske Stone to straighten out the mess left over from the Teapot Dome scandal. One of the results was the appointment of J. Edgar Hoover as head of the (not yet Federal) Bureau of Investigation. Thirty-seven years later, Hoover was still there. His Bureau, now expanded twentyfold, comprised half of the Department of Justice workforce— although most of the time the FBI did not consider itself part of the DOJ. Since 1933, when new laws and directives had given it a major law enforcement role, Hoover's well-publicized exploits against "public enemies," Nazi spies, and Communist subversives had made him a national icon. His high profile gave him job security: Any administration that tried to fire him would have sustained significant political damage. Successive attorneys general had allowed him an unusual degree of autonomy in running his agency, and even presidents were respectful. As combative a man as Harry Truman was careful to keep his distance, though he was no admirer of Hoover. As president-elect, John Kennedy's first act was to request publicly that Hoover and CIA director Alan Dulles remain in office.

The differences between J. Edgar Hoover and Robert Kennedy were both stylistic and substantive. They were men of different worlds. Hoover, the son of a midlevel federal civil servant, was born in the late Victorian era. His whole life had been spent in Washington, D.C., which until World War II was a sleepy Southern city. He entered government service after high school, working his way through college and law school. His success was based on his bureaucratic skills and his ability to garner favorable publicity. Robert Kennedy was more than thirty years younger. He had been exposed to the cosmopolitan worlds of Boston, New York, and London at an early age, but did not become a playboy. He married young and fathered a brood of children. Official Washington was a stuffy place, but as attorney general, Kennedy did not concern himself too much with decorum. Despite regulations to the contrary, he brought his giant Labrador dog, Brumus, to the office. In meetings he would sometimes toss a football around with his lieutenants, and if he wanted to talk to a subordinate he might phone him directly, even if it meant bypassing several layers of command. Once he popped into Hoover's office unannounced and in shirtsleeves, interrupting the director's nap. He had an intercom installed on Hoover's desk and made it clear that he expected Hoover, not the secretary, to answer it. Kennedy even took to coming into the office on Saturdays and asking the FBI duty agent to bring him confidential Bureau files. This infuriated Hoover, but a mere agent could not refuse a request from the attorney general. In an effort to protect his turf, Hoover began to come in on Saturday himself. And with the director in the office, FBI SACs across the country also found it expedient to work on that day.

The stylistic differences between the two men, however, were not insurmountable. If, like other attorneys general before him, Kennedy had adopted a laissez-faire attitude toward the FBI while praising its director at every opportunity, the two might have gotten on well enough. Hoover had always had a friendly relationship with Joe Kennedy, Sr. If his son had followed precedent, Hoover would have been happy to furnish Bobby voluntarily with choice FBI files, such as those describing the sexual peccadilloes of various VIPs. As old Washington hands knew, politicians, including presidents, enjoyed reading titillating accounts of their enemies' misdeeds. And they enjoyed reading about their friends' embarrassments even more.

But Robert Kennedy had no interest in granting Hoover carte blanche—his concern about organized crime alone guaranteed that. Kennedy's experience with the McClellan Committee had given him an unfavorable opinion of the FBI. After the Apalachin raid, he asked for information on the participants, and was incredulous to learn that the Bureau had very little. For example, its file on the shooting of Frank Costello consisted of newspaper clippings. As he would frequently tell people, "The FBI didn't know anything, really, about these people who were the major gangsters in the United States. . . . that was rather a shock to me." The more probable explanation is that the Bureau did not give him "the good stuff," since it included secret sources. However, Kennedy was essentially correct that the FBI had far less knowledge than it should have had. By 1961, the Bureau had more information but was still short on cases. Treasury agents had convicted Vito Genovese on narcotics and Tony Accardo on taxes (though the latter conviction was later reversed). However, neither case had much impact on the mob families. The FBI's tentative attack on the Mafia was already being scaled back, and the DOJ's organized crime and racketeering section was a small backwater with just seventeen attorneys.

Robert Kennedy was not one to spend a lot of time reading think pieces or debating technical legal points. When government lawyers complained about the imprecision of such terms as "Mafia" or "organized crime," his response was, "Don't define it, do something about it." He largely concentrated on improving organization and generating greater efforts. He ordered the FBI's organized crime squads beefed up and changed the name of the program from Top Hoodlum to Criminal Intelligence. He also quadrupled the number of attorneys in the racketeering section. Kennedy intended to mobilize not only the Justice Department, but the entire federal law enforcement establishment, in an all-out war against the Mafia. Twenty-seven different agencies, ranging from the FBI to the Social Security Administration, had some jurisdiction over organized crime activities. Few were eager to exercise it. As a spur, Kennedy formed an interdepartmental committee with himself as chairman—a repellent approach to bureaucrats who jealously guarded their territory and did not share information with others. If the attorney general had not been the president's brother, most agencies would have ignored his directive, but instead his commands were often carried out with unusual alacrity. When Bobby became attorney general, the immigration commissioner was retired lieutenant general Joe Swing, a soldier in the Patton mold. As an Eisenhower administration holdover, he feared for his job, so when Kennedy ordered Marcello deported it was "Yes, sir," no questions asked. Even Kennedy was a bit shocked when the deportation was carried out like a commando raid.

The style and vigor (pronounced "vigah" by JFK) of the new administration attracted bright young people to Washington. Thirty-year-old Henry Ruth, then practicing civil law in an elite Philadelphia firm, was a typical recruit. He circulated his résumé to various agencies and was eventually taken by the organized crime section, where he soon found himself prosecuting mobsters in the field. His service under Kennedy would lead him to a career of public service assignments, culminating in his appointment as Watergate special prosecutor.

While the organized crime section functioned as a sort of commando team, success in the war on the Mafia would depend on the generals who led the DOJ line troops—the ninety-four local U.S. attorneys. Appointed to four-year terms by the president and confirmed by the Senate, they supervised the staff of lawyers that conducted most of the prosecutions brought by the Department. The typical U.S.A.—as they were known— was a lawyer of standing in his community, most likely a senior partner in a corporate firm. Appointment was also proof of political finesse, being among the most prized of federal patronage posts. Normally a U.S. senator who belonged to the party controlling the White House sponsored the appointee. If neither senator of the state was of the president's political persuasion, the post would be within the gift of a governor, big-city mayor, senior congressman, or political boss who had the ear of the White House. Many U.S. attorneys saw the job as a stepping-stone to the federal bench or higher public office, and thus were not inclined to upset too many applecarts—which prosecuting politically connected mafiosi was very likely to do. Denial was often the smarter career move. In the early 1950s, Otto Kerner, the U.S.A. in Chicago, publicly stated that there was no organized crime in the city; a few years later he was elected governor.[1] Others were simply not interested in the subject, or were busy pursuing what they regarded as more important agendas. Without the cooperation of the U.S. attorneys in Mafia-dominated cities, Kennedy's efforts would fail. The FBI and other agencies could arrest, but they could not prosecute.

1 In 1973, while serving as a judge on the U.S. Circuit Court, Kerner was convicted of receiving bribes from gamblers during his term as governor and sent to prison.

Organized crime section attorneys could prosecute, but in addition to be-ing spread thin, they risked offending the local U.S.A. and being seen as carpetbaggers by judges and juries.

The most important federal prosecutor's office in the United States was the Southern District of New York. Its jurisdiction included the financial and corporate heart of the nation, as well as the leading element of the American Mafia. New York's Democratic senator was Herbert Lehman: for-mer governor, name partner in a prominent Wall Street investment bank-ing firm, and member of high society. His choice for U.S. attorney was his nephew, Robert M. Morgenthau, son of FDR's secretary of the treasury. Morgenthau had another backer in Eleanor Roosevelt, grande dame of the Democratic Party. In 1940, when Joe Kennedy, Sr., had been ambassador to the Court of St. James, he had offended President Roosevelt and the strongly interventionist Secretary Morgenthau by opposing American aid to Britain. The wounds were not entirely healed, and during Jack's cam-paign Mrs. Roosevelt had made some derogatory comments about the amount of money Joe was spending on his son's behalf. Another problem was that Tammany boss Carmine DeSapio and Bronx boss Congressman Charlie Buckley both claimed a say in selecting the Southern District head.

When Bobby Kennedy interviewed Morgenthau he was not impressed. The Kennedys admired people who were "tough," and Morgenthau did not look the part of a racket-buster. Slim and bespectacled, educated at Amherst and Yale Law School, he had the gentlemanly manner of a well-bred New Yorker. "He wouldn't have the nerve to tell someone to get out of his own office," was Robert Kennedy's comment to Deputy Attorney Gen-eral Byron "Whizzer" White. Yet as executive officer of an American de-stroyer sunk by German bombers in the Mediterranean during World War II, Lieutenant Morgenthau had rallied the crew and managed to save many lives. Later he was on a destroyer hit by a kamikaze off Okinawa. There was also the legacy of his father, the treasury secretary who had sent T-men after corrupt political bosses like Tom Pendergast in Kansas City and Huey Long in New Orleans. In the end, Kennedy's lack of enthusiasm for Morgenthau was outweighed by a pronounced dislike of DeSapio and Buckley. To get them to back off, he threatened to appoint a man from Connecticut to the New York vacancy. At Morgenthau's swearing-in, the attorney general of the

United States was notably absent. But once in office, Morgenthau proved to be very tough indeed on mobsters, crooked politicians, and other assorted criminals, and he quickly became the Kennedy brothers' favorite U.S.A.

Not surprisingly, one of Robert Kennedy's major goals as attorney general was to bring Jimmy Hoffa to justice. Breaking organized crime's hold on the Teamsters would deal a heavy economic blow to the Mafia. Bypassing established procedures, he created what became unofficially known as the "Get Hoffa Squad," appointing Walter Sheridan, formerly chief investigator for the McClellan Committee, as his special assistant. Sheridan was put in charge of a staff of twenty lawyers who were supplemented by thirty investigators, including FBI agents—another breach of protocol, as Sheridan was not an attorney. Of course, Kennedy valued Sheridan precisely because he did not think like a lawyer. Lawyers were too cautious, too inclined to wait until they could assemble an ironclad, copper-riveted, unsinkable case, the kind that might take years to develop. Some observers thought Sheridan was actually a lot like Hoffa: hard-driving, jut-jawed, with crew-cut hair, and given to wearing inexpensive solid-colored suits. Sheridan also possessed Jimmy's taste for personal conflict. On February 14, Hoffa's birthday, the Get Hoffa Squad decorated its door with a valentine that bore their target's photo, along with the inscription, "Always thinking of you." A former FBI agent, Sheridan was familiar with Hoover's dicta, but showed little deference to standard procedures. He did not hesitate to communicate directly with Bureau officials when necessary.

Under Sheridan the investigation quickly moved into high gear, and soon thirteen grand juries across the country were busy scrutinizing the affairs of the Teamsters union and its leader. In the run-up to the 1960 election it was widely rumored that Vice President Nixon had headed off a Justice Department indictment of Hoffa, who was supporting the Republicans against Kennedy. The case had involved allegations that Teamsters were being steered toward a Florida retirement development in which Hoffa had a hidden interest. After the election, but before JFK took office, Hoffa was indicted by a federal grand jury for participation in the scheme. While that was pending, Sheridan's investigators latched onto a case in which Hoffa had allegedly received kickbacks. In 1952 he and another union official had incorporated a truck leasing company in their wives' names. Over the years the firm—called "Test Fleet"—had received money from a Detroit car-hauling company that employed union drivers. Under the Landrum-Griffin Act, union officers were forbidden to accept money from employers they were negotiating with. The government argued that paying the money to the wives was just a way of funneling it to Hoffa and his partner. It was only a misdemeanor charge, but both Hoffa and the government put vast resources into the prosecution. Tried in Tennessee, the case ended in a hung jury, though that led to Hoffa and some of his lieutenants being indicted for attempting to bribe jurors. Next, Jimmy and various associates were indicted in Chicago, on charges of making fraudulent loans from the Central States Pension Fund.

Kennedy had been right to think that a typical lawyer would have qualms about the government's tactics against Hoffa. After all, how many people in the business world or public life were so squeaky clean that a small army of lawyers and detectives, aided by thirteen grand juries, could not find something to nail them on? Hoffa had previously been acquitted on a charge of wiretapping his employees in New York and of bribing Investigator Cheasty in Washington, yet the government kept after him. What distinguished Hoffa, head of the IBT, from the average citizen, though, was his alliance with the Mafia. Given the political and economic power of the two entities and their capacity for employing violence, only an all-out assault could bring Hoffa down: Spreading the effort over many fronts increased the chances that somewhere there would be some jury that could not be bribed, some witness who could not be intimidated, and some charge that would stick. If the government was not prepared to undertake such an effort, it would amount to a concession that racketeers were effectively beyond the law.

Marcello's deportation in April 1961 was only the start. In September, President Kennedy signed laws outlawing Interstate Transportation in Aid to Racketeering (ITAR), Interstate Transportation of Wagering Information (ITWI), and the Interstate Transportation of Wagering Paraphernalia (ITWP), giving the FBI its first major jurisdiction in the bookmaking and numbers-lotteries area. ITAR, ITWI, ITWP—any charge that might be employed against mobsters was pressed into service, even environmental protection laws. When Chicago hoodlum Joey Aiuppa shot some doves that were on the prohibited list, he was prosecuted for violating the Migratory Bird Act and sentenced to six months in jail. As always, taxes proved the most effective weapon. Between 1961 and 1963 the number of organized crime convictions increased from one hundred to more than three hundred, with about 60 percent from tax charges. More than half were obtained by Bob Morgenthau in New York. Mobbed-up politicians felt the weight of Kennedy's DOJ as well. James Keogh was a New York State Supreme Court justice, a former U.S. attorney, and the brother of a congressman who was close to the Kennedys. In 1962 it was learned that Ducks Corallo of the Lucchese family had given him and an assistant U.S. attorney $35,000 to bribe another judge into awarding a lenient sentence to a defendant convicted of bankruptcy fraud. Despite appeals to the Kennedys from Keogh's supporters, both Corallo and the judge were indicted, found guilty, and given two-year prison sentences.

One of the Department of Justice's principal targets was Sam Giancana of Chicago, at the time probably the leading mob boss in the country. Carlo Gambino might have been the top man in New York, but he had to share his turf with four other bosses. And Carlo wisely kept a low profile. Giancana, on the other hand, was the boss of the entire Chicago area (courtesy of Tony Accardo) and cavorted in plush spots from Florida to Vegas. He made a much easier mark for the Feds. FBI agents served as a welcome committee one night when he and his girlfriend, singer Phyllis McGuire, arrived at O'Hare Airport. Furious, Giancana began berating them, especially Bill Roemer, who gave it right back to him. After he called Roemer a number of four-letter words, the G-man, by his own account, "lost my cool." Roemer began shouting to the passengers in the airport concourse, "Take a look at this piece of garbage! This piece of scum! You people are lucky you're just passing through Chicago. But we have to live with this slime. This is Sam Giancana, the boss of the underworld here. Take a good look at this jerk!" Roemer was so out of control that his supervisor stepped in, kicking him in the shins and ordering him to "shut up and back off."

During the altercation Giancana made some puzzling remarks, such as

"I know all about the Kennedys." The G-men didn't know it then, but Giancana had his reasons for feeling angry and betrayed by the administration. When Jack Kennedy campaigned for the 1960 Democratic presidential nomination, Frank Sinatra had been of great assistance. He considered himself a personal friend of the candidate, and Kennedy's brother-in-law Peter Lawford was a member of the crooner's Rat Pack. Sinatra enlisted his close pal Paul "Skinny" D'Amato to help Kennedy in West Virginia, a crucial primary that would test whether he could carry a heavily Protestant state. D'Amato was the front man for one of organized crime's watering holes, the 500 Club in Atlantic City, New Jersey (he had also served a prison sentence for violating the Mann "white slavery" act). From the 1940s on, every name entertainer played the 500 Club's thousand-seat house. And long before legal gambling came to the boardwalk, the 500 Club had a flourishing illegal casino in the back room. The 500 was also the place where the mob made deals with politicians—whose tabs were always comped. So highly did Sinatra regard Skinny and his backers that all five times he performed at the club, he played a grueling four shows a night and waived his fee. In West Virginia, county sheriffs were men of great power and influence. They had control over the election machinery, and Skinny knew how to win their favor. With D'Amato's connections and Joe Kennedy's lavish infusion of cash, Jack won a sweeping victory, forcing his rival, Hubert Humphrey, out of the race.

Illinois was a key battleground in the general election, so Sinatra sought Giancana's support. It was not an easy sell. When Sam appeared before the McClellan Committee, he had taken the Fifth Amendment. As was his practice, Robert Kennedy continued to ask questions in order to put various accusations on the record. During the one-sided interrogation, he noticed Giancana engaging in some laughing asides with his lawyer, and sharply remarked, "I thought only little girls giggled, Mr. Giancana." Mob bosses did not like to be humiliated. Based on his experience with Bobby, Sam saw no reason to support Jack. Frank managed to convince Giancana that if Kennedy was elected, the attacks on the Mafia would cease. As a result, the Chicago mob raised money for the campaign and passed the word in the wards where its influence was strong.

Kennedy won a narrow victory in Illinois. Giancana apparently thought it was principally his doing, and since Illinois' electoral votes had helped push Kennedy over the top, he told people he was responsible for electing the president. Anyone familiar with the Chicago election practices of that time would find it a doubtful thesis. The wards under strong mob influence were also those that were always carried overwhelmingly by the Democratic machine. (When good-government groups or federal investigators would point to certain irregularities, such as voting dead people, the standard answer was that downstate, the Republicans did the same thing.) Cook County Democrats needed no help from Giancana to carry the river wards.[2]

Giancana had other reasons to feel that he was owed some favors. Prior to the 1960 election, a CIA liaison man named Robert Maheu approached a friend of his named Johnny Roselli for help in overthrowing the Castro regime in Cuba. Johnny had been the Chicago mob's Hollywood overseer in the '30s. In 1944, he was sent to prison along with five top Chicago bosses for extorting money from the movie industry.[3] Well-groomed and impeccably dressed, with a handsome, distinguished appearance, Roselli became an intimate of celebrities and society people and for a while was married to the beautiful actress June Lang. Despite his polish, Roselli (né Sacco) bore a dark secret. Like Marcello, he had been brought to America as a young boy and had never acquired United States citizenship, which made him vulnerable to deportation. Roselli took Maheu's Cuban proposition to Giancana. While Johnny, who always fancied himself a Hollywood-type hero, may have wanted to respond favorably for personal or even patriotic reasons, Giancana's agreement was based on business. When Castro took power he expropriated Mafia-owned casinos, and naturally the organization was anxious to get them back. It also occurred to Giancana that helping Uncle Sam would provide the mob with a very valuable marker that could be called in at a later date.

When Kennedy assumed office, plans to assassinate Castro were already

2 In addition, even if Illinois had gone Republican, the Democratic victory in LBJ's home state of Texas would have been enough to elect Kennedy.
3 The defendants were sentenced to ten years but served only three. Their parole was rushed through with such lightning speed that it sparked a congressional investigation to determine whether political influence had been used on their behalf. In order to avoid questioning, the parole board resigned en masse.

well advanced. In May 1961, shortly after the failure of the Bay of Pigs invasion, Attorney General Kennedy learned of the mob's involvement through
a Keystone comedy caper involving Giancana. Suspecting that Phyllis
McGuire was fooling around in Las Vegas with *Laugh-In* TV star Dan Rowan,
Giancana asked Maheu to have the comedian's phone tapped. When the
private investigator brought in to do the job was caught, he implicated
Maheu, who was then indicted by the United States government. This led to
the CIA's approaching the Department of Justice to have the charges against
their man dropped. When informed of the request, Kennedy supposedly
expressed vehement disapproval of using the Mafia. (Despite this, a year
later Roselli was still working with a top CIA official on plans to kill Castro.)

In Giancana's eyes, he had helped elect Kennedy president and had assisted the CIA in a plot to kill one of its enemies. In recompense he had expected the government to turn a grateful blind eye, but instead he was
under heavy scrutiny from its agents. And he wasn't alone—the FBI also
succeeded in planting a bug, known as "Shade," in the headquarters of
Chicago's First Ward Democratic organization, located in an office building near City Hall. The First Ward, run by its secretary, Pat Marcy (né
Pasquale Marchone), was the conduit through which the Chicago Outfit
sent orders to its political lackeys. Between Little Al on Michigan Avenue,
Mo in Giancana's Amory Lounge, and Shade on LaSalle Street, the FBI was
able to develop an accurate picture of how the politics–organized crime alliance in Chicago worked.[4]

Giancana's betrayal (as he saw it) had theatrical precedents. In the 1945
film *Nob Hill*, George Raft (a longtime close associate of the mob off-
screen) played a San Francisco Barbary Coast gambler named Tony Angelo
who falls in love with a society girl from Nob Hill. When the girl's brother
runs for district attorney, Angelo agrees to support him despite warnings
from other dive owners, who predict that the brother will crack down on
them once in office. When Raft goes to the D.A.'s victory party on election
night he is snubbed, and must acknowledge to his friends that he has been
double-crossed. It is a movie that should have been required viewing for
hoods who thought their cooperation would win them acceptance in the

---

4 Though it is suspected that after a while, the mob had begun to tumble to the fact that
Uncle Sam was listening to some of their conversations.

upper strata.[5] With the appointment of Robert Kennedy, Giancana and Sinatra found themselves, like Tony Angelo, bounced from the party. On a golf course, Giancana vented his feelings to Johnny Roselli while an FBI mike listened in. Describing Sinatra's relationship with the Kennedys, he said, "They don't want him. They treat him like they treat a whore." As for himself, he complained, "If I ever get a speeding ticket, none of these fuckers would know me." Some of Giancana's friends suggested a hit on Sinatra. But Giancana eventually forgave Sinatra, who also managed to maintain his friendship with Kennedy for a time after the election.

Giancana would be in the middle of another embarrassment for the Kennedys. In February 1960, candidate Jack Kennedy had dropped in to the Sands Hotel in Las Vegas, one of the mob's casinos. There Frank Sinatra introduced him to a pretty dark-haired woman named Judith Campbell, ex-wife of a minor movie star. Later in the year the two allegedly began an intimate relationship. Early in 1961, Sinatra introduced Campbell to Sam Giancana at the Fontainebleau Hotel in Miami, and he too began an intimate friendship with her. It was an interesting situation, to say the least: The president of the United States was sharing a mistress with a top Mafia boss. To further complicate matters, the president's brother, the attorney general, was trying to jail the mob leader, while the CIA was relying on Giancana to get rid of Fidel Castro, whose ouster was a high priority of the Kennedy administration. It would seem that between the White House, the CIA, and the American Mafia, some signals had been crossed.

During Kennedy's first year as president, the White House switchboard logged seventy calls to him from Miss Campbell. In 1962, FBI agents overheard conversations linking Giancana to Campbell and Campbell to Kennedy. Though Robert Kennedy had already learned of it from DOJ sources and passed it on to his brother, J. Edgar Hoover went to the White House to tell the president personally. Immediately all contacts, including telephone calls, between President Kennedy and Judith Campbell ceased. Kennedy also canceled a plan to stay at Frank Sinatra's house during a visit to Palm Springs, California, bunking with Bing Crosby instead. Frank was so upset that he took a sledgehammer to the landing pad he had installed

5 Though, in typical Hollywood fashion, a happy ending was tacked on to the story.

to accommodate the president's helicopter. The Campbell affair may have persuaded the Kennedys to be more accommodating to J. Edgar Hoover. Not long after he informed them of her relationship with the mob, Hoover finally managed to get the attorney general to sign an order authorizing electronic eavesdropping on civil rights leader Dr. Martin Luther King, Jr.

The anti-Castro plots and Judith Campbell affair would hamper the Kennedy efforts against the Chicago mob. In 1963 the FBI set up a lockstep surveillance of Giancana, on Robert Kennedy's orders. When Giancana was chauffeured around town, an FBI car kept on his tail, and on the golf course a foursome of G-men (including Giancana's bête noire, Roemer) would tee off right after his party. So he sued the FBI. When the local special agent in charge of the Chicago office was called to testify, Attorney General Kennedy ordered him not to answer questions. The federal prosecutor in Chicago was unable to respond adequately, for fear that during court proceedings Sam might blurt out what he knew about the plot against Castro or the president's relationship with Campbell. The SAC was fined $500 for contempt of court and Giancana obtained a federal court order compelling the FBI to stay several cars—and several foursomes— back with their tails. The judgment (though later overturned) was an embarrassment to the Bureau, and did not improve relations between Hoover and Bobby Kennedy.

Another potential setback for the Outfit was the revival of the old Chicago police Scotland Yard squad. In 1960, in the aftermath of a police scandal, Mayor Daley had appointed O. W. Wilson, dean of the University of California School of Criminology, to head the police force. On recommendation of the FBI and the Chicago Crime Commission, Wilson had named Joe Morris a deputy superintendent of police and Bill Duffy director of a vastly expanded intelligence division. In their new posts they would work closely with the FBI organized crime squad. In 1962 Dick Ogilvie, who had prosecuted Tony Accardo on tax evasion, was elected sheriff of Cook County. Ogilvie was a legitimate mob buster, but for some unexplained reason he appointed as his chief investigator a Chicago detective named Richard Cain (né Scalzitti), against the advice of people like Duffy. Cain was a close associate of Sam Giancana, and he used his new post to advance the Outfit's interests—going as far as to avail himself of the polygraph facilities to interrogate a holdup man he suspected of supplying information to the FBI. Eventually Cain himself was convicted in a burglary case and sent to prison.

The high point of the Kennedy war on the Mafia came in the fall of 1963. New York drug dealer Joseph Valachi, a.k.a. "Joe Cago," had been sentenced to Atlanta prison with his boss, Vito Genovese. There Genovese became suspicious that he might turn informer and gave him the ceremonial kiss of death. Assuming—wrongly—that a convict who approached him was the assassin, Valachi beat the innocent man to death with an iron bar. He was sentenced to life. His only way out was to cut a deal with the government, so his lawyer approached the Feds. Valachi's knowledge was largely limited to New York and his perspective was that of a low-level soldier, yet with a little coaching he could serve an important purpose. He provided a mouthpiece through whom extensive information about the American Mafia could be made public, without revealing that much of it had been obtained though legally questionable electronic eavesdropping. After exchanging information with FBI agents, he incorporated what they told him into his own knowledge. Attorney General Kennedy arranged to have him testify before the Senate's McClellan Committee, where he spoke with authority about persons, events, and high-level decision making in many cities. Much of what he related had already appeared in print over the previous twenty-five years and/or been revealed by mob turncoats such as Dutch Schultz's lawyer Dixie Davis and Abe "Kid Twist" Reles, a crew chief in Anastasia's Murder Inc. *Time* magazine, not impressed by a sixty-year-old "squealer with a sunlamp tan sucking a juice-filled plastic lemon," dismissed his testimony as "stale underworld gossip." *Newsweek* thought his tone of remorse over the murders he had committed was that of "a martini-tipsy lady who had just trumped a partner's ace."

The magazines may have dismissed him, but TV did not, and that was important. When Jack Kennedy first took office, national magazines like *Time* and *Newsweek* provided the largest audience for a president. By 1963, the television networks had supplanted them, and Valachi's appearance on TV made a major impact. In the past, mobsters had either taken the

Fifth Amendment or been evasive at the Kefauver and McClellan hearings. Valachi took the opposite approach, telling more than he knew.

A new name for the Mafia emerged out of the hearings. Wiretaps had picked up made men talking about *cosa nostra* ("our thing"). Many mob watchers had never heard the expression—it was actually a generic term used by some New York gangsters—but it was eagerly embraced by J. Edgar Hoover. It permitted him to say he had been right all along to insist that there was no Mafia—there was a La Cosa Nostra (*The* Our Thing?), and it had taken the FBI to discover it.

Valachi's testimony did nothing to help him personally. He might have been able to win his release from his original drug charges, but to beat the murder rap he needed to give information that would put bigger murderers behind bars, and he had no hard evidence. Valachi would spend the rest of his life in a federal correctional facility in Texas, where he was given some modest comforts. After his death in 1971, other noted mob turncoats would be housed in what would become known as the "Valachi Suite."

In November 1963, Attorney General Kennedy held one of the regular conferences of his organized crime working group. At the midday break, he invited U.S. Attorney Morgenthau and some of the others to join him for lunch at his home in nearby Virginia. As they sat by the pool eating clam chowder and tuna sandwiches, the attorney general was called to an outdoor phone. At the same time, a housepainter carrying a small radio began shouting something about the president. Glancing at Kennedy talking on the phone, Morgenthau observed him suddenly clasp his hand to his mouth, and instantly grasped what the painter was saying. When Kennedy returned to the group he told them that the call was from J. Edgar Hoover, informing him that his brother the president had been shot in Dallas. Though Kennedy remained as attorney general for another year, the organized crime group never met again. Jimmy Hoffa's first act after the assassination was to reprimand a Teamster official who lowered the IBT headquarters flag to half-mast, and his public response was to observe that Bobby Kennedy was now "just another lawyer."

Robert Kennedy and Lyndon B. Johnson had never gotten along—Bobby had frantically tried to dissuade his brother from making Johnson his running mate in 1960. With LBJ's ascension, Kennedy's power to make the federal bureaucracy dance to his tune ended. Hoover quickly established a close liaison with Johnson, effectively restoring the Bureau's traditional autonomy within the DOJ. Heartsick, Robert Kennedy went through the motions until August 1964, when he resigned to run for U.S. senator from New York.

Before he resigned, Kennedy did have the satisfaction of seeing Jimmy Hoffa convicted in the Nashville jury tampering and Chicago loan fraud cases. Hoffa was sentenced to eight years on the former charge and five years on the latter, for a total of thirteen. He appealed the Nashville conviction all the way to the Supreme Court, on the grounds that the government had engaged in illegal eavesdropping and planted an informer among his defense team's inner circle. The informer was a Teamster slugger who, after getting wind of plans to bribe jurors while he was guarding the door at Hoffa's meetings with his attorneys, had alerted Walter Sheridan. The U.S. Supreme Court upheld the convictions in 1966, and Jimmy began serving his sentence in 1967.

The year after Kennedy left the Justice Department, Sam Giancana was jailed on a contempt of court charge for refusing to answer questions posed to him by a grand jury after being granted immunity. Giancana sat in a jail cell for nine months until the grand jury session ended. His mob colleagues, disgusted by his antics and the federal pressure that he had brought upon all of them, passed the word via Tony Accardo that Giancana should step down and leave town. So in 1966 he and his pal Dick Cain went off to Mexico for an extended stay.

In June 1968, while seeking the Democratic nomination for president, Robert Kennedy was assassinated in Los Angeles. He was the first cabinet-level official since Treasury Secretary Henry Morgenthau to take organized crime seriously, and he had infused the drive with his own passion and energy. As a result, he did more to combat the American Mafia than any single person before him. Prior to Kennedy, there had been no coordinated attempt to break the mobs. Commissioner Anslinger went after the narcotics traffickers, the DOJ attempted to put the Apalachin group in jail, and J. Edgar Hoover's Top Hoodlum Program was gathering intelligence. But none of these made a major dent in the organized crime families. As attorney general, Kennedy coordinated and accelerated the attack on the mobs.

He did not have adequate laws on the books to do more than make tax or gambling cases, and his victories were tactical rather than strategic. The damage to the Mafia was not great, but it was thrown on the defensive and badly shaken by such things as Marcello's deportation and the full-court press on Giancana. If Jack Kennedy had lived and (as was very likely) been elected to a second term, Robert Kennedy would undoubtedly have been succeeded as attorney general by someone like Robert Morgenthau, who shared his commitment to fighting organized crime. A second Kennedy term with expanded intelligence data, increasingly skilled field agents, new laws, and perhaps a comprehensive strategic approach would have seen much more effective government efforts. If the administration of Jack Kennedy had been followed by a few years of President Robert, the American Mafia might have been crushed. Later some would assert that this prospect was real enough to make the mobs take the removal of the Kennedys into their own hands. More than a decade after Dallas, the question would become a contentious issue leading to a congressional investigation. And the names of Robert Kennedy's old adversaries—Carlos Marcello, Jimmy Hoffa, and Sam Giancana—would figure prominently in that inquiry.

CHAPTER 5

HAIL COLOMBO:
THE MAFIA MAKES A COMEBACK

In New York City, celebrations of ethnic pride are not only festive occasions but major political events. High officials such as the mayor, governor, or U.S. senators can always be found marching in the St. Patrick's or Columbus Day parade. Events of lesser magnitude also attract politicians—even if they don't attend, they often send messages of support to be read aloud at the ceremony. During the three and a half years he served as U.S. senator from New York, Robert Kennedy attended many such rituals. By June 1970 he had been dead for two years, but even if he had been alive he would not have sent congratulations, much less attended the rally being held on the twenty-ninth. Most likely he would have denounced it, and perhaps if the Kennedys had still been in power it would not have been held at all. Joe Colombo, Sr., boss of one of New York's five families, was staging a protest against the war on the Mafia that the Kennedy brothers had accelerated. Only half a dozen years had passed since the mobs had been shaken by assaults from Attorney General Kennedy's Justice Department, the country riveted by Joe Valachi's tales about life in the Mafia, and bosses like Carlos Marcello and Sam Giancana blanketed by law enforcement. Now a Mafia leader proclaiming himself an Italian version of Dr. Martin Luther King, Jr., was being taken seriously.

It had all started two months earlier, when Joe Colombo, Jr., had been arrested by the FBI in a case involving some melted-down silver coins. An enraged Joe Senior and his gangsters began picketing FBI headquarters, then located on the fashionable Upper East Side of Manhattan. Agents entering and leaving the building had to brush past demonstrators, and sometimes clashes occurred between G-men and pickets. Agents of Italian descent were specifically singled out for harassment and taunted as traitors. A few years earlier, Colombo and his boys might have been hauled away in a patrol wagon. In the climate of the time, though, claiming to be civil rights protesters gave them a certain immunity. Instead of being jailed or denounced, Colombo began to receive considerable media attention, much of it sympathetic. Buoyed by his new image, he decided to hold a rally at Columbus Circle, adjacent to Central Park in the heart of Manhattan. From his standpoint, the symbolism was perfect—Joe Colombo as an Italian hero, in the tradition of the great Christopher. Flyers were distributed in Italian neighborhoods, and local businessmen were "encouraged" to close their places on the day of the event. The longshoremen's union was headed by the son-in-law of the late union president Anthony Anastasio (brother of Murder Inc.'s lord high executioner, Albert Anastasia, despite the different spelling), Anthony Scotto, and he shut down the waterfront for the day. An organization that can draw that kind of backing is treated respectfully by politicians. Mayor John Lindsay's first deputy, Richard Aurelio, extended official greetings to the crowd (estimated at fifty thousand) that gathered in the Circle, and four congressmen were in attendance. At the rally's conclusion, the crowd marched across town to FBI headquarters to continue the protest. The press played the event up and declared that it had been a great success. Colombo announced that he was forming an Italian-American Civil Rights League to carry on the good work. In November, a black-tie audience of five thousand people turned out to hear Frank Sinatra and other stars perform at a benefit in the Felt Forum at Madison Square Garden. They raised half a million dollars for the league's coffers.

Joe Colombo had succeeded to leadership of Brooklyn's Profaci family in 1964 when he was only forty, the youngest of the New York gang bosses at the time. His ascent was the culmination of three years of intrafamily warfare. Joe Profaci had been a longstanding member of the national syndicate: In 1928 he was seized at a national mob conclave in Cleveland, and twenty-nine years later he was among those apprehended at Apalachin. A devout churchgoer, he contributed substantial sums to his local parish. When a thief stole a crown laden with expensive jewels from a statue in a Brooklyn church, Profaci ordered it returned. The thief complied, but three of the diamonds were missing. Not long after, a man's body was found with a set of rosary beads wrapped around his neck. In the eyes of the faithful, symbolic justice had been rendered.

Despite his popularity with his neighbors, Profaci's last years had been troubled by the usual problem of a long-serving CEO. Young Turks in the family became restless, complaining that most of the earnings went to the boss, his relatives, and his close friends. For example, Profaci collected a hefty street tax, charging hijackers up to $1,800 per truck, but he did not spread the money around to the troops. In 1961 a rebellion broke out. The most prominent of the insurgents were "Crazy Joe" Gallo and his brothers Larry and Albert. Joe Gallo had earned his nickname by his odd behavior. He told off-color stories in the presence of fellow mobsters' wives and openly smoked marijuana or chewed hashish. During the McClellan Committee hearings he strode into Robert Kennedy's office dressed like a movie gangster—black shirt, black coat, and black pants. Feeling the carpet, he declared it would be nice to use for a crap game. Then he offered one of the secretaries a job, telling her she could supplement her salary by taking "as much as you want from the till."

From their headquarters on President Street in Brooklyn's Red Hook section, where Crazy Joe kept a pet lioness in a cage, the Gallos ran a paper local of the Teamsters called the Automatic Coin Machine Union. Owners of jukeboxes and pinball machines were forced to pay them a $25 initiation fee and dues of six dollars a month per machine. The Gallos' sales methods were simple and direct. One jukebox distributor told a congressional committee, "They came out with steel bars and split my skull open." Another said, "They tried to twist my nose into a horseshoe." It was the Gallos who were thought to have carried out the assassination of Albert Anastasia for Carlo Gambino. Between 1961 and 1963 a dozen men either were killed or disappeared in the Gallo-Profaci war. Larry Gallo was lured to a bar where an attempt to strangle him was halted only by the unexpected appearance of a police sergeant who happened to walk in off the street. Gallo had already turned blue by the time the sergeant noticed his feet protruding from behind the bar. A shoot-out erupted and a patrolman was wounded, but thanks to the sergeant, Larry survived. A few months later, brother Joe was sent to prison for extortion. The battle was still raging in 1962, when Profaci died of old age and was succeeded by his brother-in-law Joe Maggliocio. During the Gallo insurgency, Carlo Gambino and Tommy Lucchese had appeared to favor the rebels against the family boss. So Profaci ally (and in-law) Joe Bonanno proposed to Maggliocio that they should retaliate by killing Carlo and Tommy.[1] Maggliocio delegated his lieutenant Joe Colombo to do the dirty work, but instead Colombo betrayed the plot to the intended victims. In 1963, in the midst of the intrigue, Maggliocio died, supposedly of natural causes, though it was rumored he had been poisoned.[2] Gambino backed Colombo to be head of the family, leaving the Gallos out in the cold.

An additional result of the failed plot was that Joe Bonanno was ordered to appear before the other bosses to answer charges against him. Bonanno knew how such affairs usually ended, and hurriedly left town. When he came back to New York, U.S. Attorney Morgenthau subpoenaed him to testify before a federal grand jury. It was an uncomfortable situation for Bonanno, with both the Feds and the family bosses pressuring him. On the day he was scheduled to show up at the grand jury, he was "kidnapped" from the streets of New York and not seen again for two years. Neither the Feds nor the other bosses bought the kidnapping story. From his exile, Bonanno sought to make his son Bill the family leader; instead it too broke into dissident factions, who battled for supremacy in what the cops labeled "the Banana wars." In 1966 some family rivals cut loose on Bill with a machine gun (they missed). Deprived of his seat on both the New York and the national commissions, Joe Bonanno eventually settled in Arizona, where he continued his racketeering activities.

1 In 1956 Bonanno's son Salvatore, called "Bill," married Profaci's niece Rosalie. Their lavish wedding has sometimes been cited as the model for the Corleone family wedding in the opening scene of *The Godfather*. In fact, the Bonanno affair was held in a Manhattan hotel, while the Corleone wedding took place at the family's suburban enclave.
2 An autopsy conducted five years after his death failed to disclose any traces of poison.

From the mobsters' viewpoint, the post-Kennedy administration of Lyndon Johnson was a great relief. Johnson had no interest in carrying out a war against the Mafia, and J. Edgar Hoover's commitment had always been lukewarm. G. Robert Blakey, one of Kennedy's prosecutors, who would later become a top organized crime expert, has related how the Department of Justice quickly reverted to its "lackadaisical pre-Kennedy days." The Johnson administration cut back on significant portions of the government's antimob drive.[3] In 1965, Edward Bennett Williams sued the FBI over electronic eavesdropping in Las Vegas. When Williams won his case, Johnson ordered an end to the practice. Across the country, bugs like Chicago's "Little Al" were turned off. Agent Bill Roemer later recalled, "We were devastated. We were so much better off now than we had been in 1959, when we knew so little about who the mobsters were and how they operated . . . now we were back to ground zero. . . . July 11, 1965, was one of the worst days of my life, I tell you that!" J. Edgar Hoover would attempt to blame Robert Kennedy for authorizing the bugging, but it had been standard practice long before 1961. For his part, Kennedy would try to deny that he knew it was happening, although as attorney general he had listened to tapes played by FBI agents.

It is not clear that the administration had to abandon electronic surveillance. It could have argued that the activities of a secret criminal organization like the Mafia constituted a clear and present danger to national security, citing, for example, the Teamsters' ability to paralyze transportation. By 1965 the American Mafia was far more of a threat to the United States than some old-line Communists. Another justification for the eavesdropping might have been to determine whether the Mafia had any role in the assassination of the president of the United States. Certainly that would have constituted a national security matter. Sitting justices of the Supreme Court Tom Clark and Byron White had been attorney general and

---

3 On the day of Kennedy's death, a high Justice Department official was seen weeping. When a colleague sought to console him he explained that he was not crying because Kennedy was dead but because Johnson was president, since it would mean the end of the organized crime drive.

deputy attorney general of the United States, respectively, and as such they had authorized eavesdropping in national security investigations. Thus the Supreme Court might well have upheld the practice, albeit with certain restrictions. But not even a halfhearted attempt to save the bugs was made.

Years later the FBI would admit to Congress that after the departure of the Kennedys, "the steam went out of the drive against organized crime." Many accounts put the blame for the slowdown on Attorney General Ramsey Clark, identifying him as Bobby Kennedy's successor. However, after Kennedy left office in August 1964, he was succeeded by his deputy, Nicholas deB Katzenbach, who held the post until 1967 and was in turn succeeded by Clark. Perhaps Clark's later career as a prominent leftist lawyer has caused people to place the onus on him. But as president, Lyndon Johnson proved that he had the will to keep an unpopular war like Vietnam going strong. It would have been much easier to maintain a popular one against the Mafia. If he had wanted it to continue at full strength, it would have. Responsibility for the fact that it did not must be placed on the man in the White House. It was not that the government completely stopped fighting the Mafia—Apalachin and the Valachi testimony made it politically impossible to do that. From 1964 to 1968, attacks on the mob continued, but they were pinpricks. Most of the convictions obtained were for violating antigambling laws or the old standby, tax evasion. These did little to cripple an organization that was heavily involved in drug trafficking, loan sharking, labor racketeering, infiltration of legitimate businesses, and murder. Typically, a convicted gambler received a fine or a sentence of a few months in jail. For mafiosi, an occasional jail sentence was just an occupational hazard, similar to a professional football player's acceptance of physical injury as part of the game. Since most Americans did not think gambling was a particularly serious matter, attacking the Mafia on that front played into the notion that they were essentially sportsmen. And tax violations were white-collar crimes that many otherwise respectable people engaged in.

The Mafia's real threat to the public was not that the gangs did a bit of wagering, but that they had obtained significant economic and political power and were not averse to killing ordinary citizens to advance their interests. For example, about the time Kennedy left the DOJ, a Genovese family big shot named Jerry Catena approached the giant A&P grocery chain to carry a detergent that he had an interest in. The company tested the product but declined to accept it. In 1964, four A&P stores in the New York area were burned to the ground. The next year, the manager of a Brooklyn store found a flat tire on his car. Because he was a law-abiding person, he did not realize that flattening a tire was a common way for mob assassins to set up their victim. When he undertook to change it, he was shot dead by three men. A month later a Bronx A&P manager was killed in his own driveway. Catena was no out-of-control rogue like Joey Gallo. He was a top figure in the family, who sometimes deputized for the imprisoned Vito Genovese in dealings with the commission. Robert Morgenthau was still U.S. attorney for the Southern District of New York—he had remained in office after Kennedy left the Department of Justice, and was too powerful to be dismissed by President Johnson. Though there was only suspicion against Catena, Morgenthau summoned him for a grilling before a grand jury, after which the attacks on the A&P suddenly stopped.

The mobs began to display a distinct disregard for law enforcement. In September 1966, Santo Trafficante of Tampa and Carlo Marcello of New Orleans had a sit-down at the La Stella restaurant in Queens with Carlo Gambino, Joe Colombo, and some other New York City mob leaders. Federal narcotics agents who had trailed Marcello to New York reported the meeting to the NYPD, which raided the place and arrested the thirteen participants. A week later, while awaiting disposition of the case, Trafficante, Marcello, their lieutenants, and two of their lawyers went back to the same restaurant for lunch. This time they notified the press. When a newspaper photographer showed up to take a picture, the participants raised their wine glasses in a mock toast. For the benefit of some plainclothes officers nearby, Marcello loudly proclaimed, "Why don't they arrest us now?" The cops did not take up the challenge. When the photo appeared in newspapers across the country, readers perceived that the authorities were backing down from the mob.

In his 1964 challenge to LBJ, Senator Barry Goldwater seized on the problem of crime in the streets. Though Johnson won in a landslide, it was clear that the issue had resonated with a good portion of the electorate. Street crime had not been a national concern since the Dillinger days, when President Roosevelt had scored significant political points by declaring, and then winning, a national war on crime. In the 1960s, the issue was much more complex than a few gun-happy small-time hoodlums shooting up banks and kidnapping rich men. A large element of the Democratic core constituency suspected that demands for law and order were simply code words for cracking down on black protesters. Still, it was true that between 1960 and 1965 the number of violent crimes (murder, rape, robbery, aggravated assault) jumped 60 percent.

When a high official is faced with an issue that he does not know how to deal with, a common response is to appoint a group to study it. In 1965, Johnson named nineteen notables to serve as members of a presidential commission on law enforcement and administration of justice. Since the president assumed he would be running for reelection in 1968, it was important that his crime commission deliver a balanced report. In this case, "balanced" would mean one that did not alienate minority and liberal voters by calling for harsh repressive measures, while still offering enough positive proposals to support law enforcement and prevent a Republican candidate from using the crime issue against Johnson. The president selected Attorney General Katzenbach to be the chairman, and the other members included the presidents of Yale, the Urban League, the League of Women Voters, and the American Bar Association (the head of which was Lewis Powell, later an associate justice of the U.S. Supreme Court); Mayor Wagner of New York; a former governor of Minnesota; and Johnson's close confidant, Leon Jaworski. Task forces were appointed to consider crime, police, courts, corrections, juvenile delinquency, narcotics, and alcoholism—every conceivable aspect of the problem except organized crime, because Johnson did not want to touch the subject. Some analysts have attributed sinister motives to LBJ's reluctance to fight the Mafia, citing, for example, the corruption of his top aide, Bobby Baker. Perhaps a simpler explanation is that for Johnson, attacking the mobs was bad politics. It could, as the Kefauver Committee had demonstrated, lead to embarrassing revelations about LBJ supporters. As a junior senator, he had seen Democratic majority leader Scott Lucas of Illinois lose his seat when the committee exposed links between the mob and the Cook County Democratic machine. Lucas, a downstater with no connections to the Mafia, was caught up in the voter outrage and swept out of office. Organized crime was also Robert Kennedy's signature issue, and Johnson had no intention of promoting the agenda of a man whom he not only disliked but who might challenge him for the White House.

The deputy director of the president's task force was Henry Ruth, who had served as an attorney in Kennedy's antiracketeering section. He was disturbed by the exclusion of organized crime from the agenda and insisted that there be a task force on the subject. So eighteen months into the commission's work, a modest $30,000 was made available to retain a small staff under the direction of Charles Rogovin, chief assistant district attorney of Philadelphia. Rogovin had developed an interest in organized crime, and his approach to the problem was innovative for the time. Instead of proceeding on a case-by-case basis, he had assembled a staff of county detectives, installed them in a location away from the D.A.'s office, and set them to work collecting basic intelligence.

In 1967 the president's commission released an overview report supplemented by individual reports from each task force. The commission did not dismiss fears of crime as racist, but it recommended solutions that emphasized "Great Society" social welfare programs. As it turned out, the report was of no help to Johnson in the 1968 presidential election. By then, protests over the Vietnam War had driven him out of the race. Ironically, the three major candidates that year—Richard Nixon, Hubert Humphrey, and George Wallace—to greater or lesser degrees adopted Goldwater's hard line on the crime issue, causing some observers to remark that they all seemed to be running for sheriff.

Given its limited funding, its short working life, and the political constraints it operated under, it is not surprising that the report of the commission's stepchild, the task force on organized crime, was largely a restatement of the Kefauver and McClellan committee conclusions. The most significant finding was in fact an affirmation of the status quo: Since the 1950s, very little had changed in the world of the American Mafia, and the same people were in the same rackets. As with Kefauver, the task force reported:

[The] core of organized crime in the United States consists of 24 groups operating as criminal cartels in large cities across the nation. Their membership is exclusively Italian. . . ."

J. Edgar Hoover was quoted describing the organization that only a few years earlier he had claimed did not exist:

La Cosa Nostra is the largest organization of the criminal underworld in this country, very closely organized and strictly disciplined. They have committed almost every crime under the sun. . . .

In a subtle reference to LBJ's reluctance to fight the Mafia, the report notes: "In 1965, a number of factors slowed the momentum of the organized crime drive."

Everyone in the organized-crime-fighting field recognized that electronic eavesdropping was a vital tool, but Johnson had warned the commission that he would not accept a report that endorsed it. Nevertheless, the task force recommended the enactment of federal laws permitting it. When the full commission considered the recommendation, Johnson's allies sought to block its approval. To their surprise, members like Whitney Young, head of the Urban League, supported it as a weapon against the Mafia's exploitation of ghetto dwellers. For a while it appeared that Johnson would not consent to receive the final report, and some commission officials suggested that they should notify TV networks that they were going to deliver it by throwing it over the White House fence. Finally Johnson agreed to accept it, with the electronic eavesdropping recommendations standing. Charles Rogovin would go on to create an organized crime unit in the office of Massachusetts attorney general Elliot Richardson that would become a model for similar operations in other states. Later, as a professor, writer, and consultant, he would become a leading expert on organized crime.

In 1968 Senator McClellan's committee prepared the Omnibus Crime Control and Safe Streets Act that provided for the use of electronic surveillance under court authorization. There was some resistance within the administration to signing the bill into law. In April, riots swept American cities after the assassination of Martin Luther King and two months later Robert Kennedy was killed. Public opinion demanded national action on crime. The McClellan Committee bill contained funds to assist state and local law enforcement, so to secure these, President Johnson signed the law. The omnibus bill was largely the work of the chief counsel to the committee, G. Robert Blakey, who had begun his government service in 1960 as an attorney in the organized crime and racketeering section. A North Carolinian who graduated from the University of Notre Dame's college and law school, Blakey quickly became a disciple of Robert Kennedy. Later he served as a consultant to Rogovin's task force. When *Time* magazine published a picture of the participants at the second La Stella sit-down, identifying them as mobsters, it neglected to mention that two of the diners were defense lawyers. Frank Ragano of Tampa, who represented Santo Trafficante, was one of them, and he sued. The magazine retained Blakey as an expert witness, and his testimony—that Ragano was effectively house counsel for an organized crime figure—helped *Time* win the case.

While the government was rediscovering effective tactics like electronic eavesdropping, it still lacked a winning strategy. Strategic planning was not the Department of Justice's strong suit. Prosecutors saw themselves as gunslingers going mano a mano against top defense lawyers in dramatic trials, not theorists. Rogovin's organized crime task force had contained consultants from the social sciences who emphasized the importance of thinking about the Mafia as an organization rather than just individuals. One of them, criminologist Donald Cressey, had revised Valachi's testimony into sociological jargon as an appendix to the task force report, titled "The Function and Structure of Criminal Syndicates." Influenced by the social scientists, in 1970 Blakey would draft an organized crime control law, which included a so-called RICO (Racketeer Influenced and Corrupt Organizations) statute. It was meant to emulate the 1890 Sherman Antitrust Act, which had been passed to make corporations subject to criminal penalties. Despite later belief, the law was aimed not simply at the Mafia but also at white-collar crime and political corruption.[4] As with antitrust laws, the RICO statute contained provisions authorizing civil suits for damages, and it permitted the freezing of a defendant's assets before trial. This too was not an approach that the macho world of law enforcement greeted with enthusiasm—filing a lawsuit against a hoodlum was seen as the act of a 98-pound weakling who whimpered when a beach bully kicked sand in his face. In time RICO would provide the tool by which the Mafia could be attacked as an organization, but it would take ten years before Blakey could persuade prosecutors to consider using it.

The Vietnam War, civil rights protests, and campus unrest made it fashionable to question the received wisdom on any subject, and the menace of the Mafia was no exception. Scholars began to produce articles and books debunking the very existence of such an organization. In 1970, University of Chicago professor Norval Morris and a research colleague, Gordon Hawkins, published a book with the cute title *The Honest Politician's Guide to Crime Control*. One of its chapters, entitled "Organized Crime and God," was written as a rebuttal to the work of Cressey and officials like Robert Kennedy. In it the authors describe the belief in organized crime as a "seductive and persistent . . . myth . . . belong[ing] to the realm of metaphysics or theology." Their principal recommendation in the area was "All special organized crime units in federal and state Justice and police departments shall be disbanded." Morris would go on to become dean of the University of Chicago Law School and a member of the Chicago Police Board. Yet his concept of organized crime seemed to be the notion that mobsters simply furnished people with goods that they desired. Forty years earlier, another Chicagoan, Al Capone, had argued that he was only providing a service by selling beer to a thirsty public. He omitted to mention such things as the Valentine's Day massacre. Missing in Morris's for-

---

4 The popular name of the RICO Act is often taken as a play on Edward G. Robinson's character, Caesar Enrico "Rico" Bandello, in the 1930 movie *Little Caesar*, who, as he lies dying, mutters, "Mother of Mercy, can this be the end of Rico?" While Little Caesar dies, the head of the criminal organization he belongs to, "Big Boy," continues to operate. Though Blakey has never confirmed that the title RICO was based on the movie, he has stated that the law was written to ensure that the Big Boys would be punished along with the Ricos.

mulation was any recognition of organized crime's extortion of legitimate business, including the killing of innocent people like the A&P managers, or the brutal exploitation of members of mob-controlled unions.

Even Donald Cressey was prepared to temporize with the Mafia. He expanded his work on the organized crime task force into a book in which he suggested "appeasing" the mob. He wrote, "It is . . . not inconceivable, that Cosa Nostra would agree to give up its political involvements and its illegal operations of legitimate businesses . . . if it could be assured that it would be permitted to keep the profits after payment of taxes, on bet-taking." At about the same time, the *Godfather* novel became a runaway bestseller. Written by a man with no real knowledge of organized crime, it presented a composite New York mob family, stressing their fidelity to old-fashioned virtues like honor, loyalty, and respect.

The Beautiful People had always found it amusing to socialize with gangsters (this was especially true in the 1920s, when the mob's social cachet was further bolstered by its ability to furnish the best brands of illegal liquor). For a mobster to mingle with the swells, however, he could not advertise his violent methods too broadly, or openly peddle drugs. Instead he had to project himself as a "good" bad man. In accordance with the spirit of the times, after his release from prison, Crazy Joe Gallo took to presenting himself as a thoughtful intellectual. The popular actor Jerry Orbach and his wife invited Gallo to parties, where he joined celebrity guests in discussions of Camus and Sartre. The Orbachs allowed him to use their home for his wedding.

In the face of President Johnson's rollback of the government's efforts, scholarly debunkers, proposals for an organized crime version of Munich, and Joey Gallo spouting philosophy, the war might have been called off or at least put on the back burner. One reason it was not was that the Mafia's leadership was incapable of exploiting the opportunity presented. Frank Costello of the New York family and Chicago's Murray Humphreys were able to fix politicians and charm influentials. But the leaders who had replaced them were much less shrewd and circumspect. Upon his return from the La Stella meeting, Carlos Marcello assaulted an FBI agent at the airport and was prosecuted.[5] Sam Giancana sued the FBI and projected a

5 Eventually he was sentenced to two years in prison, though the actual term served was only six months.

public-be-damned attitude. After Giancana went off to Mexico, the Outfit named Milwaukee Phil Alderisio as its chief. A well-known enforcer was not the ideal person to convince people that the mob was harmless. Carlo Gambino, the most important boss in New York, had been smuggled into the country at the age of nineteen and spent most of his subsequent career as either a Prohibition-era bootlegger or a wartime black marketeer. A good moneymaker, he lacked the political skills to fill Costello's shoes. And though mild-mannered and physically unintimidating himself, he encouraged violence in other families in order to enhance his own power. After Jimmy Hoffa went to prison, instead of distancing themselves from the Teamsters, the mob became much more involved with them, exercising even greater influence with his successor. Given the economic threat this posed, government was bound to keep investigating the IBT-organized crime alliance.

Familiar discoveries of mobsters in bed with politicians also served to remind people of the Mafia's threat to governmental integrity. In 1965, Mayor Wagner decided not to run for reelection after twelve years in office. For his successor the voters chose John Lindsay, a tall, handsome thirty-eight-year-old socialite and liberal Republican who represented Manhattan's "silk-stocking" district in Congress. At first Lindsay seemed like the kind of dynamic leader who could master the problems besetting the city and move on to higher office. Many people not normally attracted to municipal jobs sought to join his administration.

One of Lindsay's prize recruits was thirty-five-year-old James Marcus, son-in-law of former Connecticut governor John Lodge (of the Brahmin Lodges). Marcus was a member of Lindsay's social circle and had worked as a campaign volunteer. After the election he was tapped to run the city's department of water supply, gas, and electricity. Like many wealthy men who entered government service, he agreed to work for a nominal dollar a year. Soon he was part of the inner circle of the administration, and the dollar was replaced by a commissioner's full salary—which, as it turned out, Marcus badly needed, since he was in debt due to business misjudgments and worse (in some instances he had sold stock and failed to deliver it to the purchaser). Seeking union endorsements for Lindsay during the campaign, Marcus had met with a labor lawyer named Herb Itkin, who in turn arranged for Marcus to have an interview with Ducks Corallo, the Lucchese family capo who controlled several Teamsters locals. It is hard to believe that in 1965 Marcus was unaware of the problems in the Teamsters union, or that Corallo's name could be unfamiliar to anyone who read the newspapers. Three years earlier, Corallo and Judge Keogh had been convicted in a highly publicized trial. The election passed without incident, but once in office, with his troubles mounting, Marcus turned to Itkin and Corallo for financial assistance. Over lunch in a tony New York restaurant, Ducks agreed to lend him $10,000 in return for Marcus's awarding an $835,000 no-bid contract for cleaning the Jerome Park Reservoir to a friend of Corallo's. The contractor would then kick back a portion of the money, $16,000 of which would go to Marcus. Not only was the contract let, but Marcus got Mayor Lindsay to hold a press conference at the reservoir explaining that an emergency contract was required because debris had accumulated and was a threat to the city's drinking water. The press, still in a honeymoon phase with Lindsay, portrayed the affair as indicative of the new administration's dynamic approach to problem solving.

Unfortunately for Marcus, he could not fool his creditors the same way he did the mayor. They complained to New York County district attorney Frank Hogan's office about undelivered stocks, and Marcus was called in for questioning. When he stonewalled, Hogan notified the mayor. Marcus duped Lindsay once again, explaining that he needed to resign to take care of his business affairs. The gullible mayor wrote a letter thanking him for his services and mentioning their close friendship. The district attorney's investigation continued, with little cooperation from Marcus. Gradually, however, the pieces began to fit together. When an assistant district attorney asked him if he was in debt to Corallo, Marcus realized the game was up. He went to Itkin, who (unbeknownst to Marcus) was a paid informer for the FBI. The clever Itkin suggested that they make a clean breast to the Feds so as to head off a state prosecution. In December 1967, Marcus, Itkin, and Corallo were all indicted by U.S. Attorney Morgenthau. When the mayor was informed of the charges, Lindsay warned Morgenthau that he was "making a terrible mistake." Marcus would serve fifteen months in a federal prison and then turn government witness.

The Marcus case also spelled disaster for another New York politician, though in the case of Carmine DeSapio he had already been removed from office, having been defeated for district leader by a reform candidate. When DeSapio tried a comeback he was beaten by Ed Koch, who would later become mayor of New York City. Koch was one New Yorker under no illusions about DeSapio. He would write, "I didn't want to run for district leader. Who wants to run against Carmine DeSapio? You literally worry about getting killed; you do." One night during the campaign, a flowerpot mysteriously dropped out of a window and barely missed Koch's head.[6] Corallo had enlisted Marcus in a scheme to shake down the giant utility Con Edison. As gas and electricity commissioner, Marcus had the authority to issue permits to the company, and he demanded that in return Con Ed contracts be let to firms favored by Corallo. To assist in the shakedown, DeSapio was engaged as an intermediary among the parties. Morgenthau brought charges against them, and in 1968 DeSapio and Corallo received prison sentences.[7]

While Joe Colombo's antics fit the time, not everyone fell for his oppressed minority act—Senator John Marchi of Staten Island, one of the most respected members of the state legislature, constantly warned his ethnic compatriots that they were being "conned." Yet Colombo's rantings touched a nerve with law-abiding Italian Americans, who were tired of being stereotyped as gangsters and listening to jokes about themselves on television. The stereotype caused more than hurt feelings—it limited their advancement. It was extremely rare to find an Italian American who was a partner in a Wall Street law or banking firm. Outside the automobile industry, there were not many Fortune 500 executives with multiple vowels in their names. So while most Italians did not support Colombo, he was saying things that many of them thought needed to be said. Under pressure from Colombo's group, the producers of the *Godfather* movie agreed to delete any reference to the Mafia or La Cosa Nostra. Attorney General John

6 In fairness to DeSapio, he must have possessed some excellent personal qualities. In research for this book, everyone I spoke to recalled him fondly. When he died in 2004, at the age of ninety-five, the obituaries were generally respectful.
7 Under laws in effect at the time, Corallo's sentences in the Keogh case (see chapter 4) and the Con Ed extortion were relatively light. Senator McClellan was so outraged by this that he pushed for the RICO Act and legislation that eventually led to laws that mandated stiff sentences.

Mitchell ordered the Justice Department to purge the words from its reports. New York's Governor Rockefeller gave similar orders to the state police. Senator Marchi denounced the "preposterous theory that we can exorcise devils, by reading them out of the English language." Under the circumstances it was probably fortunate that Colombo did not demand that the name of the village of Apalachin be changed to Columbus.

But while Colombo was winning some hearts and minds within and without the Italian community, he was incurring displeasure inside the Mafia, an organization he claimed did not exist. Most bosses held to the traditional view that it was best to keep a low profile, avoiding the heat that publicity could bring. They also believed that the FBI should not be directly confronted. This was in line with the notion that cops weren't personal enemies, but just people doing their jobs. When a young mob punk mouthed off to a detective, his boss, Tommy Lucchese, slapped him across the mouth and ordered him to apologize—sincerely. For Colombo to picket FBI headquarters flew in the face of Mafia convention.

When Colombo scheduled a second Colombus Circle rally in June 1971, Carlo Gambino passed the word that people should not attend or close their shops, and this time the waterfront did not shut down. As a result, attendance was much lower than in the previous year. One man who did show up was not there to offer support. Before the event could get under way, in broad daylight and surrounded by his supporters and scores of cops, Joe Colombo was shot in the head by a twenty-five-year-old black man posing as a photographer. The shooter, Jerome Johnson, was immediately tackled by a flying wedge of cops and Colombo men. When the pile was untangled, Johnson was dead of a bullet wound from a gun dropped at the scene. Colombo survived but remained comatose until his death in 1978. Johnson was an ex-convict about whom little was known—detectives believed that other mobsters had used an African American as the hit man because he could get close to the target without arousing suspicion. Among the suspects were the Gambinos and Joey Gallo, still on the outs with his former associates. During his prison stretch Gallo had made friends with some black gangsters and had talked about forming an alliance with them.

Influenced by his celebrity status, Gallo began discussing the possibility of a book and movie about his life—another Mafia taboo. When the great Lucky Luciano, exiled to Naples, had begun similar discussions, he received a warning from his colleagues in America that such a venture would be very bad for his health. He shelved the idea.[8] In April 1972, while celebrating a family birthday at Umberto's Clam House in Lower Manhattan, Gallo was shot to death and his bodyguard wounded.[9] Some claimed it was revenge by Gallo's enemies, the Colombos. Others said Joey's buddying up to the media called too much attention to the Mafia. The NYPD version of the hit was that a mob wannabe spotted Gallo and his party when they walked into the restaurant and alerted the Colombos in an attempt to ingratiate himself with the family. Gallo provided entertainment for chic New Yorkers even in death: Bob Dylan wrote a song about him, and for a time it was fashionable for a party of in-crowd types to drop into Umberto's and ask the waiter, "What time is the next shooting?" It provided a laugh and a good story to tell at parties.

Four months after Gallo's death there was another shooting in a Manhattan restaurant. A gunman killed four respectable businessmen at the bar of an upscale place called the Neapolitan Noodle. The men had sat down to wait for their table at seats just vacated by some Colombo gang members. Detectives believed that a mob spotter had summoned gunmen to kill the Colombos, and by the time they arrived, the targets had departed and the victims had taken their seats. This time chic New Yorkers did not see the killings as particularly humorous.

The six or seven years following the murder of President Kennedy was a crucial time in the war against the Mafia. Had it not been for the efforts of a cadre of Kennedy-era mob fighters like Robert Morgenthau, Henry Ruth, Charles Rogovin and G. Robert Blakey, and the strong support of the powerful Senator John L. McClellan, the war might have been abandoned. Instead, by the '70s it had been revived. In 1972 death would remove J. Edgar

8 After Luciano's death, a book of his supposed recollections appeared, but organized crime experts dismissed it out of hand.
9 Jerry Orbach and his wife had been seen with Gallo earlier in the evening and could not explain where they were when the hit occurred. When Orbach died in 2004, the writer Pete Hamill recalled in *The New York Times* that it was commonly believed that the Orbachs had been present when the shooting took place. Later Jerry would star as a detective in the popular TV show *Law and Order*.

Hoover, something no president had been able to do. In assessing his forty-eight-year career as head of the FBI, one can level many criticisms at him, not the least of which is his prolonged refusal to become involved in the attack on organized crime. However, it also has to be conceded that the Bureau he created was the most honest and efficient law enforcement agency in America. Hoover's critics cannot have it both ways. If the failures of the FBI can be blamed on him, then he must be credited with its accomplishments. Post-Hoover, the Bureau would become the leading force in the fight against organized crime.

The year 1972 also saw the movie version of *The Godfather* appear, with Marlon Brando in the title role of Don Vito Corleone. The film made a star of Al Pacino, who portrayed the younger son of the Corleone family. Like Brando's Terry Malloy character in 1954's *On the Waterfront,* Michael Corleone, a decorated Marine in love with a respectable girl, is associated with the mob by blood but not conviction. In this telling, though, the hero does not turn against his heritage. Instead he rejects the straight life, embraces the family's values, and becomes boss. The film caught the antihero spirit of the time, presenting mafiosi as more honorable than ostensibly respectable people. The story depicts events real, distorted, and false. The strangling of a hoodlum in a bar is obviously based on the incident involving Larry Gallo. No one has any difficulty identifying the troubled singer whose career is boosted by mob intervention (though in real life it was not necessary to plant a horse's head in the bed of studio chief Harry Cohn to get Frank Sinatra a part in *From Here to Eternity*). The scene in which Michael Corleone kills another mobster and a corrupt police captain is meant to depict a virtuous act; in fact a New York police captain was never assassinated by Mafia gunmen.[10] Many mobsters loved the movie, seeing it over and over again and constantly playing the theme song on jukeboxes. Some even tried to shape their behavior to fit the screen characters, and it was probably a boon to mob recruitment. Of course, the admiring light it cast on gangsters made many organized crime fighters critical of the film. In retrospect, they were wrong. The *Godfather* movie, with its sequels and

10 The closest was an honest lieutenant murdered in 1909 while on an investigation in Sicily.

constant showings on television, has done more to convince the public of the Mafia's existence than all the presidential commissions and congressional committees combined. As the saga progressed and Michael Corleone brought about the psychological destruction of his wife and sister, and the murder of his own brother, it offered a powerful counter to its earlier portrayals of mob bosses as honorable men. In the last quarter of the twentieth century, the decline of the Mafia's image on the screen would be paralleled by the public's increasing disapproval.

CHAPTER 6

FROM HAVANA TO DALLAS:
THE SUNBELT MAFIA AND THE KILLING OF JFK

Luigi Santo Trafficante, Jr., was one of several Americans who remained in Cuba after Fidel Castro took over at the beginning of 1959. To leave would have meant abandoning his lucrative holdings, which included the ownership of or interest in four hotel/casinos. At one of them, the Capri, washed-up Hollywood star George Raft glad-handed customers and strolled around pretending he owned the place—a real-life reprise of his role in *Nob Hill*. Only the tourists were fooled, but before 1959 there were plenty of them. Just ninety miles off the Florida coast, Havana had been a mecca for visiting Americans since the 1920s. Its luxury hotels offered exotic tropical drinks, dancing to Latin rhythms, and old-world charm and elegance amid palm trees. The city also provided plenty of gambling and prostitution, making it an attractive target for American gangsters. In the 1930s Meyer Lansky cut a deal with dictator Fulgencio Batista to open the island to the Mafia. There was a brief intermission during World War II, when travel restrictions ended tourism, and Batista went into exile in 1944, the loser in an honest election forced on him by the United States government. The Mafia's reentry after the war was a little rocky: When Lucky Luciano tried to set up his headquarters in Havana, Commissioner Anslinger of the Bureau of Narcotics compelled the Cuban authorities to deport him back to Italy. But Batista's return in 1952 gave the mob families carte blanche.

Havana had everything: dog tracks, horse racing, blackjack, poker, dice, roulette. Women were readily available, ranging from beautiful courtesans to young girls who walked the downtown streets. Drugs were plentiful, for recreation and as a commodity that could be smuggled into the United States. The range of attractions was endless. Santo Trafficante (he rarely used Luigi) summed up the delights of Havana succinctly: "You want opera, they have opera. You want baseball, they have baseball. You want ballroom dancing, they have ballroom dancing. And if you want live sex shows, they have live sex shows." The last were heavily patronized by American visitors seeking to absorb the "local culture."

A short, stocky man with piercing green eyes behind his horn-rimmed glasses, Trafficante was boss of the Mafia family in Tampa, Florida. Anyone who wanted to run an organized crime operation there had to "see the man with the green eyes." He inherited his domain from his father, a Sicilian immigrant (also known as Santo) who had gotten a foothold in the rackets as a bolita operator. A game of Cuban origin, in a typical version balls numbered 1 to 100 are placed in a sack and shaken up, and the winning one is drawn out. With wagers as low as a penny, it appealed to poor people. The center of the Tampa bolita racket was the Italian-Hispanic Ybor City district. There Santo Senior worked closely with Cuban Americans and became fluent in Spanish. When father and son began coming to Havana in the '30s, their affinity with Cubans and mastery of the language made it easy for them to gain a foothold.

In the 1940s Santo Senior became boss of the Tampa Mafia; after his (natural) death in 1954, Junior, then forty, succeeded him. The rich pickings in Cuba and a fondness for the lifestyle led him to spend most of his time there. He installed a beautiful showgirl as his Havana mistress while his wife remained home in Tampa. By the late '50s he was second only to Meyer Lansky in the Cuban world of the American Mafia. By 1957 he had achieved an enviable position in the mob: He was among those invited to Apalachin by the national commission, yet he was still virtually unknown to law enforcement—when arrested at the conference, he managed to be booked as Louis Santo.

On New Year's Day 1959, Batista fled the country and the Cuban government collapsed. Before Castro's army could arrive in Havana, mobs began rioting and invading casinos. One group wrecked the Capri, sending George Raft packing. But some of Trafficante's other places were spared, and he stuck around. He had reason to think that he might be able to make the same kind of arrangements with the new rulers that he had with the old. Prior to the revolution, he had been secretly funneling money to the rebels as a form of insurance. However, the early days of the new regime were not encouraging. According to Trafficante, he was frequently harassed by Castro's men, who raided his apartment, tore up his furniture, and took him into the woods in attempts to persuade him to tell where he had money hidden.

In the mountains, Castro had made statements to journalists about getting rid of mob figures, sometimes threatening to shoot them when he came to power. But when he took over, he did not immediately make his official policies clear. In the uncertain conditions, tourists stopped coming to Havana. Trafficante closed his places for lack of business. Then soldiers with submachine guns came to his apartment one night and ordered him to reopen at least one of his clubs—Cuba could not afford unemployment. The government promised to unfreeze some of his assets if he cooperated. So for a while, fifty musicians played nightly to an audience of chorus girls and waiters who were standing around with nothing to do. Not a single customer showed up. Batista supporters were being summarily executed, and Cubans with enough money to gamble were afraid to enter the casinos lest they be arrested as enemies of the revolution.

In June, Trafficante was picked up and taken to Trescornia Detention Center, where "undesirable aliens" were being processed. The place was an old mansion without guards or bars on the windows, yet the sound of firing squads at work down the road had a chilling effect on detainees. Alarmed, Trafficante called his Tampa lawyer, Frank Ragano, who made several trips down to try to secure his release. Another man who may have visited Trafficante in prison was Dallas nightclub owner Jack Ruby, though both men would later deny that they had met then. Ruby's story was that he had visited a friend named Lewis McWillie on a pleasure trip.

One day Trafficante heard that he had been put on the death list as a drug dealer. When Ragano asked officials for proof of the charge, one explained that the prisoner's name gave him away: In Spanish it meant "trafficker." The lawyer countered that it was his given name, Santo (or saint), that signified his real character. Finally, in August, Trafficante was released. Whether it was Ragano's efforts, mob connections, or, most likely, a deal Trafficante himself struck with the Castroites is not clear. He had lost an estimated $20 million in investments and could only return to Tampa to bide his time and hope for the regime to change.

Trafficante did not have long to wait for a chance to strike back at Castro. In 1960, after CIA cutout Robert Maheu made his initial approach to Johnny Roselli, he was introduced to Trafficante, the Mafia boss with the most contacts in Cuba. Roselli, Sam Giancana, and Maheu briefed Santo on the plot to kill Castro. Enlisting underworld figures to carry out secret missions in hostile territory was standard operating procedure for intelligence agencies. Criminals had the skills and access to clandestine channels that enabled them to evade security forces, and the nerve and greed to take on dangerous tasks in return for a financial reward. Mafia groups like Trafficante's had many Cuban connections and a great desire to see the man who had appropriated their properties removed from power. They also were skilled killers. From a field officer's point of view, they were ideal for the job of eliminating Castro.

In a wartime situation, no intelligence agency would think twice about using gangsters to carry out missions. After the United States entered World War II, U.S. naval officers sought the assistance of Lucky Luciano and his capos in securing the Port of New York and later in collecting information for the invasion of Sicily. When the Americans occupied southern Italy in 1943, they utilized mafiosi to assist them in their administration. Vito Genovese, then hiding out in Italy from a New York murder rap, became an aide to U.S. officials and was even given his own jeep to run around in. When an Army sergeant questioned Genovese's position, he was stonewalled by his superiors.

But in 1960 the United States was in a state of cold war, in which the rules were not as clear as they had been in World War II. Though the goals at field officer level may have been unchanged, from the higher perspectives there should have been some hesitation about enlisting the services of mob figures. At the very least, someone ought to have stopped to ask how would it look if *The New York Times* revealed that the agency was not only planning to murder a head of state, but had brought in the Mafia to do it. CIA director

Allen Dulles was a man of sophistication with an Ivy League education and membership in high society. His late brother, John Foster Dulles, had been President Eisenhower's first secretary of state. In his own career, Allen had carried out secret operations in Europe during both world wars. Like most old intelligence hands, his views were shaped by his wartime experiences. After World War II, when it was revealed that U.S. intelligence had enlisted the services of the Mafia in New York City, some disapproval was expressed, but not much. Dulles okayed the assassination plan.

While the CIA developed various schemes to poison Castro at his favorite restaurant or slip something into his cigars, Trafficante sent assassination teams onto the island, where they got into firefights with the Cuban forces and had boats shot out from under them—or so he claimed. Later Roselli would allege that Trafficante made up the stories, pocketing as much as $150,000 of the funds that the CIA had allotted for the effort. He even suspected that Trafficante might have played a double game, informing Castro of the plot. Pulling such a stunt in order to put himself in the Cuban dictator's good graces was something a Mafia boss would not hesitate to do. In April 1961, the CIA-controlled Bay of Pigs invasion failed, much to the embarrassment of the Kennedy administration. Later that year, Allen Dulles was eased out. After the Bay of Pigs, the president put Robert Kennedy in charge of Operation Mongoose, the plan to overthrow the Castro regime.[1] After Castro learned of the plot against him, he made public statements warning of possible retaliation.

In October 1962 the Cuban missile crisis almost led to nuclear conflict. As part of the ensuing negotiations, President Kennedy promised not to invade Cuba. The government also began to crack down on anti-Castro activists who used the United States as a base for attacks on the island. The administration's actions angered the Cuban exile community. Thus, in less than three years, United States policy toward Cuba caused government

---

1 There has always been debate over the extent to which the Kennedys knew of plots against Castro. The distinguished Cambridge University historian of intelligence operations Christopher Andrew has stated, "It is difficult to believe the President was not informed the plot was underway even if he was not told (and probably did not wish to know) all the details." Michael Beschloss, a leading historian of the American presidency, has commented, "If Kennedy knew that the CIA's (assassins) were loose in Cuba and ready to strike, this would help explain his approval of an invasion plan [the Bay of Pigs] that otherwise seems so implausible."

agents to become involved with the Mafia, and drew the ire of both pro- and anti-Castro forces. Rightly or wrongly, the Kennedy administration bore the brunt of their wrath. On November 22, 1963, the president was assassinated in Dallas.

Suspicions of a foreign-directed plot began to form immediately after the murder of President Kennedy, fueled by the news that the man accused of killing him, Lee Harvey Oswald, had been a defector to the Soviet Union and an open supporter of Fidel Castro. The fact that the United States had almost been at war with the Russians over Cuba hardly a year before gave added credence to this line of thinking. Then, almost before the public could absorb the news of the assassination, Jack Ruby killed Oswald on national television. Ruby's apparent mob ties raised questions about possible gangster involvement. The fact that Ruby had been allowed to enter Dallas police headquarters with a gun, and get so close to Oswald as to make a kill virtually certain, suggested some sort of official connivance in the affair. In a poll taken a week after the assassination, only 29 percent of the respondents believed that Oswald had acted alone.

In December, President Johnson appointed a commission of seven prominent Americans, chaired by U.S. Chief Justice Earl Warren, to investigate the assassination.[2] In September 1964, the Warren Commission, as it was popularly known, issued a report declaring that after obtaining the cooperation of all government agencies and thoroughly exploring the relevant files, it concluded that Oswald carried out the assassination without the assistance of other parties. At first, the report was acclaimed by the media and widely accepted by the public. Then doubts began to surface. For example: Was Oswald capable of firing three shots from a sixth-floor window of the Texas School Book Depository building, at a moving target, in the five-second time frame the commission posited? Given Oswald's and Ruby's backgrounds, how could the commission dismiss the notion

2 The other members were Senators Richard B. Russell of Georgia and John Sherman Cooper of Kentucky; Representatives Hale Boggs of Louisiana and Gerald R. Ford of Michigan; former director of the CIA Allen W. Dulles; and John J. McCloy, who had served as president of the World Bank.

of a conspiracy? Had its seven Washington insiders suppressed certain information for reasons of state, or to cover up derelictions by U.S. agencies? In 1914 a small group of Serbian conspirators, aided by some of that country's officials, carried out an assassination that led to World War I; a finding that Russian or Cuban agents were involved in the Kennedy murder might have led to World War III. As a former defector to the Soviet Union, an outspoken supporter of Castro, and a visitor to the Cuban and Soviet embassies in Mexico City, Oswald had drawn attention from both the FBI and CIA. Had these agencies dropped the ball, ignoring information that could have prevented Oswald from carrying out his plan? Several of the president's policies, such as his support for civil rights legislation, had created domestic foes. To some critics, the notion of an alliance between rogue government agents, American right-wing elements, and/or anti-Castro forces in a plot against the president did not appear outlandish. In time, the questions became assertions that the president was murdered by foreign agents or domestic enemies, who benefited from the mistakes or deliberate acts of U.S. officials.

In 1966, New Orleans district attorney Jim Garrison opened a very public investigation of the assassination. Garrison had briefly served as an FBI agent and was an elected official in a major American city; his action gave legitimacy to the commission's critics. But after three years of sensational claims, Garrison finally charged New Orleans businessman Clay Shaw with conspiracy to murder the president. At his trial the prosecution presented virtually no evidence, and it took less than an hour for the jury to acquit the defendant.

The ignominious ending of Garrison's case might have silenced most critics if other events had not fanned the conspiracy flames. Jack Ruby, who had been convicted of the murder of Oswald, died in jail in 1967 at the age of fifty-five while awaiting a court-ordered retrial. In 1968, Dr. Martin Luther King, Jr., and Senator Robert Kennedy were both assassinated. The Vietnam War caused many Americans to become highly critical of their own government. The Watergate scandal of the 1970s demonstrated that some officials were capable of authorizing lawless acts (and then lying about it). In 1975 a Senate committee investigating the CIA, headed by Frank

Church of Idaho, revealed that the agency had recruited the Mafia in its efforts to topple Castro. The fact that Castro knew the Kennedy administration was trying to kill him suggested that he had a motive for striking first in a similar fashion. Though former CIA director Allen Dulles had been a member of the Warren Commission, he supposedly did not inform it of his agency's role in the plot. It was also revealed that the FBI had failed to disclose some of its contacts with Oswald. In one instance, after the assassination, an agent acting on the orders of his superior had destroyed a threatening note Oswald had previously left for him. Nor had the Bureau admitted that it had been conducting electronic eavesdropping of many organized crime figures, and through that surveillance had picked up conversations about the desirability of assassinating President Kennedy and/or Attorney General Robert Kennedy. Many people wondered what else Allen Dulles and J. Edgar Hoover (both dead by then) might have withheld from the assassination inquiry.

In 1974 Sam Giancana had come back to Chicago from Mexico. That disturbed the Outfit leaders, who feared that he might be looking to get his old job back. Giancana should have known better. His aide, Richard Cain, had been murdered in Chicago the year before because he displeased the bosses. In 1975 Sam was scheduled to testify at hearings of the Senate committee probing the CIA plot to kill Castro. Before he could do so, he was shot in the back of the head while cooking up a late-night snack in his suburban Chicago home. Investigators believed that the killer must have been a friend of Giancana's, or else Sam would never have turned his back on him. The fact that he also took a bullet in the mouth suggested that some kind of message about not talking was being delivered.

Johnny Roselli, down on his luck, did testify, and also spoke to journalists like columnist Jack Anderson.[3] In 1976—shortly after a visit to Santo Trafficante—his body was found in an oil drum in the Miami harbor. Since all three men had been involved in the CIA Mafia plot, it was

3 Johnny had been caught cheating at card games at the Friars Club in Beverly Hills, California. Over a four-year period he cleaned up $400,000 at gin rummy through a scheme involving electronic signals from observers stationed at peepholes. Roselli had been sponsored for the club by Frank Sinatra and Dean Martin, so he was disgraced among his friends. In 1971 he began serving a sentence in federal prison.

suspected that Giancana had been killed to ensure his silence, and Roselli as a warning to others to keep their mouths shut. West Coast mafioso Jimmy Fratianno, who had good connections among midwestern mobsters, never bought the story that the deaths of Giancana and Roselli had anything to do with the CIA plots. Instead, he believed that they involved settling old scores within the Chicago Outfit. Other equally knowledgeable people still see a link between the two men's deaths and the CIA-Cuban relationship.

The House of Representatives formed a select committee to investigate the assassinations of both Kennedys and Dr. King in 1976. Owing to many false starts, including twice changing the chief counsel and chairman, the investigation was not completed until 1978. Then, under the chairmanship of Congressman Louis Stokes and with organized crime expert G. Robert Blakey as chief counsel, the committee confirmed that Oswald had fired three shots at the president. But based on the findings of acoustical experts, the committee concluded there had been a fourth shot fired. According to the committee, Oswald missed his first shot, then hit the president and Texas governor John Connolly with the second. Another bullet, which missed, was fired from an area known as the "Grassy Knoll." The committee found credible the testimony of five witnesses who reported hearing a shot from there. Oswald then fired his third shot, which struck President Kennedy in the head.[4]

As a result of its findings, the committee posited that there had to have been a conspiracy. It then proceeded to theorize about who might have been behind the assassination, and concluded that while there was no direct evidence to link the Mafia to the president's murder, certain facts suggested the involvement of Carlos Marcello, Mafia boss of New Orleans, and other mob figures.

Fifteen years later, Tampa attorney Frank Ragano presented a version of the assassination that supported the congressional committee's

4 Blakey believes that the man who fired the shot from the knoll might have been assigned to kill Oswald when he exited from the Texas School Book Depository (though he was unable to do so), and that when the shooter saw Oswald's first shot had missed, he opened fire himself. After the committee completed its work, other scientific examinations called into question the acoustical evidence for the fourth shot.

hypothesis and pointed more directly at the involvement of Marcello and others. Ragano had been Trafficante's lawyer since the mid-1950s and was the man Santo had turned to when he was incarcerated in Cuba. Because of his success in representing the Tampa Mafia, Ragano was retained as part of Jimmy Hoffa's legal team in his battle with Robert Kennedy's Justice Department. In a book co-authored by Selwyn Raab, a top *New York Times* investigative reporter, Ragano claimed that in 1963 Hoffa had used him to relay a request, through Trafficante, that Carlos Marcello kill the president. At first Ragano did not take the notion seriously, lightheartedly telling Trafficante and Marcello over dinner in a New Orleans hotel, "Marteduzzo [Italian for "Little Hammer," a name by which they referred to Hoffa] wants you to do a little favor for him. You won't believe this, but he wants you to kill John Kennedy." As Ragano later recollected, "I waited for the laughter." To his surprise, neither man cracked a smile. Instead they stared at him, as if to indicate he should not have mentioned such a thing in a public place. According to Ragano, after the assassination he never dared to ask Santo whether Marcello had carried out Hoffa's wishes, though several times Trafficante pressed demands for Teamsters loans on the grounds that Hoffa owed him a very large debt.

In the years that followed, Ragano was convicted of crimes, disbarred, and served jail sentences. He claimed that Trafficante never tried to help him, and the two men ceased their friendship. Then in 1987, Ragano was supposedly summoned to the dying mafioso's home. There Trafficante, dressed only in pajamas, insisted that Ragano take him for an automobile ride—by then a standard practice to avoid hidden FBI microphones. Ragano's story was that during the ride, Trafficante confessed that Carlos Marcello had carried out the assassination as a favor to Hoffa and as a way of getting Robert Kennedy removed as attorney general, thereby lessening the pressure on himself and other mobsters. By the time Ragano's book was published, Trafficante, Marcello, and Hoffa were all dead, and his account offered no other evidence to support the allegations. The Trafficante family produced hospital records showing that on the day that Ragano recollected as the one on which he took the alleged automobile ride, Santo Trafficante had been a dialysis patient in a Tampa hospital. Many organized crime experts found Ragano's assertions difficult to accept.[5]

Over the past forty years, several thousand books and articles have been published on the Kennedy assassination. No theory of the case has received general acceptance, and no one has been prosecuted at a real trial.[6] Some theories of the case are based on facts; others are a product of misperceptions, emotion, or a generalized belief that the world is controlled by hidden forces. Persons unfamiliar with firearms often doubt Oswald's ability to get off the shots during the time frame stipulated. In fact it was not a particularly difficult task for a man who was a former Marine sharpshooter. Accounts that theorize that Oswald acted alone face a major psychological hurdle: Many people cannot accept that a single insignificant sociopath could murder the most powerful man in the world, thereby changing the course of history. Instead they look for alternative explanations, such as an attempt to influence national policy or exact some type of revenge. Others simply do not trust official sources, so they posit a conspiracy and assign the blame to Castro, the CIA, or any number of favorite villains. Accounts of the case often rely on supposed witness testimony. Yet since many of their statements are contradictory, it is obvious that some of them must have been lying, delusional, or honestly mistaken. A casual reader of the assassination literature will quickly recognize that depending on the author's point of view, certain witnesses are accepted as telling the gospel truth while others are dismissed as lying phonies. Inconvenient facts such as Oswald's public statements supporting Castro, his visit to the Cuban and Soviet embassies in Mexico City, or his attempted assassination of retired general Edwin Walker are explained as efforts to conceal his

5 In his book, Ragano also related that he had once accompanied Hoffa to a meeting in Attorney General Kennedy's office during the course of which Jimmy assaulted Bobby and had to be pulled off him by his lawyers. Supposedly, no Justice Department personnel were present and Kennedy did not take any retaliatory action. Individuals familiar with procedures in the Department of Justice during Kennedy's administration find it highly questionable that he would meet alone with defendants and their lawyers, and that an altercation such as the one described would not have drawn the attention of the office staff.
6 Jack Ruby was convicted of killing Oswald, but this did not settle disputes over why he did it or who killed Kennedy. The Shaw trial in New Orleans was a farce.

real sentiments, the actions of a double—or simply ignored. Even completely discredited notions linger on: Jim Garrison's investigation forms the basis for Oliver Stone's *JFK*. Starring Kevin Costner as Garrison, the film is probably now the principal source of information on the assassination for most Americans.

While neither official inquiries nor extensive media investigations have been able to reach a definitive conclusion about the death of President Kennedy, there are theories that do conform to the facts, such as the possibility of mob complicity in the assassination. If the Mafia was behind the murder of the president, it is likely that the key person in the conspiracy was Carlo Marcello, the most important organized crime figure in the southern states. Marcello had a hand in every illicit enterprise in the New Orleans area—gambling, bars, professional burglaries, holdups, and prostitution— as well as legitimate enterprises. The Town and Country Motel just outside the city limits served as headquarters for his empire. In 1967, *Life* estimated Marcello's personal wealth at $40 million. He also provided a link to Santo Trafficante and his Cuban connections as well as the Dallas mob world, which was controlled by Marcello's lieutenant, Joe Civello. When Marcello, angry about the attempt to kill Costello, boycotted the 1957 Apalachin conference, he sent Civello in his stead. Based on an analysis of the known facts, it is possible to assemble an inferential case against Marcello, one that goes beyond mere suspicion but is insufficient to have formed the basis for a prosecution.

In the first instance, Marcello was in a unique position to order the assassination of Kennedy without informing the national commission. As the oldest Mafia group in the United States, dating back to the late nineteenth century, the New Orleans family enjoyed great prestige among its peers. Given its seniority and geographical isolation, it had always operated outside the oversight of northern gangsters. Frank Costello might have been the prime minister of New York, but he entered New Orleans only at the invitation of the local organized crime–political nexus.

Marcello was clearly a man who saw murder as a useful tool. His philosophy was summed up by a sign on his desk that said, "Three people can keep a secret, if two of them are dead." His putative motives for murdering the president comprised a combination of survival and revenge. Robert

Kennedy's efforts to jail or deport him were a serious threat, not only to Marcello's operations, but to his dignity and person. Marcello was embittered by the bum's rush out of New Orleans that he had received. In addition to the embarrassment, it could have cost him his life. His trek through the jungle and his periods of incarceration by hostile local authorities had placed him in very real danger. At the time of President Kennedy's assassination, proceedings against him were still pending. Coincidentally, on November 22, he was acquitted of some immigration charges in a New Orleans courtroom amid allegations that a juror had been bribed. There was every expectation that John Kennedy would be reelected president of the United States in 1964 and that Robert Kennedy would continue as attorney general—or ensure the appointment of someone who would carry on his work with the same vigor (one reason for assassinating the president, rather than the attorney general). Thus in November 1963, Marcello and his Mafia allies faced the prospect of five more years of assault by the Kennedy administration, or even longer if Robert Kennedy succeeded his brother.

During his investigation of the Kennedy assassination, District Attorney Jim Garrison did not probe any ties between Oswald and the underworld. Garrison frequently declared that there was no organized crime in Louisiana. The high-spirited prosecutor was no stranger to French Quarter night life, and on occasion he accepted complimentary accommodations and a $5,000 gambling advance at the Sands Hotel Casino in Las Vegas, where Marcello was a silent backer. In 1967, after critical articles appeared in *Life* magazine, Garrison responded by initiating a grand jury investigation and promising to resign if organized crime was found to be flourishing. According to the executive director of the New Orleans Crime Commission, "Garrison conducted a parody of a grand jury investigation."

Both Marcello and Garrison would become targets of law enforcement. In June 1971, Garrison was arrested by federal agents for taking bribes from the operators of pinball gambling devices. One of the alleged payoffs, a thousand dollars in fifty-dollar bills coated with fluorescent powder, had been delivered to his home just prior to the arrest and was found in a drawer. Garrison admitted receiving the money, but claimed it was the repayment of a loan. At a 1973 trial he did not take the stand in his own defense, instead delivering a stirring jury summation. Thus he had the advantage of addressing the jurors without being subject to cross-examination. Garrison was acquitted. In November of that year he was defeated for reelection as district attorney.

In the late 1970s the FBI initiated Operation Brilab (bribery of labor). They established a fictitious insurance company, with a professional con man as the front and Bureau agents as managers. The con man arranged a scheme with Carlos Marcello in which they would bribe public officials to obtain insurance contracts. In 1981 Marcello was convicted and given seven years in prison. Later the verdict was reversed by higher courts after a Supreme Court decision in another case invalidated a portion of the statute under which he had been convicted.

Suspicions of the mob's involvement have also been raised by Lee Harvey Oswald's actions in New Orleans. He had spent much of his youth in the city and returned to live there from April to September 1963. During that time he resided with his uncle, Charles "Dutz" Murret, a gambler who had ties to Marcello's organization. While in New Orleans, Oswald publicly expressed sympathy for Castro and was arrested during a scuffle with anti-Castroites. One informer reported Carlos Marcello called for the assassination and suggested that a "nut" be used to do it. (When questioned by the assassination committee, Marcello denied ever having made such a statement.) If he had been hoping to use someone to kill Kennedy, Oswald was a prime candidate. He was a Marine sharpshooter, had defected to the Soviet Union, and was an open supporter of Castro. Marcello may even have learned through Dutz Murret about Oswald's attempt to shoot General Walker. Such a man would have been an ideal "nut" to assassinate the president.

It has also been alleged that Oswald might have been recruited for the assassination under false pretenses. Handbills for his "Fair Play for Cuba Committee" (of which he seemed to be the only member) listed an address in a building that also contained the offices of a private investigator named W. Guy Bannister (a former SAC of the Chicago FBI office). Bannister was widely believed to have worked on behalf of anti-Castro Cubans. An activist named Sylvia Odio, whose testimony the House assassination committee found credible, would later claim that in September 1963 some fellow exiles came to her Dallas apartment with a man whose name she recollected as "Leon" Oswald. Scenarios in which a patsy is used to carry out a mob hit had allegedly been used by the Mafia in the past. Mayor Anton Cermak of Chicago was killed in Miami in 1933 by a man named Giuseppe Zangara, who was allegedly shooting at president-elect Franklin D. Roosevelt. Cermak had cracked down on what was still called "the Capone gang" while favoring the remnants of Bugs Moran's group, which had nearly been wiped out on St. Valentine's Day. He rebuffed attempts by Capone's successor, Frank "The Enforcer" Nitti, to cut a deal. In December 1932, a detective who worked directly for the mayor shot and seriously wounded Nitti, who was unarmed and offering no resistance. It was rumored that Ted Newberry of the Morans had put a bounty on Nitti. Three weeks later Newberry was murdered, and the following month Cermak was killed. Nine days after Cermak died, Zangara was put to death by the state of Florida. Supposedly he was a psychotic with a grudge against high officials, though what prompted him to violence at that particular time and place was never explained. Reportedly Zangara was dying of cancer, and it was rumored that he may have been paid by the Chicago mob to commit the murder. Though nothing was ever proven, for the next thirty or more years, most people in Chicago believed that the mob had killed Mayor Cermak. The 1971 killing of Joe Colombo in New York City by an African-American gunman, Jerome Johnson, was thought to have been arranged by Joe Gallo or Carlo Gambino. Since Johnson was immediately shot to death in a pileup of cops and hoodlums, he could not be questioned.

G. Robert Blakey believes that Oswald may have been tricked into believing that he was working for Castroites and that the failure of the Grassy Knoll shooter to kill him necessitated that Oswald be murdered by someone else before he could reveal details of the plot.[7] Jack Ruby had a long history of mob associations. Some investigators believe he was sent to Dallas in 1947 to help pave the way for the Chicago Outfit's attempt to enter

---

7 Officer J. D. Tippett, a uniformed policeman on motor patrol, stopped Oswald, supposedly based on a radio description of the assassin. During the encounter, Tippett was fatally wounded by Oswald. Some writers have suggested that Tippett was assigned to kill Oswald, but that the target turned the tables on him. However, the assassination committee found nothing in Tippett's background to suggest any ties to organized crime or corruption and did not see him as involved in the assassination. The officer's hesitancy to shoot Oswald, as noted by witnesses, suggests that he did not know whether he was confronting a guilty or an innocent person—which would not be the approach of a mob hit man.

that city. The more likely story is that he was chased out of Chicago by the Outfit sub-boss, Lenny Patrick, after finding himself on the losing side in a war between West Side gamblers. In Dallas he continued to maintain contacts with organized crime. He often dined at the Egyptian Lounge, owned by Joe Civello's lieutenant, Joe Campisi, and mob-connected visitors to the city frequently dropped in at Ruby's strip club. On the night before Kennedy's assassination, Ruby dined with Campisi at the Egyptian.[8]

In the days just before the Kennedy assassination, Ruby placed phone calls to people such as Irwin Weiner, the Chicago bail bondsman close to Allen Dorfman, and Teamsters slugger Barney Baker. Some have connected these calls to the Kennedy assassination, while others explain them as attempts by Ruby to get help in resolving problems that he had with AGVA, the union that represented his strippers. Even if his calls were about legitimate business, the fact remains that men like Weiner and Baker were unlikely to waste time talking to anyone who did not have mob connections. Ruby also had close ties to a gambler named Lewis McWillie, who had associated with Trafficante in Cuba. When attempts were being made to get Trafficante out of jail in 1959, Ruby met with McWillie in Havana. A person who has over many years associated with mobsters is by definition a mob associate, or at the very least a wannabe. Certainly Ruby was a man whom they might have considered calling on to perform a task for them.

If the conspirators needed someone able to get into Dallas police headquarters, to report on what Oswald might be telling the police and/or to kill him, Ruby was an ideal person to use. He had a very close relationship with the Dallas Police Department, many of whose officers had been guests at his strip club. On Friday night, after Oswald's arrest, Ruby managed to enter headquarters twice. One time he stood outside the door of the room where the suspect was being interrogated. On a second occasion he sat in on a midnight press conference in which Oswald was displayed to reporters. On Saturday, he was again in police headquarters, and on Sunday he managed to enter the building despite the high security that was in

8 Ruby also had a propensity for assaulting people—including customers—with his fists, a blackjack, or a gun. This led to arrests and license suspensions, yet he continued to operate a nightclub. Though the matter has not been probed, it is difficult to accept that a dive owner from the North could have behaved as Ruby did in Dallas and still continued in business without mob backing.

effect because the suspect was about to be transferred to the county jail. Some investigators have characterized Ruby's movements during this period as "stalking" Oswald. It was then that Ruby got close enough to Oswald to shoot him at point-blank range.

Marcello's desire for survival and revenge was shared by other mob bosses and their allies. Sam Giancana of Chicago faced imprisonment because of the full-court press that Robert Kennedy had ordered the FBI to put on him. He was also angry over the failure to honor the debts of gratitude he thought he was owed for his assistance in the 1960 election and the plot to kill Castro.[9] Jimmy Hoffa was another who feared and hated the Kennedys. According to Frank Ragano, he was the one who instigated the assassination scheme. In 1963, many northern mob leaders were under heavy electronic surveillance by the FBI or, like Jimmy Hoffa, had government informers in their camp. At the time, Angelo Bruno, Steve Magaddino, Giancana, Hoffa, and Trafficante were all heard expressing on either bugs, or to informers, a forecast or hope that Kennedy would be killed. However, there was no mention of any specific plan. After the assassination, neither bugs nor informers disclosed any mob bosses' awareness of a plot.

More than forty years of investigations have yet to disprove the Warren Commission's theory that President Kennedy was killed by Oswald, alone and unaided. Therefore, hypotheses that posit organized crime involvement in the assassination do not provide a case provable in a court of law, though it may eventually be accepted by the court of history. Even at this late date, it is possible that some startling new information might emerge. There are still serious investigators that believe they can link Mafia figures to President Kennedy's murder. If so, it would not be the first time history would have had to be revised. In 1975 a retired British intelligence officer published *The Ultra Secret*, in which he revealed that between 1940 and 1945, Allied code-breakers had been reading Germany's top-secret messages. The disclosure rendered obsolete many histories of the European war. It also caused embarrassment in high places, since some generals had claimed credit for victories that were essentially handed to them on a silver

9 In his 1999 autobiography, *Bound by Honor*, Bill Bonanno, son of Joe, claimed that Giancana and the Chicago Outfit ordered the assassination and that Johnny Roselli was the shooter! Students of the case give no credence to his account.

platter (and a few even managed to lose battles that they should have won hands down). Until the 1990s, many Americans did not believe that Alger Hiss or Julius Rosenberg had engaged in espionage for the Soviet Union. Since the release of previously intercepted secret communications from Soviet spies in America, there are far fewer people who hold that view. And after thirty years of denials, in 2005 retired FBI official Mark Felt finally admitted that he was Deep Throat.

One source that has not yet been heard from is Havana. Both the Kennedys and the Mafia had been linked to attempts to overthrow Castro. When his regime ends, information may emerge that will shed new light on the death of President Kennedy. While it may someday be shown that organized crime had nothing to do with the president's murder, perhaps the Kennedys' final victory over the American Mafia is that so many people believe that it did.

CHAPTER 7

ACTORS ON THE SAME STAGE:
ORGANIZED CRIME AND CORRUPT POLITICIANS

t was the kind of event that can make Florida seem like the American Riviera. On a pleasant evening in late March, with snow still on the ground
in other parts of the country, a group of happy revelers were preparing to
board a yacht moored in the marina at Delray Beach. Not only were they
going to partake of Chivas Regal and thick steaks, but there would be opportunities to discuss business with well-connected people. In the year
1979, the host alone would have drawn a crowd. He was an oil-rich Arab
emir, of the type that OPEC had catapulted into the forefront of international wealth and glamor. Tonight he was giving a party for an important
American politician from the great state of New Jersey: Angelo Erichetti
was both the mayor of Camden and a state senator in the legislature at
Trenton. Best of all, Erichetti had access to a veritable gold mine—the casinos that would soon dot the boardwalk in Atlantic City.

The guests were thrilled when Emir Habib Yassir alighted from his lim-
ousine in the manner of one born to the purple. Accompanied by his bodyguards and retinue, he strode down the pier. The yacht's crew snapped
to attention; the captain—dressed in an immaculate white uniform with
shining gold braid—rendered a sharp salute. When the mayor was introduced to him, the emir presented his guest with a gleaming ceremonial

knife of friendship handed down from his noble ancestors. Genuinely touched, Erichetti responded with a short speech that ended with the emotional affirmation, "Friendship is everything." Then an even more important guest was introduced to the emir: an American aristocrat and senior United States senator named Harrison Arlington Williams, known to the voters of New Jersey as "Pete."

The emir had to leave early, but through his interpreter he entreated the guests to continue enjoying his hospitality. They did, and much business was discussed, to the delight of the real host of the party: the FBI. Agents acted the part of the emir, his retinue, and the ship's captain, and the Bureau had even supplied the $2.75 dagger to give to Erichetti. The white Chinese-built yacht, one of only two or three of its kind, was also the property of the United States, courtesy of a drug dealer who had abandoned it on the ocean. Formerly known as the *Grand Hotel,* it had been renamed *The Left Hand,* which pretty well described the circumstances of the affair. Mayor Erichetti and Senator Williams would later learn that not only was Uncle Sam their host, but their fellow guests had been a motley collection of con men, pornographers, forgers, drug smugglers, and gamblers whom the FBI had also been measuring for handcuffs.

The FBI operation known as Abscam would snare Mayor Erichetti, Senator Williams, six congressmen, a host of lesser officials, and other assorted crooks before it ended. What was conceived as a simple sting aimed at swindlers evolved into an investigation of organized crime and corruption in Atlantic City. There its agents encountered Erichetti, a hungry politician who led them to others of his kind. Finally it reached the U.S. Capitol. When the case broke, Congress was not pleased, and many officials—including some federal prosecutors—questioned the tactics employed by the FBI and the Brooklyn-based organized crime strike force, which had supervised the operation. The strike force had been created to prosecute organized crime, yet most of the defendants ultimately convicted in Abscam had no direct mob ties. But it was corrupt politicians who allowed the Mafia to exist in the first place. Abscam and other criminal investigations in New Jersey would illustrate the truth of that assertion.

When the Johnson administration left office, the federal government resumed its attack on organized crime. One of the first battlegrounds was New Jersey. Large portions of the state contain suburbs of the two great cities just beyond its borders: Northeastern New Jersey is closely linked to New York City, and much of the south is part of the Philadelphia metropolitan area. Jersey's only homegrown Mafia family was the DeCavalcantes from Union County, but all five New York City gangs and the Philadelphia family had powerful semiautonomous subgroups operating in the state. Since the 1920s, New Jersey had been known as a place where organized crime and political corruption were rampant. Whether it was deserving of its reputation is another question.

In the 1960s the situation in New Jersey was probably no worse than in some other states. Its tarnished national image was due in part to the legacy of its longtime political czar, Frank Hague. From 1913 to 1947, New Jersey politics were dominated by Hague, who as mayor of Jersey City ruled his city and the surrounding Hudson County with an iron hand. His control of the populous county enabled him to swing the balance of power in the state.[1] Every governor was either a Hague ally or at least willing to do business with him. One of them appointed the boss's thirty-four-year-old son to the state's highest court despite the fact that the young man had flunked out of two law schools. Once when an official protested that the law forbade him to carry out Hague's orders, the mayor replied, "I *am* the law, do it." From then on the press always referred to him as Frank "I Am the Law" Hague. By the '60s he was long gone, but the corrupt political system remained.[2]

In 1968, fresh from serving on the staff of the president's crime commission, G. Robert Blakey and Henry Ruth were called to testify before the New Jersey state senate on a proposed electronic eavesdropping law. In answer to a question posed, Blakey declared, "I think New Jersey has as large a corruption problem as any state in the union." Ruth stated, "Organized crime

1 In one instance a Republican candidate for governor carried New Jersey's other twenty counties by a total of 84,000 votes, but lost Hudson County by 129,000. A canvass found that in one Jersey City precinct there were 433 Democratic votes counted and only one Republican. Yet at the primary election earlier in the year, 103 Republican votes had been cast.
2 Though the state court system, which had been reformed in 1947, was a national model.

is so powerful in New Jersey that they can have almost anything they want." Their remarks caused a furor. The state's attorney general branded them irresponsible and announced that he would ask a special grand jury to look into the allegations. To head the investigation he appointed William Brennan, Jr., son of a sitting justice of the U.S. Supreme Court. After conducting an inquiry, Brennan found no reason to disagree with Blakey and Ruth. In an address to the state chapter of Sigma Delta Chi, the society of professional journalists, young Brennan declared that organized crime had infiltrated virtually every facet of life in the Garden State, with the exception of the church. "Too many local governments are responsive more to the mob than to the electorate that put them in office," he charged, declaring that some legislators were "entirely too comfortable with members of organized crime."

One way to cripple organized crime's control of the state was to strike at its corrupt politics. In 1969 President Nixon appointed Frederick Lacey U.S. attorney for New Jersey. His first target was its largest city, Newark. There a coterie of corrupt white officials and their gangster allies ruled a largely black population. After a 1967 riot that left twenty-six people dead, a state investigating commission laid part of the blame on the city government's neglect of its minority residents. Newark's mayor was Hugh Addonizio, nicknamed "the Pope." But the real powers were the Boiardos, father and son. Ruggiero "Richie The Boot" Boiardo was the longtime Genovese family overseer of Newark organized crime. Nearing eighty, he still ran numbers in the area while spending most of his time at his palatial estate in Livingston. *Life* magazine described the style of the Boiardo homestead as "Transylvanian Traditional." The main house was constructed of dark Italian stone, and to enter one passed through wrought iron gates flanked by pillars topped with bronze swans. The comparison to Dracula's homeland made for a good joke, but in fact the estate had more in common with the North Shore of Long Island or Fairfield County, Connecticut. Like some other nouveau riche Americans, the Boot styled himself as a country squire. Along the driveway were statues, starting with one of himself attired in full hunting regalia astride a noble steed, followed by sculptures of his three children mounted on ponies. And to show he had not forgotten his background, the vegetable patch that

Boiardo attended with loving care bore a sign proclaiming it "Godfather's Garden."

As boss of the First Ward in the 1920s, the Boot had waged a war over control of organized crime in Newark with Abner "Longy" Zwillman, boss of the Third Ward. In 1930 the Boot was hit by thirteen slugs. According to legend, the one that "would have torn his guts out" was stopped by the Boot's five-thousand-dollar diamond belt buckle. Perhaps chastened by the close encounter, Zwillman and Boiardo reached an agreement to divide the spoils during the '30s. Facing pressure from the McClellan Committee, Longy had supposedly committed suicide by hanging himself in 1959; Boiardo no longer had to share the wealth.[3]

Day-to-day operations in Newark were run by the Boot's son, Ruggiero Junior, known as "Tony Boy" and a chip off the old block. In addition to overseeing the rackets, Tony Boy was the man to see if you wanted to obtain a city contract. The kickback required was 10 percent, no exceptions permitted. As he explained to one supplicant who tried to haggle over the price, "We've got a lot of mouths to feed down at City Hall." When a contractor who cut back his payoffs because the city still owed him for another job appealed to Addonizio, the mayor advised him he would have to take up his case with higher authority—Tony Boiardo. Tony, in turn, warned the contractor to pay the full 10 percent or he would break both his legs. For a Boiardo it was a rather mild threat. A bug once picked up Tony describing how he and dad had dealt with another recalcitrant: "The Boot hit him with a hammer. The guy goes down and he comes up. So I got a crowbar this big . . . eight fucking shots in the head." Everybody "in the know" was aware of the murders the family was reputed to have committed, and had heard about the private crematorium on the Boot's estate. It was rumored that as a favor to other mob bosses like Tommy Lucchese, Boiardo would take dead bodies off their hands. Nobody in Newark wanted to become dust on his well-manicured grounds, so what the family said went.[4]

In 1969 the public heard about the relationship between politics and

---

3 Many people have never accepted the suicide story. As one knowledgeable Jerseyite told the author, "They are still trying to find the guy who pushed the chair out from under him."
4 Some commentators have claimed that Boiardo's family served as the model for the TV show *The Sopranos*.

organized crime from conversations unknowingly furnished by Simone DeCavalcante, who ran his mob family from a plumbing store in Kenilworth, New Jersey. The son of a Sicilian immigrant–turned–American bootlegger, he was commonly referred to as "Sam the Plumber," though he preferred to be called "Princeton Sam" for the upscale university town in which he resided. He also liked to claim he was descended from nobility and did not mind associates referring to him as "the Count." With his silvered black hair, neat graying mustache, and hoarse asthmatic whisper, he resembled Brando's Godfather. Once, while being questioned by state investigators, Sam gave one of the officials a cigarette and graciously told him to keep the pack. After DeCavalcante was gone, an investigator noticed it did not have a federal tax stamp. Though his family was small— only fifty members—and did not have a seat on the national commission or a public profile, Sam was highly respected within the Mafia.[5] During the Bonanno family wars, the commission designated Sam as mediator between the contending factions.

Before the government turned off its bugs in 1965, DeCavalcante had been monitored by a hidden microphone referred to in FBI reports as "criminal informant 2461 c." In 1969, DeCavalcante's attorney sought to stage a preemptive strike on federal investigators by filing a motion to review the pre-1965 conversations. If the motion was made in the anticipation that the government would drop the charges so as not to reveal its eavesdropping, it did not succeed. The response of Lacey's office was to accede to the request, entering two thousand pages of transcripts into court records. Though not admissible as evidence, the information obtained proved exceedingly embarrassing to many public figures in New Jersey. The government followed up by releasing tapes from a bug planted on another mobster, Angelo "Gyp" de Carlo. The conversations from the two plants mentioned the names of congressmen, mayors, politicians, and police chiefs and their alleged relationships with mobsters. While leading political figures from the governor of New Jersey on down denounced the release of unsubstantiated and "scurrilous" remarks, the tapes were credited with being the decisive factor in securing public support for the federal

5 The DeCavalcantes too would later be reputed to be the model for *The Sopranos*.

probe. Title III of the 1968 Organized Crime Control Act authorized the attorney general of the United States to apply to federal judges for a warrant to engage in electronic eavesdropping. Unlike the pre-1965 era, when information garnered from Elsurs could not be admitted at trial, the new law permitted both taps and bugs to be used as evidence in a court of law. However, there were limitations on the scope of information that could be gathered. The government had to state which specific violations of federal law it would be investigating, and why electronic eavesdropping was the only means available to do so. Once President Johnson left office, FBI agents and prosecutors were allowed to submit Title III (T3) applications to the courts for the okay to listen in on conversations of organized criminals and corrupt politicians.

During the course of the Newark investigation, Tony Boiardo's boys warned people to keep their mouths shut if they valued their families' health. One who got the warning was a city engineer named Paul Rigo, who acted as a middleman between contractors, corrupt politicians, and the mob. One of Boiardo's henchmen told Rigo, "Keep your mouth shut and remember you have a pretty daughter." Later he found a note in his car: "This could have been a bomb. Keep your mouth shut." Though worried, Rigo decided to tell the Feds all he knew, and through him they were led to others who agreed to become informers. Mayor Addonizio was handed a grand jury subpoena as he alighted from a plane at Newark Airport. When he appeared before it and was asked if he knew Tony Boiardo, the mayor invoked the Fifth Amendment.

In December 1969, a federal grand jury indicted Addonizio and seven current or former members of the Newark City Council on extortion charges. Included with them was Tony Boiardo. The city officials were convicted—Addonizio received ten years—but young Boiardo suffered a heart attack and was never brought to trial (he died a few years later). The Boot lived on until 1984, when he expired at the age of ninety-three.

When U.S. Attorney Lacey was appointed to the federal bench, he was succeeded by his chief assistant Herb "The Hawk" Stern, who targeted Hague's old machine, the Hudson County Democratic organization then led by boss John Kenny. It was Kenny who had sponsored the career of

Senator Pete Williams, later to be involved in Abscam. When the Feds began closing in on Kenny, Williams publicly described him as a "great humanitarian." Stern indicted both Kenny and Jersey City mayor Thomas Whalen. The boss received seventeen years for tax evasion but died before he could serve his time. Whalen, convicted of extortion and bribery, was given fifteen years.

Beginning in 1969, the New Jersey authorities too began to move against organized crime. The state enacted an electronic eavesdropping law and established a statewide grand jury. The first bug was put in the offices of "Bayonne Joe" Zicarelli of the Bonanno family, mob overseer of Hudson County organized crime. In 1968, *Life* magazine published a story about a bizarre incident that linked Zicarelli and local congressman Cornelius Gallagher. It reported that in 1962 a loan shark named Barney O'Brien had died while visiting the congressman at home. Gallagher did not wish to explain why he was entertaining a known criminal, so, according to the *Life* story, he called a notorious mob enforcer named Harold "Kayo" Konigsberg to his home and asked him to get rid of O'Brien's body. Konigsberg, whom *Life* characterized as an "uncaged killer who ranged up and down the Eastern Seaboard," declined to help without the approval of Zicarelli. Only when that was forthcoming did the hoodlum dispose of the body. Officially O'Brien was listed as a missing person. In 1967, Konigsberg, then in the midst of serving a lengthy prison sentence, decided to talk. He led investigators to a mob burial ground where O'Brien's shoes and the remnants of other gangsters' bodies were found. When the story appeared, Gallagher denied it.

New Jersey troopers, under the direction of Deputy Attorney Generals Pete Richardson and Edwin Stier, spent fifty-five days listening to the bug in Zicarelli's office. On it he discussed his relationships with local officials and even plotted a murder. As a result of the state task force investigation, Zicarelli was indicted on multiple charges, along with local police officers and municipal officials. In 1971 he was convicted and sentenced to prison, and ceased to be a presence in Hudson County.

By the time the federal and state prosecutors were done, ten New Jersey mayors had been convicted, along with two secretaries of state, two state treasurers, the assembly speaker, and the senate president. Among those brought down by the Feds were Sam DeCavalcante, who received a five-year sentence (of which he served two) on an interstate gambling charge, and Congressman Gallagher, who pleaded guilty to income tax evasion.

The assault on the political organized crime nexus in New Jersey scored an impressive number of convictions, but it only scratched the surface. Organized crime continued to flourish, and in the late 1970s the New Jersey and Philadelphia mobs struck a bonanza. Atlantic City had been dying for years. Once a glamorous spa favored by the well-to-do, it eventually became a mass-market tourist spot. By the 1960s its only residual claim to glamor was the Miss America pageant held there every September. It was said that the typical visitor was a very old lady, accompanied by her mother. In the 1970s the population that inhabited the city of forty thousand behind the boardwalk was mostly seniors and minorities. The crime rate was so high that visitors were warned not to stray from their hotels.

Because Atlantic City's prosperity had been built on its resort status, it seemed obvious that attracting large numbers of visitors would be one way to restore its economic health. With the success of Las Vegas as a model, it was argued that the answer was legalized casino gambling. In 1974 a statewide referendum was held on whether to allow casinos in New Jersey. Amid widespread rumors that organized crime was behind the proposal, it lost three to two. Two years later another referendum was held, and this time the measure limited gambling to Atlantic City. When U.S. Attorney Jonathan Goldstein opposed it on the grounds that it would bring in organized crime, Governor Brendan Byrne conceded the possibility, but claimed, "When you have it in the open and regulated and accounted for, I think the ability to deal with those problems is there." Colonel Clinton Pagano, the superintendent of the state police, had a different view. Legalized gambling, he said, "will bring to New Jersey more problems than it will cure." Nevertheless the proposal to permit casinos passed three to one. When Byrne signed the casino gambling bill on the Atlantic City boardwalk he concluded his speech by shaking his fist and proclaiming, "I've said it before and I will repeat it again to organized crime: Keep your filthy hands off of Atlantic City! Keep the hell out of our state."

Politicians' rhetoric was never taken seriously by the Mafia bosses, who were capable of making pious statements themselves. One who was especially good at this was the man who controlled the penny-ante organized crime that already operated in Atlantic City: Angelo Bruno, boss of the Philadelphia family. In 1977, when it was clear that casinos would be coming to the boardwalk, the New Jersey Commission of Investigation called him in for questioning. Asked directly, "What are your intentions with Atlantic City, Mr. Bruno?" the boss replied, "Stay away from it. That's my intentions." In fact, not only did he mean to defy Governor Byrne, but he also intended to allow other mob families to get in on the action by agreeing that Atlantic City be open territory.

The Philadelphia Mafia did not have the political clout of its New York or Chicago counterparts. Until the 1940s, organized crime in the City of Brotherly Love was run by Jewish gangsters, and the Italian mob stuck to their enclave in South Philadelphia. Even when the Italian faction became paramount, it did not control City Hall. After Philadelphia boss Joe Ida was seized at Apalachin in 1957, he fled to Italy. Angelo Bruno (who dropped his last name of Annalore) was next in the line of succession, but he had to struggle to claim his inheritance. One rival for the top job tried to murder him. Finally, at the urging of Carlo Gambino, the national commission threw its support to Bruno and made him a member of the commission itself to enhance his standing. In 1963, after Robert Kennedy's Justice Department got an indictment against him for extortion, Bruno fled to Italy, then came back and was acquitted.

As boss, Bruno believed in keeping his business out of the papers and away from police heat, so he usually preferred to negotiate rather than fight. He even forgave the rival who plotted his murder, and the press began referring to him as "the Docile Don." Bruno essentially sought to maintain a détente with the authorities. While Bruno's policies may have stemmed in part from his own personality, they were also dictated by the local situation. With limited political clout, he did not have carte blanche to do as he pleased. So he kept things cool: During his twenty-year rule, no made men were hit.[6] Bruno's boys were also forbidden to peddle drugs. The Philadelphia Mafia did not even collect a street tax on numbers operators and bookmakers. In the matter of both drugs and street taxes, though, some mob guys quietly did their own thing. Bruno himself maintained a low profile. The only time he put on a public display was on the Fourth of July, when he would hang out a large American flag. He had considerable wealth from his extensive legitimate holdings, including real estate in three states and investments in restaurants, motels, and a foreign casino, but he lived in a modest South Philadelphia row house. His only extravagance was a taste for well-tailored clothes—though he chose to wear a cap rather than the sharp fedora favored by most of his peers.

Bruno expected his lieutenants to follow his example. He allowed no drunks, high-rolling gamblers, or hotheads in his inner circle. In 1963 Nicodemo "Nicky" Scarfo, a Philadelphia mob soldier, got into a dispute with a longshoreman who would not give up his seat in a restaurant booth. "Little Nicky"—he was only five foot five—promptly stabbed the longshoreman to death. Later he boasted, "I took a knife and stuck it into an Irish M——f—— and twisted it into his guts." He served only a few months of his manslaughter conviction, but when he was released, Bruno exiled him to Atlantic City. Scarfo lingered in the dull backwater for the next dozen years, having to content himself with looking after the Philadelphia family's petty rackets in the area.

A decade later, when the gold rush at Atlantic City began, Scarfo, who kept pictures in his house of his heroes Napoleon, Benito Mussolini, and Al Capone, proved that he was a man who knew how to dig out the treasure. The key was the labor unions, who would provide construction workers to build the casino hotels and employees to service them. With the leverage provided by the threat of labor difficulties, Scarfo could demand major payoffs from the owners. He already had control of Local 54 of the hotel, restaurant, and bartenders union, but his expansion to construction was

6 According to one account, a police commissioner warned Bruno that he would be held personally responsible if any dead bodies were found in Philadelphia. So when an occasional corpse was found in South Jersey, detectives speculated that the hit might have originated in Philadelphia.

frustrated by "Big John" McCullough, head of the Philadelphia roofers union. McCullough moved in on the Atlantic City roofers local, using it as a wedge to take over the city's all-encompassing Building Trades Council. Then he started his own bartenders union and began stealing members from Scarfo's local. Next, McCullough organized a union for casino security guards. It was a clever move: The law required a full complement of security officers on duty during operating hours, so a strike by the guards would automatically close a casino down. Scarfo was furious with McCullough, but he could not twist a knife in *his* guts. This Philadelphia Irishman was well connected politically and had a good relationship with Scarfo's boss, Angelo Bruno. By the late 1970s, Bruno realized that more than ever he had to be cautious. The FBI, under the direction of an aggressive SAC, was on the move in Philadelphia.

Since Hoover's death in 1972, the winds of change had begun to blow through the FBI. Clarence Kelley, former Kansas City SAC (and later that city's police chief), was named director, and in 1975 he reorganized the agency to make organized crime a major priority. Yet when Neil Welch arrived as special agent in charge of the Philadelphia FBI office in that same year, he found that the Feds too were maintaining a détente with Bruno's family. So cooperative was the Docile Don that he had agreed to furnish the FBI information when one of the Bureau's primary crimes like kidnapping or bank robbery went down. It was a relationship that didn't sit well with Welch, a forty-nine-year-old midwesterner who had developed a reputation as a hell-raiser during his twenty-four years in the Bureau. As SAC in Buffalo he had constantly raided Steve Magaddino's gambling operations. Another time he "invaded" Canada to rescue a young girl kidnapped from the American side—it was typical of Welch not to let a little barrier like an international border get in his way (even when critical questions were raised in the Canadian parliament, Welch did not apologize). In Philadelphia he immediately served notice that the détente period was over. Following Kelley's lead, he announced that bank robbery was no longer the top priority of the office; organized crime was. He arranged for a bug to be installed in a steakhouse where Bruno family members met to discuss business. And when he overheard a subordinate complaining to headquarters about his orders, he took a pair of scissors and cut the phone wire.

Welch was the kind of leader who would bring the post-Hoover FBI into the late twentieth century. In 1978, a selection committee appointed by President Carter chose him as one of five finalists to be director of the Bureau. For a time it appeared that the job was his, despite the fact that the Old Guard of the agency considered him too much of a maverick. In the end none of the finalists was chosen, and the president turned instead to William Webster, a St. Louis–based judge of the U.S. Court of Appeals. Welch was given a consolation prize: promotion to the rank of assistant director in charge of the Bureau's largest office, New York City. Oddly, Welch's new job in New York would put him in charge of an investigation that would impact both the Philadelphia Mafia and New Jersey politics at their intersection in Atlantic City. Some FBI office heads might have figured that they had enough to do in their own bailiwick—why get involved in another jurisdiction? For Welch, who had ignored an international border, a mere state line was no barrier.

The seeds for the investigation were first sown in 1977, when a New York con man named Melvin Weinberg was arrested by the FBI for a securities fraud. Weinberg, then fifty-two, was a veteran swindler. His principal con was obtaining advance payments for phony loans, then disappearing. Following his arrest he sought to avoid jail time by becoming an informant. After reviewing the case, an FBI supervisor named John Good decided to put Weinberg to work. His first task was to gather evidence against a Long Island swindler and his accomplice, an organized crime muscle man. Weinberg balked at getting involved with mob guys—particularly after he learned that four potential witnesses in the case had already been murdered. But he didn't have much choice, and within three months sufficient evidence was assembled to charge the suspects.

Weinberg's initial success led to further assignments. At the time, oil-rich Arab sheiks were making acquisitions of expensive assets all over the world. Weinberg spread the word around that he had a wealthy client, Emir Kambir Abdul Rahman, who was interested in putting some of his Middle Eastern dollars to work in the United States. The problem was that to circumvent Arab laws against usury, he needed phony certificates of deposit showing that the money was not out on loan but reposing in United States banks. At other times, Weinberg announced that Abdul was interested in buying works of art, no questions asked. To provide a façade for the scheme, the agents created Abdul Enterprises, Inc., with Weinberg as president and FBI agents as chairman of the board and vice presidents. In Bureau records the operation acquired the name Abdul Scam, or Abscam. The Abscam team took steps to establish their bona fides. In anticipation of suspicious art buyers checking up on them, they deposited a million dollars in government funds in the Chase Manhattan Bank and alerted one of its vice presidents to the scheme. Whenever potential targets wanted a reference they were given his name, and he would duly certify that Abdul Enterprises had a substantial sum on deposit.

Weinberg's expanded activities required the blessing of another federal agency, the organized crime strike force for the Eastern District of New York. The strike force had jurisdiction over the arrest of the first con man and his mob partner Weinberg had hooked. Informers always prefer to remain out of sight. In Weinberg's case, though, the government required his testimony. At the trial he would have to take the stand, revealing his undercover role. His FBI handlers appealed to the strike force chief, Thomas Puccio, to hold off prosecution until Weinberg's other investigations were completed. When FBI agent Jack McCarthy brought Weinberg to the strike force headquarters in Brooklyn to explain Abscam, Puccio was not impressed. The short, stocky con man spoke with an accent that betrayed his Bronx origins, while the G-man, according to Puccio, looked like the grand marshal of a St. Patrick's Day parade. Hardly the types to be top aides to an Arab sheik, he thought. Nevertheless he gave his blessing to the operation.

In the 1960s the Department of Justice had established strike forces in selected judicial districts across the country that would take their orders directly from the organized crime section in Washington rather than the local U.S. attorney's office. Though some U.S.A.s (like Bob Morgenthau of New York's Southern District) pushed organized crime investigations, many did not. They feared political repercussions, or simply had other priorities. Strike forces were meant to pick up the slack, providing a permanent and dedicated staff to make organized crime cases, one that would be less subject to local political pressures. If the Abscam team had not hooked a mob figure on Weinberg's first assignment, it would not have become involved with the strike force.

With a slick con man as its spearhead, the Abscam investigation needed tight control. Informers—or, in FBI parlance, "209s" (from the form used to file reports on them)—always presented problems for law enforcement. Some took advantage of their role to carry on criminal activities; a few had been known to commit murders while supposedly helping to keep the community safe. Con men are among the most difficult informers to control: Typically, they're quick-witted individuals whose success is based upon the degree to which they can fool people. A bunco artist always wants to be in charge. He is not only an actor, he also writes the script and directs the play. On the other side, "Never let your informant take control of the case" is a law enforcement maxim. In his work for the FBI, Weinberg was handed a script and given directions. Yet to be successful, he had to exhibit a high degree of spontaneity: If his delivery or actions seemed rehearsed, it would be obvious to the target. To further complicate the situation, many law enforcement officers found it hard to conceal their contempt for "stool pigeons" who committed the crime but were not willing to do the time.

Emir Abdul was scheduled to meet with a seller of stolen art in a hotel room at New York's Plaza. The meeting was hastily set up, and an FBI agent was detailed to impersonate the Emir. He spoke no Arabic, though he managed to memorize a simple phrase of greeting. Agents rented Arab dress from a local theatrical costumer, but the robes arrived so wrinkled that the emir had to settle for wearing a headdress with an ordinary business suit. The emir and his entourage—played by other agents—did not give Academy Award performances. At times some of them had to leave the room hastily, unable to suppress their laughter. The art seller was puzzled by the levity displayed and by the fact that the emir was continually munching on hors d'oeuvres purchased from a Jewish deli.

The FBI's stock company was then recast. An agent who had been raised in Lebanon and actually spoke Arabic was brought aboard. Since one of the targets had already seen Emir Abdul, the newcomer took the name of Emir Yassir. Another addition to the team was Special Agent Tony Amoroso. Meyer Lansky supposedly said that he could always tell an FBI agent by his cheap watch and college ring; he might also have said by his buttoned-down, clean-cut appearance. But post-Hoover, the Bureau had loosened up. It now accepted women, and agents were sometimes allowed to dress like hoods, go undercover, and pretend to be crooks. Amoroso was one of the new breed: He wore a mustache, open-necked shirts, and plenty of jewelry. Like Weinberg, he had been born and raised in the Bronx. After college he joined the FBI and was assigned to work on organized crime cases, including a stint undercover in Detroit. He was also like Weinberg in that he preferred not to follow a script, instead operating according to his instincts. Once while Amoroso was posing as an engineer (a subject in which he had no training), one of his targets casually asked what school he had attended. A more conventional agent might have given the year he supposedly graduated from MIT (thereby facilitating a check with the alumni office). In typical wiseguy style, Amoroso answered, "None of your fucking business," a response that clearly marked him as a fellow crook. During the course of the investigation, Amoroso and Weinberg would sometimes express concern to a target that some other suspect might be an undercover FBI man. It helped establish their credibility, since the targets reasoned that real G-men would not be worried about the law.

Abscam's wide-ranging investigation of theft, fraud, and organized crime eventually led it to Atlantic City. A con man friend of Weinberg's suggested that he get the sheik to invest in the Atlantic City casino boom. When the New Jersey Casino Control Commission was established, it adopted a rule that a preliminary license was required to build a casino, and then a second one had to be procured to operate it after completion. Meant to screen out organized crime, it had the reverse effect. No lender would finance construction of a casino if there was a possibility that the borrowers would not be able to open it. By 1978 only one casino was operating, and its permanent license was being held up because of questions about its affiliations. The Abscam team let it be known that the emir was interested in building and operating a casino himself, and might even be willing to buy land and lend money to other operators to build their own places. It was an offer too good to refuse, and one that brought Abdul Inc. into contact with Mayor/Senator Angelo Erichetti.

The team's first meeting with the mayor was held in the Long Island office of Abdul Enterprises. Erichetti, a handsome man with a marked resemblance to screen actor Richard Conte, was a tough hustler who sprinkled his conversations with scatological phrases. In old-time thieves' argot, he was the kind of bold crook who "would steal a hot stove with the fire still in it, and then go back and look for the smoke." His bailiwick, Camden, was another decaying New Jersey city with a large minority population run by a corrupt politician. A few years earlier Erichetti had beaten an indictment for fraud and perjury. As Tom Puccio would later write, "Erichetti's idea of economic development was to use the Port of Camden to smuggle guns and drugs into the country." He also had very good mob connections. His main man was Paul Castellano, who had recently become head of Carlo Gambino's mob family upon the latter's (natural) death. Since the Gambinos had been instrumental in installing Angelo Bruno as Philadelphia's boss, they had plenty of IOUs to call in. Erichetti, with his connections in the Mafia and the New Jersey State Capitol, was also in a powerful position. At the very first meeting he laid it on the line, saying, "I'll give you Atlantic City; without me you have nothing." After he left, one of his middlemen remained behind to explain that it would take $400,000 in bribes to secure a casino license and that Erichetti would require $25,000 up front to get the ball rolling. The mayor would eventually prove to be the key figure in Abscam, providing the team with names of other officials who could be bribed, including U.S. congressmen and Senator Williams.

In retrospect it is difficult to understand how a man like Erichetti could have been taken in by the FBI team. Throughout the investigation, Abscam was replete with implausible situations and obvious gaffes that any experienced crook should have recognized immediately. The whole rich-Arab ploy had several incongruous components. For one thing, it was hardly likely that an Arab would have a Jew representing him, given Middle Eastern tensions. And then, Abdul Enterprises rented a cheap office on Long Island in order to establish jurisdiction in the Eastern District of New York. An oil-rich Arab would have maintained a deluxe suite of offices in Manhattan, and retained an established firm of lawyers or consultants to service him. A female agent occasionally used in the sheik's retinue got her picture in the paper when she responded to an airport hijacking incident. One of the targets saw it and raised the alarm, but Weinberg and Amoroso managed to convince him that the woman in the picture was a different person. An informer whom the Florida FBI had sent onto the yacht at Delray Beach passed the word that it was an FBI sting, and it got back to the targets. Somehow the agents persuaded them that he was mistaken. Otherwise sharp operators were blinded by the large amounts of money the Abscam team waved in front of them, allowing their greed to overcome their suspicions.

When the investigation moved from garden-variety swindlers to public officials, alarm bells sounded in Washington. Arresting a con man was one thing; a mayor or senator was very different. The FBI had come into existence seventy years earlier when Congress punished the U.S. Secret Service for making a case against a U.S. senator. J. Edgar Hoover always knew where to draw the line. One of the primary reasons he did not want to investigate organized crime was that it always went hand in hand with crooked politics. As Neil Welch would later write, "I defy anyone to investigate organized crime apart from political corruption—the actors play on the same stage." If Hoover had still been director, Abscam might well have been terminated as soon as it began to involve federal legislators. Neil Welch and Director Webster were not as concerned about offending politicians as Hoover had been. Over the FBI, though, was the U.S. Department of Justice. Senator Williams and most of the congressmen who became targets were Democrats. With the election of President Carter in 1976, the Democrats were in control of the Department of Justice. No president could be expected to welcome the prospect of his own Department of Justice locking up his congressional supporters, particularly in a case that the department itself had initiated. The whole affair was fraught with political peril. But in the end, with the approval of Attorney General Griffin Bell, a fellow Georgian and close associate of the president, Abscam was given the green light to proceed.

Politicians on the take usually do not accept money directly, preferring that it be passed through intermediaries—or, as they are less politely known, "bagmen." Yet cases against small-fry middlemen would be of little value. Unless they talked—which was unlikely—there was no way to prove that the money actually went to the public official. In many instances the intermediary was a lawyer or businessman who could claim that the money he requested was a retainer for his professional services. Therefore, the investigators sought to deal directly with the officials.

Nor could anyone be entrapped. The idea for the crime had to originate with the target, not the law enforcement officers.[7] To ensure that there would be no entrapment, all of the conversations were not only taped but filmed by hidden cameras and monitored from a nearby room by a strike force attorney to ensure that statements made by agents were within the law. In some cases the attorney would phone the agent's room to suggest particular questions that should be asked of the target so as to produce legally admissible evidence.

After a couple of months of negotiations, Erichetti personally accepted $25,000 from the Abscam team. The investigators were also able to pass a $100,000 bribe to Erichetti in the presence of an official of the New Jersey Casino Control Commission. Senator Williams too was snared. Where Erichetti was bold and brash, Williams, chairman of the powerful Senate Labor Committee, was hesitant and ill at ease. At a meeting scheduled in a Washington motel, Weinberger intercepted Williams in the lobby before he went up to the room and advised him what to say. Later, defense lawyers would claim that he put words in the senator's mouth. But in the meeting that followed, Williams made it clear that he would work to obtain government funds for a titanium mine in which he secretly held shares.

As the investigation drew in various congressmen whom Erichetti and other targets identified as amenable to bribes, the basic sting was the same. The congressmen were told that the emir would like to obtain permanent residence in the United States. They would then agree to introduce a private bill to allow him to do so in return for a bribe. One of the first to be caught on

---

7 During Prohibition an undercover federal agent solicited a fellow war veteran to obtain some illegal liquor for him. Though initially unwilling, the man finally succumbed to the agent's pleas. When the case reached the U.S. Supreme Court, it overturned the conviction on the grounds that an innocent person, with no previous disposition to commit an offense, was lured into it by repeated and persistent solicitation, and hence by the exploitative and questionable use of friendship. Sorrells v. United States 287 U.S. 438 (1932). On the other hand, it is not entrapment for a law enforcement officer simply to provide the means for someone to commit a crime for which he has already formed the intent. A classic example is that of a husband who asks an acquaintance to recommend a hit man to kill his wife and is introduced to an undercover cop.

camera was Ozzie Myers, a former longshoreman who represented South Philadelphia. Congressman Myers did not exactly fit the image of a distinguished statesman. The day he took the oath of office, he got arrested for punching out a Washington cocktail waitress. On camera, he offered this classic bit of advice to the Abscam team: "I'm gonna tell you something real simple and short. Money talks in this business and bullshit walks. It works the same way down in Washington." He was also filmed accepting a bribe of $50,000 cash, though he later complained that he had expected $100,000. Another congressman stuffed his pockets with bills as the camera rolled. Finally one congressman became suspicious and sent a private detective to investigate Abdul Enterprises. The investigator quickly concluded that they were government agents. It was too late. In February 1980, with newspapers about to break the story, the FBI went public with the sting. In the end, Senator Williams and six congressmen were convicted of bribery and given sentences in the two-to-three-year range. Various lawyers and lesser officials were also convicted; Mayor Erichetti received a six-year sentence.

Despite the successful prosecutions, Abscam was not without critics. One complaint was the tactics it employed, such as Weinberg's coaching of Williams. There was also the broader issue of the separation of powers. Did the executive branch have the right to test the integrity of the legislative branch? Some members of Congress thought Abscam was conceived as revenge for the curtailment of presidential power in Watergate's aftermath. Melvin Weinberg would later claim if Abscam had continued, it would have bagged one-third of the members of Congress (though crooks always justify their conduct as being no worse than that of most respectable people). One of the names of bribable legislators that Mayor Erichetti had provided was that of New Jersey congresswoman Millicent Fenwick, an elderly patrician lady who served as the model for Congresswoman Lacey Davenport in the comic strip *Doonesbury*. As Tom Puccio later observed, "The mayor might as well have added Mother Teresa to the list." Another time, Erichetti brought a supposed deputy commissioner of the U.S. Department of Immigration to the Abscam team to receive a bribe. The agents were suspicious when the man did not resemble pictures of the commissioner and was unable to spell his own name correctly. It turned out he was a lawyer from Philadelphia looking to make a quick score.

The dénouement of Abscam coincided with a changing of the guard in the Philadelphia Mafia. In March 1980, Angelo Bruno was driven home by a substitute chauffeur named John Stanfa. As they pulled up to Bruno's house two men came out of the shadows. One fired a 12-gauge shotgun into Bruno's head, killing the Docile Don. The hit was reputedly set up by Bruno's consigliere, Tony Caponigro, who was looking to move up. Stanfa was slightly wounded by pellets and glass fragments, and some investigators suspected he was in on the plot. But in retrospect that notion has been discounted. The most commonly accepted explanation for Bruno's murder is that some of his lieutenants were unhappy with him for allowing other families to operate in Atlantic City. Caponigro spread word that he had cleared the hit with some national commission figures in New York City. Apparently he had not. A month later he and his brother-in-law, the suspected triggerman, were found murdered in New York City. The New York bosses then sent word that family underboss Phil Testa was to succeed Bruno. As a result, Atlantic City remained open territory.

"Chicken Man" Testa, who ran a poultry store as a front, named Nicky Scarfo as consigliere. With Bruno gone, Scarfo was able to solve his Atlantic City union problems. Scarfo's boys hired an ex-con named Willard "Junior" Moran to kill John McCullough. Moran, like Scarfo, had been sent to prison for murdering a man during a dispute in a public restaurant. Also like Nicky, he served only a brief sentence. Moran was anxious to ingratiate himself with the Philadelphia mob, so he accepted the assignment for five thousand dollars. Shortly before Christmas he posed as a delivery man and brought flowers to McCullough's home in northeastern Philadelphia. McCullough's wife answered the door and told Moran to wait while she went to get two dollars for a tip. McCullough, busy talking on the phone, told her, "It's Christmas, give him three." In return Moran gave McCullough a bullet in the head, then stood over him and pumped five more into his body. The miscalculation of using an outsider to carry out a hit was demonstrated by Moran's post-assassination behavior. After leaving the murder scene, he and a friend stopped at a go-go bar to celebrate, and Moran ordered three shots of whiskey. After he and his companion each consumed one, he ordered the bartender to throw the third down the sink. It was a classic toast to a dead man. A few years later Moran's gesture would be remembered by witnesses and included in a case that earned him a sentence to the electric chair. To avoid death he turned government witness against some of Scarfo's lieutenants.

The new regime was not accepted by Bruno loyalists. In 1981, Chicken Man Testa was blown up on the front steps of his home by a remote-controlled bomb, and Nicky Scarfo ascended to the leadership. He immediately imposed a street tax on the city's independent bookies and other freelance criminals, sending strong-arm squads to deal with recalcitrants. The diminutive Scarfo was much feared for his murderous temper, and when his men relayed messages from him they would hold their palms across their chests, well below eye level, to indicate that they were speaking for "the little guy." Wild and reckless as ever, he began ordering hits left and right. No one in his organization felt safe; over a period of four years an estimated two dozen murders were carried out under his direction. Scarfo would also prove that the family had learned nothing from Abscam, even after it had taken down two Pennsylvania congressmen, two Philadelphia City Council members, and the mayor of nearby Camden. In 1986 Willard Rouse III, a nationally known developer, sought to build a half-billion-dollar shopping and entertainment complex known as Penn's Landing on the Delaware River at the foot of Market Street. Scarfo saw an opportunity to get a share. He had one of his lieutenants, Nick Caramandi, tell a Rouse representative, Jim Vance, that a million-dollar bribe was necessary to ensure that City Councilman Leland Beloff gave the necessary approval for the development to commence. Scarfo anticipated it was only the start of the payoffs. As in Abscam, greed blinded the conspirators to danger. Rouse was known to be so honest that he did not even make political contributions, yet he was expected to give a million-dollar bribe to the Mafia. When Jim Vance turned out to be FBI agent Jim Vaules, Caramandi and Beloff were arrested. After Caramandi turned government witness, Scarfo himself would be brought down.

In the end the Mafia families were never able to get control of the Atlantic City casinos themselves, though they operated in ancillary areas, such as bribing public officials to award contracts to mob-controlled companies.

In 1984, one of those convicted in a federal sting operation was the mayor of Atlantic City, Mike Matthews. He too had ignored the lessons of Abscam. As Matthews told the federal judge who sentenced him to prison, "Greed got the better of me." The Mafia had not heeded Governor Byrne's injunction to keep its dirty hands away from Atlantic City. He should have given the same warning to the politicians.

CHAPTER 8

STRAWMEN: SKIMMING VEGAS

Small and compact, Tony Spilotro did not look the part of a mob enforcer. Yet despite his appearance, he was one of the most feared
strong-arm guys in the Chicago Outfit. In 1971, just thirty-three years old
and already a made man, his bosses handed him a big promotion: Spilotro
was to be the watchdog for their western operations, headquartered in Las
Vegas. It was another bad decision from a mob family that had been making a lot of them ever since Tony Accardo had stepped down as boss fourteen years earlier. Spilotro had a fatal flaw—he was too confrontational,
especially with law enforcement officers. He once sued the IRS and Chicago
cops after they relieved him of $12,000 in gambling proceeds. The suit
went nowhere.

During his early apprenticeship in the Outfit, Spilotro learned his trade
from some of the city's master gangsters and their associates. For a time he
was a gofer for the mob's favorite bail bondsman, Irwin Weiner. The job allowed him to poke around the criminal courts, examining records and
keeping an eye on lawyers and defendants who might be thinking of cutting a deal with the prosecution. Anyone the Outfit suspected might be
trying to lighten his sentence by sharing information was liable to be terminated with extreme prejudice. In his spy job, Spilotro once trailed FBI
agent Bill Roemer to a secluded area of a public park, hoping to observe

him meeting with an informer. According to Roemer he turned the tables on Spilotro, emerging from the bushes with his gun drawn to inquire, "Looking for me, pal?" Spilotro was well aware of Roemer's reputation as the Feds' muscle guy, but even with a revolver in his face he did not back down, refusing to answer questions or produce identification. The burly Roemer grabbed Spilotro, twisted his arm behind his back, and forcibly extracted his wallet—while making sure he was not carrying a gun. When Roemer was through examining the contents of the wallet, he threw them down on the ground. The two men then began exchanging unpleasantries, and Spilotro declared, "I seen your house. Big shot! Live in a little dump out there by the steel mills." That was a violation of the rules of engagement: By revealing that he had cased the house, Spilotro was making an implied threat to Roemer's family. "Listen, punk," Roemer shouted, "If I ever see you around my house, I'm coming after you!" The encounter ended with the FBI man calling Spilotro a "piss ant." Roemer spread the story around among his reporter friends, and from that time on Spilotro was known as "Tony the Ant" in Chicago's newspapers.

By his mid-twenties Spilotro was a debt collector for Sam De Stefano, Chicago's premier "juiceman"—a loan shark who lent out money at 20 percent interest per week on the principal. At those rates a thousand-dollar loan could escalate to two thousand in less than a month. If a borrower forgot to pay, his memory would be prodded with an ice pick. De Stefano was one of the best known local mob characters of his time, a man who had come to Chicago from downstate Illinois as a teenager and still retained the accent of his youth. Generally, people who spoke in a rural twang sounded friendly; De Stefano's midwestern folksiness blended with a Chicago gangster snarl made him seem especially menacing. He was so vicious and unpredictable that he frightened fellow mobsters, changing from amiable to maniacal in midsentence. Known by everyone as "Mad Sam," his business practices—such as hanging a debtor from a meat hook or repeatedly stabbing him—seemed more like expressions of some deep psychological problem. On occasions when Bill Roemer dropped by to have a chat, De Stefano usually displayed his amiable side by having his wife brew up a nice cup of coffee for the G-man. When Roemer would remark that it seemed strong, Sam explained that it was a special blend.

Finally Captain Bill Duffy of the Chicago police alerted Roemer that the flavoring in the coffee was De Stefano's urine.

Spilotro's other mob mentor was "Milwaukee Phil" Alderisio, chief enforcer for the Chicago Outfit. Alderisio and his partner, Chuckie Nicoletti, were responsible for carrying out the major hits. While on a job they usually prowled the city in a "work car," an ordinary-looking Ford or Chevy equipped with hidden gun compartments, heavy metal sides, and bulletproof windows. The license plates flipped over to confuse witnesses, the taillights could be turned off, and the engine was souped up for maximum-speed chases. One of their other tasks was to collect the street tax from robbers, burglars, and hijackers. Chicago's garden-variety criminals were a tough lot, but only a few refused to pay—and those only once. Phil served as outfit boss from '67 to '69, when the Feds convicted him of bank fraud. Sent to the maximum security prison at Marion, Illinois (the modern equivalent of Alcatraz), he died there of a heart attack. Chuckie was murdered in 1977.

Spilotro got started on the Outfit's fast track by assisting Alderisio and Nicoletti in carrying out a double murder in retaliation for a triple murder—the kind of event that gave Chicago a certain reputation. Billy McCarthy and Jimmy Miraglia were small-time stickup guys. In May 1962, the two were worsted in a barroom fight with two mob associates, the Scalvo brothers, Ron and Phil. Afterward, McCarthy and Miraglia waited outside, and when the Scalvos and the club's female singer exited the place they shot and killed all three of them. Mob bosses suspected Billy McCarthy of being one of the shooters, and Tony Spilotro was used to lure him into an ambush where he could be seized by Alderisio and Nicoletti. They took him to a workshop where they beat and kicked him and used an ice pick on his private parts. While Alderisio and Nicoletti watched, Spilotro squeezed McCarthy's head in a vise. Finally, after one eye popped out, McCarthy identified Miraglia as his partner. A few days later, both men were found in a car trunk with their throats cut.[1]

This was the man chosen to represent Chicago in the most glamorous

---

1 Nick Pileggi describes the incident correctly in his book *Casino*. The movie version retains the eye-popping but changes the precipitating event to a robbery and the locale to Las Vegas.

tourist resort in America—Las Vegas. It was a place where the Outfit operated on sufferance of the local authorities. In such a setting discretion was
required. Yet even before he left Chicago, Spilotro proved he was still a
reckless hoodlum. As he was packing up to leave for Las Vegas, he got into
a row with IRS agents, who seized a truckload of his family's belongings to
satisfy a tax assessment.

It was Bugsy Siegel who had first brought the Mafia to Vegas in the 1940s.
Siegel spent mob money lavishly in building the Flamingo Hotel and
Casino, and what he did not spend, his mistress Virginia Hill stole. When
the till ran dry he got more money from eastern mobsters like Meyer Lansky, Lucky Luciano, and Frank Costello. In addition, he sold shares—many
times over—to various investors. When the Flamingo opened to disappointing business, Bugsy was murdered in Los Angeles on orders from the
eastern bosses whose money he lost. Lansky then stepped in and used his
superior business acumen to make the place a success.

Vegas was designated a "open city"—one that any mob family could operate in. Several of them secured Teamster loans to build casinos that they
controlled through fronts, or "strawmen." Frank Sinatra and his Rat Pack
buddies were regulars on the local scene. Their 1960 movie *Ocean's Eleven*,
a lighthearted story about a group of war buddies who attempt to rob the
casinos, was virtually a commercial for Vegas. Knowledgeable people
found it even more amusing than did the general public. In the film, the
casino owners ask a mob boss, played by Cesar Romero, to help recover
their money. In a scene in which he makes calls around the country to connected guys, seeking information, one of the names he uses was the real
name of a mob associate and friend of Sinatra's.

One form of Vegas heist the movie omitted to show was "the skim," the
system used to keep some of the casino's profits hidden from the official
owners and tax collectors so they could be funneled to gangsters. While the
mobs often got a cut of the casinos' profits from the owners, their real stake
was in the skim. They utilized "skim men," usually veteran gamblers who
knew numerous ways to steal even though state officials and tax collectors
were watching the operation. As a chief skimmer explained to a mob boss,

Jimmy Hoffa, *right*, then midwestern boss of the Teamsters Union, squaring off with Robert Kennedy, *left*, counsel for a Senate rackets investigating committee, 1957. In 1961 when Kennedy became attorney general he mounted a "Get Hoffa" drive that led to Jimmy's imprisonment and the end of the longtime Teamsters president's career. (AP/WORLDWIDE PHOTOS)

Joseph Barbara, *left*. His Apalachin estate was the site of a Mafia conclave that was raided in November 1957 by New York State Police under the command of Sergeant Edgar Croswell, *right*. The "Apalachin raid" would be the opening shot in law enforcement's war against the Mafia that would continue for the next half-century. (AP/WORLDWIDE PHOTOS)

Chicago Outfit boss Sam Giancana and the singer Phyllis McGuire in a London nightclub, 1962. In contrast to most Mafia chieftans, Giancana maintained a high public profile. Because of the intense pressure put on him by the federal government his mob underlings forced him to step down and go into exile in Mexico. Later they would murder him. (AP/WORLDWIDE PHOTOS)

Mafia chieftain Anthony "Big Tuna" Accardo. The low-profile Accardo, who was never shot and never spent a night in jail, was the most prominent figure in the Chicago Outfit from World War II until his death in 1992. (CHICAGO CRIME COMMISSION)

Jerome Johnson (with camera) taking a motion picture of Joseph Colombo Sr. at an Italian-American civil rights rally in New York's Columbus Circle, 1971. A few minutes later Johnson allegedly shot Colombo and was himself immediately killed by an unknown gunman. Colombo, head of the family that bore his name, remained comatose until his death in 1978. (AP/WORLDWIDE PHOTOS)

"Crazy Joe" Gallo, the man suspected of arranging Colombo's shooting, testifies before a Senate rackets investigating committee in Washington, D.C., 1959. Despite being a killer, Gallo liked to socialize with artists and intellectuals. His 1972 murder in a Manhattan restaurant passed into mob legend. (AP/WORLDWIDE PHOTOS)

Anthony "Tony Ducks" Corallo, future head of the Lucchese crime family leaves FBI headquarters in New York, 1961. He and a state supreme court justice would be convicted of attempting to fix a federal court case. Eight years later Corallo and a former boss of Tammany Hall would be found guilty in another bribery case. (AP/WORLDWIDE PHOTOS)

Robert M. Morgenthau, *left*. From 1961 to 1970 as United States Attorney for the Southern District of New York, Morgenthau spearheaded the government's war on the Mafia. From 1975 on, as district attorney of Manhattan, he demonstrated that he was not afraid to prosecute any defendant, however powerful. *At right*, John Moscow who led the Bank of Credit and Commerce International investigation. (DANY)

G. Robert Blakey, *left*, staff counsel to a Senate subcommittee, and its chairman Senator John L. McClellan, *right*, testifying on a proposed Racketeer Influenced Corrupt Organizations (RICO) law, 1970. The federal government would eventually use this statute to bring down mob bosses all over the United States. In 1978 Blakey would serve as chief counsel to a congressional committee that probed possible Mafia involvement in the assassination of President John F. Kennedy. (AP/WORLDWIDE PHOTOS)

Carlos Marcello, 1981. The most prominent Mafia figure in the South, his enmity toward Attorney General Robert F. Kennedy caused congressional investigators to suspect him of ordering the assassination of President Kennedy. (AP/WORLDWIDE PHOTOS)

"The Docile Don," Philadelphia Mafia boss Angelo Bruno. Under his twenty-year reign violence was held down. In 1980, a year after this picture was taken, the low-profile Bruno was murdered by dissident members of his own family. (AP/WORLDWIDE PHOTOS)

Bruno's eventual successor, Nicodemo "Little Nicky" Scarfo (in handcuffs). His violent style of leadership led not only to his own imprisonment but also to the decline of the Philadelphia Mafia family. (AP/WORLDWIDE PHOTOS)

A video of U.S. Representative Michael Myers, *second from left*, accepting an envelope containing $50,000 from undercover FBI agent Anthony Amoroso, *far left*. In 1980, as part of the Abscam sting, FBI agents made bribery cases against a United States senator, half a dozen congressmen, and various state and local officials. (AP/WORLDWIDE PHOTOS)

Anthony "Tony the Ant" Spilotro, the Chicago Outfit's overseer of its Las Vegas interests, 1980. His reckless behavior helped to end the practice of skimming from casinos. In 1986, while under indictment, Spilotro was beaten to death by Chicago gangsters, who dumped his body in an Indiana cornfield. (CHICAGO CRIME COMMISSION)

Anthony "Tony Pro" Provenzano, in the custody of federal agents, 1976. A Genovese family capo and longtime power in the Teamsters union, Provenzano was a principal suspect in the disappearance (and presumed murder) of Jimmy Hoffa. In 1978 Provenzano was sentenced to life in prison on a different murder charge. (AP/WORLDWIDE PHOTOS)

Teamsters president Jackie Presser is rolled in on a red chariot at a 1986 conference in Las Vegas. For years the Cleveland-based Presser managed to serve as both an FBI informant and a Mafia associate, finally becoming head of the union. In 1988 he died while under federal indictment. (AP/WORLDWIDE PHOTOS)

The body of Bonanno family head Carmine Galante in the garden of the Brooklyn restaurant, July 1979, where he was murdered by members of his own crime family. The cigar clutched in his mouth was reportedly planted by photographers. (AP/WORLDWIDE PHOTOS)

Anthony "Fat Tony" Salerno in the custody of a United States Marshal. In 1986 Salerno was convicted of being the leader of New York's Genovese family though, in fact, he was only the number two man. (AP/WORLDWIDE PHOTOS)

Vincent "Chin" Gigante, 1997, was the real boss of the Genovese family. For years he was able to avoid being brought to trial by pretending to be mentally ill. After the government proved otherwise he was sentenced to prison where he died in 2005. (AP/WORLDWIDE PHOTOS)

Rudolph Giuliani, United States Attorney for the Southern District of New York, 1983 to 1988. Giuliani brought the commission case in which leaders of the five New York families were convicted, as well as a number of other high profile Mafia indictments.

Ron Goldstock, director of the New York State Organized Crime Task Force, *right*, with Governor Mario Cuomo. Goldstock demonstrated that a small state agency could play a significant role in bringing down New York's five families.

The body of Gambino family boss Paul Castellano (on a stretcher) and, *below*, his bodyguard Tommy Bilotti, lying outside of a steak house in Manhattan, December 1985. This photo is also on the book jacket. The killings were ordered by John Gotti so that he could grab Castellano's title. (AP/WORLDWIDE PHOTOS)

John Gotti, head of the Gambino family, is arrested by the FBI in New York City, December 1990. Though he was acquitted in three previous trials, after this arrest he was convicted and sent to a maximum-security federal prison where he died in 2002. (AP/WORLDWIDE PHOTOS)

The senior Gotti reportedly passed the leadership of the family to his son, John A., known as "Junior." Junior would later be imprisoned and, after his release, would face new indictments. In this 2006 photo he is running up the steps of a courthouse where he was a defendant in a case that resulted in a hung jury.
(AP/WORLDWIDE PHOTOS)

Jim Fox, New York FBI head from 1987 to 1993. Under his administration cases were made against major mob figures including the one that finally sent John Gotti to prison.
(AP/WORLDWIDE PHOTOS)

FBI TEN MOST WANTED FUGITIVE

RACKETEERING INFLUENCED AND CORRUPT ORGANIZATIONS (RICO) - MURDER (18 COUNTS), CONSPIRACY TO COMMIT MURDER, CONSPIRACY TO COMMIT EXTORTION, NARCOTICS DISTRIBUTION, CONSPIRACY TO COMMIT MONEY LAUNDERING; EXTORTION; MONEY LAUNDERING

JAMES J. BULGER

Photograph taken in 1994   Photograph taken in 1994   Photograph retouched in 2000

Aliases: Thomas F. Baxter, Mark Shapeton, Jimmy Bulger, James Joseph Bulger, James J. Bulger, Jr., James Joseph Bulger, Jr., Tom Harris, Tom Marshall, "Whitey"

DESCRIPTION

Date of Birth:	September 3, 1929	Hair:	White/Silver
Place of Birth:	Boston, Massachusetts	Eyes:	Blue
Height:	5' 7" to 5' 9"	Complexion:	Light
Weight:	150 to 160 pounds	Sex:	Male
Build:	Medium	Race:	White
Occupation:	Unknown	Nationality:	American
Scars and Marks:	None known		

Remarks: Bulger is an avid reader with an interest in history. He is known to frequent libraries and historic sites. Bulger is currently on the heart medication Atenolol (50 mg) and maintains his physical fitness by walking on beaches and in parks with his female companion, Catherine Elizabeth Greig. Bulger and Greig love animals and may frequent animal shelters. Bulger has been known to alter his appearance through the use of disguises. He has traveled extensively throughout the United States, Europe, Canada, and Mexico.

CAUTION

JAMES J. BULGER IS BEING SOUGHT FOR HIS ROLE IN NUMEROUS MURDERS COMMITTED FROM THE EARLY 1970s THROUGH THE MID-1980s IN CONNECTION WITH HIS LEADERSHIP OF AN ORGANIZED CRIME GROUP THAT ALLEGEDLY CONTROLLED EXTORTION, DRUG DEALS, AND OTHER ILLEGAL ACTIVITIES IN THE BOSTON, MASSACHUSETTS, AREA. HE HAS A VIOLENT TEMPER AND IS KNOWN TO CARRY A KNIFE AT ALL TIMES.

CONSIDERED ARMED AND EXTREMELY DANGEROUS

IF YOU HAVE ANY INFORMATION CONCERNING THIS PERSON, PLEASE CONTACT YOUR LOCAL FBI OFFICE OR THE NEAREST U.S. EMBASSY OR CONSULATE.

REWARD

The FBI is offering a $1,000,000 reward for information leading directly to the arrest of James J. Bulger.

www.fbi.gov

August 1999
Poster Revised November 2000

An FBI Ten Most Wanted poster on James "Whitey" Bulger. In return for information that Bulger supplied to rogue FBI agents about the Boston Mafia, he was given virtual carte blanche to carry out his own criminal activities including eighteen murders. Since his flight from Boston in 1994 he has been reported seen in many locations but has yet to be apprehended. (FBI) there were "at least twenty-two holes in the [money] bucket." Among the more popular techniques was using a duplicate key to open the locked cash boxes when they were being transported from the gaming tables to the count room; better yet was planting skimmers in the count room itself. One time the FBI spotted a skimmer entering the count room through a hidden door. Slot machines could be rigged to show more payouts than occurred. The casino's banks of overhead cameras known as "eyes in the sky," which constantly scanned the gaming floors and the count room, could be made to malfunction, or be left unattended for a few minutes if a maintenance man or security guard was paid off. Skimming had been around as long as casinos themselves. In the 1950s it had been used to pay off the late Bugsy Siegel's creditors. In the early '60s it was estimated that individual mob bosses were receiving fifty to seventy thousand dollars a month from the Vegas skim.

In the freewheeling atmosphere of Vegas, some employees who knew what was happening figured they might as well cut a little slice of the pie for themselves. If a guest paid for his reservation in cash, the room clerk could pocket the money and destroy the records. Dealers palmed chips from the tables. Casino managers came up short in the count. It was understood that employees, including ones doing the skimming, stole a little. One chief skimmer told a mob boss (while an FBI tape recorded him), "Sometimes people are going to steal even from you . . . you gotta give them some leeway."

In addition to skim bosses, Vegas needed someone who could keep the troops in line and deal with dishonest employees or freelance hustlers such as jewel thieves or extortionists attracted by the presence of so many well-heeled chumps. The friendly blonde a big spender picked up in the casino and took to his room might well be setting him up for a burglary or shakedown. This was a job for a troubleshooter—sometimes in the literal sense—and Chicago, as the principal family in Vegas, supplied the man.

Johnny Roselli had been Chicago's Las Vegas watchdog in the 1950s, after he finished serving time in prison for his part in the attempted Hollywood extortion. The mobs did not want gunplay on the Strip, lest it scare off the tourists, and Roselli knew how to be tough without going overboard. If someone got out of line, Johnny would talk to him and suggest that he should leave town immediately—for health reasons. If that was not sufficient, some outside boys would be brought in to solve the problem. When violence was necessary, it was preferable that it be done away from Vegas. In 1958, when Gus Greenbaum, the manager at the Riviera, was suspected of holding out on his employers, it was arranged for him and his wife to be killed in Phoenix, Arizona. The soft sand of the vast desert also made it easy to dig holes in which bodies could be disposed of. The Vegas casinos that were under mob control were usually avoided by professional criminals.

The Nevada authorities did not pose a serious problem to the mobs. Gambling had been legalized in 1931 as a means of boosting the state's economy, and officials did not want to kill the goose that laid the golden eggs—particularly since the eggs often found their way into the pockets of some officials. The local culture also posed an obstacle to vigorous law enforcement, especially by the Feds. Cities like San Francisco, New Orleans, and Chicago had never been puritanical. Most people in such places were ready to tolerate gambling and a certain amount of vice; reformers who criticized these activities were never popular. The attitude in Vegas was the same, and further bolstered by the traditional Western hostility to regulation by the federal government. Until the '50s the FBI did not have a field office in Vegas, only a few resident agents who mostly worked days while the mob guys cavorted at night.

Then things began to change. The Bureau made Vegas a full-fledged field office and assigned some of its top people to work there. The state too cracked down. It created a gaming control board and circulated a black book with the names of undesirables who were forbidden to enter the casinos. The FBI commenced an investigation of skimming. Mob-controlled Vegas casinos were an ideal target for the Department of Justice, whose principal strategic focus at the time was arresting gamblers or tax evaders. In 1965, though, the government received a major setback when FBI agents were caught engaging in illegal eavesdropping.

At the same time that the FBI was strengthening its operations, the mob was growing increasingly lax. In the 1960s, Chicago boss Sam Giancana sent Marshall Caifano out to Vegas to supersede Roselli. Elder statesman Tony Accardo advised Caifano not to be too visible, but Giancana himself was not setting a very good example by parading around the casinos with his girlfriend, singer Phyllis McGuire (in 1963, Frank Sinatra lost his license at a resort he owned on the California-Nevada border for allowing Giancana, reportedly his hidden backer, to frequent the place). Instead of heeding Accardo's counsel, Caifano carried on as if the law could not touch him. He appeared openly in casinos, defying state authorities to do anything about it. When they penalized the casinos, he sued the control board. After Caifano was recalled, it was Spilotro's turn.

When he got to Vegas, Spilotro proved that he had no more of Roselli's savoir faire than Caifano. He immediately imposed a street tax on burglars, pimps, and other freelancers, enforcing it with the methods he had learned from Milwaukee Phil. He imported his own crew of Chicago muscle guys and burglars to pull jobs. His boys became known as "the Hole-in-the-Wall Gang" from their method of chopping through walls to avoid burglar alarms when they broke into houses. Another specialty was sticking up maître d's. In crowded Vegas restaurants, free-spending gamblers thought nothing of dropping big tips to get a table. Many headwaiters went home at night with thousands of dollars in cash, and some of them got grabbed by the Hole-in-the-Wall crew.

No shrinking violet himself, the Los Angeles strong-arm man Jimmy "The Weasel" Fratianno could only shake his head at Chicago sending someone like Spilotro to Vegas. He attributed it to the bad judgment of Joey Aiuppa (a.k.a. O'Brien), the Chicago mob boss at the time. Aiuppa had made his own reputation running clip joints in Cicero. There, a patron who got out of line would get a blackjack over his head.[2] But what played in a blue-collar factory town would not fly in Vegas, and Spilotro's tactics caused both the local cops and the FBI to swarm all over him. When he opened a jewelry store under the name of Tony Stuart, the FBI immediately planted a legal Title III bug in it. Defiant as always, Tony hired technicians to set up a radio system so he could monitor Bureau transmissions.

In 1973 another new player appeared on the Vegas scene. Allen Glick was not a gambler or a mob guy. He was a thirty-year-old lawyer and real estate developer from San Diego, who acquired the run-down Hacienda

2 It was an old custom—back in the 1920s, Capone had done the same thing to the mayor of Cicero, sending him sprawling down the steps of City Hall.

Casino. A year later his corporation, known as Argent (for Allen R. Glick Enterprises, or in French, "money"), took control of three more casinos, including Chicago's flagship, the Stardust. His financing came from Allen Dorfman's Central States Pension Fund, the mob's bank. The short, balding Glick seemed like the perfect strawman. With a clean record that included Vietnam combat service and a conservative appearance, it would be easy for him to obtain a license. He was a square, and his backers expected he would take orders like a good little boy. The problem was that Glick did not fully realize what kind of people he was dealing with. He had initially been introduced to Frank Balistrieri, boss of the Milwaukee family. Later Glick would claim that he hadn't known of Balistrieri's mob affiliations. But when his lawyers did a background check and informed him who Frank was, that would have been the right time to back out. Glick probably thought he could keep the mobsters at bay. What he didn't know was that a Teamster loan also needed approval from the Chicago, Kansas City, and Cleveland families, all of whom had their hands in the pension fund. As part of the deal, Glick was required to take Chicago gambler Frank "Lefty" Rosenthal as one of his top managers.

Rosenthal's expertise was in calculating the odds on sporting events. In the postwar era, sports betting began replacing horse racing as the most popular form of gambling. The secret of success in oddsmaking was inside information, such as knowing that a team's star quarterback had injured his arm in practice. Success was even more likely if a key player could be bribed to hold back a little. When Chicago had sent Lefty out to Vegas to learn the casino business, the Chicago Crime Commission followed up by forwarding a character reference to the Nevada authorities—a very *bad* reference. Rosenthal's sins included taking the Fifth before the McClellan Committee, gambling arrests, and pleading no contest to a charge of fixing a college basketball game. With that background he would never be licensed to manage a casino. Instead, operating under titles like Food and Beverage Manager, he ran the skim at the Stardust. Nick Pileggi, to whom Rosenthal later told his story, has described how Lefty came to control everything from the famed Lido stage show to how many blueberries the cooks put in each muffin. With Rosenthal as the skim man and Spilotro as the muscle, Chicago's Vegas team was complete. The two had previously gotten along fairly well together in Chicago and Florida. There, though, they had been under tough bosses. Given their enhanced status and the greater distance from their Chicago masters, there was potential for conflict between them.

The whole setup in Vegas was an object lesson in how not to manage an enterprise. One problem was that Spilotro kept being hauled back to Chicago every couple of years to face old murder charges. Sam De Stefano was his co-defendant at one in 1973. At the preliminary hearings "Mad Sam" acted as his own lawyer, causing a media sensation. The Outfit's leaders weren't eager to see the case turn into a circus, and Sam was shotgunned to death. In his absence the trial proceeded quietly, and Spilotro was found not guilty. Two years later Spilotro was charged in a Teamsters extortion scheme along with Allen Dorfman. This time the government's chief witness had his head blown off in front of his wife. Without him, the prosecution's case collapsed.

The ultimate overseers of Vegas were four absentee owners of different mob standing, and their uneven footings added to the confusion. Nick Civella of Kansas City and Frank Balistrieri of Milwaukee ran their families with an iron hand but did not have seats on the national commission. In Cleveland, after the death of family boss John Scalish in 1976, an all-out war broke out between two competing factions. This distracted the local mob's attention from Las Vegas. During Spilotro's time in Vegas, Chicago was basically run by a committee. Joey Aiuppa was the boss and Jackie Cerone the underboss. Cerone too had a misleading tag, "Jackie the Lackey." In reality he was almost coequal with Aiuppa, much in the same way that the late Paul Ricca had been with Tony Accardo. Accardo had stepped down from day-to-day operations, but he was still the most respected figure on the scene. It was Aiuppa who personally received the skim money that a courier brought from Vegas every month. In the 1980s, federal prosecutors would estimate that a minimum of $160,000 a month, and probably a lot more, was being skimmed and cut up by Cleveland, Milwaukee, Kansas City, and Chicago, with the largest share going to the last.

Dorfman may have been the money power behind Vegas, but he was not a made man. Like Spilotro, he reported to a captain, Joe Lombardo, whom the newspapers had taken to referring to as "the Clown." It was one of the least apt nicknames ever bestowed. Lombardo was smart and tough, and in time he would become the top boss of the Outfit. When Dorfman visited Vegas, he swaggered through the casinos like a Marine top sergeant, issuing profanity-laden directives. But in Lombardo's presence, Dorfman became a meek civilian.

In Vegas itself, Allen Glick, whom one observer characterized as "a little man who hid behind a big desk," didn't know how to control mob guys. He let Rosenthal (who was not a made man) defy him: Lefty wandered around hiring and firing employees on his own authority. Reportedly, on one occasion he even tried to fire Glick's secretary because she would not spy on her boss. Balistrieri of Milwaukee was the one who originally told Glick to hire Rosenthal, yet when Glick and Rosenthal clashed, it was not Balistrieri or Spilotro but Kansas City's Nick Civella who laid down the law. According to Nick Pileggi, one night Rosenthal suddenly informed Glick that they had to attend an emergency meeting in Kansas City. When Glick declined, it was made clear to him that it was a command performance. Glick was flown there in a corporate jet, and when he landed at about 3 A.M. was met by the local underboss, Carl "Toughy" DeLuna, who drove him to a meeting with Civella. Glick knew he was in for a rough time when Civella declined to shake hands, declaring that if it were his decision, Glick would be dead. Civella thought he had been cheated out of the $1.2 million promised him for helping to get the Teamsters' okay on the pension fund loan. Glick had no idea that there had been any such promise; Civella assured him that he could bet his life that there had. When Glick protested that he did not know how the corporation could make the payment, Civella told him that Lefty would take care of it. The money would come out of skim.

To run its Vegas operations, the mobs needed someone with both business acumen and prestige within organized crime. Nearby Los Angeles was the base of lawyer/labor consultant Sid Korshak, a man with plenty of clout. Korshak was a product of Chicago's West Side and had risen to power with the support of the Outfit. This did not deter his corporate clients, particularly those in the entertainment business, who came to him to handle their problems. If they had labor trouble, there was no better attorney to retain than Korshak. A man with his connections could always persuade union heads to be reasonable. Sid became a major presence on the Hollywood scene; not to be invited to his annual Christmas party was social death. While Korshak had prestige among mob guys, he kept them at a distance to maintain his respectability. Anyone who wanted to deal with him had to go through the Chicago Outfit. Jimmy Fratianno once made the mistake of confronting Sid in person, feeling that the lawyer was not moving fast enough on some favor he wanted done. Chicago mob bosses quickly informed "the Weasel" that they had invested too much in keeping Sid above the fray: Under no circumstances was he ever to go near him again. Jimmy had done hits for Chicago, and he knew what happened to people who disobeyed such injunctions. He kept his distance.

Spilotro's job called for a veteran capo who had both a reputation that commanded respect, and the good sense not to throw that weight around too openly. When people know you are a killer, you can speak softly and they will obey. In a town that was starting to have an FBI agent behind every bush, it was not wise to scare folks—they had only a short sprint to the nearest G-man. Nor was it sensible to threaten the local cops. The metropolitan Las Vegas sheriffs' force retained many of the traditions of the old Western days. Pileggi related how when one of its commanders learned from his local informants that two of his detectives were on a mob hit list, he went right to the top. He and an aide hopped on a plane for Chicago and burst into the homes of Aiuppa and Lombardo. They found only the men's wives. Undaunted, the two cops hung around Chicago passing the word that if any of their men were killed, the next time they visited the Aiuppa and Lombardo households they would gun down anybody they found. Soon the detective commander received a call at his Chicago hotel, informing him that the contract had been canceled.

In 1975 things began to turn bad for the Mafia in Vegas. Glick's California real estate empire went bankrupt, causing an investor to sue him. As part of her suit she demanded to see all the legal documents concerning Glick's corporations. The mob couldn't afford to let her get hold of Argent's records. Not long afterward, she was murdered in her California home, by either Spilotro or one of his boys. In 1976, Rosenthal was ousted from the Stardust by the state control board. Instead of lying low, he instituted a series of actions to have the commission declared illegal, and began hosting his own TV show, which he used as a platform to attack the Nevada authorities. As if that weren't enough, he got into public altercations with his ex-showgirl wife, Gerry, who began carrying on an affair with Spilotro.[3] The last was a no-no in the Mafia, punishable by death. Not only was it dishonorable, but a jealous man might do something crazy like start talking to the FBI. The Feds offered mob guys shoulders to cry on, and cozy witness protection programs in which they could retire from life's vicissitudes. When rumors about Mrs. Rosenthal's affair drifted back to Chicago, Spilotro's friends managed to cover up for him. It was another example of how out of touch Chicago was.

Joe Agosto, Kansas City's skim boss in Vegas, was so upset that he called Toughy DeLuna and complained that Rosenthal was going to bring everybody down. Joe had a lot to worry about. His real name was Vincenzo Pianetti, and he was a Sicilian who had entered the United States illegally by assuming the identity of the son of a Cleveland mob guy who had died in Italy in 1951. After a number of scrapes with the law, Agosto was overseeing both the skim and the popular Folies Bergère show at the Tropicana. In his conversation with DeLuna, which the FBI recorded, he said that Rosenthal would "pull everybody into the mud. . . . I mean if he committed suicide, he should accept the fucking deal, that's all, don't put another half-dozen fucking people in the firing line. . . ." Agosto made clear that he wanted Rosenthal hit, telling DeLuna that if he hadn't known who Rosenthal's backers were, "I would take action myself, without asking anybody's permission."

In January 1980, Joe Yablonsky took over as SAC of the Las Vegas FBI office. Yablonsky had previously served in New York and Miami, becoming so adept at undercover work against organized crime that he became known as "the King of Sting." In the post-Hoover era, he was called to Washington to establish the Bureau's undercover operations program. After a stint in charge of the Cincinnati office he was sent to Nevada. Yablonsky, like any

---

3 Later the film *Casino* would portray characters based on Rosenthal, his wife, and Spilotro, played respectively by Robert DeNiro, Sharon Stone, and Joe Pesci.

new SAC, tried to develop community support for his agency. He became active in his local synagogue and gave frequent speeches to civic groups. However, in those talks he openly charged local politicians with responsibility for the Mafia's free rein in Vegas, and his remarks were not well received. Powerful officials such as Senator Paul Laxalt, an intimate of President Reagan, began protesting to Washington. Some politicians feared that the FBI was going to work an Abscam-type sting on top local officials, and they demanded that Yablonsky be removed as SAC. But when their complaints reached FBI Director William Webster, they fell on deaf ears.

Back in the Midwest, Kansas City FBI agents Bill Ouseley and Lee Flosi of the organized crime squad were investigating a feud between the Civella mob family and the Spero brothers. They were uniquely qualified for the assignment: Ouseley's Italian-born mother had taught him to speak her native tongue, and Flosi had acquired street smarts about the mob while growing up on Chicago's West Side. In May 1978, three Speros were shot in a local bar, one of them fatally. As part of the investigation, the agents obtained a court order to plant a bug in the back of a pizzeria where the Civella leadership was known to talk business. In June it picked up a conversation between Nick Civella's brother Carl, known as "Corky," and Toughy DeLuna (Nick was unable to participate in the discussion because he still had a couple of weeks to serve on a gambling sentence). The conversation the G-men heard in the pizzeria was not about murder, but Vegas casinos. The Civella family was trying to get "the Genius" to sell his casinos to a group that included "Caesar," as opposed to one that included "Lefty." Eventually, it became clear that the speakers were talking about compelling Allen Glick to sell to the group Joe Agosto belonged to rather than one that Lefty Rosenthal was part of. The agents found it hard to believe that two guys in windbreakers sitting in a tiny restaurant in Kansas City could have such power. Yet eight days later Glick held a press conference to announce that he was selling his casinos.

The FBI put all-out surveillance on DeLuna, who was not an easy man to follow. Like many veteran hoods, he would drive through parking lots, make sudden turns, and double back to shake tails. A spotter plane was brought in to follow him around town, and soon the agents discovered his improvised message center: DeLuna was using the public phones at a local hotel to make his calls, confident that they were not tapped. The FBI stationed a platoon of agents, secretaries, and clerks near the phones so that they could overhear DeLuna's conversations, thereby providing enough evidence to obtain T3 warrants to install taps on all of the hotel's dozens of public phones. In addition, they tapped or bugged the residences of the Civellas and any relatives who allowed them to meet in their homes. Nick Civella knew that recording a suspect's conversations with his lawyer was not permitted, so as "Mr. Nichols" he used a room at his attorney's office to conduct business. Nick's understanding of the law was incomplete: Talking to a lawyer and using his office to conduct one's own business were not the same thing. A judge issued a federal warrant to bug Nick at the law office. Finally, the FBI had enough evidence to move. On Valentine's Day 1979, they intercepted $80,000 in skim money being brought in through the Kansas City airport and followed up with a search of DeLuna's house. There they found meticulous records that he had kept over the years, detailing all of the mob's business operations—including some involving families in other cities. The investigation, named "Strawman I," would lead to the indictment of the Civella brothers, DeLuna, and Agosto. Toughy DeLuna and Corky Civella each received thirty-year sentences. Nick died before he could be brought to trial, and Joe Agosto flipped over and became a government witness (shortly after the trial he also died, of a heart attack).

Another blow to the Vegas operation came from Chicago. In 1979 FBI agents commenced Operation Pendorf (for "penetrate Allen Dorfman"). Dorfman had been a federal target since the 1950s, and in 1972 he had been removed as head of the pension fund after being sent to prison for extortion. A CPA and former Notre Dame football star named Dan Shannon was appointed to run the fund, but Dorfman continued to keep a discreet hand in. When Shannon proved troublesome, Dorfman put out a contract on him. Chicago was always a Notre Dame town, and someone in the mob must have realized that killing Shannon, a city hero since his days at Mount Carmel High School, would, as the Notre Dame's fight song proclaimed, "Shake down the thunder from the sky." Dorfman was overruled. Instead, through some complex maneuvering, Shannon was forced out, and Dorfman continued to run the fund from behind the scenes.

Chicago organized crime squad agents Pete Wacks, Art Pfizenmayer, Richard Houston, and Jim Wagner secured a court order to plant a bug in Dorfman's office. It proved difficult to install: Surveillance by the FBI was something Dorfman took for granted, and he surrounded himself with tight security. The insurance company he owned maintained offices in a building patrolled by private guards twenty-four hours a day. By the late 1970s the FBI had a great deal of experience with elsurs, and a special "black bag" team from Washington was dispatched to Chicago. Its technicians made a duplicate master key to the building and used it to enter the outer offices of Dorfman's company. Though the key did not work on the door to his private office, agents managed to slip inside briefly while a maid cleaned it. There they noted a sophisticated alarm system and a security camera. The team managed to neutralize Dorfman's security devices long enough for them to plant bugs, including one in the bathroom. Toilets were normally off limits, but because Dorfman was known to take people in there for private conversations, it was permitted. Every morning Dorfman and Lombardo would meet in the office to talk business like a couple of regular CEOs. Listening FBI agents were surprised that Lombardo, though not an educated man, was the clever Dorfman's equal when it came to understanding complex financial issues.

Eventually the bug tossed a hot potato into the FBI's lap. Until 1977, the Interstate Commerce Commission (ICC) had set freight rates and restricted entry into the trucking business. As a result, the Teamsters were able to obtain hefty wage increases, because employers could pass the cost on to the shippers by gaining rate increases from a compliant ICC. As an anti-inflation measure, the Carter administration proposed deregulating the industry. Faced with competition, the established firms might have had to pay lower wages. Defeating the deregulation bill became a major IBT priority, and Allen Dorfman and Roy Williams—soon to be named general president of the union—took the lead in opposing it. On the bug, agents heard Dorfman, Williams, and Joe Lombardo discussing a deal whereby they would let the chairman of the U.S. Senate Commerce Committee, Howard Cannon of Nevada, purchase some Teamsters property in Vegas at a discounted price in return for his help in blocking the deregulation bill. Despite Allen Dorfman's reputation, Senator Cannon had approached him about buying the property and had met with Dorfman and Williams in his private Las Vegas office.

When the investigation was completed, Dorfman, Williams, and Chicago bosses Aiuppa, Cerone, and Lombardo were indicted and eventually convicted. Some prosecutors, reviewing the evidence, thought that Senator Cannon should be charged too. The Department of Justice, fresh from indicting Senator Williams of New Jersey in the Abscam investigation, was not eager to prosecute another U.S. senator. Instead, Cannon was allowed to testify as a government witness. The publicity from the case probably contributed to his defeat when he stood for reelection in 1982, ending twenty-four years of service in the Senate.

Strawman I, Pendorf, and an additional skimming investigation involving Chicago and the Stardust (which would become Strawman II) had the midwestern bosses worried about who among them would be the next to be arrested, and who was likely to turn government witness. In October 1982, Lefty Rosenthal came out of a Vegas restaurant, got into his Cadillac Eldorado, and started the engine. The car burst into flames, and he barely managed to get out of the vehicle before it exploded. Lefty had been saved by the old trick of keeping the car door open while he started the motor, and because that model of Cadillac had a special metal plate under the driver's seat. Frank Balistrieri was a suspect in the attack because of some remarks picked up during an electronic surveillance and his propensity for using explosives against his enemies. A bomb in Vegas might hurt a tourist and therefore be bad for business. So a boss would probably have waited until Lefty went on one of his frequent trips to Los Angeles and had him killed there. Most investigators believed it was Spilotro who arranged it. When Rosenthal was asked who he thought did it, he replied, "It was not the Boy Scouts of America." In January 1983, while awaiting sentencing a month after his conviction in Pendorf, Allen Dorfman was murdered outside a suburban Chicago restaurant.

When Strawman II broke, charges were brought against Balistrieri, Aiuppa, Cerone, DeLuna, and Spilotro. Named as co-conspirators were Nick Civella, Allen Dorfman, and Joe Agosto, all of them by this point deceased. Allen Glick was granted immunity and testified for the government. With his mastery of precise detail and his mild manner, "the Genius" proved to be a potent witness. Aiuppa and Cerone received twenty-eight years. Balistrieri and DeLuna, already under sentences for other crimes, received lesser terms. Lefty Rosenthal was never charged in the Strawman cases, and he has steadfastly denied any wrongdoing. Nevada authorities have not permitted him to return to a management post in the casinos.

In addition to the Strawman investigations, under Joe Yablonsky the FBI went all out to nail Spilotro, whom one agent later recollected—with considerable understatement—as having "a nasty attitude." One characteristic of "the Ant" did please the G-men. While Rosenthal was an astute handicapper, Spilotro was a terrible one, virtually never winning a bet. Some agents used to note his choices in sports contests and then hurry out to get their own (legal) wagers down on the opposing team.

The agents managed to trap Spilotro's Hole-in-the-Wall Gang in the act of carrying out a burglary and one of them turned government witness against Tony; the case ended in a mistrial. Spilotro was not to face any more charges. Though only in his mid-forties, it was determined that he required heart bypass surgery. Proceedings against him were postponed until he was deemed physically fit. Released on $2 million bail, during his recuperation he spent most of his time in the Chicago area. By any reckoning, Spilotro had done more than enough to get himself hit. The heat generated from his gangster behavior in Vegas, and some uncomplimentary remarks about his bosses picked up on FBI bugs, were all marks against him. Yet he did not run, hide, or flip.

On a June night in 1986 he and his brother Michael left the latter's suburban Chicago home. As they were departing, Michael told his wife, "If we are not back by nine o'clock, we're in big trouble." Ten days later the two men's bodies, stripped to their undershorts, were found buried in an Indiana cornfield sixty miles southeast of Chicago. The site was about four miles from a farm owned by Joey Aiuppa, who was then in prison for the Vegas skim. A pathologist's report indicated they had died of blunt force to the head and neck. Only by sheer chance had their bodies been discovered: A farmer had spotted signs of digging and notified game officials, thinking it was an animal carcass buried by a hunter. A couple of weeks later the corn would have grown so high that no one would have noticed the site. From the nature of the wounds and the way the bodies were disposed of, investigators concluded that whoever killed them was not try-ing to extract information, nor were they sending a message to others. Yet because they had not used something quick like a pistol shot, they must have wanted the victims to suffer before they died. Seven years later a Chicago newspaper account would claim that on the day that the Spilotros disappeared they told an informer that they were attending a meeting with the Outfit's new boss, Sam Carlisi. Another informant claimed that a mob heavy had kept in close contact with them by telephone, as if tracking their whereabouts, right up to the day before they disappeared. The article stated that the authorities believed Carlisi's men killed the brothers and handed their bodies over to a suburban crew chief for burial.

The mob's poor management of its glamor capital had been a disaster. Once it was the Mafia that was well run, while law enforcement plodded along in its old-fashioned ways. The situation was now reversed. In the '60s the FBI had recognized that Vegas was no mere desert backwater, but the Mafia never did, and it still resorted to using resident watchdogs like Tony Spilotro. In the 1980s the last Teamster loans in Vegas were paid off and the big corporations began to take over the casinos, including those that had previously been run by the mob families.

Perhaps a time will come when reenactments of Vegas's mob past are staged for tourists the way some casinos put on pirateship battles and hourly eruptions of Vesuvius. Though none of them were killed locally, the deaths of Bugsy Siegel, Allen Dorfman, and Tony Spilotro, along with the bombing attack in Vegas on Lefty Rosenthal, were gory enough to suit con-temporary public taste. But the most illustrative tableau would be one showing mob guys talking while FBI agents listened in. It was bugs, not bullets or bombs, that brought down the Vegas skim and dealt heavy blows to its midwestern Mafia overlords.

CHAPTER 9

THE MOB AND THE TEAMSTERS:
JIMMY'S FATE, JACKIE'S DILEMMA

When the legendary Neil Welch was appointed SAC of the FBI's Detroit field office in 1970, he immediately secured the transfer of a hundred additional agents to his command to work on organized crime. One of those he received was twenty-eight-year-old Jim Esposito, fresh from his rookie year in Oklahoma City. Welch assigned him to work gambling and loan sharking, and later he joined the labor racketeering squad. The latter was a key unit, because Detroit was the home base of the former IBT president, Jimmy Hoffa. In December 1971, Hoffa was paroled after serving five years of his thirteen-year consecutive sentences for jury tampering and pension fraud. Under the terms of a commutation granted to him by President, Richard Nixon, he was forbidden to hold any union office until 1980. While Jimmy formally had to accept the conditions, he immediately began plotting to regain control of his union. It was a prospect that was not welcomed by the top leadership of the IBT or their gangster allies. Over the next few years the conflict between Hoffa and his former friends grew into a virtual war.

By mid-1975, Welch was gone and Esposito was relief supervisor of the labor racketeering squad. On July 31, he received a phone call from an attorney assigned to the Detroit organized crime strike force who reported a rumor that Hoffa was missing. Esposito immediately assigned agents Bob

Garrity and Bob Newman to check it out with their sources in Teamster Local 299. Within half an hour they confirmed that the rumor was true. Esposito alerted his superiors and flashed word to Washington. Though the FBI had no jurisdiction in missing person cases, its long-standing policy was to informally investigate where there was a possibility that a victim might have been kidnapped and taken across state lines in violation of the federal "Lindbergh Law." Even if the policy had not existed, the FBI would have been motivated by its interest in Hoffa. In addition, a few days after Jimmy disappeared, his family contacted FBI director Clarence Kelley to request the Bureau's intervention.

The initial information was sketchy. When Hoffa left his vacation home in Lake Orion at one o'clock the day before, he told his wife, Josephine, that he was meeting someone at 2 P.M. at Machus Red Fox Restaurant in Bloomfield, a suburb of Detroit. At 2:15 he called her to say the person he was supposed to meet had not arrived yet. It was the last time she heard from him. When he had not returned home a few hours later, Mrs. Hoffa began phoning family and friends seeking information; she notified the Bloomfield Township Police Department the next morning. Within a short time, the police located Hoffa's green Pontiac in the Red Fox parking lot. Jimmy was not a man who stayed out at night: If he had not come home, it was because he couldn't. Esposito assigned an agent to go to Lake Orion and obtain from the family some of Jimmy's personal effects. The hairbrushes and worn underwear he secured were later used to provide dogs with his scent. An examination of Hoffa's office appointment book showed a listing on July 30 of "2:30 P.M., Fox rest Tony G." Tony G. was assumed to be Anthony Giacalone, a.k.a. "Tony Jack," a Detroit mob captain long associated with Hoffa.

From the earliest stages of the investigation, federal agents and police suspected that Jimmy Hoffa had not been kidnapped for ransom, or to scare him into agreeing to something—the man was too tough for that. Anybody who roughed up Hoffa and let him go would spend the rest of his life looking over his shoulder and starting his auto ignition by remote control. Thus the most likely assumption was that he was dead, and it was not hard to figure out who was behind his murder. Since the 1950s Hoffa had defied the United States Congress, the FBI, and the Kennedy and Nixon administrations. Recently he had been battling the Mafia, and it appeared they had done what the others could not—get rid of Jimmy Hoffa.

When Hoffa entered federal prison at Lewisburg, Pennsylvania, in March 1967, he did not resign as general president of the IBT. Instead, he designated his loyal supporter Frank Fitzsimmons to keep his seat warm. The plan was that Fitzsimmons, who had risen through the ranks from truck driver to general vice president through Hoffa's favor, would mobilize Teamster money and influence in an all-out effort to win his leader's early release. Hoffa's initial efforts to gain freedom were concentrated on legal maneuvers to overturn his convictions. In 1968 the U.S. Supreme Court denied his appeal. The following year Richard Nixon took office as president. Like most labor unions, the IBT had supported his opponent, Hubert Humphrey, but after a couple of years, the Nixon administration started courting the Teamsters. In 1971 the president himself dropped in at an IBT executive board meeting. Cabinet members began attending Teamster receptions, and White House counsel Charles "Chuck" Colson was assigned to act as liaison man with the union leadership. Fitzsimmons was invited to the White House, where he was given VIP treatment. By 1970, the Teamsters' two and a half million members made it the largest union in the country, comprising 10 percent of all organized labor. IBT support would mean a major boost to Nixon's reelection campaign in 1972. On the Teamsters side, an alliance with the White House might lead to the granting of many favors to the union, not the least of which would be an end to federal law enforcement pressure. Another might be to let Jimmy Hoffa out of prison—or, conversely, to keep him in.

Under Hoffa's regime, power had been centralized in the president's office and all decisions were made by him. Fitzsimmons returned to the old system, under which regional and local union heads were allowed to run their duchies and baronies without interference and the executive board of the IBT approved major decisions. It was an arrangement that permitted organized crime—which already controlled a number of Teamsters affiliates—to increase its influence in the union. One illustration of the decentralized system was the process for handling loan applications to the Central States

Pension Fund. Under Hoffa, every loan required his signoff (for which he normally received a kickback). Fitzsimmons was much more willing to accommodate the mob than Hoffa was. He allowed Allen Dorfman and Ohio Teamster leader Bill Presser, chairman of the executive board's loan committee, to make the final decision. In practice, this meant that the Chicago and Cleveland mobs (which backed Dorfman and Presser respectively) got a piece of the action. After a few warning shots whistled past Dorfman one night, some other families were also given a share of the pie.

Another post-Hoffa innovation was an arrangement whereby employers who made deals with people like the northeastern Pennsylvania family head Russ Bufalino, or Genovese capo "Tony Pro" Provenzano of New Jersey Local 560, could use Teamsters to haul their freight without paying them union wages. Under this scheme, businesses (including some Fortune 500 companies) would terminate their in-house truck drivers, who were immediately rehired at lower wages by a mob-backed leasing firm. The leasing firm would then sign a sweetheart contract with the old employer. When some drivers protested and demanded to look at the contract, they were shown the cover sheets of the standard IBT master freight agreement—with the new provisions sandwiched in between. Drivers who persisted in complaining were intimidated into silence.

Ironically, the principal rationale for the Department of Justice's "Get Hoffa" drive had been to break the power of organized crime in the IBT. Yet with Jimmy in Lewisburg, the Mafia's influence in the union was stronger than ever. Fitzsimmons spent a good deal of time playing golf and enjoying the good life. The rumor was that he would soon take Hoffa's job on a permanent basis. When word of what was happening reached Jimmy in prison, he became increasingly unhappy. The boss of the Mafia prisoners in Lewisburg during Hoffa's stay was Carmine Galante of the Bonanno family. He was a small man, but the other prisoners were frightened of him. Naturally, he had special privileges, and sometimes he cooked for a few guests. On occasion, Hoffa would join Galante for a meal after he finished work in the mattress factory. Other times, he preferred to remain in a maximum security cell, fearing some of the non-Mafia prisoners might attack him. To make himself popular, he utilized his contacts to help inmates get jobs, without which they could not be paroled.

When Jimmy entered the prison, Tony Provenzano was already there on an extortion conviction. At first he and Hoffa were friends, and Jimmy used his outside influence to force the prison authorities to provide necessary medical attention for Provenzano. Then trouble developed between them. Despite his criminal conviction, Hoffa was slated to receive an IBT pension, while Provenzano had been denied his. When Tony Pro asked Hoffa to use his clout to force the IBT to reconsider their decision, Hoffa refused, and Provenzano became furious. Hoffa in turn began berating Provenzano and mob bosses in general for his own troubles. The two men reportedly got into a brawl in a prison workshop. When he was released, Provenzano went from being a Hoffa loyalist to a fierce foe, badmouthing Jimmy to other mobsters.

Frank Fitzsimmons might have preferred to see Hoffa remain in Lewisburg, but he was under pressure from Jimmy's family and friends to get him out. Hoffa's release under the provision prohibiting him from holding office until 1980 gave Fitzsimmons the best of both worlds: Hoffa out of jail but also out of union office. How Fitzsimmons managed to pull off such a deal has been the subject of speculation. In his 1978 book on the Teamsters, Steve Brill wrote that sources close to Allen Dorfman and Tony Provenzano told him that each man collected half a million dollars and arranged to have it delivered to Chuck Colson. In return, President Nixon was to impose restrictions on Hoffa's release and grant a few other favors as well. Colson always denied the allegation, and no evidence has been produced to support it.[1] The IBT supported Nixon in the 1972 presidential election, and Fitzsimmons remained loyal to him throughout the Watergate investigation. When Chuck Colson left the White House, Fitzsimmons removed the union's legal business from Edward Bennett Williams's firm and gave it to the one that Colson joined.

In 1973 Hoffa sued to invalidate the parole restrictions that forbade him to hold union office, on the grounds that the president's imposition of additional penalties on a judicial sentence was a violation of the Separation of Powers provision of the Constitution. A worried Fitzsimmons began moving to block Hoffa from returning. To run for Teamster president, Hoffa

1 On one Oval Office tape, when an aide estimates that it would take $1 million to keep the Watergate burglars from talking, Nixon mentions that he knows a source that could easily provide the money. Some people have inferred that he was talking about the IBT.

would have to hold union office. Dave Johnson, the head of Jimmy's old Local 299 in Detroit, was a loyal supporter who could be depended upon to appoint him to a post such as business agent whenever the restrictions were lifted. Johnson had even postponed his retirement in order to stick around and help Jimmy. As an inducement for him to depart, shots were fired at Johnson's office window and a boat he owned was blown up. In 1974 Fitzsimmons' son Richard challenged Johnson for the presidency of the local. The acrimony generated by the contest drew so much unfavorable publicity that a compromise was reached, whereby Johnson would remain as president and young Fitzsimmons would be designated vice president of the local. The Hoffa side could play rough too: In June 1975, Richard Fitzsimmons' car was blown up while he was drinking in a nearby bar.

After Gerald Ford succeeded Nixon he appointed Edward Levi, the president of the University of Chicago and former dean of its law school, to be his attorney general. Levi was a man impervious to political influence. In 1975 rumors began to circulate that Department of Justice lawyers who reviewed Hoffa's pardon agreement had concluded that the restrictions were in fact unconstitutional. As the prospect of Hoffa's return became more likely, mob bosses such as Tony Giacalone and Russ Bufalino sought to persuade him to back off. Both men were initially restrained in their arguments. They pointed out that Jimmy was sixty-two years old and well fixed financially: He should go off and enjoy himself. In contrast, Hoffa's erstwhile jail buddy Tony Provenzano threatened not only to tear Jimmy's guts out but to kidnap his little granddaughter. Hoffa refused to listen to pleas or threats, and warned the mobsters that when he returned to the IBT and got hold of the Teamster records, he would expose their crooked dealings.

For all his street smarts, Hoffa seemingly never really understood the world of the American Mafia. He thought they would not dare to kill him. If the issue were simply that his return would cost them some money through the loss of their rackets, they might indeed have hesitated to murder someone so prominent. But when he threatened to expose their crimes—in effect, to put them in jail—killing him became a matter of their own survival. If the mob could discuss murdering a sitting president of the United States because his brother, the attorney general, was a threat to them, they would hardly shrink from killing an ex-president of the

Teamsters union. With the situation so tense, some of Jimmy's friends advised him to carry a gun or surround himself with bodyguards, but he refused. He drove to the Red Fox alone and unarmed.

More than thirty years after the fact, precise details of Hoffa's disappearance are still not fully known, though there is agreement among most investigators on the basic scenario. At the outset the two leading suspects in the case were Tony Pro, who was known to be Hoffa's bitter enemy, and Tony Jack, who had been the most active in trying to dissuade Jimmy from seeking to regain the IBT presidency. In addition, mob protocol required that a hit on Hoffa in Detroit be approved by the local boss, Joe Zerilli, whose interests Giacalone represented. Both Tonys had alibis that were verified by the FBI. On the afternoon of the thirtieth, Provenzano was playing cards in Local 560's headquarters in Union City, New Jersey. Giacalone spent the afternoon at a club in Detroit, where he seemed to go out of his way to call attention to his presence (for instance, though there was a clock on the wall, he continually asked people what time it was).

In 1978 Steve Brill laid out an account of the case, which appears to have been based on authoritative information. According to Brill, Hoffa drove to the Red Fox expecting to be picked up by Giacalone and taken to a meeting with Provenzano. At the restaurant he supposedly entered a car driven by his foster son, Chuckie O'Brien, whose mother had once been Hoffa's girlfriend.[2] For a time after the death of her husband, she and Chuckie had lived with the Hoffas. During that period she reportedly kept company with Tony Giacalone. O'Brien addressed Jimmy as "Dad" and called Giacalone "Uncle Tony." By 1975, however, O'Brien was on the outs with Hoffa. After Jimmy's wife and son were fired from union positions, Chuckie was spared because he pledged loyalty to Fitzsimmons. According to Brill, there were two other men in the car, Sal Briguglio and either his brother Gabe or Tom Andretta. All three were lieutenants of Tony Provenzano and were thought to have arrived from Detroit that day by chartered plane, two of them going to the Red Fox while the other remained at the

---

2 The car, a maroon Mercury, was owned by Tony Jack's son Joe and had been lent to O'Brien. Trained dogs found Hoffa's scent in the area of the Red Fox parking lot, where witnesses had reported seeing Hoffa in the Mercury. In 2001, DNA tests, which were not available in 1975, also confirmed Hoffa's presence in the vehicle.

airport. In Brill's narrative, one of Provenzano's men knocked Jimmy out with a gun butt in the backseat of the car. They then drove him to the place where he was killed and his body disposed of—possibly by Frank Sheeran, a Delaware Teamster official. Additional sanction for the murder came from Russ Bufalino, who, in company with Sheeran, was due in Detroit on August 1 to attend the wedding of a friend's daughter.[3]

While agreeing on the previous general outline, most journalists and investigators have differed on certain specifics. FBI agents doubt that Hoffa was knocked unconscious in the car. Rather, they believe he was driven to the building where he was killed and entered it unaware of what was about to happen. Some investigators assign a role in the case to Tony Jack's brother Vito, who, as Jim Esposito has observed, "was as invisible that day as Tony was visible." Some would also include on the suspect list a self-confessed hit man, Charles Allen, who had been in prison with Hoffa.

Other scenarios have been largely discounted. The 1992 movie *Hoffa* depicts him being shot to death while sitting in his car in the parking lot of a small diner, after which his body was taken away in a truck by a backup team. The Red Fox was a large upscale restaurant, and a shooting and abduction on its grounds in broad daylight would have attracted attention. Stories that Hoffa's body was flown out of Detroit seem equally unlikely. Over the years various individuals have claimed to know where Hoffa's body could be found. A professional con man named Harry Haler duped investigators for a Senate committee into digging up fields in the vicinity of Pontiac, Michigan. CBS News laid out $10,000 to explore the ocean bed near Key West, Florida. Some tipsters claimed that the body was shipped to New Jersey in oil drums and buried in the Meadowlands. The FBI believes that Hoffa's body was compacted or otherwise disposed of in Detroit, probably at a sanitation firm the local mob used for such purposes.

With Hoffa gone, Frank Fitzsimmons was easily reelected president of the IBT in 1976. Supposedly he confided to intimates that he had really wanted

---

3 In 2004 a published account claimed that before his death, Frank Sheeran admitted killing Hoffa at a house in Detroit. However, DNA tests on the house in 2005 revealed no traces of blood.

to retire, but remained in office at the mob's insistence. Beset by federal law enforcement pressure over Teamster corruption and suspicion that he may have been involved in the Hoffa disappearance, Fitzsimmons' health began to decline. He spent even more time traveling around the country playing golf. His most likely successor was Roy Williams of Kansas City, whose career had been sponsored by Nick Civella. Williams and Civella had met back in the early 1950s when they both headed Democratic political clubs. Williams would later claim that at the time he did not know of Civella's mob affiliations; if so he was one of the few people in Kansas City politics who didn't. Williams also told a story of his children being threatened when he resisted mob penetration of the local. According to him, when he consulted Hoffa he was advised to go along.[4] Williams had been an interstate truck driver, hauling livestock from Missouri to the Chicago stockyards. As a soldier in World War II, he had been awarded the Silver Star for gallantry. After the war he began working as a union official. It was Williams who took Hoffa to the parking lot at Soldier Field in Chicago and taught him to drive an eighteen-wheeler so that Jimmy could be one of the boys. And Williams had been instrumental in approving the casino loans, for which he received $1,500 a month from the skim. Like Fitzsimmons, Williams was not a workaholic. He chose to spend a great deal of time at his country estate. In mob circles, his preference for the rural life earned him the sarcastic nickname "the Rancher."

A second rising star of the IBT was Jackie Presser, who replaced his father, Bill, in 1976 as international vice president, head of the Ohio Teamsters, and a pension fund trustee. He was also named national director of communications for the union, with a combined annual salary of $270,000. Bill Presser's mob connections had been so well known that it was commonly remarked that his Cleveland IBT Joint Council was "a Who's Who of organized crime." Jackie owed his career to his father (although his work experience after dropping out of school in the eighth grade was largely confined to membership in an interstate auto theft gang). He was made business agent for the Hotel and Restaurant Workers Local in Cleveland in

---

4 Stories about innocents who unknowingly get mixed up with mobsters and are then forced to accept career advancement and cash largess must be received with considerable skepticism.

1947 at age twenty. Mostly the job involved union organizing via strong-arm tactics, and settling labor-management disputes in return for a payoff. Within a few years Jackie was made president of the local. Despite his girth (he weighed 300 pounds) and fondness for orange suits with green shirts and ties that gave him the appearance of a Halloween pumpkin, Jackie was a Lothario, managing to collect a string of wives and mistresses. In 1957 he was removed for using union funds to pay his personal expenses.

After Jackie was booted from the union, Bill Presser arranged for him to receive a Teamster loan to build an entertainment complex. By the mid-'60s it had failed. So forty-year-old Jackie was made secretary-treasurer of a newly chartered Teamsters local, created by raiding other locals. His union job brought him into contact with Tony Hughes (Uzzi), an ex-prizefighter and mob associate who became Jackie's close associate. In the '70s, as Presser became a man of substance, he began to dress like a banker and involve himself in civic affairs. He also fancied himself a journalist and PR expert, editing the monthly *Ohio Teamsters,* a house organ put out by his father's union.

The world of labor racketeering in which the Pressers moved was a dangerous place. One problem was the instability of the Cleveland mob family to which they were ultimately beholden. John Scalish had been the boss since the late '40s, when there were about sixty made members in the family. By the mid-'70s the number had dwindled to around twenty, because Scalish did not induct replacements when older members died off. It was his way of ensuring that the money coming in would be kept in just a few hands, and one of the reasons that Scalish himself was very wealthy. Contented with things as they were, Scalish even allowed nonfamily members to run gambling operations without paying the street tax. But with no new blood, there was a dearth of successors if anything should happen to him. The underboss of the family was nearing ninety, and the captains were mostly senior citizens. Scalish himself was beset by serious health problems, and it was clear to everyone that he could not last much longer. The stage was set for a leadership struggle. Jackie Presser could never be sure which faction would win, and how he would stand with them.

The FBI was threatening Presser from the other direction. In the late '60s an agent named Marty McCann began contriving occasions to bump into Tony Hughes, with a view toward making him an informer. About that time a loan shark Hughes collected for got on the wrong side of the Cleveland mob. One day when the shark was playing golf at a suburban country club, a sniper with a rifle picked him off at the sixteenth tee. Shaken, Hughes agreed to accept McCann's proposal. Through Hughes, McCann was also able to recruit Presser as a top echelon informer, supplying information on high-ranking mobsters. Presser was so special he was not given the usual informer number—whereas Hughes was CV (Cleveland office) 882 TE (Top Echelon), Presser was given the code name "Tailor" and his file was kept at Washington headquarters.[5] It was a fortuitous decision, because a civilian clerk in the Cleveland FBI office would later steal the informer list and sell it to some mob guys, one of whom was a man who had served twenty years for killing two Cleveland cops. Becoming an informer gave Jackie the usual insurance policy in the event that criminal charges were brought against him. As long as he kept supplying information, the FBI would not be eager to see him go to jail. In his case, it also provided life insurance. The Bureau had so many informants, bugs, and wiretaps in Cleveland that they were usually able to pick up advance warning if someone was falling afoul of the mob bosses. In that case they could alert Presser and through their contacts move to abort the hit.

In 1976 John Scalish died after an unsuccessful operation, and as predicted, war broke out between two mob factions. One group was the Scalish supporters headed by James Licavoli, a.k.a. Jack White, who had reluctantly agreed to take the top job. Another member of this group was Maishe Rockman, the family's liaison in the Vegas skim. Rockman was part of both Cleveland mob worlds. Like the Pressers, he came from the Jewish organized crime milieu, and as a brother-in-law of Scalish he was an honorary mafioso. The rival group was led by Teamsters official John Nardi and an odd character named Danny Greene, who was active in waterfront unions. A sort of professional Irishman, the flamboyant red-headed Greene habitually wore a green suit, drove a green car, and wrote in green ink. His crew was a collection of Irish hoodlums and Hell's Angels biker types. The first time Jimmy Hoffa met Greene, he commented that

5 After a while, FBI officials realized that Tailor—a related occupation to a presser—was a bit obvious as a code name, and it was changed to Alpro.

there was something wrong with the guy and warned his followers to keep away from him. It was good advice—Greene was also an FBI informant.

Thirty-seven bombs exploded in the Cleveland mob war over the course of 1977, and Danny Greene was a prime target of attack. He was a man of great self-confidence and considerable luck: In an earlier war, a bomb had blown Greene and his girlfriend from their second-floor bedroom into the basement, but both emerged unscathed. Now, after each unsuccessful attempt he would go on TV and challenge his opponents to "come and get me." In one instance, Greene was strolling through a park when a sniper fired at him from a car. He missed, but Greene got off a lucky return shot, which killed his assailant. The shooting was ruled justifiable homicide.

Jackie Presser cast his lot with Licavoli and Rockman's group, though he constantly worried that he might have chosen the wrong side. In May 1977, Greene's partner, John Nardi, was blown up by a remote-controlled bomb as he was getting into his vehicle in the parking lot of the Cleveland Teamsters headquarters. Next, the Licavoli group took a page from the FBI and put a tap on Danny Greene's phone. They overheard his girlfriend making a dental appointment for him, and in October Greene was killed by a remote-controlled car bomb after leaving the dentist's office. When the cops got to the scene they literally could only pick up the pieces. A witness took down the bomber's license and the police captured him. After the suspect turned government witness, Licavoli and the other top bosses were charged with murder in state court. Though some underlings were convicted, the bosses were acquitted.

In 1980, presidential candidate Ronald Reagan came out against deregulation of the trucking industry, and Presser persuaded the IBT to endorse him. When he was elected, Reagan chose Presser to be a member of his transition team. It was the beginning of another close relationship between the White House and the IBT. Though the president publicly described organized crime as "the evil enemy within," somehow Presser was not included in that category.[6] It was the same story as in the Nixon era: A Republican administration with few friends in the labor movement could not resist the prospect of winning support from a powerful union.

6 The president's phrase was a combination of his own description of the Soviet Union as "the Evil Empire," and the title of Robert Kennedy's book *The Enemy Within*.

Presser had come a long way in just a few years, and he now began to see himself as a potential general president of the IBT. In 1981 it was clear that Frank Fitzsimmons' health would prevent him from standing for re-election at the upcoming Teamsters convention. The favorite to succeed him was Roy Williams. As Hoffa had done with Dave Beck, Jackie began supplying the FBI with information on Williams, including some that helped them to snare Williams and Allen Dorfman in the Pendorf investigation. When Fitzsimmons died in office in May, Presser threw his support to Williams—by then under indictment in Pendorf—knowing he would probably not be around for long.

As Presser came close to realizing his dream of being IBT president, new troubles developed. In August 1981 the Cleveland *Plain Dealer* published an article declaring that he was a government informant. The story put Presser in great danger. If his mob backers believed it, they would try to kill him. Under the circumstances, Jackie had two choices: Enter the witness protection program, which would mean the end of his union career, or deny the allegation and try to persuade his mob allies to believe him. Presser chose the latter option. It was the act of a man who had been getting away with a triple life for nearly a decade. In public, he posed as an upstanding union leader. In private, he was both a pawn of organized crime and an FBI informer.

Mob bosses had a general understanding of how the news business worked. A major paper like the *Plain Dealer* could not publish such a story without extensive research, thorough checking by editors, and a review by the corporation's lawyers. A mere "I swear it's a lie" from Presser would hardly be sufficient to overcome a Mafia death sentence. Jackie turned to Maishe Rockman, a friend of the Pressers for decades. Rockman knew that Bill Presser (who had died just a month earlier) had always been a standup guy, and he couldn't believe Bill's son was an informer. Nevertheless, he too realized that mere denial would not be enough to keep Jackie healthy. Since John Scalish's death, Cleveland was represented on the commission by Tony Salerno of New York's Genovese family; Maishe reached out to him. Salerno trusted Rockman, and he contacted a man who sometimes worked miracles—lawyer Roy Cohn. Cohn had gained both fame and infamy in the 1950s as chief counsel to Senator Joe McCarthy's Red-hunting committee. It turned out that Cohn was able to obtain a front-page retraction of the charges. Many of the papers' reporters were so outraged that they established an informational picket line outside the *Plain Dealer* building, but the retraction was sufficient to restore Presser's standing with the mob.

A companion article to the informer piece had accused Jackie of taking kickbacks from a public relations firm that received a contract from the IBT. IRS agents had tried to bring a case against him in the 1970s for doing so, but the Department of Justice declined prosecution because it was largely based on the word of Harry Haler, the career con man whose scams included claiming to know where Jimmy Hoffa was buried. In Haler's long record of criminal conduct, one incident stood out to Justice Department lawyers: He had once taken money from a man under federal investigation, promising he could get the charges dropped in return. Though not a lawyer, he managed to secure an appointment with the chief of the organized crime section of the DOJ. While alone in the man's office, Haler had stolen some official stationery. He prepared a letter stating that the charges would be dropped, and forged the section chief's signature to it. Putting Haler on the stand would allow defense attorneys to have a field day impeaching his credibility and embarrassing the Department of Justice.

After Haler's name surfaced in the *Plain Dealer* story, he was contacted by agents of the Department of Labor who were already investigating Presser. From leads he supplied them, they began to develop a case based on Presser allowing relatives and friends like Tony Hughes to hold no-show jobs in his Cleveland Teamster local. Over the years the Department of Labor had frequently been accused of ignoring union corruption. On the labor beat, DOL was the good cop and DOJ the bad cop. In 1978, Congress passed a law requiring cabinet departments to appoint inspectors general to ferret out misconduct. Now the Labor inspector general's office sought to refute the department's critics by going all-out in an investigation of Jackie Presser, a major target. The DOL investigation added to an already strained situation in the Cleveland federal law enforcement community. The FBI and the local strike force were not on good terms, so the Bureau had not told the prosecutors that Presser was an informant, adhering to the maxim that the fewer people who know a secret, the more likely it is to be kept. When DOL agents investigating Presser approached the FBI, they were not told of his status either. The DOL investigators were new kids on the block and they did not carry firearms, which in the culture of the law enforcement world meant they weren't really cops. The Bureau declined to take them into their confidence. Later, in testimony before a U.S. Senate committee, a witness alleged that an FBI agent had referred to the DOL agents as "a couple of clowns who couldn't even carry a gun." When Presser expressed concern about the DOL investigation, his FBI handlers supposedly assured him that no charges would be brought against him.

Although the Senate Subcommittee on Investigations (whose previous head had been John McClellan) would be highly critical of the FBI, looking at the big picture, the Bureau's position becomes understandable. For a quarter of a century it had been investigating organized crime's relationship with the IBT. Some of the most important cases in the history of the FBI had been developed in connection with the IBT/OC relationship. Now the FBI had an investigator's dream situation: An organized crime associate was about to become head of the target organization. Was he to be sacrificed over a few no-show jobs in a union local? If Presser were slated to take over an undercover Soviet spy network, the FBI would undoubtedly be able to block an IRS criminal prosecution against him for tax evasion. The difference was that international espionage was not viewed the same way as organized crime. In the eyes of some government officials, the FBI was obstructing justice.

At higher levels, broad governmental policy considerations had to be taken into account. If Presser became IBT president and his informant status were later revealed, the FBI could be accused of running the union. The rank and file of the Teamsters and industry employers might then argue that the IBT's position on wage negotiations or other matters was dictated by the government. In addition, given Presser's relationship with the Reagan administration, the Bureau could be accused of having a spy in the White House. In 1983, after his conviction in Pendorf, Roy Williams resigned and Presser was named as his successor. FBI Director William Webster ruled that Presser could no longer be given assignments by the Bureau, but his handlers were still permitted to receive information from him.

In 1984 the IBT backed the reelection of President Ronald Reagan. Presser even rigged a poll of union members to show their support for the president when the ballots cast had actually favored Walter Mondale. In 1985, a presidential commission appointed by President Reagan to investigate organized crime criticized his administration's ties to Presser. The mounting criticism of Presser and the IBT led to a reversal of administration policy. The Department of Justice indicted Presser for the no-show jobs. His FBI handler at the time was Special Agent Robert Friedrick, head of the Cleveland organized crime squad, an Annapolis graduate and Vietnam veteran who also commanded the office's SWAT team. He was known as a man of high integrity. While some investigators are able to keep their distance from informers, a man with Friedrick's background might very well have seen the situation in military terms, akin to an officer sending a spy on a dangerous mission. This seems borne out by his later explanation, "When you are in combat with someone you become close to them." Friedrick allegedly told prosecutors that the FBI had authorized Presser to allow the no-show jobs as part of their investigation. The prosecutors did not accept this claim, and Friedrick was fired from the Bureau and indicted for obstructing justice. (A judge later dismissed the charges on the grounds that Friedrick believed that a statement he gave had been made under a grant of immunity.)

When the Senate Subcommittee on Investigations examined the Presser affair, the respected senator Sam Nunn complained, "Lo and behold, we now find that the very people who were complaining about lack of Labor help back five, six, seven years ago . . . are now doing what they can to stifle the Labor Department and to prevent them from being effective in law-enforcement." A *Washington Post* editorial declared:

> We are led to believe that Mr. Presser was some kind of informant for the FBI and that indicting him would jeopardize some other—more important?—cases. But who authorized this arrangement and why didn't the strike force know about it?

At the 1986 Teamsters convention held while he was under indictment, Presser, the self-styled public relations expert, was rolled in on a red chariot by Teamsters dressed as Roman soldiers. When a picture of the spectacle appeared in newspapers, it was viewed as an example of the IBT leadership's excess and arrogance. Presser would die in office in 1988, still under indictment.

Despite many problems, Cleveland became one of the success stories of the federal government's war on the mob. In the 1970s, Jimmy "The Weasel" Fratianno, an ex-Clevelander who functioned as the Mafia's West Coast enforcer, became acting boss of the L.A. family. Even before he got the top job, Fratianno decided to buy some insurance and began supplying information to the FBI. At the time he was not the only California mafioso doing so. Tony "Bomp" Bompensiero, boss of San Diego, had been giving information to the Bureau since the mid-'60s. When Jimmy Licavoli was challenged by the Nardi-Greene faction after Scalish's death, Fratianno was called back to his hometown to help the regulars. While he was there he learned about the corrupt FBI clerk who was supplying names of informants to the Cleveland mob. Though she had not yet obtained Jimmy's identity, she did have Bompensiero's. Shortly afterward, Bomp was cut down by a shotgun blast, and Jimmy knew it was only a matter of time until he too was outed and murdered.

Over the previous three years, Fratianno had given the FBI tidbits for which he received total payments of $16,000. Now he began funneling information to the Bureau regularly. It was his tip that led to the arrest of the corrupt clerk. But he still tried to play games, refusing to admit his role in the killings of Nardi and Greene. Only after the FBI arrested him on two counts of conspiracy to commit murder did he agree to enter the government witness program and become a full-time informant. In a federal trial, Licavoli and other bosses were convicted of the Nardi and Greene murders based upon information from Fratianno and other informers. Cleveland underboss Angelo Lonardo, who was sent to prison, opted to secure his freedom by testifying for the government at various trials and committee hearings. An even greater victory was scored nationally, when the United States government brought a civil suit against the IBT under the Racketeer Influenced and Corrupt Organizations Law (RICO). Despite the fact that the IBT was headquartered in Washington, D.C., and much of its criminal activity had revolved around Dorfman in Chicago, Hoffa in Detroit, Williams in Kansas City, and Presser in Cleveland, the case was filed in the Southern District of New York. Rudy Giuliani, the U.S. attorney there, was known as a man who would tolerate no nonsense and insisted that all the agencies involved in a case work as a team (with himself as captain). The prospect of a government takeover of the Teamsters brought forth opposition from a number of powerful interests. The AFL-CIO, which had expelled the IBT thirty years earlier, took it back in a gesture of union solidarity. Presidential candidates as diverse as Jack Kemp, Al Haig, and Jesse Jackson announced their opposition to the takeover. At first the IBT executive board put up a fight, but faced with the prospect of extensive individual civil liability, they agreed to accept supervision by monitors appointed by the government.

For more than thirty years, IBT executives had ridden roughshod over members. Now the shoe would be on the other foot. Judge David Edelstein (in whose court the suit had been brought) appointed former New Jersey U.S. attorney Frederick Lacey, the man who had cleaned up Newark in the 1970s, as an independent administrator of the union with the same powers as the IBT president and executive board. Other monitors were appointed to conduct investigations or to oversee individual locals. At the outset, the IBT sought to limit the monitors' authority, filing suits in federal courts around the country. The effort to bog the government down in a multiplicity of cases was defeated, and all the suits were consolidated in Judge Edelstein's court. The IBT executive board believed that charges would not be brought for actions predating the consent decree, but this was not the monitors' view. Officials were dismissed or punished for practices that had previously been widespread, such as using union funds to pay personal expenses or to purchase a new car as a gift for a retiring officer. Union officials who associated with organized crime figures were removed from their posts. When they appealed the monitors' decisions to Judge Edelstein, he usually upheld them—and in some cases increased the penalties. When one union official filed suit against a monitor, the judge held him in contempt of court.

Under the consent decree all union officers had to be elected by the vote of the rank and file. In 1991 Jimmy's son James P. Hoffa, who had served as a lawyer for the union for twenty-two years, sought to run for president of the IBT. Judge Edelstein ruled that he did not meet the requirements of two years' service as a Teamster, and a New York union official named Ron Carey was elected. Though he was hailed as a reformer, Carey's regime would eventually end in scandal leading to his removal from office. In 1999 young Hoffa would be elected to head the union.

No one has ever been charged with murdering Jimmy Hoffa, though a number of suspects were convicted of other crimes. In 1976, Tony Provenzano and Sal Briguglio were indicted for a 1961 murder in New York. Provenzano was given a life sentence and Briguglio was killed before he could be tried, possibly because someone thought he was about to break down and confess his role in the Hoffa disappearance. Also in 1976, Tony Giacalone was convicted of income tax fraud and given a ten-year sentence. The next year, Russell Bufalino was convicted of extortion and sentenced to jail for four years. After he got out in 1981, he was found guilty of plotting a murder and given a fifteen-year sentence (he was later transferred to a nursing home, where he died at the age of ninety). Frank Sheeran served prison terms on various charges. As recently as May 2006, the FBI dug up a farm seventeen miles from the Red Fox restaurant on a tip that Hoffa's remains were buried there. Although they found nothing, a Bureau spokesperson said the investigation would continue. She noted, "There are still possible defendants, and they know who they are."

In the second half of the twentieth century, significant resources of the strongest union in the United States were wasted on kickbacks to mobsters, loans to organized-crime-backed enterprises like casinos, and battles with the United States government. The Teamsters' problems coincided with, and contributed to, the decline of union membership and influence. In the 1950s one out of three American workers belonged to a union. By 2000 the figure was one out of eight. A generation earlier, AFL-CIO president George Meany was one of the most powerful men in America. Few would make similar claims about his successors.

At the time of his disappearance, Jimmy Hoffa was telling everyone that he was going to expose the gangsters and drive them out of the IBT. Accomplishing that would have required him to cooperate with the United States government, and considering his antipathy toward that quarter, it is not clear whether he would have made good on his threats. But the Mafia believed he would, which is undoubtedly why he was killed. In his last years, Hoffa may well have had second thoughts about his 1957 dinner with Robert Kennedy that went so badly. As it turned out, he probably had more in common with Kennedy than he did with Tony Jack or Tony Pro. Despite their dislike of each other, the Harvard rich kid and the rough-hewn union leader were in some ways more alike than either supposed. In politics, Kennedy championed the underdog, not the fat cats. Giacalone's and Provenzano's commitment was strictly to their own pockets. Hoffa might have taken kickbacks, but he was always available to any truck driver with a problem. If Hoffa and his successors had not been aligned with organized crime, the story of the labor movement in the second half of the twentieth century might have been very different. The Mafia's infil-tration of the IBT changed the course of American history.

. . .

CHAPTER 10

FROM THE FRENCH CONNECTION TO THE PIZZA CONNECTION: DRUGS, THE MAFIA, AND ITS WOULD-BE SUCCESSORS

The second half of the twentieth century witnessed constant change in American institutions. In the 1960s, even bastions of tradition like Ivy League schools broke sharply with the past. Among the very few organizations that retained their old-fashioned way of doing things was the American Mafia.

On an afternoon in July of 1979, Carmine Galante, pretender to the title of boss of the Bonanno family, was dining on the patio of Joe and Mary's Restaurant in an out-of-the-way section of Brooklyn. At the table with him were two bodyguards, one of his drug dealers, and the restaurant owner. Around 2:45 P.M., while waiting for his coffee and dessert, Galante lit up a cigar. Suddenly three men in ski masks burst in, shot and killed Carmine and two of his companions, and wounded the restaurant owner's son. When the cops arrived, Galante was lying on the floor with the cigar still clenched between his teeth.[1] Somehow the bodyguards had emerged unscathed.

To anyone familiar with the history of the American Mafia, Galante's murder had a familiar ring. Forty-eight years earlier, in another out-of-the-way Brooklyn restaurant, Joe "The Boss" Masseria had been lunching with

---

1 Most New York mob watchers believe the cigar was planted in his mouth by photographers to create a more dramatic picture.

his lieutenant, Lucky Luciano. After Lucky excused himself to go to the men's room, four gunmen entered and killed Masseria. Lucky emerged unharmed, and when questioned by cops could only moan, "Who would want to kill poor Joe?" Detectives suspected that he could find the answer by looking in the mirror. Like Masseria's, Galante's murder looked to be a classic setup. The investigation of the case also demonstrated that a Bonanno family tradition was still being maintained: obtaining recruits from the old country. Galante had formed a palace guard of young gangsters from Sicily known as "zips."

Carmine "Lilo" (Little Cigar) Galante was sixty-nine at the time of his murder. He was born in East Harlem of parents who had emigrated from the Sicilian Mafia stronghold of Castellammare del Golfo. In his teens Galante became a member of a gang led by Joe Bonanno, who had come to New York from Castellammare in 1924. Back then it was Castellammare men, under Sal Maranzano, who provided the principal opposition to Boss Masseria.[2] Galante missed the mob war. While fleeing a holdup in 1930, he shot at a detective, missed, and hit a six-year-old girl. He spent the next nine years in prison. Upon his release he rejoined Bonanno's family, where he worked under capo Frank Garofalo, another Castellammare man.

In 1943 Galante made the big time when he became the leading suspect in the murder of the world-famous anarchist Carlo Tresca. At 9:30 on the night of January 11, Tresca was shot and killed on a Lower Manhattan street by an assailant who fled in a dark sedan. About ninety minutes before the hit occurred and a mile away, Galante had made his weekly report to his parole officer. When he left, another officer assigned to follow him saw Galante entering a black sedan, license IC9272. Shortly after midnight a black 1938 Ford with that license number was found abandoned a few blocks from the scene of Tresca's murder. The victim had been an outspoken antifascist and was a vociferous opponent of Mussolini. The talk on the street was that the hit had been carried out at the request of Vito Genovese in an attempt to curry favor with Il Duce, though there were also other scenarios and suspects. Tresca's many influential leftist friends demanded that his killer be brought to justice, but no case was ever made

2 Though Masseria's assassins were the Neapolitans Joe Adonis and Vito Genovese, the Calabrian Albert Anastasia, and the Jewish Bugsy Siegel.

against Galante. A jailhouse informer put in a cell with him allegedly obtained a confession, but it could not be used because the informer had already testified in so many cases that the courts would no longer accept his word.[3] Galante was turned loose.

After Genovese returned to New York in 1945, he picked up where he had left off at the time of his flight, importing heroin from Italy to distribute in the United States. Drug trafficking was always the area where relations between the Italian and American Mafias were the closest. This led some law enforcement officials wrongly to conclude that the two were a single organization. Galante became one of Genovese's lieutenants, and from that time on they were close associates. In 1956 Bonanno and Galante met with Joe Barbara upstate in Binghamton to discuss drugs. Afterward Galante, riding with Garofalo, had his run-in with New York State police sergeant Croswell. In October 1957, Bonanno, Galante, and other American importers met with Lucky Luciano and Sicilian suppliers in Palermo. The following month they were slated to report to their American Mafia colleagues at the Apalachin conference. When the Genovese drug operation was taken down in 1959, Galante was one of those indicted. After a time in hiding he was apprehended. It took a while to convict him—one attempt ended in a mistrial when the jury foreman mysteriously fell down a flight of stairs and broke his back. Eventually Galante was convicted and sent to the federal penitentiary at Lewisburg, Pennsylvania, where he served twelve years. While there he bossed the Mafia inmates and helped protect Jimmy Hoffa from other cons. Released in 1974, he returned to the drug business. It was Galante who is reputed to have invented the notorious "black man test." In order to determine the quality of a quantity of heroin, an African-American addict would be kidnapped and injected with a double bag; if he became comatose within a specified time, the narcotic was judged to be of the correct purity. In 1977, Galante was charged with violating parole by associating with known gangsters. He spent some time in and out of jail until his lawyer, Roy Cohn, managed to get the charges dropped. His legal troubles resolved, Lilo spent the two years leading up to his murder plunged back into international drug trafficking. Unlike

3 The informer provided the model for the Nick Bianco character, played by Victor Mature, in the 1948 movie *Kiss of Death*.

previous big-name mob hits like Joe Masseria's, this one would be solved. Law enforcement was learning how to combat the Mafia. It was even putting its own agents inside the organization, including one in the Bonanno family.

Drug dealing was always controversial within the Mafia. Some bosses, like Frank Costello, forbade their members to get involved. Drugs carried a stigma that would make Costello's many political friends wary of doing favors for the mob. Frank himself didn't care who knew about his gambling interests, but when some overzealous lawmen accused him of being a drug trafficker he volunteered to testify before a grand jury, without immunity, to deny the charge. His offer was not accepted, because higher authorities knew he was clean. However, the fact that a boss might be against drugs did not mean that all family members would share his scruples. Genovese paid no attention to Costello's directives. Joe Bonanno liked to have it both ways. He piously declared that his family was not mixed up in drug trafficking. In the 1980s, after Bonanno wrote his autobiography, which contained his claim of not being involved in drugs, a Bonanno capo scornfully told a DEA agent, "He was the one who started it." When Bonanno repeated his denial on *60 Minutes,* the next day Ducks Corallo was heard on a police bug scoffingly saying "He [Bonanno] was the biggest drug dealer of them all." In some families drug dealing was carried on "off the books." Others justified the business on the grounds that the addict population was mostly made up of minorities. Attitudes like that of Tommy Lucchese, who told Costello that heroin was "only going into the veins of niggers," were common. On the other hand, Tony Accardo made drug dealing a capital offense for members of the Chicago Outfit. Even so, some members of Accardo's family were able to get away with drug-related activities. Bosses were realistic. There was too much money to be made in narcotics. An absolute across-the-board ban might have caused some of the troops to revolt or defect to another leader who, rich with drug money, could become a serious rival.

In the 1950s the principal drug smuggling operation was the so-called "French Connection." The morphine component of Turkish opium was shipped to laboratories in Marseille to be refined into heroin. From there it was smuggled into the United States through way stations like Montréal, where Carmine Galante helped establish relationships with French-Canadian organized crime gangs. A family like the Luccheses would then further refine the product. Their base in the Pleasant Avenue neighborhood of Manhattan's East Harlem was dotted with apartments where crews of women worked in the nude—to prevent them from secreting any of the powder—diluting the heroin with milk sugar and placing it in plastic bags. It was then sold on the street for a nickel or a dime ($5 or $10). A kilo purchased for $30,000 from the French suppliers, after being cut, could bring ten to twenty times that amount on the streets of New York.

At the beginning of the 1950s, sentences for drug trafficking were still relatively light. In 1956, through the efforts of federal narcotics commissioner Harry Anslinger, Congress passed the Narcotic Control Act, which imposed ten to twenty years for a first offense and twenty to forty for the second. Penalties of that magnitude provided a powerful incentive for individuals to turn informer, which was another reason some bosses did not want their members to become involved in drugs. Despite the risks, the narcotics business took off in the 1960s. In addition to the ghetto clientele, drugs also returned to the widespread popularity they had enjoyed in the Roaring Twenties, this time as part of the counterculture. Between 1960 and 1970 it is estimated that the number of heroin addicts in the United States grew from fifty thousand to half a million. Eighty percent of the supply was controlled by the American Mafia.

If drugs were a lucrative business for the dealers, they also proved profitable for some law enforcers. A drug dealer caught with a load of heroin faced twenty years in jail and a loss of product that might run into the millions. Under the circumstances, a $50,000 bribe was a drop in the bucket. In 1962, Commissioner Anslinger retired at the compulsory age of seventy (only J. Edgar Hoover was able to secure a waiver when he reached that milestone). In Anslinger's time, his bureau had been small enough that he could infuse it with his own stern morality. Expansion of federal and local narcotics enforcement brought in inexperienced people, some of whom succumbed to temptation. In the late '60s, a number of agents in the New York FBN office were found to be taking bribes. At the heart of the scandal was the usual story: Investigators got too close to their informants and started doing business with them.

When President Nixon declared a war on drugs, he was looking for quick results in the form of increased arrests, which it was expected would lower crime rates before the 1972 election. The president issued an executive order creating the Office of Drug Abuse Law Enforcement (ODALE), which was assigned personnel from the FBN (by then renamed the Bureau of Narcotics and Dangerous Drugs, BNDD), Customs, and IRS agents, as well as local police and intelligence analysts from the Defense Department and the CIA. ODALE task forces were deployed to thirty-three cities to make street-level arrests, using tactics like "no knock" raids. Instead of pounding on the door, shouting "police," and demanding entrance, raiders would announce their presence by smashing the door down and entering with guns drawn. ODALE became operational at the beginning of 1972, and soon precipitated a disaster that destroyed the agency. In Collinsville, Illinois, a raiding party broke into the private homes of innocent citizens who they mistakenly thought were drug dealers. This led to a congressional investigation and criminal charges against the agents. The repercussions of the Collinsville raid and the collapse of the Nixon administration brought on by the Watergate scandal—another ill-conceived investigative operation—led to the abolition of ODALE. In 1973 it and the BNDD, along with a number of customs agents, were absorbed into the Drug Enforcement Administration (DEA).

Local drug cops became involved in scandals too. The NYPD's elite anti-narcotics squad, known as the Special Investigations Unit (SIU), saw forty-seven of its sixty detectives indicted and the unit abolished. Among the more spectacular fiascoes was the disappearance from the NYPD property room of confiscated French Connection heroin with an estimated street value of $73 million. The theft was never solved, though suspicion fell on some members of the SIU who were later jailed for other offenses.

In 1972 the Turkish government banned the production of opium. Turkey was not the only opium producer, but the action did upset the French

Connection. As a result, the way was opened for heroin from Mexico or cocaine from South America to enter the United States market. At the same time, black and Hispanic distributors began to assert their independence from Mafia overlords, making their own deals with suppliers. Up to this time, African-American dealers like Ellsworth "Bumpy" Johnson, long known as America's premier black gangster, had played ball with the mob. Characters sporting Johnson's trademark look—shaved head, sunglasses, and fierce aspect—have appeared in many films, slugging or shooting Mafia hoodlums. In real life, Johnson was actually a Harlem lieutenant of the Genovese family. He demonstrated his loyalty to the mob after he was arrested for drug dealing, when he served eleven years in federal prison rather than inform on his bosses. In the late '60s he was allowed to operate his own small cocaine distribution network before the drug became popular. He was arrested again for drug dealing, and he died of a heart attack in 1968 while awaiting trial.

In the 1920s, Italian-led street gangs had pushed aside the more established Irish and Jewish gangs in many cities. There were signs of a similar ethnic shift in the 1970s. Harvard professor Daniel Bell had long argued that Italian dominance was simply the result of a natural progression, with one immigrant group succeeding another in the hierarchy of organized crime. In 1974, Columbia University professor Francis Ianni predicted, "We shall witness over the next decade the systematic development of what is now a scattered and loosely organized pattern of emerging Black control in organized crime into the Black Mafia."

Frank "Pee-Wee" Matthews, a black heroin dealer, broke with his Gambino suppliers and started purchasing heroin directly from the French Connection. Soon he was furnishing drugs to black dealers all over the eastern half of the United States. At the tender age of twenty-eight, Matthews was a walking model of success for ghetto kids. He strode around in sable coats, owned five luxury apartments, and maintained a fleet of expensive cars. When threatened by the Gambinos, he allegedly told them, "Touch one of my people and I'll load my men into cars and drive down Mulberry Street and shoot every Wop we see." In 1971 he hosted a meeting of forty black drug dealers from around the country in Atlanta, Georgia. There they discussed the formation of a separate black crime syndicate. Before any further steps could be taken, Matthews was arrested by federal authorities. He jumped bail and disappeared with $20 million.

The next kingpin, Leroy "Nicky" Barnes, started by receiving his heroin from the Luccheses and the Gambinos. While in prison for drug dealing he met "Crazy Joe" Gallo, the Brooklyn gangster who had led a rebellion against the Profaci family. The two men became friends and began discussing the creation of a Black Mafia, with Gallo as adviser. After Joe was paroled he hired a lawyer who secured Barnes's release from prison. Nicky then convened a meeting in Harlem of ten African-American crime leaders to consider forming a Black Mafia in partnership with Gallo. The proposal was turned down by a vote of seven to three. Barnes went ahead without Gallo, forming his own group of black kingpins known as "the Council." It imitated the Mafia's corporate form by creating divisions to deal with legal, financial, and security matters. The Barnes Council received its heroin directly from foreign suppliers and used intermediaries who were able to tap in to the American Mafia distribution sources. The Council operated a network extending through several states and Canada. With millions flowing in, Barnes not only adopted a lavish lifestyle, but diversified his portfolio by investing in legitimate businesses. In 1977, he and some of his fellow Council members were indicted by the Feds. Instead of emulating Matthews and disappearing, Barnes stood trial; he was convicted and sentenced to life in prison. In 1982 he cut a deal to inform on other drug dealers and had his sentence shortened to thirty years. His former colleagues were so incensed that they put out an eight-million-dollar contract on him. In 1998 he was released.

In Philadelphia a gang involved in extortion and loan sharking actually called itself the Black Mafia. In the 1970s another local dealer, Roland Bartlett, had begun by obtaining his heroin from the Gambinos but then set up his own operation, which was so strong that he was able to get away with refusing to pay tribute to the Mafia. Eventually the Feds smashed both the Black Mafia and Bartlett's group.

The careers of black drug kingpins like Matthews, Barnes, and Bartlett resembled that of many white Prohibition-era beer barons who were essentially independent entrepreneurs. When the top figures were jailed, their gang collapsed. In contrast, Lucky Luciano and Al Capone led corporate organizations. If the leader went to prison, the organization continued. Black gangs with more potential for creating a lasting organization developed in Chicago. Starting in the early 1960s, a group of teenagers who called themselves the Blackstone Rangers began to emerge.[4] The Rangers did not come together to sell drugs for the Mafia, but were products of an urban ghetto in ferment. Living amid violent conditions, many young men opted to join a gang as a form of protection. The gangs, in turn, fought to protect their turf. In the mid '60s the Rangers were drawn into the political affairs of their local Woodlawn neighborhood. As a result they became involved in a federal grant program designed to prevent riots. While helping to "keep the ghetto cool" they acquired considerable political savvy. Soon the group was nationally famous under a dynamic leader named Jeff Fort. In 1967, Senator McClellan's investigations committee heard testimony from former gang members that the Rangers were extorting money from individuals involved in an unemployment program they ran. Fort was sent to jail for the embezzlement of federal funds. While there he began calling himself Prince Malik and formed a group called the El Rukns, which he identified with the Black Muslim movement (though there was no real connection). In this new incarnation the gang became major drug traffickers. In the 1980s, Fort was sentenced to thirteen years in prison for participating in a cocaine conspiracy.

The crack explosion hit American cities in the mid-1980s. Easily ingested, the cocaine derivative was both potent and cheap. A kilo could be purchased for less than $20,000, melted down, and sold for several times that amount. The only other piece of equipment needed to go into business was a firearm, preferably a machine gun. As some remarked, "Anyone bold enough to shoot a gun qualified as an entrepreneur."[5] Open warfare broke out between drug crews, who used methods that made the Mafia look like Boy Scouts. Gangs with automatic weapons would spray a street corner, not only killing the intended target but hitting five or ten bystanders. Innocents gunned down were referred to as "mushrooms" (because they

4 The name originated from the South Side street where the gang originally hung out.
5 In some publications this remark has been attributed to me. While I sometimes repeated the phrase, it was already in coinage.

popped up underfoot). In some neighborhoods, gunfire could be heard all night long, and shots went through the windows or walls of private residences. Little children sometimes slept in bathtubs to protect them from bullets. Nursery school youngsters were taught to drop down flat when they heard a popping noise. The murder figures in New York rose dramatically. In 1985 the city recorded fewer than 1,400 murders; by 1990 there were 2,245. Virtually the entire increase could be attributed to the drug-related killings. One drug gang in Queens dared to do something that the New York Mafia had never done: They assassinated a police officer, as a warning to the NYPD to cease interfering with its activities. Across the country, many other cities experienced similar warfare and increases in the body count. The cocaine wars were a replay of Prohibition's beer wars with much greater carnage.

While most crack crews rose and fell with great rapidity, some drug gangs did achieve a degree of permanence. Another Chicago group, the Black Gangster Disciples, had an estimated thirty thousand members and ran a $100-million-a-year drug business. In the 1990s it engaged in extensive political activity, registering voters and supporting candidates in city elections. When its leader, Larry Hoover, sought a parole—he was serving two life sentences for murder—many politicians backed him, including a former Chicago mayor. Though some community residents were willing to accept "King Larry" and his troops as a civic group, in 1997 the federal government convicted Hoover and many of his members on drug conspiracy charges.

Latin American groups also moved onto the American drug scene. The most prominent were the Colombian-based Cali and Medellín cartels. When cocaine became popular, the Colombians were ideally situated to dominate the trade. They were located near coca-producing areas such as Bolivia and Peru, and their position on the northern coast of South America—facing both the Caribbean and Pacific—facilitated their ability to smuggle the drug into the United States. Using Cubans, Dominicans, and other Latin Americans as middlemen or street distributors, the cartels dominated the cocaine trade. Their marketing activities, such as developing cheap crack, helped to make the drug popular, and their incomes soon exceeded that of the wealthiest Mafia groups. The leader of the Medellín cartel once offered to pay off the entire national debt of Colombia in return for being released from custody.

The Colombians' use of violence was worse than that of other drug gangs. Women, children, and infants were deliberately killed. Victims' throats were slit and their tongues pulled through and left to dangle—a practice known as "a Colombian necktie." At the same time, the efficiency of the Colombians' operation in the United States frustrated law enforcement. In one instance, a New York City woman waiting for a supply of cocaine to be delivered to her apartment heard muffled voices in the hallway. She immediately contacted her supplier on a cell phone and told him the men were probably police. While DEA agents listened to his phone conversations, he was able to redeploy his entire operation to Los Angeles within a few hours.

Based on Prohibition's precedent, ethnic succession in organized crime should have occurred during the drug wars. The new ethnic gangs not only had vast sums of money, they had more guns at their disposal than the Mafia.[6] The body counts of the 1980s dwarfed the toll of the 1920s. However, the obstacles to black or Hispanic groups' achieving the kind of power that the American Mafia had acquired in the '20s and '30s were formidable. Gangs that developed strictly to sell drugs quickly fell apart after their leader was taken down by law enforcement. And while some black gangs such as the Rangers or Disciples did have strong preexisting organizational ties, the fact that their principal product line was drugs made it difficult to win acceptance. Most Americans of the 1920s did not attach the same negative connotations to liquor that Americans of the 1970s or '80s did to narcotics. In the 1920s most of the victims of gun battles were hardened gangsters. In the drug wars they were much more likely to be young boys and innocent bystanders. Many politicians openly criticized Prohibition, and bootleggers were often seen as local heroes. In the drug era, the combined effect of widespread public fear of the product and the indiscriminate violence associated with its distribution made it impossible for its purveyors to garner significant community support.

6 Although according to law enforcement sources, when a black gangster threatened to send fifty gunmen into South Philadelphia, a local Mafia boss was reported to have told his troops, "If they come I will have five hundred guys with guns waiting for them and they will never be heard from again."

The Mafia continued to be active in the drug trade up through the last quarter of the twentieth century, though they were not the most important group. Colombian cartels, with their access to South American cocaine and multi-billion-dollar annual profits, were at the top of the pyramid. Even so, the Hispanic or black gangs did not replace the Mafia as the most important element in American organized crime. Instead, they remained glorified street gangs. Unlike the 1930s-era Mafia, the minority gangs did not move into alternative fields like gambling, labor racketeering, and loan sharking. They may have had the guns and the money, but they did not have the established base, the political clout, and the requisite organizational skills.

Half an hour after Galante's murder occurred, an NYPD team observing the Ravenite Club on Mulberry Street in Lower Manhattan saw a Bonanno family delegation arrive. The Ravenite was the headquarters of Aniello Dellacroce, underboss of the Gambino family. The cops realized that this visit was akin to a group of KGB spies showing up at a People's Republic of China outstation. Anthony "Bruno" Indelicato was among the visitors seen exchanging high fives with the Gambinos. Eventually an examination of the getaway car used by Galante's killers would turn up Indelicato's palm print. Detectives quickly grasped that the hit had been part of a deal between the Gambinos and a Bonanno faction.

In prison, Galante had constantly badmouthed Carlo Gambino as a coward. It was reported that he promised to make Gambino "shit in Times Square." Boston hoodlum Vinnie Teresa, who had served time in Lewisburg with Galante, published a tell-all book in 1973 titled *My Life in the Mafia*. In it he predicted that when Galante was released he would try to take over the Bonanno family and "wipe out the Gambinos in a drive to become boss of bosses." Teresa even forecast that Galante would use Sicilian immigrants to carry out his plans. Additional support for the intrafamily dispute theory was the fact that titular Bonanno boss Rusty Rastelli, then a prisoner in a federal lockup, had received an inordinate number of mob visitors shortly before the hit on Galante. A forensic investigation disclosed that in addition to fire from the gunmen who stormed the restaurant,

Galante, who had been sitting next to a bodyguard named Cesare Bonventre, had been hit by slugs in the back of his head.

Establishing that Galante had been killed by members of his own family as part of a deal between mobs did not explain the full story. Then police surveillance of Bonventre disclosed that he was partners in a pizzeria with a fellow Sicilian named Salvatore Catalano. The twenty-eight-year-old Bonventre was from Castellammare del Golfo. Catalano, ten years older, had come to the United States from another Mafia stronghold near Palermo. The two were linked to other Sicilians of similar backgrounds. Eventually investigators determined that there was a group of Sicilians within the Bonanno family that were doing more than just making pizza. Some were observed shuttling large sums of money back and forth across the Atlantic. Galante had been running a huge heroin smuggling operation, importing the drug from Italy and distributing it through legitimate businesses like pizza parlors in New York and other cities. The Sicilians, known by the American Mafia as "zips,"[7] were professional killers whose talents were sometimes employed in the United States. Although the zips had been the losers in conflicts within the Italian Mafia, they were much feared because they were quicker to violence than Americans and reputedly would not refuse an assignment to kill a cop or a judge. Another figure in the ring was Gaetano Badalamenti, a mafioso from the Palermo district. He had been driven from Sicily by the Corleones (not the movie family, but a faction of the Sicilian Mafia from the town of that name) when they emerged as winners in the island's intramural wars. From a base in Brazil, Badalamenti was supplying heroin to the zips. During the course of the investigation he planned to ship twenty-two kilograms of heroin to the zip captain Salvatore Catalano in the United States. Some feds immediately set a trap to catch Badalamenti. Others were aghast at the prospect of permitting such a quantity of heroin into the United States. Before the deal could take place, however, Badalamenti fled to Spain, where he was captured by DEA agents.

7 There are as many explanations for the name as there are organized crime experts. It has been said to denote a Sicilian term for bumpkin, zip guns, the Italian dish ziti, or the newcomers' rapid speech. Crime historians are still arguing over whether "hoodlum" comes from a family of toughs named Hodlum or a gang rallying cry "Huddle 'em," and whether "cop" is derived from the copper buttons on a London bobby's coat or the abbreviation COP for constable on patrol.

In employing the Sicilians and attempting to usurp family leadership, Galante had violated protocol in the New York Mafia world. After the difficulties that caused Joe Bonanno's withdrawal from New York in the 1960s, the other mob bosses had placed the family in a sort of receivership. The commission should have been consulted before Galante made his moves. Some of his own Bonanno capos and soldiers feared that Galante would replace them with zips. Instead, it was his zip bodyguards Bonventre and Baldassare Amato who had joined the conspiracy against Galante.

The investigation of Galante's murder and the activities of the zips were greatly helped by the fact that the FBI already had one of its agents established within the Bonannos. Four years before the Galante killing, Special Agent Joe Pistone had managed to infiltrate the family. Though not the first FBI penetration agent, he would prove to be one of the most successful. Pistone did not look like a stereotypical G-man of the Hoover era. He was dark-complexioned, wore a mustache, and could easily pass for a street hoodlum. He had joined the Bureau when he was nearly thirty years old, after working as a schoolteacher and then an investigator for naval intelligence. In 1974, with five years' service in Florida and Virginia behind him, he was transferred to the hijacking squad of the New York FBI office. After a year there, on the strength of his appearance and his knowledge of trucking crime, he was given an undercover assignment investigating East Coast car theft rings. Upon successfully completing that assignment, he was detailed to infiltrate the New York City organized crime scene.

Under Hoover, the Bureau had employed civilian informers, such as the individuals who penetrated the Communist Party. While some of them were popularly referred to as "FBI agents," they had never actually been appointed to that status or gone through the academy at Quantico, Virginia. Hoover feared, with some justification, that men who lived and worked alongside hoodlums would cross the line and compromise the Bureau. This was particularly true of anyone who went undercover in the Mafia. They might be asked to commit a murder. While FBI rules authorized agents to ignore certain nonviolent crimes if that would further their mission, there was no way that they could do the same for a violent crime. After it was revealed in the 1960s that a civilian FBI informant had been riding in a car with some

Klansmen when they killed a female civil rights worker, the Bureau was severely criticized.

Only a particular type of agent could work successfully undercover. As Pistone would later observe:

> Take a regular agent and put him in an undercover capacity. Suddenly no one tells him when to go to work. Nobody tells him what kind of clothes to wear. . . . He comes and goes as he pleases.
>
> If you don't have a strong personality and ego, a sense of pride in yourself, you're going to be . . . consumed by the role you're playing. The major failure among guys working undercover for any law enforcement agency is that they fall in love with the role. . . . They forget who they are.

Pistone had grown up around mob guys. As a teenager he played cards, dice, and pool. He also became aware of certain harsh facts of life and death. As he recalled, "Even as a kid I knew guys that were here today gone tomorrow, never seen again, and I knew what had happened."

Unlike the CIA, the FBI was not a spy agency, and it was at a disadvantage when using its agents in undercover roles. FBI recruits were allowed to tell people who their employer was, while in the CIA, individuals enlisted for spy duty were instructed from the beginning of their service never to reveal that they worked for "the company." Pistone had been raised in the nearby states of New Jersey and Pennsylvania and was assigned to work undercover in an area where he had already functioned as a law enforcement officer. There was a chance that he would run into criminals or legitimate citizens who knew that he was a G-man. In fact, that did happen to him and to other undercover agents during the course of the investigation. In those instances the agent either tried to beat a hasty retreat or bluffed it through.

Pistone began hanging around mob joints posing as a jewel thief named Donnie Brasco. In time he became loosely affiliated with members of the Colombo family. When his contacts with the Colombos did not appear to lead anywhere, he took up with a new group—a crew of thieves from the Bonanno family. Some of his new associates were suspicious of him and required references. Pistone furnished them the name of a Florida thief who was an informer for the FBI. The man had been briefed on what he was supposed to do and he gave a favorable reference for his pal Donnie, quelling the suspicions. Most of Pistone's time was spent in playing his role, and he saw his wife and children only at infrequent intervals. Periodically he would meet his FBI contact agent at some place like a museum: As the two men pretended to be looking at exhibits, the contact man would slip him money to live on. One thing was missing from his life that presented a real credibility problem: women. Most mob guys liked to show off a sexy girlfriend or two, but Brasco always appeared alone. In the Mafia world, a man who didn't seem to like the company of women was an object of suspicion for two reasons. First, gangsters came from backgrounds where homophobia was endemic. Being gay was not an acceptable lifestyle. And secondly, the only alternative explanation for someone who didn't seem to have a girlfriend was that he had a wife or girlfriend hidden away, thereby suggesting that he was not what he semed to be.[8] When asked about his situation, Brasco claimed to have a sweetheart in California and another in Florida. One time he told his gang buddies that his girlfriend's brother had arranged for him to take them aboard a fancy yacht off the Florida coast (the same one used in the Abscam sting). Even then he invented excuses for why his girlfriend couldn't make the party.

Only the leader of the crew Pistone hung around with was a made man, and so the closest Pistone got to mob bosses was one time when he stood guard with other family members outside a restaurant where Galante was dining. As Pistone peered in through the window of the place at the hawk-nosed and almost bald gangster, he was not particularly impressed. One of his new buddies, Benjamin "Lefty Guns" Ruggiero, wised him up:

> Lilo is a mean son of a bitch, a tyrant. . . . Lots of people hate him. . . .
> There's only a few people that he's close to. And mainly that's the zips . . .
> he brought them over from Sicily and uses them for different pieces of
> work and for dealing all that junk. They're as mean as he is.

Eventually Pistone was taken under the wing of capo Dominick "Sonny Black" Napolitano, who had earned his nickname from his dyed jet-black

8 Sometimes mob bosses would arrange for a suspected informer to spend the night with a beautiful prostitute. If she reported that he had failed to perform, he would be killed.

hair. Often his mood was equally dark—as Pistone recalled, "He could freeze anybody." The muscular capo who "would kill you in a minute if you crossed him" took a liking to Brasco and made him his protégé. After Galante's murder, Sonny Black became one of the top capos in the Bonanno family. Through Sonny, Pistone was able to meet mob big shots like Santo Trafficante of Tampa and and Frank Balistrieri of Milwaukee.

Brasco played his role so well that the inevitable happened. Sonny Black assigned him to kill Bruno Indelicato, promising to put him up for induction as a fully made man if he succeeded. It was the signal for the Bureau to bring Pistone in from the cold. In order to discourage a hit being ordered on Pistone, agents visited Mafia bosses to inform them that he was not a turncoat but a bona fide FBI agent whose murder would bring severe repercussions. Even when shown a picture of Pistone in company with other G-men, Sonny Black could not believe it. He continued to insist to the Bonannos that the man they knew as Brasco could not have been a Fed. His protests were unavailing. Seventeen days after the Bureau notified the Mafia about Pistone, Napolitano was summoned to a mob conclave. It was the last time he was seen alive. A year later his badly decomposed body was found in a Staten Island creek. Despite the warning against going after Pistone, a $500,000 contract was put out on him.

The zip investigation eventually extended to other groups in Italy and Switzerland. In 1982, American and Italian police compared notes at a conference in the Quantico, Virginia, FBI facility, and three months later, 153 Italian mafiosi were arrested. In April 1984, more than four hundred FBI and other federal agents fanned out throughout the Northeast and Midwest arresting members of the Pizza Connection. Of thirty-five named defendants, only twenty-two were available for trial: The others were fugitives, murdered, or had been found guilty in other jurisdictions. Their trial would be one of the cornerstones of the federal government's war on the Mafia.

Pistone's success in infiltrating the Bonannos and the use of zips illustrated some of the problems besetting the American Mafia. One was demographic. The exodus of the older immigrant groups from the city weakened the mob's recruitment base. East Harlem had become a largely Puerto Rican area, Brownsville was African-American, and Manhattan's Little Italy was rapidly filling up with Chinese. Like other groups, Italian families that moved to the suburbs had middle-class aspirations for their children. Many young Italian Americans were graduating from college and entering professions or business. There were no longer legions of street toughs clamoring to join up. While some suburban men took up mob activities, on balance the exodus from the cities was a negative for the Mafia. In the old days it would have been unlikely that a man like Pistone could have infiltrated the mob. They would never have trusted someone who had not been recommended by a person who knew his family and had watched him grow up. Once only full-blooded southern Italians could belong to the Mafia, and even then some Sicilians never trusted Neapolitans or Calabrians and vice versa. In the 1970s, in order to overcome the shortage of recruits, some Mafia bosses allowed any son of an Italian father to become eligible for membership, including those whose roots were in central and northern Italy.

Then there was the generational problem. Young men everywhere no longer gave automatic respect to their elders, and the Mafia was no different. Young guys thought the old-world traditions of ceremonial kissing, bowing, and scraping were silly and demeaning. Nor were they willing to wait years to become made men or get a chance at the big money. The zips, with their Sicilian upbringing, seemed like ideal recruits. But in the late twentieth century, immigrants rapidly became Americanized. A Sicilian of the past might have been willing to die for his family and chief. Now, like young professionals everywhere, he would think nothing of jumping ship if it meant a few more dollars in his pocket. Young men were also likelier to use drugs, and some who peddled narcotics became their own best customers. As in the business world, stoned employees were more likely to make bad decisions.

Still, the American Mafia was a long way from being finished. Though Pistone was honored by the Department of Justice for his work against the Bonannos and celebrated in print and film, he had to constantly move his family and hide his identity. In his bestselling account of his adventures, he mused on what he would say if he ran into an old colleague like Lefty Guns (by then doing twenty years). Instead of apologizing, he would tell him,

"I'm proud of what I did, Lefty. If I had to do it all over again, yeah, I would. I exposed the Mafia. We got over a hundred convictions." To which he imagined Lefty would say, "That's real nice, good for you. You exposed us, but if you did so good exposing us, Donnie, whyzit you and your family gotta live a coverup for the rest of your lives?"

CHAPTER 11

RICO: DECOMMISSIONING
THE COMMISSION

F ive years earlier, no one would have believed it could happen: In February 1985, the top figures of New York City's five families, including the leaders of the local commission, were simultaneously indicted. For years the existence of a Mafia—or, as the FBI had referred to it since 1963, La Cosa Nostra—had been subject to debate. Recently, however, thousands of hours of recorded conversations and witness testimony heard in courts across the United States had confounded the skeptics. And having seen endless reruns of *The Godfather* and scores of similar films, the public had no trouble envisioning a commission of sharply dressed, sinister-looking men sitting around a table debating life and death issues.

At dawn on the twenty-fifth, posses of federal agents and cops raced across the New York City area arresting the individuals indicted. The names were no surprise. Some of them had been in the newspapers for thirty years. In the mob world, many were so well known that even a casual mention by nickname evoked instant recognition—and considerable fear. In some cases the nickname was all that had been heard on conversations recorded by the government. In order that the accused be fully identified, the indictments supplied both their given names and their street monikers.

In law enforcement's eyes, the most prominent of the accused was Paul Castellano, a.k.a. "Pauly," "Mr. Paul," or "Big Paul," boss of the Gambino family. Some law enforcers considered the Gambinos, with three hundred made members and as many as ten times that number of associates, to be New York's most powerful family. Castellano had inherited the top job in 1976 when his brother-in-law, Carlo Gambino, died of old age. Within the family Paul was called "the Pope," and the three-million-dollar mansion he lived in was known as the "White House." Neither term was complimentary. To his troops, Castellano was as remote and unapproachable as the pontiff in Rome, and when Paul wanted to talk to his capos, he summoned them to his residence as though he were the president of the United States. The mansion was located on a hill in Staten Island that the old Dutch settlers had named Todt (death)—a fitting coincidence, since the meetings there often involved discussions of who needed killing. Indicted with Castellano was underboss Aniello Dellacroce, a.k.a "Neil" or "O'Neill." The latter came from Dellacroce's work as a gunman for Albert Anastasia, when he sometimes went out on hits disguised as a Catholic priest.

Back in 1976, most family members had thought Neil should be made boss. If Dellacroce had not been in jail for failure to pay taxes on $123,000 he had obtained in an extortion scheme, Gambino might have had to bow to popular sentiment and name him as his successor. As it was, Paul agreed to give Neil control over half of the family's twenty-odd crews. The burly, rugged Dellacroce was not inaccessible. He could always be found at the Ravenite Club in Manhattan's Little Italy District. When the Bonanno crew that killed Carmine Galante reported to Dellacroce at the Ravenite after the hit, it was an indication of the power realities in the Gambino family. Divided authority was often an invitation to trouble in the mob world, but Paul and Neil had coexisted for nine years, neither daring to challenge the other. Now Dellacroce was terminally ill with cancer.

The best known of those arrested was Anthony Corallo, a.k.a. "Tony Ducks," boss of the Lucchese family. Though it had only a few more than a hundred made members, the Lucchese family was the Tiffanys of the mob world, thanks to the immense income generated by its holdings in the garment center and extensive drug trafficking. And unlike the other four families, the Luccheses had never experienced internal warfare. Corallo had been making news since the 1950s, when he had clashed with Robert Kennedy at the McClellan Committee hearings and helped Jimmy Hoffa become president of the Teamsters. In 1962 he and state Supreme Court justice James Keogh were convicted of trying to bribe a federal judge. When Tommy Lucchese died in 1967, Corallo was the consensus choice to be boss. The only problem was that Ducks was being sent to prison for the extortion scheme he had worked with Carmine DeSapio. Corallo was so popular that the family decided he would be made boss anyway, and an elderly capo was designated to keep his seat warm. Three years later Ducks was paroled into the top job. Indicted with Corallo were his underboss Salvatore Santoro, a.k.a. "Tom Mix," and Lucchese counselor Christopher Furnari, a.k.a. "Christy Ticks." Santoro had come up from the streets of the same East Harlem area that produced Lucchese and Corallo. In 1959 he got nineteen years for drug dealing. When he was released, he convinced Ducks that he was through with drugs and was assigned to labor racketeering. Ticks Furnari was a Brooklyn hoodlum who had done time for armed robbery and rape. He didn't join the Luccheses until 1962, when he was thirty-eight. His ability to earn $25,000 a day for the family through loan sharking fueled his rise and made up for his late start.

Also indicted was Anthony Salerno, a.k.a. "Fat Tony," ostensible boss of the Genovese family. As he weighed in at 230 pounds, his nickname was self-explanatory. With a ubiquitous cigar in his mouth and a cloth cap perched on his head, he looked the part of an old-time mafioso. The Manhattan-based family had been led by such high-profile mob figures as Lucky Luciano, Frank Costello, and Vito Genovese (who gave it its lasting name). Historically it was the most prestigious Mafia group. Estimates of its strength ranged above three hundred made men. Fat Tony acted as liaison between out-of-town mobs and the New York City commission. In vouching that Jackie Presser of Cleveland was not an informer and backing him for Teamsters international president, Salerno had recently made a colossal mistake.

Though few knew it, Salerno was not the real boss. Within the family he was second to Vincenzo "Chin" Gigante, the man who had shot Frank Costello in 1957.[1] Afterward he was promoted to capo, in charge of the Genoveses' interests in Lower Manhattan. By the 1980s he had risen to

---

1 Supposedly his mother called him by the diminutive "Cincenzo," which his playmates on the street shortened to Chin. In photos, however, his lantern jaw stands out.

boss. As a cover for his real status, Chin posed as a poor, mentally ill no-body who lived with his mother in a cheap Greenwich Village walkup. He once accepted a subpoena standing in the shower, dressed in a raincoat and holding an umbrella. Other times he would wander the streets in his pajamas, so seemingly oblivious of his surroundings that he would relieve himself in broad daylight. When examined by psychiatrists, Gigante might pretend that he thought he was at a wedding, asking "Where is the bride?" His family, which included a brother who was a prominent Catholic priest, explained that the ex-light-heavyweight boxer had taken one too many punches in the head. Prosecutors despaired of ever having him declared fit to stand trial. Somehow Gigante got the mistaken notion that FBI agents did not work after midnight. Trailing his chauffeured limo as it raced through the streets late at night, agents eventually discovered that Gigante led a triple life. The second one was with his wife in an expensive suburban New Jersey home, and the third played out in an uptown Manhattan town-house he shared with another beautiful lady (curiously, and perhaps con-veniently, both women were named Olympia). None of these arrangements were illegal, and there was no solid evidence against him. The walls inside his Triangle Civic Association Club on Sullivan Street were plastered with signs that read, "Don't talk, the enemy is listening." His troops were told never to mention his name in conversation, only to point at their chin. Sometimes eavesdropping Feds would hear references to a mysterious "Aunt Julia," which they finally figured out was a code name for Gigante.

While Carmine Persico, boss of the Colombo family, was listed as "Ju-nior," most people referred to him as "the Snake"—though only his girl-friend "Tootsa" dared call him that to his face. Since the Gallo-Profaci war more than twenty years earlier, the Colombos had been a troubled family. Persico owed his survival to the fact that although he began by supporting the Gallos, at a critical moment he had switched to the other side and was one of the assailants who participated in the strangling of Joey Gallo's brother. Joe Colombo's ill-advised demonstrations against the FBI and his wounding in 1971 further upset the family equilibrium. After the comatose Colombo died in 1978, Persico had emerged as boss. Under his regime the family, which numbered about 125 made men, had been more successful. Indicted with Persico was his underboss, Gennaro Langella, a.k.a. "Gerry

Lang," and one of their soldiers, Ralph Scopo. Langella was the man who oversaw the family's one-third interest in the garment center rackets. Scopo made the list because as a key figure in the "concrete cartel," he played an important role in a racket that was a prime target of the indictment.

The Bonanno family was represented by its boss, Philip Rastelli, a.k.a. "Rusty," and capo Anthony Indelicato, a.k.a. "Bruno." The Bonannos had been in turmoil since founding father Joe's expulsion from the commission and exile to Arizona back in the '60s. Still, they numbered over 150 members. The 1979 murder of the would-be boss, Carmine Galante, was another important part of the indictment. Indelicato had been one of the shooters.

The man who, as architect of the indictments, was the cause of the bosses' predicament also had a nickname and a family. He was U.S. attorney Rudolph Giuliani, a.k.a. "Rudy," boss of the Southern District Feds. Counting prosecutors, G-men, cops, and other staff, his family had several hundred members. The task before Giuliani was not only to prove that there was a criminal organization known as the Mafia, but to destroy its foundation—New York's five families.

A few years earlier, the mobs had been flourishing and law enforcement floundering. According to a 1977 *Time* magazine cover story (written by a reporter known to have a direct pipeline to FBI intelligence), nationally the Mafia was grossing an annual $48 billion, of which half was net profit. Only Exxon, with $51 billion in sales, made more—but its net was just 5 percent. In some respects it was surprising that the Mafia had managed not only to survive but to thrive. Since the 1960s, federal law enforcement had been making major efforts to destroy it. The FBI had been restructured to make organized crime a major priority. Across the country more than a thousand agents, combining the street smarts of big-city cops and the legal and investigative knowledge of the FBI, were staffing organized crime squads, led by hard-charging supervisors and SACs. Many of the new recruits were gung-ho types who had served as officers in the Marines, Special Forces, and other elite outfits during the Vietnam War. More than a few were quietly determined not to repeat the humiliations of Vietnam by losing the war against the Mafia. Under Hoover, agents had been forbidden to go undercover; now they were posing as Mafia associates. In New York, agent Joe Pistone was about to be put forward for initiation into the Bonanno family. Federal strike forces composed of career prosecutors were active in most cities where there was a Mafia problem. In others, activist U.S. attorneys made organized crime a priority.

Congress had provided law enforcement with many tools. Electronic eavesdropping had become so pervasive that the Mafia was hard-pressed to find private places to conduct business. The government established a witness protection program to provide sanctuary for those who testified against the mob. An informer might not only be able to have his charges dismissed by informing on others, he could avoid retaliation by disappearing and reemerging elsewhere as an entirely different person. Long before the witness protection program, it was an American tradition that an individual could go off someplace (usually out west) and reinvent himself. Often, he left his creditors and spouse behind. Now, under witness protection, an informer could obtain money and other assistance from the federal government, for his family as well as himself. By the 1980s, nearly four thousand individuals had availed themselves of it.

Many mob figures had been jailed. In some ways, convicting bosses actually helped the Mafia by pruning deadwood. As in a compulsory retirement program, when an old boss received a stiff jail sentence, it allowed young Turks to move up. Despite a large number of tactical successes, though, there had not been a strategic victory. To borrow a phrase from the Vietnam experience, in the 1970s the Department of Justice was compiling an impressive body count while still losing the war. As long as the mob families existed, there would always be people to fill vacancies.

New York City was the crown jewel of the Mafia, and the mob's hold on it was so complete that almost anybody who ate a meal there was probably paying tribute to at least one of the five families. If the dinner was fish, it came from the Genovese-dominated Fulton Fish Market. Beef and poultry were controlled by the Bonannos, Luccheses, and Gambinos. Paul Castellano had an interest in a couple of grocery chains; when chicken mogul Frank Perdue sought to enter the New York market, he quickly learned that Big Paul was a major player. Clothes purchased anywhere in the United

States had probably passed through the New York garment center, where the Gambinos, Colombos, and Luccheses held sway. Tommy Gambino, twice blessed as the son of Carlo and son-in-law of Tommy Lucchese, was the most important figure, through his control of trucking. Clothing manufacturers and designers were in effect "married" to a particular trucking company. If a customer ceased to do business with his assigned hauler, no other trucking firm would service him, and he could not move his merchandise. Independent truckers seeking garment center business were discouraged by harassment and intimidation.

The construction industry was another mob bonanza shared by various gangs. One of the most important figures in the industry was a Teamsters union leader, John Cody, who was an associate of the Gambinos. Every year he gave $200,000 to Castellano. Genovese associate Edward "Biff" Halloran controlled concrete suppliers, and Colombo soldier Ralph Scopo ran the cement and concrete workers union. On concrete jobs under $2 million the Colombos took a 1 percent cut. Jobs between $2 and $15 million were divided among seven contractors who submitted rigged bids and paid off 2 percent to the New York commission. An FBI bug caught Scopo explaining to an outside contractor why he could not do a multi-million-dollar job:

SCOPO: You can't do it. Over two million you can't do it. It's under two million, hey, me, I tell you go ahead and do it.

CONTRACTOR: Who do I gotta go see? Tell me who I gotta go see?

SCOPO: You gotta see every family. And they're going to tell you no. So don't even bother.

On jobs over $15 million, the payoff belonged exclusively to the Genovese family. The mob's control was so tight that during the Manhattan construction boom of the early '80s, Biff Halloran was able to charge $85 a square foot for concrete, the highest price in the nation.

Mobbed-up unions were an accepted part of the city's life. In the 1970s the Department of Justice had mounted an operation known as UNIRAC (union racketeering) aimed at the International Longshoremen's Association. It led to the conviction of 130 individuals up and down the East Coast.

One of those charged was Anthony Scotto, boss of the Brooklyn water-front. Scotto had acquired a reputation in New York as a progressive labor leader who was active in civic affairs. At his 1979 trial, New York governor Hugh Carey and former New York City mayors Abe Beame, John Lindsay, and Robert Wagner all testified to his good character. Their support apparently did not outweigh the government's evidence, including some recorded conversations, and Scotto was found guilty. As one juror explained, the character witnesses "did not listen to the tapes." He was convicted, sentenced to prison, and barred from union activity for life. When Scotto was released after serving three years in prison, many New York politicians attended his welcome-home dinner. FBI director Louis Freeh was then a young agent assigned to UNIRAC, and in his 2005 memoir he wrote, "All that was a lesson for me . . . in how politics can sometimes destroy judgment and corrupt moral sense."

The New York mobs felt that they could act with impunity, and that conviction seemed justified. In 1979, the largest cash heist in American history was pulled off at a mob-dominated airport complex named for a president whose brother was once the scourge of the Mafia. Lucchese chiefs like Ducks Corallo and Johnny Dio had established the family's hold at JFK back in the 1950s. Their control of the unions allowed them to extort money from employers. It also permitted hijacking crews, acting on inside information from drivers or freight handlers, to steal valuable cargoes directly from the airport or during transit to and from it. In some instances drivers would arrange in advance to surrender their loads without resistance. When questioned by the police, they would claim they were unable to recall any details of the robbers' appearance. Among detectives, such holdups were known as "giveups." The pickings at JFK were so lucrative that every family had a piece of the action.

In the 1970s the king of the hijackers was Jimmy "The Gent" Burke. On any heist that was not a setup, his first move was to take the trucker's driver's license and tell him, "Now we know who you are and where you live." Then, to show what a good fellow he was, Burke would shove a hundred-dollar bill into the driver's shirt pocket. The Irish Burke was in the mold of such old-time gangsters as Chicago's Dion O'Bannion or New York's Owney "The Killer" Madden. All three were smiling, jovial individuals who would kill friend or foe without a moment's hesitation. Not a made man, Burke was treated as a virtual crew chief whose services were available to the families. In the Lufthansa case, his principal contact would be Lucchese capo Paul Vario.

When a freight supervisor for the German airline Lufthansa, Louis Werner, fell behind on his gambling debts in 1978, he began shopping around information about the vulnerability of his cargoes. One night Burke and six accomplices held up the Lufthansa terminal and took $5.3 million in cash and $875,000 in jewelry. They were able to bypass the security devices and had called some of the loaders by name, making it obvious that the heist was an inside job. Burke was an immediate suspect, and informers soon confirmed to investigators that his crew was indeed responsible. A full-court press was put on the suspects, including aerial surveillance by an FBI helicopter. The key to breaking the case was to get some of the people actually involved to turn informer. One who began blabbing was Louis Werner—though not to the cops. Instead he told everyone else, bragging about the money he was going to make. His loose talk led to his arrest. Though he had no direct connection to Jimmy Burke and his holdup crew, Werner could testify against others who did. Burke knew that, and to ensure that other possible informers could not talk, he began having them killed. Some accounts claim thirteen people, including participants, accomplices, associates, and a couple of their girlfriends, were murdered.[2] If Werner had any intention of turning government witness, he waited too long. By the time he was convicted and sentenced to eight to twenty-five years, the only people he could implicate were dead.

Another man aware of Burke's role in the robbery was Henry Hill, who had worked scores with him for many years. The two had recently completed a prison sentence in Florida for a robbery and assault carried out while they were trying to collect a debt for a friend. As a known associate of Burke, Hill was subject to the same close surveillance as Jimmy and his holdup crew. For a time, Hill would drive with one eye on the FBI helicopter that tailed him. When he was arrested for drug dealing, he decided to

2 Knowledgeable law enforcement sources believe that number is too high. In the months after the robbery, the media had a tendency to assume that any apparent hit was connected to Lufthansa.

cut a deal and give up Burke. He was unable to connect Jimmy with the Lufthansa robbery directly, but the court testimony he provided led to Burke's conviction for the murder of a small-time hustler and drug dealer. In return for his cooperation, Hill was permitted to enter the witness protection program. Burke received a life sentence and eventually died in prison.[3] Only $100,000 of the Lufthansa loot was recovered. According to investigators, Burke spread it around among various mob families and used his own share to invest in drug deals and purchase small businesses. As Eastern District strike force chief, Ed McDonald, who led the Lufthansa investigation, has observed, "Everyone focused on the $6 million stolen. The real losses at JFK were the money the mobs were able to extort from employers and ultimately the public."

The futility of the government's attacks on the Mafia continued into the 1980s. In 1983, President Reagan named a commission to advise him on "actions which can be taken to improve law enforcement efforts against organized crime," naming federal appeals court judge Irving Kaufman as chairman. Other than being the trial judge who had sentenced the Apalachin defendants to prison (a decision later reversed), Kaufman had very little involvement with the subject and proved to be an ineffective leader. The commission included some top experts on organized crime, such as Charles Rogovin, but unlike the 1967 Presidential Task Force on Organized Crime that Rogovin had directed, the Kaufman Commission had virtually no impact on policy and sometimes took on the appearance of a circus. Witnesses like Jimmy Fratianno testified from a closed booth, supposedly for security reasons—a dubious justification, since he had previously appeared on television without a disguise. In its final report a majority of the commission members, including Rogovin, criticized the effort as "a saga of missed opportunities."

At the rate of progress the federal government was making, the American Mafia would still be going strong well into the twenty-first century.

---

3 Hill's story was eventually told by bestselling author and mob expert Nick Pileggi in the book *Wiseguy*, which later became the basis for the movie *Goodfellas*. *Wiseguy* and *Casino* have become primers on mob life for millions of Americans.

What was needed was some means of simultaneously taking down the leaders and key players of a Mafia gang, thereby crippling their entire operation. In fact a strategy for victory was already on the law books. In 1970, G. Robert Blakey had drafted the RICO law, which made it illegal to participate in an organization or enterprise involved in a pattern of racketeering. Under RICO, a pattern could comprise as few as two of thirty-four common state and federal crimes committed within a ten-year period, and an individual could be convicted of both the substantive crime and conspiracy with a twenty-year maximum for each offense, and a life sentence if a murder was involved.

Most law enforcement officers either did not understand RICO or were reluctant to use it. Learned attorneys did not feel it could possibly be held constitutional, because it appeared to stand traditional legal concepts on their head. Before RICO, prosecutors could not introduce evidence that defendants had been involved in crimes other than the specific ones they were charged with, nor could they allege that the defendant was part of a criminal organization. In New York, police officers who were members of an organized crime squad could not identify their unit when testifying lest it be seen as prejudicial to the accused. Under RICO, previous crimes could be cited to prove that the defendants were members of a racketeering organization. Even if they had been acquitted, it did not matter. They could be charged with the offense of carrying out the activity on behalf of an organization. To prove that there was an enterprise, or at least an association that engaged in a pattern of racketeering, the jury might be given the criminal history of the organization—including offenses committed before some of the defendants had joined the group. Some lawyers thought the act applied only to racketeers who had infiltrated a legitimate organization such as a labor union. A criminal gang was of course not a legitimate business, so under that rubric it would be exempt from RICO. However, the U.S. Supreme Court would rule that a criminal gang did indeed constitute an organization or association under RICO.

Even those who grasped RICO did not embrace it. Lawyers and cops were used to working on cases that involved individuals: Arrest the bad guy for a specific crime, prosecute him, and move on. Prosecutors were reluctant to use RICO because it could require a vast commitment of

resources over a long period of time, only to result in a massive and unwieldy trial that the government could very well lose. Assembling a RICO
case required investigators to collect and piece together many disparate
pieces of information. In the FBI, analytic types willing to spend years conducting surveillances and filing reports gravitated to counterintelligence
work, while the more action-oriented went to the criminal squads where
they could clear up the latest bank robbery or hijacking.

Blakey took it upon himself to sell RICO, and in 1972 he arranged to
brief the staff of the U.S. attorney for the Southern District of New York.
Under Robert Morgenthau the district had secured half of the organized
crime convictions in the entire nation, so Blakey expected a sympathetic
hearing. If the Southern District were to bring a successful RICO case, the
rest of the country would inevitably follow suit. However, Morgenthau
was no longer in office—his resignation had been requested in 1969, when
President Nixon appointed John Mitchell attorney general. Though he
managed to hold on for a year, he could not force the Nixon administration
to reappoint him. His successor was Whitney North Seymour, Jr., a former
New York State senator from the "Silk Stocking" district. As Blakey related
to journalist Selwyn Rabb, in the midst of his presentation Seymour terminated the meeting, calling it a waste of time, and ordered Blakey to leave
the room. RICO would not be used in the Southern District until nearly a
decade later. Despite humiliation and rebuff, Blakey was not discouraged.
As he would later tell people, the Sherman Anti-Trust Act was passed in 1890
and not used successfully in a case until 1911. He continued his mission-
ary efforts from his position as a professor at Cornell Law School, where he
established an organized crime institute.

When Neil Welch was appointed head of the New York FBI in 1978, he
declared the office a disaster and promised to rebuild it brick by brick.
The flagship office of the FBI was still devoting most of the efforts of its
thousand agents to the Bureau's traditional (and necessary) task of combating foreign espionage. As the economic capital of the United States
and host city to the United Nations, New York swarmed with spies, some
of them illegals, others working under diplomatic cover. So hundreds of
New York FBI agents spent their time trailing Soviet agents and their Eastern European and Chinese counterparts. In contrast, only a couple of

dozen agents were assigned to work full-time on the Mafia, although New York was also the capital of organized crime. Welch immediately beefed up the organized crime squad and established a joint task force with the NYPD. He also realized that a case-by-case approach would never make a serious dent in the five families. Welch knew about Blakey and RICO, and in the summer of 1979 he assigned Jim Kossler, his coordinator of organized crime investigations, and a top supervisor, Jules Bonavolonta, to attend one of Blakey's two-week seminars at Cornell. At first they chafed at having to participate in an academic tea party in upstate Ithaca, hundreds of miles from the action in New York City. Once there, though, they quickly grasped that RICO was a way to take out whole mob families. After a series of meetings between prosecutors and agents, the FBI initiated Operation GENUS. A separate squad was assigned to each of the five families and directed to identify the leaders, chain of command, and racket areas in which they were involved. To put the organized crime squads closer to their targets, satellite FBI offices were opened in the outer boroughs.

At the state and local level, when Robert Morgenthau became district attorney of New York County in 1976, he made organized crime a high priority of the office. A former chief of his criminal investigations bureau, Ron Goldstock, later became Blakey's top assistant at Cornell. In 1982, Goldstock was appointed to direct the New York State Organized Crime Task Force (OCTF). The operations of OCTF would illustrate that a small agency is sometimes in a better position than a large bureaucracy to develop innovative programs. One head of the New York FBI office described OCTF as "an elite vanguard in the fight against organized crime; imaginative and unencumbered by bureaucracy, it can move quickly and decisively, scoring important victories in uncharted territories."

One of the accomplishments of OCTF was to conduct a comprehensive study of racketeering in New York City's vast construction industry. To do so, Goldstock utilized not only prosecutors, lawyers, and detectives, but also social scientists. The study found that the New York mobs actually provided a "rationalizing influence," which regulated competition and enabled developers to cut through the labyrinth of regulation that often stifled construction in the city. Thus to eliminate racketeering would require more than simply convicting some gangsters, but rather an overhaul of the economic and regulatory structure of the industry.

The FBI bosses were rapidly moving in the right direction, but some agents assigned to the organized crime squads were not quite up to the job. One was unable to find his way to Staten Island, despite having served two years in New York. Another complained that he could not keep straight the names of the Italian suspects he was investigating. Less laughably, some supervisors were beginning to suspect that mob moles were privy to their secrets. It would take several years for them to determine that a clerk in the Southern District federal court and an NYPD intelligence squad detective were passing information to the Gambinos.

FBI listening devices began recording reams of information on the five families, under the direction of the head of the Bureau's special operations group, Jim Kallstrom, a former Marine captain in Vietnam.[4] Kallstrom's troops became experts at setting up surveillance devices on short notice and in the most unlikely locations. For the impossible tasks he could call on the Bureau's foreign counterintelligence operatives, who had such advanced equipment that, to keep its details secret, only a few specialists were allowed to employ it. On jobs where there was a possibility of running into mob gunmen, Kallstrom obtained assistance from the Bureau's "half-dollar club." These were agents who could put six shots into a target so closely spaced together that they could be covered by a fifty-cent piece. While one team worked on electronic devices, their colleagues peered through sniper scopes, covering their flanks. A device in the Palma Boys Club in East Harlem picked up the conversations of Tony Salerno. Another bug was inserted in a restaurant where the Colombo family held meetings. The FBI even managed to plant a device in the Staten Island "White House" of Gambino boss Paul Castellano.

The Luccheses were too clever to hold their meetings at a regular location that could be spied on or bugged. Instead they established a mobile command post in a $120,000 black Jaguar owned by family soldier Sal Avellino. When Ducks Corallo wanted to talk to a couple of his capos, Sal would drive them around. Ron Goldstock's OCTF investigators bugged the car.

4 In 1996 Kallstrom, by then director of the FBI's New York office, would become a familiar figure on national TV as he led the investigation into the explosion of TWA Flight 800.

Avellino had an inquiring mind and would frequently quiz his boss about the workings of mob enterprises such as the Long Island garbage hauling racket. The task force agents found Corallo's explanations very illuminating.

The ultimate goal was to assemble the information into court cases. In 1983, thirty-eight-year-old Rudy Giuliani was appointed to head the Southern District U.S. attorney's office. In his new post he was following in the footsteps of such famous Americans as Henry Stimson, who went on to be secretary of state and twice secretary of war; Thomas Dewey, three-time governor of New York and two-time Republican candidate for president; and Robert Morgenthau, who held the post for nine years before becoming the country's leading local D.A. Being an assistant in the office provided a lifelong cachet equivalent to that of a Rhodes scholarship. Its alums filled the federal bench in the New York area, held partnerships in major law firms, and occupied important government offices. Giuliani himself had started as an assistant, developing a reputation as a tough prosecutor (though in the movie *Prince of the City* he is portrayed as a sympathetic one who manages to turn a rogue cop into a government witness). When he left the DOJ he became a partner at a prestigious New York law firm. Giuliani's background was different from that of most Southern District assistants and big-firm partners, who were Ivy League graduates from solid upper-middle-class backgrounds. His father was the owner of a Brooklyn tavern/restaurant and Giuliani attended Catholic schools through college, though he went on to top-ranked New York University Law School.

In 1981, the incoming Reagan administration had named Giuliani associate attorney general, the number three post in the Department of Justice. By that time he had made up his mind that someday he would run for public office in his home state. From his vantage point in Washington he became aware that major organized crime cases were being developed in New York. Giuliani thought he was the right man to lead the main battle in the war against the Mafia. So he secured the appointment as U.S. attorney for the Southern District, though on paper it was ranked below his Washington post. As it turned out, Giuliani's experience dealing with Justice Department brass and his hard-driving, take-charge personality were ideally suited for the job. Soon the handsome, boyish-looking prosecutor was all over TV, locking up everyone from Wall Street brokers to street-level drug dealers. In one instance, he and New York senator Al D'Amato, in casual clothes and dark glasses, went on a highly publicized drug buying expedition. It was Giuliani's way of showing that drug dealing was rampant in New York City. He followed up by establishing "Federal Day": Once a week, all drug arrests by city cops were taken to the Southern District instead of being sent into the state courts. In U.S. courts, defendants who could normally expect to get a six-month state sentence were more likely to get six years. As word of the new program began to get back to the streets, drug dealers took note. When they were arrested, they would ask whether it was Federal Day. If they were told it was not, they would go along quietly. If they were informed that it was, they would assault the arresting officers and attempt to flee.

In his efforts against the Mafia, Giuliani obtained valuable intelligence from a general in the opposing army. In 1983 Joe Bonanno, deposed head of the family that still bore his name, wrote a memoir titled *A Man of Honor*. In it Bonanno, like many men of the older generation, made the familiar charge that things were not what they used to be, complaining that young mafiosi no longer adhered to the traditions of the organization. He also declared that there was both a local and a national commission, which brought him criticism from his peers. Their dismay was well founded: Upon reading this admission, Giuliani declared, "If he can write about it, I can prosecute it." When later summoned before a grand jury and asked to tell about the commission, a more reticent Bonanno declined. As a result, he spent fourteen months in jail for contempt of court.

Professor Blakey had developed the RICO law. The FBI and federal prosecutors had reorganized their operations to concentrate on families rather than individuals and had collected vast amounts of evidence. And a dynamic leader who knew how to fuse the various elements had arrived on the scene.

Two major cases serve to illustrate Giuliani's efforts against the New York mobs. The first was the pizza case, initiated by the murder of Carmine Galante. The defendants could be divided into two factions: the Bonanno zips, led by Salvatore Catalano, and the smugglers, of whom the principal was Gaetano Badalamenti. The trial commenced late in 1985 and continued for seventeen months.

The lead prosecutor for the Southern District was Louis Freeh. A native New Jerseyan, during his law school days he had held a summer job unloading trucks, which required him to obtain a union card from Tony Pro's Teamsters Local 560. Like other 560 members, he was shaken down by a job foreman. After graduation he became an FBI agent, working the organized crime beat in New York City, where he would play a major role in the UNIRAC investigation. Sometimes Freeh's adventures bordered on the hilarious. During the UNIRAC investigation, one mob capo, Mike Clemente, was so security conscious that he would take payoffs from businessmen only while they were standing nude in the sauna of a Brooklyn health club. Freeh was assigned to stand around naked and observe the goings-on.[5] On another occasion, one of Freeh's informers entered a mob social club with a tape recorder strapped to his groin. He managed to pass a cursory frisk, but the sound of the whirring tape was picked up by the sharp ears of a watchdog who went over and buried his nose between the informer's legs. Before any mob guys could act, the spy ran off down the street to his FBI handlers, who quickly put him into witness protection. An hour later, when Freeh and other agents drove past the club, the mobsters were partying in the street and feeding steak to their canine hero. Freeh would later switch to the prosecutorial side, then become a federal district judge and later director of the FBI.

In the pizza case, in addition to the drug and money laundering offenses, the defendants were also charged with RICO conspiracy and a related offense of managing a continuing criminal enterprise. Because no drugs had been seized, Freeh and his co-prosecutors had to rely on the voluminous tapes from electronic eavesdropping. To spare the jury boredom, professional actors were hired to read the transcripts to them. So jurors could understand the reenactments, veteran narcotics agents were called to testify

5 Freeh eventually struck up an acquaintanceship with Clemente in the club's coffee shop. Later, at Clemente's trial, the defendant noticed Freeh sitting in the courtroom and wondered if the young man had been dragged into the case because of their association. He ordered his lawyer to inform the judge, "The kid had nothing to do with it." The lawyer grasped the real situation at a glance and asked Freeh point-blank if he were an FBI man. When Freeh confirmed that he was, Clemente's conscience was relieved.

as to the meaning of the various code words—for example, "boy" meant heroin and "girl" cocaine, and "sixty cents" was actually $60,000. The many defendants were often at cross purposes, as the alibi strategy of one might provide further evidence against another. One defendant became so exasperated with his own lawyer that he put out a contract on him. After six days of studying the 120-page indictment, 350 pages of charges and instructions, 410 pages of charts and summaries, and the 59-page verdict sheet, the jury found all but one defendant guilty. Sentences for ten of them, including the two principals, were in the twenty-to-thirty-five-year range, and for most of the others, twelve to fifteen.

The second case was the commission trial. Giuliani set the tone, saying "[This] is an attempt . . . to dismantle a structure which has been used from the beginning of organized crime in the United States." Certain Department of Justice officials were skeptical that a prosecution that embraced all five families would succeed. They thought that it would be better to proceed one family at a time, but Giuliani argued for doing it all in one fell swoop. To overcome his superiors' doubts he promised to prosecute the case personally. Simultaneously, he was confronted with a huge political corruption scandal in New York City. The prominent defendants caught up in it succeeded in having their case moved to New Haven, Connecticut, to avoid fallout from headlines in the city. The political defendants were supported by many public figures, and even some journalists tended to root for them. An acquittal was a definite possibility, so Giuliani opted to prosecute this case himself, which meant he would not be available to present the commission case. The commission prosecution was led by Michael Chertoff, another assistant in whom Giuliani had great confidence. Chertoff would later serve as U.S. attorney for New Jersey, then judge of the U.S. Court of Appeals for the Third Circuit. In 2005 President George W. Bush would name him Secretary of Homeland Security.[6]

By the time the commission trial commenced in September 1986, Gambino boss Castellano had been murdered, and Rusty Rastelli of the Bonannos was severed from the proceedings because of pending charges elsewhere. As Giuliani had signaled with his comments on the Bonanno

---

6 The careers of prosecutors like Freeh, Chertoff, and Giuliani illustrate why berths in the Southern District are so eagerly sought after by young attorneys.

memoir, the trial began with a history lesson. To prove that the commission was an organization in fact, the prosecutors tracked the story of the American Mafia from 1900 on, evoking long-forgotten episodes. In 1911, New York mob bosses "Lupo the Wolf" Saietta, Joe Morello, and six of their gang had been convicted in a southern district courthouse; now their ghosts were on trial again. To buttress its presentation, the government brought in mob turncoats to describe the Mafia, such as Angelo Lonardo, former underboss of the Cleveland family, and Jimmy "The Weasel" Fratianno, onetime acting boss of the Los Angeles family. Since the Cleveland mob's contact man in New York City was Tony Salerno of the Genovese family, Lonardo's testimony was devastating. Fratianno backed up his account with photographs of himself in New York posing with such mob luminaries as Carlo Gambino and Paul Castellano (and Frank Sinatra). New York State troopers who had been present at the Apalachin raid twenty-nine years earlier were called to testify. FBI agent Joe Pistone, a.k.a. Donnie Brasco, was another witness. Defense lawyers objected to the history lessons and claimed that there was no such thing as the Mafia—until one admitted in open court that it existed. In so doing he sought to explain that the commission was not a criminal organization, but one that engaged in interfamily mediation. Since the murder of Carmine Galante was part of the RICO charge, the jury heard about the kind of decisions that arose out of "interfamily mediations."

Carmine "The Snake" Persico acted as his own lawyer, a ploy that permitted him to address the jury without being sworn as a witness or subjected to cross-examination. Persico illustrated the truth of the legal maxim "He who acts as his own attorney has a fool for a client." Though the Snake dressed in the expensive suits of a high-priced lawyer, his "dese, dem, and dose" vocabulary and his confused phrasing—such as referring to "Mr. Persico and myself"—constantly reminded the jury he was a defendant. While cross-examining one witness, he accused the man of having a grudge against him because of a beating Persico's brother had administered over an unpaid loan-sharking debt, saying, "You was angry because you was beat up, and you was beat up because you didn't pay back the money." He also tried to show that another government witness was untrustworthy by claiming that he had failed to make a promised payoff to the mob. The prosecution enjoyed his performance immensely, but his co-defendants (and their lawyers) were distinctly displeased. They could not voice their unhappiness, though, because he was a boss. According to mob protocol, his actions could not be questioned.

At the heart of the government's case was the "concrete cartel." Some of the defense lawyers argued that it was the contractors who should have been charged with bid rigging, instead of their clients for extortion. Ultimately the most damaging evidence was the tapes. The defendants convicted themselves from their own mouths. In November 1986, they were found guilty, and all but one were sentenced to a hundred years in prison. The verdict was upheld on appeal. Since many of the defendants were senior citizens, or close to it, their careers were over. Carmine Persico took the verdict hard, allegedly putting out a contract on Giuliani. When a prison informer reported it to the FBI, they began visiting mob bosses, and the contract was canceled. Each New York family would also be charged and convicted in its own separate RICO case. Across the country, mobs in cities from Boston to Los Angeles were receiving similar treatment. In the same year as the commission verdict, the Southern District clerk who served as a mob mole stood trial, having been caught up in an FBI sting. She would be sentenced to one year under house arrest and still be allowed to receive her government pension.

Corallo, Salerno, and some of the other commission bosses spent part of their remaining years in a federal medical facility in Springfield, Missouri. By that time they had largely been forgotten by their New York friends and received few visitors. They were so lonely that they even welcomed occasional visits by an FBI agent from the Kansas City office. He, at least, appreciated what big shots they had once been, so they were happy to converse with him—though they never did reveal any Mafia secrets.

CHAPTER 12

THE DEFECTOR AND THE DON:
TAKING DOWN JOHN GOTTI

T he commission case would deal a heavy blow to the Mafia, but even before the trial commenced, the government learned that the mobs were not going to fold up their tents quietly. On the evening of December 16, 1985, Professor Blakey was scheduled to give one of his RICO seminars for law enforcement at NYU Law School in Greenwich Village. Blakey and his theories were no longer ignored; now his talks were banner events and law enforcement officials flocked to them. Shortly before six o'clock a pre-event cocktail party was in progress. At the John Jay College of Criminal Justice three miles to the north, a Christmas party was in full swing. Suddenly beepers began to go off in both places. Some revelers headed for the door, and at NYU, Blakey stood wondering why so many people were not sticking around to listen to his lecture. As it turned out, they had been notified that Big Paul Castellano and his bodyguard chauffeur, Tommy Bilotti, had just been gunned down outside Sparks Steak House in midtown Manhattan. Racing uptown from NYU and across town from John Jay, cops and FBI agents streamed to the murder scene.

Dressed in identical fur caps and tan trench coats to frustrate eyewitness identification, four gunmen had killed the two men as they were alighting from their car outside the restaurant. The immediate questions before the detectives were who was behind the crime, and why it was carried out.

Would the bosses waiting to be tried in the commission case have been foolish enough to sanction such a hit? It did not take too long for the investigators to get answers: It was an unauthorized killing, arranged by a Gambino capo named John Gotti. As he would soon prove, it was a bit premature to celebrate the downfall of the New York Mafia.

For someone who would rise so high in the firmament of organized crime—at least in the eyes of the media—John Gotti came late to prominence. Lucky Luciano had been the premier boss of New York at thirty-four, and Capone was just twenty-six when he took over in Chicago. Born in 1940, at age forty-five Gotti was still only a midlevel capo. In the 1960s he had advanced from a street tough to a petty burglar and auto thief in a Brooklyn crew run by capo Carmine Fatico. Eventually he established himself as a hijacker at Kennedy Airport. He took up with a fellow thief named Wilfred "Willie Boy" Johnson, a huge, part–Native American bruiser with a reputation for violent behavior. Willie Boy became Gotti's faithful retainer.

Late in 1967 the FBI arrested Gotti for an airport hijacking. He was charged with two more hijackings in New Jersey while out on bail. The charges led to a four-year sentence in Lewisburg. Carmine Galante was then serving as boss of the Mafia wing of the prison, and Gotti complained to him about not getting a sufficient share of T-bones and Scotch. Impressed by the young man's nerve, Galante asked Gotti if he would like to join the Bonanno family when he got out. Instead, after serving a little over two and a half years, Gotti returned to the Fatico crew. By that time they had abandoned their previous base in East New York, Brooklyn, in favor of a spot nearer to the airport, in Ozone Park, Queens. Fatico took over a couple of adjacent storefronts on 101st Avenue that he named the Bergin Hunt and Fish Club (perhaps a reference to Bergen Street with an *e* back in Brooklyn). Gotti, then thirty-two and married with children, moved into the nearby Howard Beach area.

In 1973, Neil Dellacroce gave Gotti a career boost. A freelance hoodlum named James McBratney was identified as one of the men who had kidnapped the nephew of Carlo Gambino, demanding $100,000 to release him. Carlo took a businesslike approach to the problem, observing that if he paid the ransom, all of his nephews would be kidnapped. A deal was finally struck for a lesser sum, but the kidnappers killed young Manny Gambino anyway. Gotti and two mob pals, Angelo Ruggiero and Ralph Galione, were assigned to deal with McBratney. Apparently the plan was to seize him and take him someplace where he could be made to suffer before dying. In a typical example of Gotti's bravado, instead of waiting to ambush their target in some quiet spot, the three men walked into an Irish bar on Staten Island posing as police and "arrested" McBratney. Bona fide cops look, talk, and act in distinctive ways that any street guy can instantly recognize. McBratney realized that Gotti and company were phonies, and began struggling when they tried to take him out of the bar. Some of the patrons started shouting and threatened to jump in. During the mêlée, Galione shot and killed McBratney. Ruggiero and Galione were eventually arrested; Galione was murdered to prevent him from talking and as punishment for botching the job. Gotti disappeared before he could be arrested. For a year he was "in the wind," and then an informer told the FBI that they could find him in a particular bar. Agents took him without any trouble and turned him over to the NYPD.

The New York criminal justice system allowed Gotti to plead guilty to attempted manslaughter. He received a four-year sentence and served two. Thus he did less time for participating in the killing than the hijackings. One possible reason for the odd calculus is that the hijacking case was tried in a federal court and the killing in a state court, where Gotti's lawyer, Roy Cohn, was able to obtain a more lenient sentence. As a reward for his services, Gotti was inducted into the Gambino family after his release. When Fatico was taken ill, Gotti's patron, Dellacroce, named him acting boss of the crew and eventually made it permanent.

The group that Gotti led specialized in hijacking, with sidelines in gambling, loan sharking and—on the quiet—drugs. The last was a violation of Paul Castellano's orders, but some family members felt that the dictum did not apply to them. This group included Gotti's brother Gene and his friend Ruggiero. John Gotti himself did not engage in drug dealing, though he shared in the profits from it. Only five foot eight, the powerfully built Gotti developed a reputation as a tough guy among tough guys, with a violent temper. Only one thing scared him: Even though his original base of operations was an airport, Gotti drew the line at flying. In the late '70s he began to attract attention in the mob world of Brooklyn and Queens. Once while entering a restaurant he spotted a lawyer who occasionally represented him dining with Jimmy Burke, king of the JFK hijackers. When the lawyer failed to come over and pay his respects, Gotti summoned him to the Bergin and threatened to kill him.

The mob world also heard the story of Gotti's personal tragedy. While riding a motorbike, his youngest boy, twelve-year-old Frank, darted out from behind a dumpster and was killed by an automobile. The driver was a quiet family man devoted to his two adopted children, one of whom played with Gotti's kids. When he asked a local priest if he should attend the boy's funeral, he was advised not to. Later he started receiving threats and hearing whispers that he was going to be killed. He put his house up for sale, but it was too late. Walking to his car one night after work, he was seized by several men, including one whose description resembled Willie Boy Johnson, and was never seen again. The word on the street was that he and his automobile were put into a compactor and crushed beyond recognition.

When Dellacroce died of cancer in 1985, Paul Castellano did not go to his funeral. Castellano was already under indictment in the commission case and on trial in an auto theft ring case, and he figured that attending would only call attention to his boss role. In this he was acting like the racketeer-businessman he had become; but his decision was a shocking breach of protocol, deeply resented by the gangster faction of the family. Tough guys like Gotti had never respected Castellano, but Dellacroce's acceptance of the situation had kept them quiet. Now that he was gone, the time was right for a revolt. Another concern for Gotti was that his brother Gene and Angelo Ruggiero had been indicted for drug dealing. With Dellacroce no longer around, there was nobody to stop Castellano from ordering them "whacked" for disobeying his directives.

At the time, Gotti was also facing two criminal indictments himself. The first case grew out of a 1984 incident on a Queens street. A motorist began beeping his horn, annoyed because his car was blocked by Gotti's unattended double-parked Lincoln. When one of Gotti's crew emerged from a nearby tavern and took a swing at the driver, the two men started fighting. Gotti jumped in and the motorist not only got roughed up but was relieved of $325 he had in his shirt pocket. The angry man called the police, and when a sergeant and patrolman from the 106th Precinct responded, he pointed to a nearby restaurant where Gotti and his crew were sitting at a table. The cops entered and ordered Gotti and the other man who had been in the fight to stand. When the whole crew rose, the sergeant warned them firmly to sit down. Gotti asked the sergeant if they knew who he was, and he replied, "No, and I don't care." Gotti and his companion in the brawl were arrested for assault and theft. At the time, his name meant nothing to either the victim or the police. A record check showed that he was just another small-time hoodlum.

In 1981 some armored-car robbers had landed in the Eastern District federal court, where they were prosecuted by a young assistant U.S. attorney named Diane Giacalone. After she won a conviction, she sought to link the money that the robbers had paid in street tax to Gotti and Dellacroce. Her plan was to combine this with other charges, such as the McBratney killing, into a RICO prosecution. In March 1985, indictments were secured against both targets, as well as Willie Boy Johnson and eight other Gambinos.

Neither the state case in Queens nor the federal case in Brooklyn appeared particularly troublesome to Gotti. He had done two years for the killing of a man in front of a bar full of witnesses—how harsh could the sentence be for a simple street altercation? The time he had been convicted in federal court, he had been caught red-handed in a hijacking; now the charge was based on an informer's word. He might not be found guilty. From his standpoint, the situation created by Castellano's indictments, Dellacroce's death, and the plight of his brother and friends was more compelling than his own legal headaches. With his crew, he began plotting to kill Castellano and take over the family.

Part of the plan for hitting Castellano involved securing the support of Sammy Gravano, a murderous member of the family. Sammy was a man that anyone staging a coup would want to have with him, not against him. Raised in the Bensonhurst section of Brooklyn, Sammy had graduated from a membership in a street gang to hanging with the Colombo family. In 1970 he had been one of the men that Joe Colombo ordered to picket the New York FBI office. Gravano's powerful, compact build and physical strength had earned him his nickname, "the Bull." At twenty-five he made his bones by killing a gangster who had offended a Colombo capo, the first of many murders he would commit in the service of the mob. Early on,

Sammy did something unusual: He switched his affiliation from the Colombos to the Gambinos. He had the Colombos' okay, so he was not a defector, but it was an act that might have been a clue to his future behavior. At the time of Gotti's approach, Gravano and his friend Frank DeCicco suspected that if Castellano went to prison he would pass the family leadership to Tommy Gambino, overseer of the garment district, and Big Paul's slugger bodyguard Tommy Bilotti—in their words, "a dressmaker and a gorilla." They preferred Gotti and accepted his overtures, but agreed among themselves that if he didn't work out they would personally kill him.

If Gotti had been a more seasoned crew chief, he probably would not have carried out the hit on Castellano in the middle of Manhattan at the height of the Christmas rush. The streets and sidewalks were packed, Grand Central Terminal was nearby, and the headquarters of the United Nations—whose diplomats frequently ate at Sparks—was a couple of blocks east. As it turned out, he was lucky. No children on their way to see Santa Claus caught a stray bullet; no pedestrian hurrying to catch a train was mowed down by a "crash car" driver swerving to block pursuing cops; no armed guards escorting diplomats stumbled into the shooting. Afterward, Gotti called a meeting of the capos, and while his gunmen stood around eyeing those assembled, he was unanimously endorsed for family head. His official statement was that he did not know who hit Paul, and everyone he told it to managed to keep a straight face. Frank DeCicco was named underboss. Sammy Gravano was made a capo. The Gambinos were satisfied, but the other families were not. Genovese boss Chin Gigante felt that "Johnny Boy" had broken the rules by hitting Castellano without asking permission. With the Lucchese family, he cooked up a little scheme: Four months after the hit on Castellano, DeCicco and a companion who resembled Gotti were about to enter a car on a Brooklyn street when a remote-controlled bomb exploded. The Gotti look-alike lost a few toes. DeCicco lost a leg, an arm, his buttocks, and his private parts, along with his life. Gigante had hit on a clever way to confuse the Gambinos, as explosives were rarely used in New York gang warfare. Because bombs were common in Sicily, some thought it was the work of zips. Others guessed that someone within the family had sought to avenge Castellano or Bilotti. Next, an FBI bug in a ladies' room used as a meeting place by some Genovese hoods picked up word that Gigante was plotting to kill Gotti. As required by Bureau rules, agents went to John's home and informed him that the attack had come from "the West Side," the common mob term for the Genovese family.

Gotti was now widely known. Unlike most mob bosses, he was not camera-shy. He enjoyed the publicity, occasionally pausing in his rounds to say a few words to reporters. His new fame affected both his pending cases. The Queens motorist, at this point fully aware of who Gotti was, had to be compelled to testify. When questioned on the witness stand, he was unable to recall any of the events of two years earlier. A tabloid headline characterized his testimony as "I Forgotti." When the case was dismissed, both parties were satisfied: Gotti was free, and the motorist was alive. In the Eastern District, Gotti's fame had the opposite effect. Prosecutor Giacalone informed the court that he had threatened the Queens motorist and requested that he be locked up so as not to interfere with witnesses in her case.[1] The judge ordered him to be incarcerated in the Metropolitan Correctional Center in Manhattan.

Giacalone did not come from a mob-busting background, although she had been raised in Ozone Park, where she occasionally walked past the Bergin (at the time, she had wondered why all those men standing around were not out working). After graduating from NYU Law School, she took a job in the tax division of the U.S. Department of Justice in Washington, and later transferred to the Eastern District. The Eastern District fielded a separate organized crime strike force that was then also preparing a case against the Gambino family. The strike force attorneys believed it would be difficult to link Gotti to the holdups, and if he went free he would be immunized from further prosecution for the crimes he was charged with. They argued that he should be included in their case instead. Ed McDonald, the strike force chief, sent a memo to the Justice Department in Washington outlining the perceived weaknesses in Giacalone's case. Giacalone also came into conflict with the FBI when she surfaced one of their informers as a prospective witness against Gotti—Willie Boy Johnson, Gotti's longtime friend and associate. As BQ (Brooklyn Queens office) informer

---

1 There were also allegations that he had threatened a police officer.

5558 TE (Top Echelon), code name "Wahoo," Willie had been feeding information to the Bureau for more than fifteen years. It was Johnson who fingered Gotti in the McBratney killing. Willie Boy had recently made the mistake of trying to square a state charge by telling the NYPD that he was an informer for the FBI, expressing a willingness to do likewise for them, and the cops tipped Giacalone to the secret. The FBI believed that if Johnson were identified, he would be killed, so they wanted to keep him off the stand. The discussions became so heated that one agent told Giacalone that if she were a man he would punch her in the jaw. In response, she stood up and told him to take his best shot.[2] Despite the strike force's opposition, the Department of Justice permitted Giacalone to go ahead with her prosecution.

The case turned into a disaster for the government. When Gotti and Johnson were locked up in the Correctional Center, John pledged that if Willie kept quiet, no harm would come to him—so Willie Boy refused to testify. Giacalone had other witnesses, but most were career criminals whom the defense lawyers were able to tear apart. One defense witness testified that when Giacalone had tried to recruit him for her side, she had given him a pair of her underpants and told him to gratify himself in response to his complaints about lack of sex. It was outrageous, but the judge, a wealthy patrician and former politician, seemed unable to rein in the defense.[3] The jury acquitted the defendants on all charges. Unknown to the prosecution, Gotti had slipped $60,000 to a juror, using Sammy Gravano as intermediary. Some prosecutorial sources would later claim that FBI agents had learned of this through an informant and chosen not to report the bribe to the Eastern District. However, the Eastern District U.S. attorney confirmed to me that the Bureau did in fact pass on word about a possible attempt to fix a juror, but were unable to provide any specifics at the time. In any event, the other eleven jurors apparently agreed with the not-guilty verdict.

2 It might occur to some readers that the Bureau's objection to Giacalone was based on male chauvinism. In fact, across the river in the Southern District, the FBI's favorite prosecutor was Barbara Jones (now a federal judge).
3 Some accounts of the case have been highly critical of Judge Eugene Nickerson. Perhaps, as one astute former prosecutor told the writer, "He was a good trial judge, but he didn't know how to handle non-gentlemen."

Gotti's period of national notoriety began when he was released from custody in May 1986. His life followed a regular schedule: He would arise in the late morning and show up at the Bergin Club at noon, spending the afternoon talking and playing cards with the boys. He created a virtual beauty parlor in the back room of the annex with mirrors and a barber's chair. Every day a stylist came to shampoo, cut, and blow-dry his hair. He explained to his aides, "I have to look good for my public." Given his new importance, Gotti also had to have a Manhattan office, like any other successful New York executive, so around five o'clock he would arrive at Dellacroce's old hangout, the Ravenite Club. TV crews who wanted interviews knew this was the place to wait for him. The journalists generally questioned him with the same awe and respect they would accord a film superstar. If it were necessary to have a quiet talk with some of his boys, he would take them for a walk in the nearby streets. When he spotted cops or G-men following him, he would rub his forefingers together to signify "naughty, naughty." Early in the evening he would head to the glamorous Upper East Side for dinner at some chic restaurant, followed by drinking and dancing at the latest "in" place for the Beautiful People. A particular favorite was Regine's, where top models, TV personalities, and movie stars congregated. If a woman caught his eye, one of his henchmen would go over to her and ask if she would "care to join John Gotti for a drink." Most were delighted to do so. Later on there might be a discreet rendezvous with some Uptown beauty or, on a more regular basis, the wife of a Gambino soldier. This last was a violation of mob rules, which displeased Chin Gigante and other bosses.

As Gotti's celebrity grew, mob guys and wannabes began imitating his dress: Armani jacket, gray turtleneck sweater, and plenty of gold chains. Reporters dubbed him "the Dapper Don." As befitted his CEO status, he acquired closets full of well-tailored suits and exchanged his Lincoln for a Mercedes. In all of his activities and appearances, Gotti attempted to project the image of a swashbuckling, confident, charismatic boss, one whom his family—and perhaps others as well—would be proud to follow. It was a deliberate attempt to set himself apart from men like Castellano or Gigante, who kept low profiles, pretending to be either legitimate businessmen or crazy.

At home in Howard Beach, Gotti played Lord of the Manor. Every Fourth of July he hosted a huge celebration for the whole neighborhood. Six city blocks were cordoned off with dumpsters so that several thousand people could partake of food and drink, enjoy carnival rides, or play roulette. When darkness fell, a massive fireworks display would light the sky. No city permits were ever sought to do any of these things, and the NYPD did not intervene. Instead, its officers stood outside the barricades, reduced to passive spectators at Gotti's circus. No one had been paid off to keep the municipal authorities at bay. No powerful politician had gone down to City Hall to see to it that instead of cops laying down the law, the law would lie down. If anyone asked why Gotti was allowed such privileges, the usual answer would be that for many years other groups had been granted similar liberties, and besides, a crackdown would probably trigger a riot and be seen as anti-Italian. After all, it was only one night a year. Of course, the symbolic message resonated 365 days a year: Gotti was Robin Hood, making a fool of the sheriff. Signs in the neighborhood proclaimed the people's love for John.

The behavior of Gotti's neighbors probably had deeper roots than simple celebrity worship or anti–law enforcement feelings. The people of Howard Beach were typical blue-collar Americans. During the Vietnam War, instead of dodging the draft, their young men followed the dictum "My country, right or wrong" and shouldered a rifle. They were the people performing the unglamorous jobs that kept the economy running. They knew that the educated elite looked down on them, and so when one of their own rose to be rich and famous, they cheered him on even though they knew he was a criminal. After Sammy Gravano turned against Gotti he would bitterly observe, "I always wondered how fast these people would have spit out their dogs and burgers if they had known that they were being paid for from drug dealing to their own children in that neighborhood."

Some of Gotti's severest critics were found within the mob itself. His high-profile activities went against traditional practices—Mafia business was supposed to be secret, not played out on TV. In giving interviews to reporters, he was telling the world that he was a gangster and putting a face on organized crime. By demanding that his capos show up at the Ravenite, he allowed the FBI to compile a table of organization on the Gambinos.

Gotti's clockwork schedule also made it easier for law enforcement to tail him. Then there was his maneuvering within the five families: He tried to persuade the Genovese and Lucchese bosses to permit the Bonannos to have a seat on the commission once again, and advocated for the acting boss of the Colombos to be allowed to represent his family. Both men were Gotti's good friends, and if they were installed, it would give him majority control of the commission. Chin Gigante had the motion tabled. Gotti then asked Chin to make forty new men in the Genovese family. Gigante firmly reminded him that he alone would make that decision. Gigante did not want forty of his own gang feeling grateful to Johnny Boy. When Gotti proudly told the commission that his son John had just been made a member of the Gambinos, Gigante said, "Jeez, I'm sorry to hear that." Many bosses tried to keep their kids out of the mob. As Sammy Gravano would later observe, "So here was Chin, who is supposed to be crazy, saying who in their right mind wanted their son to be made? And there was John boasting about it. Who was really crazy?"

During the late '80s, Sammy Gravano began to grow increasingly close to Gotti, largely for professional rather than personal reasons. Along with murder, Sammy specialized in construction. He took great pride in the fact that he knew the technical details of the industry and enjoyed engaging in complex business negotiations. He used mob connections to get contracts, but he claimed that he made sure all the work his people did was first-rate, so his customers were satisfied. While Gotti listed his occupation as plumbing supply salesman as a means of claiming a legitimate source of income, unlike Castellano or Gravano, he was not interested in business operations. That was a negative. A Mafia family was more than just a street gang; it was a commercial enterprise, and to be successful it had to be run that way. Though he was raking in an estimated $10 million in cash annually, Gotti, a heavy gambler, was frequently broke.

After Gotti was acquitted in the Eastern District case, he named Gravano to the position of family consigliere. As a member of the "administration" he was expected to show up at the Ravenite meetings. While the other bosses dressed for such occasions, Sammy would appear in jacket and jeans, and he declined to accompany John on his late-night rambles, driving back to Brooklyn for dinner with his wife instead. Despite Sammy's new rank, Gotti continued to use him to carry out hits. One of his victims was a man who had beaten up a Gambino soldier; another had decided to talk to a grand jury. Sammy supposedly arranged the hit on Willie Boy Johnson, who was riddled with bullets as he came out of his house.[4] Johnson had naïvely believed Gotti's promise not to harm him. Despite their murderous collaboration, Gotti and Gravano did not see eye to eye on policy. Sammy thought Gotti was making the same mistake Colombo had made twenty years earlier by taunting the FBI, which would only result in the law coming down harder on them. As Gravano told his biographer Peter Maas, "Maybe he thought he was some sort of Robin Hood with the people cheering him. Hey, what is this? All of a sudden the government is the bad guy, and we are really the good guys? I don't think I'm Robin Hood. I think I'm a gangster."

Gotti continued to make mistakes. When a fancy downtown restaurant owned by the Gambinos employed some nonunion workers to do remodeling, a carpenters union official took a crew down to the restaurant and wrecked the place. Gotti was informed about the man's actions, and a bug in the Bergin complex—planted by Ron Goldstock's organized crime task force—recorded him saying "Put a rocket in his pocket." A Hell's Kitchen Irish gang known as the Westies, who sometimes subcontracted hits for the family, was given the job of shooting the leader of the wrecking crew. The man was shot, but only wounded. When a Westie gunman talked, New York County district attorney Morgenthau brought an indictment against Gotti for assault. Again one juror was bribed, and again Gotti was acquitted. The press now hailed Gotti as "the Teflon Don." Newspapers and television lived on circulation and ratings; for the first time in years they had a colorful gangster to report on. *Time* magazine put him on its cover—not a plus for a man in Gotti's position. When a gangster becomes a celebrity, it is often a prelude to his downfall. Al Capone and Frank Costello had been *Time* cover boys. Not long afterward, they went to jail.

The media attention angered the FBI agents and cops, who could not

4 According to law enforcement sources, Gravano was not the actual gunman. (See Chapter 14.)

forget incidents like the family man who may have been put into a compactor. The FBI redoubled its efforts to "get Gotti." They followed him constantly, shadowing his walks around the Ravenite neighborhood. Once, as he and Gravano strolled past a van, Sammy saw a television set inside with a picture of them on the screen. It was the FBI filming them and trying to pick up their conversation on a microphone. What the Gambinos did not know was that the FBI had a bug in an apartment above the Ravenite where Gotti discussed business.

The G-men were full of tricks. One ploy was the use of "rat patrols." Agents would place a paper bag with eyeholes over the head of an informer and drive him past locations where mob guys hung out so he could point out the players. When the gangsters spotted them, they would raise the cry "They've got a rat" and scatter. Sometimes the man in the hood would be an FBI agent pretending to be an informer just to shake the boys up. Gotti too could play games. For a price, an NYPD detective kept him informed about various investigations. William Piest had lost a leg in an off-duty automobile accident. When he was refused a disability pension because his injury had not occurred in the line of duty, he went to work as an analyst in the intelligence division. Eventually the FBI was able to set up a sting that produced enough evidence for the NYPD to fire Piest, though not enough to make a criminal case against him.

By 1990 sufficient information was available from Gotti's own mouth to develop a RICO case based on gambling, loan sharking, the Castellano murder, tax evasion, and other offenses. The only question was who would prosecute it—law enforcement officials were so eager to get Gotti that there was no shortage of candidates for the job. The U.S. attorney for the Eastern District, Andy Maloney, had begun his career as an assistant in the Southern District under Morgenthau, going on to hold a number of key law enforcement jobs. Known as a tough prosecutor, the item on his résumé that he was most proud of was his captaincy of the boxing team at West Point. Maloney had not been the U.S. attorney when Diane Giacalone commenced the Eastern District prosecution of Gotti, but he was in the job when the acquittal came down. Another man might have let her face the reporters alone; Andy Maloney stepped front and center and fielded all the critical questions. At the trial, while waiting for the jury to come in, Maloney closely observed Gotti and did not like what he saw. In his experience, even the toughest hood would display some nervousness while waiting to hear his fate. Gotti was perfectly calm, as though he knew the case was in the bag. Bribing a juror and committing perjury to humiliate an assistant U.S. attorney were crimes that no prosecutor's office could permit to go unpunished. Rudy Giuliani, who was also developing a case against Gotti, had been a young assistant in the Southern District when Andy Maloney was a senior prosecutor, and the two worked well together. Maloney went to Giuliani and explained to him why the prosecution must be returned to the Eastern District. Giuliani was agreeable, but the Southern District had been working with District Attorney Morgenthau's staff to put together a joint case. The final decision was made at the top of the U.S. Department of Justice. On orders from Washington, the Eastern District would be allowed to prosecute the entire case. Maloney agreed to participate personally, while the lead attorney would be Diane Giacalone's former co-counsel, John Gleeson.[5]

At the beginning of 1990, with the Feds closing in, Gotti made Sammy Gravano underboss. The theory was that while Gotti sat in jail during the trial, Gravano would go into hiding and continue to run the family. Gotti was betting that Sammy's reputation as a killer and his own proven ability to win acquittals would keep the troops in line until the trial was over. In October 1990, Gravano went "into the wind" for a couple of months, but he tired of it and returned to New York. On the night of December 11, Gotti, Gravano, and other family members were arrested at the Ravenite by FBI agents. The FBI was holding its annual Christmas party on the same night. Jim Fox, head of the New York office, took the stage and stopped the festivities, announcing, "I've got a Christmas present for all of us. John Gotti was arrested tonight by agents of the Federal Bureau of Investigation." A torrent of applause swept the room. After their arrests, Gravano and Gotti were taken to FBI headquarters in downtown Manhattan. During their processing an agent told them, "This is James Fox, he runs this place."

5 Knowledgeable people will note that I have omitted accounts of the "spirited" discussions among various parties seeking to prosecute Gotti and the deep disappointment felt by those passed over. The subject has been recounted in many published works in which participants give their version of events. Since I did not personally witness any of the conversations, I am unable to make any judgments about the matter.

Gotti snarled "Shame on you." In contrast, Sammy held out his shackled hand and said "Mr. Fox, pleased to meet you." Fox, who had his back to him, automatically turned and was chagrined to find himself shaking hands with the notorious Sammy the Bull.

Jim Fox looked like Central Casting's version of an FBI executive: slim, handsome, and clean-cut, with graying hair.[6] A Chicago bus driver's son, he had attended an exclusive prep school and a small midwestern college on football scholarships. At each he was both an agile halfback and a good student. He joined the FBI in 1962 after obtaining his law degree from the University of Illinois. He had learned Chinese at the Army language school in Monterey, California, and his Bureau service was largely spent in counterintelligence work. Before taking the helm of the New York office in 1987, he had spent most of his career chasing spies in San Francisco and Chicago. With a thousand agents and three SACs under him, he was at the time the only Bureau official outside Washington to carry the title of Assistant Director of the FBI. Despite his counterintelligence background, he took up organized crime fighting with great zest.

Prior to the trial, federal prosecutors managed to disqualify four lawyers for Gotti and Gravano. The judge in the case ruled that because they had been heard on bugs counseling Gotti, they might be called as witnesses, thereby creating a conflict with their duty as lawyers for the defendants. The move did not particularly disadvantage Gotti. The replacement lawyers he secured had top criminal defense credentials. The accused were entitled to hear the evidentiary tapes against them, and when Gravano listened to Gotti badmouthing him about the money Sammy was making in his construction business, he was upset. He also suspected that the defense might attempt to shift blame from Gotti to himself, bargaining on his reputation as a killer. Sammy was facing an almost sure sentence of life imprisonment, so he reached out to the FBI and offered to testify for the government. Some members of the prosecution team were against making a deal. They feared that it was a trick, and that Gravano would tell one story to the prosecutors and then take the stand and repudiate it, as Willie Boy had done. Gleeson and Fox argued for accepting his offer. Finally the

6 Some readers will remember him from his many network TV appearances at the time of the 1993 World Trade Center bombing.

Department of Justice in Washington approved it on the condition that Gravano plead guilty and receive a twenty-year sentence. After Sammy agreed to become an informer, he and Fox met on several occasions while Gravano was in protective custody on the Quantico, Virginia, Marine base, site of the FBI training center. Fox would fly down to see him, and the two men would have long talks about topics such as their children.

Gotti's trial was an anticlimax. Early in the morning on the first day of testimony, an FBI helicopter flew Sammy Gravano down from the Bureau's shooting range at Camp Smith, sixty miles north of New York City. From a landing pad in Lower Manhattan he was transferred under heavy guard to the federal courthouse in Brooklyn. Jim Fox joined him for breakfast. Over coffee and bagels, Fox asked Sammy if he realized how important his testimony would be. "It will be the beginning of the end of organized crime," Gravano replied. Later he would recall that on his entrance, the court room was so silent, "You could hear a pin drop." The front rows were occupied by members of the New York FBI SWAT team, suit jackets open, shoulder-holstered weapons visible. Behind them were the defendant's supporters, many of whom were also known to pack guns. Not today, though: U.S. marshals had screened them with metal detectors to verify that none were "carrying."

"Our next witness is Salvatore Gravano," Gleeson announced. Seated at the defense table, when Gotti caught sight of the usually casual Sammy attired in a gray double-breasted suit and red tie, he snorted, "Look, he's all dressed up." Gotti's tone was jocular and his lips formed a tight smile, but his eyes, focused intently on Gravano, were full of menace. On the witness stand, Gravano returned Gotti's hard stares and answered Gleeson's first question in a firm voice, saying, "John was the boss and I was the under-boss." During the nine days he spent on the stand, Sammy's testimony could not be shaken. Gravano had no fear of Gotti at all. Andy Maloney, a man who is a pretty good judge of fighting skill, maintains that if it had come to a physical confrontation between the two, his money would have been on Sammy. Though Gotti had able defense counsel, their task was formidable. The chief items of evidence against him were his own words and those of Gravano, who described in detail the inner workings of the Gambino family and the flow of dollars to Gotti. The defense constantly reminded the jury of Gravano's nineteen murders, with one attorney saying, "Is this where our system of justice has dropped to? Award a sick, demented serial killer his freedom for what?" And pointing toward Gotti, "In exchange for that man's head!" Calling attention to Gravano's murders might actually have helped the prosecution—the jurors may have reasoned that if Gravano was so bad, what did it say about Gotti that he had named him underboss? In any event, if Sammy was not a candidate for sainthood, neither was Johnny. When Gravano left the stand for the last time, Gotti made the sign of the cross and wiped a tear from his eye. Some Feds in the courtroom sneeringly dismissed it as an act. The jury was sequestered and none of them were bribed. When one juror tried to slip out a package with the names, addresses, and phone numbers of some of the others, she was caught and dismissed from the panel. In April 1992, Gotti was convicted. It had taken five years, three unsuccessful prosecutions, and an estimated $75 million for law enforcement to come to this moment. Jim Fox told reporters, "The Teflon is gone. The Don is covered with Velcro, all the charges have stuck." Later, as the various mob cases began bringing down boss after boss, Fox would observe, "Another day, another Don."[7]

Additional criminal cases that resulted from Gravano's information included the convictions of Detective Piest, of the juror Gravano had bribed, and of the witness who had rendered false testimony about Giacalone handing him her underpants. All three were imprisoned. Gotti was sentenced to life in the federal penitentiary in Marion, Illinois, where he would remain until his death in 2002. His funeral in New York was notable for the fact that very few mob figures turned out. In contrast, the media gave it the same kind of attention it had lavished on the funerals of Princess Diana and JFK Junior. Four television news helicopters hovered overhead. The residents of Howard Beach continued the annual Fourth of July party as a

---

7 Again, knowledgeable readers will note that I have not awarded victors' laurels to specific individuals for the conviction of Gotti. I have chosen instead to highlight the two agency heads, Jim Fox, director of the New York FBI office, and Andy Maloney, U.S. attorney for the Eastern District. In this respect I recollect the famous story about the victorious general who, when asked who really won the battle, replied, "I don't know who won it; all I know is who would have lost it."

tribute to their absent neighbor, but the city no longer treated the event as off limits to law enforcement. Instead, an army of cops policed it, making sure all laws were adhered to. Jim Fox went on to head the FBI investigation that led to the arrest of the terrorists who carried out the 1993 bombing of the World Trade Center. At the end of that year he retired from the Bureau to become an executive with an insurance company. During the six years he served as head of the New York office, he had become an extremely popular local figure, counting corporate CEOs, celebrities, and New York street cops among his friends. When he died in 1997 at the age of fifty-nine, he was given a virtual state funeral.

At Gravano's sentencing, the twenty years he had agreed to was reduced to five (or about ninety days for each murder). Released from custody in 1995, he voluntarily left the witness protection program, boasting that he had nothing to fear. He told his story to bestselling author Peter Maas in a book entitled *Underboss*. Maas, who had previously written up Joe Valachi's memoirs, struggled to make Sammy at least a little bit sympathetic, but it was a tough sell. In 2000 Gravano, his wife, son, daughter, and his daughter's boyfriend were arrested in Arizona on state and federal drug charges, accused of operating a ring that grossed about $500,000 a week selling ecstasy pills. As a result of the case, Arizona authorities seized $400,000 worth of Gravano's property and book royalties to distribute to the families of his murder victims. Gravano was later sentenced to twenty years in prison. An FBI agent involved in the Gotti takedown said of Sammy and informers in general, "Using some of these guys is like taming a wolf. You can feed them out of your hand but they're still wolves and you can never trust them."

In the years since Gotti's conviction, some people have questioned whether the government's massive campaign against him and its deal with a character like Gravano were worthwhile. John Gotti was largely a creation of the media. Most New York organized crime experts always regarded Chin Gigante as a more important figure.[8] Gotti had taken control of the Gambinos

---

8 A former federal prosecutor with long experience in New York organized crime investigations expressed a different view to me. He argued that Gigante's efforts to keep a low profile impaired the operations of the Genovese family in the same way that a remote CEO would handicap a normal business enterprise.

at a time when his own leader and the other commission bosses were almost paralyzed by the federal assault on them. Had the mobs not been in disarray, he might never have succeeded in his attempt—or even thought of it. A few months after taking over, he came close to death at the hands of other bosses. The following year he might have been convicted if the strike force had been allowed to present its case in Brooklyn. If either of those things had happened he would have been quickly forgotten. Over the next four years his high visibility and open defiance of the government made him a star on TV, but his reputation was mostly based on flash, backed with little substance. Compared with past mob superstars like Capone or Costello, or even to lower-profile ones such as Tommy Lucchese or Tony Accardo, he had little power. While they could count mayors, governors, and members of Congress among their allies, Gotti had virtually no political influence. By the time he became boss, New York politicians had learned to be wary of seeming friendly with mobsters. No members of Congress showed up at Gotti's Fourth of July celebration. Mayors or governors never appeared as character witnesses at his trials.

For a while Gotti conned himself and others into believing he could defeat the United States government. Uncle Sam had to prove him wrong, whatever the cost. He also caused other bosses to fear that he might try to move in on them, or that his antics would spur the government to even greater efforts against all of the families. Thus Gotti was in a life-and-death situation. He would either receive a life sentence from the government or a death sentence from his peers. As it turned out, the government got him first.

CHAPTER 13

DEALING WITH THE DEVIL:
THE HUNT FOR "WHITEY"

One day in January 1995, James "Whitey" Bulger was driving along Interstate 95 in Connecticut with his girlfriend, listening to the radio, when he heard a news bulletin that caused him to turn off at the next exit. Whitey's old pal and partner-in-crime, Steve "The Rifleman" Flemmi, had been arrested. It was not a wholly unexpected development. The Boston organized crime world had been tense for several months. There were whispers that a federal grand jury was taking testimony that would probably lead to indictments against mob figures. As leaders of Boston's top mob, the Winter Hill Gang, Bulger and Flemmi were prime targets, as was "Cadillac Frank" Salemme, boss of what was left of the local Mafia. For years the Mafia had reeled under FBI blows, but Whitey and Steve led a seemingly charmed life, managing to avoid indictment. To some law enforcement officers their success appeared to be more than just luck. It was as if Whitey and Steve always got a warning just in time—warnings that were rumored to come from federal lawmen. In 1988, a *Boston Globe* story declared that Whitey Bulger had a "special relationship" with the FBI, supplying information on the crimes of others in order that his own be overlooked. The story seemed too far-fetched to be true. Bulger was a notorious hard case, a graduate of some of America's toughest prisons and a suspect in a slew of violent crimes. In the clannish Irish neighborhood of South

Boston, which he had called home all his life, informers were reviled. The *Globe* account had quickly faded from public attention.

As talk about the grand jury spread through Boston during 1994, Bulger and Flemmi began to make themselves scarce. Whitey and his girlfriend traveled to Dublin, London, Venice, and the southern United States. During a brief visit to Boston in December he had been told he was about to be indicted, so they went back on the road. When nothing happened, though, they decided to return to Boston. Flemmi's arrest persuaded them to continue their travels. Finally, in late January, Bulger drove back to Boston and dropped his girlfriend off, saying "I'll call you." She never heard from him again. Instead, he picked up another, younger girlfriend and disappeared. It was a typical double cross by a man who had pulled plenty of them. He had tricked the Mafia, he had tricked his friends in the Winter Hill Gang, and worst of all, he had tricked the agency that had done the most to fight organized crime in America—the FBI.

Bulger's partner, Flemmi, had also pulled a few tricks in his day; this time they didn't work. Perhaps it was his long string of luck that had made Flemmi a little careless. He was captured when he ventured into Boston with his girlfriend and went to a restaurant in the downtown Quincy Market section. As they left the place, two Massachusetts state troopers and a DEA agent confronted them with guns and arrested Steve. He was still unconcerned when he arrived at the Federal Building, confident that after the booking was completed he would be released on bail, after which he would hop a plane for Canada. Back in the 1960s, when he was accused of planting a bomb that blew off a lawyer's leg, Flemmi had left town for four years and did not come back until the witnesses against him had recanted and the charges were dropped. Only when he learned that there would be no bail did Flemmi begin to worry.

At first the takedown appeared to be another in a series of FBI triumphs over organized crime. Cadillac Frank Salemme was tracked to a hideout in Florida. Only Whitey Bulger managed to elude capture, despite having the FBI hot on his trail. Three years later, triumph was much less certain— the defendants had yet to be tried, and Bulger was still a fugitive. During the interval, Flemmi had shocked Boston by mounting a defense that attempted to put the FBI on trial. In open court he alleged that he had been an informer for the Bureau since the mid-1960s, and that the crimes he was accused of were authorized by agents in return for his information. During the course of the proceedings, the *Globe* story was finally confirmed: Since the mid-'70s, Bulger had been an informer too.

In 1997 the judge trying the case agreed to hold an open hearing to determine whether the FBI actions required dismissal of the charges against the defendants. Government lawyers opposed the motion and fought vigorously to keep confidential files secret. They were unsuccessful. Over ten months, many law enforcement officials were summoned to testify. In 1999, Judge Mark Wolf released a 661-page finding of facts, including 384 pages devoted to the FBI's relationships with Bulger and Flemmi. The judge found that some agents had exaggerated the importance of the information that Bulger and Flemmi had furnished, shielded them from investigation by other law enforcement agencies, persuaded federal prosecutors not to charge them in a 1970s case that brought down the previous head of the Winter Hill mob, and may have tipped them off about a state police attempt to bug their headquarters in a downtown Boston garage. A few agents had socialized with the two gangsters, and one supervisor had received $7,000 in cash gifts. The most serious charges were that an agent and a supervisor had revealed to the two gangsters the identity of informants, some of whom were murdered.

It was a sensational turn of events, especially as some of the agents implicated had previously been hailed as gangbusting heroes. After the 1980s takedown of the local Mafia family, *Boston Globe* reporters Gerard O'Neill and Dick Lehr had written an admiring book about the effort. Now the same writers would publish a sequel excoriating the Boston FBI—including some of the same individuals whom they had praised just a few years before.

Lawsuits totaling over $2 billion would be filed against the FBI, mostly by the families of victims allegedly murdered by Bulger and Flemmi. Two agents would be indicted. Whitey Bulger was placed on the FBI's Ten Most Wanted list, and a million-dollar reward was posted for information leading to his capture. A decade after his disappearance he was still a fugitive, and the Bureau faced criticism that it did not actually want him found, for fear of what he might reveal. O'Neill and Lehr would write, "No amount of

FBI talk about how hard it was trying to capture Bulger could overcome the public's impression that the FBI didn't really want to." J. Edgar Hoover had always feared that going after organized crime would involve his agents in scandal and bring harsh criticism on the Bureau itself. In Boston, his fears had been realized.

The Mafia situation in Boston had presented an unusual set of problems for the FBI. The Boston family was not the absolute master of the local mob world: It shared power with Irish-led gangs, and was itself controlled from out of state. This had not always been so—from the 1930s to the mid-'50s, the New England Mafia was run out of Boston's Italian North End by Phil Bucolla and his top lieutenant, Joe Lombardo. When the time came for the senior citizen bosses to relinquish power in the early 1950s, the transition was seamless. There were no bullets, no bodies: Bucolla retired to Sicily, his birthplace, and Lombardo assumed the role of an elder states-man. Bucolla's successor was Raymond Patriarca.

Born in Massachusetts in 1908, Patriarca owed his rise to his proficiency as both a killer and a political operator. As he was making his way up, he spent some time in jail for assorted robberies and murders, but his political connections frequently helped him to get out early. In the 1930s, one precipitate parole caused a scandal leading to the resignation of a member of the Massachusetts Governor's Council. By the late '40s, Patriarca was operating out of Providence, Rhode Island. For years its top organized crime figure was Carleton O'Brien, an Irish bootlegger who had switched to gambling operations after prohibition. In 1952, Patriarca had him killed.

Unlike the New York City families, with their rich pickings from the commercial capital of the world, New England's mafiosi mostly had to content themselves with traditional mob enterprises such as gambling, loan sharking, and extortion. It also had to recognize the power of nearby New York. Patriarca developed a close relationship with the Profaci and Genovese families. In deference to them, he allowed some New York families to maintain a foothold in certain New England areas such as Hartford, Connecticut, and Springfield, Massachusetts.

Patriarca did not move his headquarters to Boston when he took over from Bucolla, remaining instead in Providence's predominantly Italian Federal Hill section. His decision to stay put was probably motivated by security concerns. The neighborhood overlooked the State Capitol, where Patriarca had many friends. Not surprisingly, he preferred to remain close to them. Given his influence in politics, he was rarely bothered by law enforcement. In the early 1960s, an FBI bug in a cigarette vending machine company Patriarca operated picked up conversations revealing his contacts with many leading New England politicians and judges. Nationally he was seen as a major boss, with a seat on the commission. Standing only five feet six inches and given to wearing cheap suits and flashy jewelry, he did not look like a big shot. But he had a fearsome reputation, and his power within his family was unquestioned. He demanded—and received—a cut of all operations. And he tried to keep his troops away from drug trafficking, perhaps one of the few marks in his favor.

Patriarca's Boston deputy was Gennaro "Jerry" Angiulo, eleven years younger than the big boss. Angiulo operated out of the North End neighborhood where he had been born, though he lived in a seaside mansion in the North Shore suburbs. Though a killer, Patriarca occasionally displayed the sunny side of his personality, smiling and waving at passersby, including police officers; but Angiulo was the opposite. His customary expression was a snarl, and if a cop walked past he would spit on the ground. He once served thirty days for punching an IRS agent, and later got the same sentence for assaulting a Coast Guard petty officer who had the temerity to stop him from racing his power boat through Dorchester Bay, swamping other craft. Yet the pudgy Angiulo was not a tough guy. As far as was known he had never killed anyone, and no one—in or out of the mob—was in awe of him as a man. Where Patriarca shot his way to the top, Angiulo bought his position. In the 1950s he had gone hat in hand to Patriarca and convinced him that he could produce more money from Boston gambling and loan sharking than anyone else. During the long relationship between the two men there was never any doubt as to who gave the orders and who took them. From time to time when Angiulo messed up he would be summoned to Federal Hill and given a stiff dressing-down.

In many other cities, non-Italian gangs had been eliminated or supplanted by the Mafia, but in Boston they continued to be powerful. Some observers attribute this phenomenon to the political strength of the Irish gangs; it may also have been due to power realities within the Mafia. Providence was not a major city, but Boston was. It was to Patriarca's advantage that his Boston overseer not have total sway in Massachusetts, lest he become too powerful and attempt to seize control of the family. Having the less-than-swashbuckling Angiulo as his Boston lieutenant made a coup unlikely. As additional insurance, Patriarca played the Irish gangsters against the Italian ones. The situation was not so different from that in Cleveland, where the local Mafia worked closely with the so-called "Jewish boys," or Chicago, where the Outfit was multiethnic. In each place it was a case of business considerations overriding fraternal loyalties. When Angiulo tried to muscle in on Jewish gangsters in suburban Revere, they invoked their own connection to Patriarca, and Jerry ended up having to apologize.

While the New England Mafia was run like a business—and known, fittingly, as "the Office"—the Irish still acted like Jimmy Cagney in gangster roles. When I was on the Boston scene in the late '60s and early '70s, I was repeatedly told that crime and corruption were carried on by Irish gangsters (and their political friends) more for fun than profit. When war broke out among the Irish groups in the 1960s, it stemmed from a barroom fight over a girl, not money or territory, and it was the Italians who had to restore order. On Labor Day of 1961, Buddy McLean's Somerville-based Winter Hill Gang and Bernie McLaughlin's Charlestown boys were enjoying an outing at Salisbury Beach, north of Boston. During the festivities, Bernie's brother George made a pass at a girl who was with a Winter Hill man. According to local lore, when she rejected him, he bit her on the breast. Her escort worked George over with his fists. A few days later, Bernie McLaughlin and another brother, Eddie (a slugger on the Boston docks known as "Punchy"), stormed into Somerville and demanded that the Winter Hill man who beat up their brother be turned over to them for punishment. Buddy McLean told them to get lost. A week later McLean's car wouldn't start, and the mechanic he called to check it out discovered that it had been ineptly wired with dynamite. Honor required a response: A month later, Buddy McLean shot and killed Bernie McLaughlin on a busy Charlestown street. Soon bodies were dropping all over the area.

At first the Mafia bosses looked on with amusement as the "crazy Irishmen" killed one another. They also saw opportunities to take over some of the operations run by the dear departed. Then McLaughlin's brothers, who had succeeded Bernie as bosses of the gang, began shaking down bookmakers to obtain funds to keep their gunmen on the payroll. Some gamblers were under the protection of Angiulo, so this constituted an attack on the Mafia. Additionally, the headlines had the cops racing around picking up gangsters on sight—including Italian ones. Patriarca sent word that if the carnage didn't stop, he would "declare martial law." It was an interesting phrase, as officially only governors had such authority. Then again, as far as organized crime was concerned, Raymond was more powerful than the governor of any New England state. He ordered his deputy, Henry Tameleo, to set up a peace conference between the McLeans and the McLaughlins. In January 1965, Buddy McLean and some of his lieutenants arrived unarmed for a sit-down at a bar designated as the meeting place. The McLaughlins, on the other hand, showed up carrying paper bags. When Tameleo asked what was in them, they replied, "We got our guns . . . we're not going to come in here unarmed, we're not crazy." Their behavior had historical justification: In 1930 two top Irish gangsters from South Boston had been invited to a meeting in the Italian North End, only to be riddled with bullets on their arrival. Still, the McLaughlins were insulting the host, and Tameleo—who had apprenticed in Brooklyn with the Bonanno gang—blew up, canceling the peace talks. When he reported to Patriarca, the boss ordered the McLaughlins wiped out. Before the war ended at least fifty men had been killed, Buddy McLean among them. The Winter Hill Gang, now led by Howie Winter, drew closer to its wartime Mafia allies. Howie began funneling $20,000 a week to Angiulo for a share of the gambling and loan sharking.

Relationships among law enforcement agencies in the Boston area were also subject to factional strife. The FBI and the Boston Police Department had been rivals for years. Colonel Tom Sullivan, who was commissioner of police from 1943 to 1957, was often not on speaking terms with FBI director J. Edgar Hoover. In 1950 there was a multi-million-dollar robbery at a Brink's garage. Though it occurred in the heart of the North End, it was not a Mafia caper. The seven heist men were a cross section of local theives. True to Boston tradition, the cops and G-men feuded while the robbers battled among themselves. Some tried to cheat the others or kill them. Eventually one turned government witness, leading to the conviction of the rest. In 1961, CBS News set up hidden cameras overlooking a Boston key shop that fronted a bookmaking operation. Though the cameras caught members of the Boston Police Department entering and leaving the place, the only raids were carried out by federal Treasury agents or Massachusetts state police. After "Biography of a Bookie Joint" aired, a local FBI agent was named police commissioner, but some elements of the department continued to operate in the traditional fashion.

Within the ranks of state and local law enforcement there were individuals skilled at fighting the Mafia. In 1967 Charles Rogovin, fresh from heading the President's Crime Commission Task Force on Organized Crime, was appointed to direct the organized crime section in Massachusetts attorney general Elliot Richardson's office. But within two years both men had moved on to jobs in Washington. In Massachusetts, as elsewhere, if the Mafia and the other gangs were going to be broken, the task would fall primarily to the FBI.

In the late 1960s, at the end of the Irish gang war, the FBI began to take down the office. Patriarca's top gun during the martial law campaign against the McLaughlins had been a vicious character named Joseph Barboza. Of Portuguese descent, he was not eligible to be a made man, but he served the Mafia in a murderous capacity. Among those he killed was Punchy McLaughlin. When Buddy McLean was murdered, it was Barboza who avenged him by gunning down his assassin. Barboza carried out more than twenty hits, then became a government witness and eventually provided testimony that led to the indictment of Patriarca, Tameleo, and Angiulo.

During the course of the bosses' trials, the Mafia had Frank Salemme and Steve Flemmi place dynamite in Barboza's lawyer's car. The resulting explosion cost the attorney part of his right leg, but it did not deter Barboza. However, the jury found his testimony against Angiulo so unconvincing that the defendant was acquitted outright (and indeed, Barboza's testimony in several other cases was perjured). In the case against Raymond Patriarca, the government cut a deal with hijacker John "Red" Kelley, who was the New England equivalent of New York's Jimmy "The Gent" Burke. Based on Kelley's testimony, Patriarca was convicted in 1968 of conspiracy to commit murder. Again Raymond was "lucky" in his prison time: He served only five years. The parole board's decision to release him may have been influenced by a letter from a high-ranking state official attesting to Patriarca's good character.

Successfully cultivating informants played a large part in the FBI's victories against the Mafia in the late twentieth century. But informants made unwieldy weapons, particularly the vicious characters who were at least as bad as the men they testified against. Government witnesses, like Jimmy Fratianno and Sammy Gravano, often got book deals along with their reduced sentences; their literary efforts seldom contained much remorse about their careers in crime. Instead they proudly recited the beatings and killings they carried out. In a 1970s as-told-to book, *My Life in the Mafia*, a Boston associate named Vinnie Teresa, who flipped over to the government, pridefully recounts invading people's homes, beating and robbing them, and killing their dogs. As an owner of race horses he would not only use electric shocks to improve their performance, but in one instance when the horse lost he beat him with his fists. Despite having twenty or more murders to his name, Barboza was paroled in 1975 and moved to San Francisco, where he lived under an assumed name. Within a year, an assassin from Boston killed him with four blasts from a shotgun. Famed Boston attorney F. Lee Bailey, who had occasionally represented Barboza, was under no illusions about men of his sort, observing, "With all due respect to my former client, I don't think society has suffered a great loss."

Any seasoned investigator knew that such men were likely to betray their law enforcement handlers. The story of Whitey Bulger is a prime example of how some FBI agents were compromised when they over-looked this basic principle.[1] Patriarca's downfall had provided an opening for Howie Winter's Winter Hill Gang. Whitey Bulger and Steve Flemmi were then among Winter's lieutenants. Born in South Boston in 1929, Bulger be-gan acquiring a police record at the age of thirteen. His early crimes in-cluded hijacking, robbery, rape, and bank holdups, one of which netted him over $42,000. He was imprisoned for nine years in such high-security facilities as Atlanta, Lewisburg, Leavenworth, and Alcatraz, spending con-siderable time in solitary confinement. After his release in 1965, he be-haved himself for the duration of his parole and then took up work as a debt collector for gamblers and loan sharks in South Boston. Whitey was a man of average height and weight, but he had honed his skills in some of America's toughest prisons and was eminently qualified for the duties of a heavy. Debtors he dunned usually paid up—fast.

Bulger's work involved him in the inevitable factional disputes between South Boston gangs, which sometimes led to killings. To increase his own chances of survival, he decided to enlist with the more powerful Winter Hill mob. On behalf of Howie Winter, he began mowing down other organized crime figures in "Southie," rising to become the top gangster in the neigh-borhood. To bolster his standing in the community he posed as a generous benefactor, delivering turkeys to needy families. In 1974 South Boston be-came known to national television audiences when many of its citizens banded together to resist court-ordered busing, sometimes violently. One of the most vocal leaders of the community protest was Whitey's younger brother, state senator Bill Bulger. After he became senate president in 1979, he was generally considered the second most powerful politician in the state.

Whitey Bulger's closest friend, Steve Flemmi, who had received his "Ri-fleman" nickname after his service as a parachute infantryman, was an-other thug whose average size belied his toughness. A few years younger than Whitey, Flemmi had worked for both the Mafia and the Irish gangs. In

1 One of Charles Rogovin's organized crime attorneys in the Massachusetts attorney gen-eral's office was George Higgins, later a bestselling author. In his 1971 novel (and later movie), *The Friends of Eddie Coyle*, he captures the tensions in the relationship between Coyle, a Boston criminal, and his federal agent handler. In the end, Coyle is murdered by his mob "friends." One character in the book resembled Whitey Bulger, but Higgins denied it was modeled on him.

the 1960s he and his pal Cadillac Frank Salemme were loan sharks and sluggers for Angiulo in the Roxbury area. Raymond Patriarca once offered Flemmi a chance to become a made man in the Mafia, but he declined, preferring to retain his independence. By teaming with Bulger in the Winter Hill Gang, he kept a foot in both organized crime camps and became the one individual trusted by both the Mafia and the Irish. Unbeknownst to either group, Flemmi also had ties to another outfit: He had become an informer for the local FBI during the great Irish mob war. For a man with so many affiliations, it was not a bad idea. The Bureau could notify him if it had picked up information that any of his colleagues were thinking of killing him. It could also help shelter him from law enforcement. According to Flemmi's later testimony, it was an FBI agent who advised him to flee town in 1969 in order to avoid arrest after one grand jury indicted him for murder and another for the bombing of Barboza's lawyer's car.

As Whitey Bulger began to appear on the FBI's radar, an attempt was made to enlist him as an informer. Though he provided tips, he refused to become a full-fledged stool pigeon. A few years later he was approached again by a different agent, one particularly well qualified for the task—perhaps, as it turned out, overqualified. John Connolly was eleven years younger than Bulger and was Southie born and raised. As a kid he had been in awe of the legendary Whitey. Once Bulger jumped in to rescue him when he was being pummeled by an older boy. Connolly also had a connection to Billy Bulger: When Bulger was first elected to the Massachusetts House of Representatives, the teenaged Connolly worked on his campaign. In 1968, after teaching high school and attending law school, Connolly was accepted by the FBI and assigned to New York. Frank Salemme would be Connolly's ticket back to Boston. At the time, Salemme, like Flemmi, was hiding from an indictment for blowing up Barboza's lawyer. In 1972, Connolly was tipped by a friend in the Boston organized crime squad as to Salemme's whereabouts. It was good information, and after spotting him on a Manhattan street, Connolly led a group of fellow agents in a pursuit that ended in the gunpoint capture of Cadillac Frank. Salemme was hauled back to Boston, where he received fifteen years, and Connolly was transferred back as well to take up an assignment on the organized crime squad.

In 1975, Bulger agreed to become an informant for Connolly. When rumors that he was a squealer eventually began to get around, few would believe it. The Irish in America had a deep hatred of informers, which they had brought over from the old country. In Ireland, a man who gave information to the British occupiers was considered damned to eternity, and his family suffered equal opprobrium. Irish South Boston's innate suspicions of outsiders were heightened by the busing controversy. To his friends and neighbors it seemed impossible that someone as deeply entrenched in the neighborhood as Whitey could be a rat. Whatever Bulger's motivation in cooperating with the FBI, it did not improve his behavior. Just five weeks after agreeing to Connolly's proposition he killed a man who had beaten him in a barroom fight. Soon Connolly inherited a second informer from another agent—Steve Flemmi. Bulger and Flemmi were code named "Charlie" and "Shogun," and the fact that Connolly controlled both of them gave him great prestige in the Boston FBI office.

Dressed in sharp suits with pointed shoes and plenty of jewelry, Connolly strode confidently through the hostile North End as though he owned it, sometimes engaging in face-to-face confrontations with Angiulo. If he disagreed with a superior's view he did not hesitate to press his own opinion, and more often than not he got his way. In 1979, when Howie Winter and twenty-one members of his gang were charged for fixing horse races, Connolly and the supervisor of the organized crime squad, John Morris, allegedly managed to persuade the Boston organized crime strike force to leave Bulger and Flemmi out of the indictment. The imprisonment of Winter and his other lieutenants paved the way for Bulger and Flemmi to take over. They transferred its headquarters to an automobile garage in downtown Boston. When the Massachusetts state police began trying to bug it, Bulger and Flemmi somehow learned about it. Many investigators suspected Connolly was the source of the tip.

Soon the two FBI men began to socialize with the two gangsters, even inviting some of their colleagues to join them. The growing closeness between Connolly, Morris, some other agents, and their supposed adversaries was evident in the gifts they exchanged. An agent who received a briefcase from Whitey gave him a fancy belt buckle in return, engraved with one of Bulger's alma maters—Alcatraz. Against his wife's objections, Morris invited Connolly and the two hoodlums to dinner at his home in suburban Lexington. It was strange behavior for an experienced lawman: Most cops prefer that criminals, particularly murderers, not know where they live or what their family looks like. Morris was a Kansan who had come to the Bureau after serving in the military police. He seemed to have no understanding of the complex environment he was entering, while Connolly was too much a part of it. Once when the agents and hoods met for drinks in a hotel, Morris reportedly consumed so much wine that he was unable to drive. Bulger drove Morris home in the agent's official vehicle. According to journalists, the gangster's nickname for Morris was "Vino" because of his liking for wine. Bulger's supposed nickname for Connolly was "Zip" because they were fellow residents of the same zip code in Southie. Morris became involved in a romance with a civilian employee in the FBI office, and when he was sent to attend a training course in Georgia, he grew lonely for her. The Wolf investigation disclosed that via Connolly, Bulger gave the girlfriend a thousand dollars to pay for her airfare so that she could join Morris.

Connolly should not have been the handler for a gangster who was so popular in the neighborhood they both resided in, particularly since he also boasted about his friendship with Senator Bulger. No agent should ever have been socializing with mob guys—much less a supervisor like Morris.[2] A supervisor in another FBI office described the correct relationship with informers: "You use them, you don't go to bed with them." Or, as a second put it, "You can be friendly but not their friend." Later, another Boston agent would tell reporters,

> Connolly just became a force unto himself . . . but he just wasn't much of an agent. He couldn't write a report. He was no administrator. He was just this brassy bullshit artist. We enabled him to some extent. No one had the stomach for examining what he was up to. We just never came to grips with that guy.

2 Ironically, Morris would get a firsthand look at how an agent/informer relationship could go wrong with devastating consequences. Enforcing drug laws was another task J. Edgar Hoover never wanted his troops to become involved in. Not until after his death did Congress assign authority to investigate drug crimes to then FBI. In 1984, Morris was detailed to Miami as part of a team investigating accusations against an FBI agent who was accused of taking bribes from a drug dealer. After the informer squealed, the agent confessed to making $1 million from his illicit operations and was given a prison sentence of ten years.

Some top managers at the Boston FBI office did raise questions about Morris and Connolly's relationship with Bulger and Flemmi. A few even suggested that Bulger should be shut down as an informer. Several times that almost happened, but Morris and Connolly were always able to argue persuasively that the two gangsters provided such vital information that without them the Bureau's work would suffer. Later, Judge Wolf's findings would allege that the informers were never as valuable as Morris and Connolly claimed. But as long as the Boston Mafia was the top target of the organized crime squad, it was not so clear to FBI managers or federal prosecutors that closing out Bulger and Flemmi was the right thing to do.

The FBI managers were also not aware of the full extent of the two gangsters' criminal activity. It was a general rule that minor crimes would be overlooked if the information supplied by the offenders would bring down bigger crooks. By about 1980, though, they might actually have become the bigger crooks. The two gangsters were so bold that they committed murders with abandon. In 1981, after a Tulsa millionaire began to suspect that a Boston jai alai operation he owned was being skimmed by some of his employees, working in cahoots with the Winter Hill Gang, Bulger and Flemmi sent a killer to Oklahoma to eliminate him. To ensure their silence, the next year, two of the skimmers were killed. One's body was found in a trunk in Florida, and Bulger himself hit the other in Boston. A Tulsa detective came to Boston to make inquiries and later reported that he got little cooperation from the FBI. Reports that Bulger and Flemmi were dealing drugs met with indifference.

In 1978, Morris's squad had commenced BOSTAR, the operation that would eventually achieve the squad's primary goal—taking down Jerry Angiulo and his whole operation. Agents managed to turn some bookmakers who were paying street tax to Angiulo. Using the information they supplied, Title III warrants were obtained that permitted the government to put Angiulo under electronic surveillance. On a freezing Sunday night in January 1981, a team of agents was able to surreptitiously enter Angiulo's headquarters at 98 Prince Street in the North End and plant a bug. Over the next four months, forty agents, working around the clock, monitored conversations from Mafia headquarters. Angiulo discussed many things, but one topic that particularly bothered him was the RICO law. He was worried that a RICO case would be brought against him and his organization. Jerry's boys were not familiar with the statute, so he tried to explain it to them. His knowledge, for that time, was fairly accurate. He stated correctly that it took only two crimes over ten years to establish a pattern of racketeering. As he put it, "If you break one of those crimes this year and within the next ten years you break the other one, they will take your fuckin' head off." But Angiulo made the mistake many other gang figures and their lawyers across the country did—he assumed RICO applied only to the infiltration of legitimate organizations. As he would put it to the troops, "We're Shylocks, we're fuckin' bookmakers, we're selling marijuana, we're illegal here, illegal there. We're every fuckin' thing. The law does not cover us." Eventually though, he came to doubt his own words and dejectedly observed, "The law was written for people like us." In his rambling discussions, Angiulo conveniently provided the government with the outline of the racketeering case that would be brought against him.

When Angiulo and some of his lieutenants were arrested in a North End restaurant in 1983, he declared to everyone within earshot, "I'll be back for my pork chops before they get cold." Instead, it was his last night as a free man. He was held in custody until his 1986 trial on RICO charges, when he and twenty-two members of his crew were convicted. Angiulo received a sentence of forty-five years. The following year he was convicted in a state court of ordering a murder, and sentenced to life without parole.

In 1988 the *Boston Globe* published their piece exposing Bulger as an informer. Though the FBI denied the story, the allegations had been privately confirmed to reporters by John Morris. His motive was to try to force Bulger into retirement. There was also the possibility that the story might impel what was left of the Mafia to retire Bulger—permanently. But the Office had been in bad shape since Angiulo and others were sent to prison. Patriarca had died in 1984, and his son Raymond Junior was not up to the job of succeeding him. In an attempt to heal factional disputes in Boston, Junior presided over an induction ceremony in 1989. It was bugged by the FBI, and the participants were arrested and eventually imprisoned. As punishment, the Mafia busted young Raymond down to an ordinary soldier.

In 1990, Agent Connolly retired. It was time for Whitey to do the same, but he did not. Other agencies who had been frustrated in their attempts to get at Bulger and Flemmi by the FBI were becoming increasingly impatient. At the beginning of the '90s, the lineup of local law enforcement changed. New men took over the Massachusetts attorney general's office, the district attorney's post in Middlesex County, and the U.S. attorney's office. Instead of engaging in factional fighting, they began to work together. Fred Wyshak, a Boston native and veteran organized crime prosecutor who had served in the Brooklyn D.A.'s office and the New Jersey strike force, became an assistant in the Massachusetts U.S. attorneys office in 1989. Reviewing intelligence reports, Wyshak wondered why there were no charges pending against Bulger—and decided to rectify the situation.

For more than a decade, the Massachusetts State Police had tried to make many cases against Bulger, but he always seemed to know about their plans. Now they began conducting quasi-secret investigations, telling as few other law enforcement officers as possible that they were making cases against bookies who were paying protection money to Bulger and Flemmi. The DEA had also been frustrated in their efforts to nail the two gangsters, and they began following the drug trail. After a while the bookies started to talk. Then a drug dealer from South Boston, tired of doing prison time, decided to tell his story. By 1995 the state police and the DEA had enough evidence to make arrests, beginning with Flemmi's. This was when Bulger traded in his girlfriend and took flight. Periodic spottings were reported in places like New Orleans or Alabama. In October 1995, he called supervisor John Morris, then assigned to the FBI Academy at Quantico, and warned him that if he were arrested he would take Morris down too. That night Morris had a massive heart attack.

During the 1998 hearings conducted by Judge Wolf, Assistant U.S. Attorney Wyshak, who handled the case for the government, sought to demonstrate that Morris and Connolly were rogue agents, and therefore any promises that they might have made to Flemmi or Bulger were not valid. By then both agents had retired from the FBI. On the stand for eight days, Morris conceded that he had supplied information to the gangsters, but denied ever authorizing them to commit crimes. Connolly, who had gotten a

high-paying job in the private sector, supposedly as a result of Senator Bulger's recommendation (though both men denied it), was a constant presence in the Boston media, vehemently proclaiming his innocence. He
characterized Morris as "the most corrupt agent in the history of the FBI,"
and had unflattering comments for any of his former colleagues who had
criticized him. He described his own work with the Bureau as "Kind of like
a circus, and if the circus is going to work, you need to have a guy in there
with the lions and tigers." Connolly declared that he would be happy to appear before the judge and waive immunity. When the court took him up on
it, he invoked his Fifth Amendment rights. Judge Wolf ruled that the agents'
promises did not confer immunity upon Bulger and Flemmi, and eventually the two would be charged with twenty-one murders. Flemmi was convicted, and his co-defendant, Cadillac Frank Salemme, pleaded guilty in
return for avoiding a death sentence.

Among those brought down was Bulger's most devoted follower, Kevin
Weeks. Even after Whitey's flight he remained loyal, channeling information to and from him. After his own arrest in 1999, he changed his mind.
Weeks led investigators to the location of three dead bodies. On the street
he acquired the nickname "Two Weeks" for the length of time it took him to
flip over. Among the bodies recovered was one of Flemmi's girlfriends—
the daughter of his mistress—who had gone missing in 1985. To frustrate
identification, after Flemmi killed her, he had cut off her feet and fingers
and pulled out her teeth. It was also revealed that in 1981 another
of Flemmi's girlfriends had been similarly murdered and mutilated. It
was becoming hard for Bulger's neighbors to see the gangsters as heroic
figures.

William Bulger retired from the Senate to become president of the University of Massachusetts. After a congressional grilling about his brother's
activities, he was forced to step down from that post. Former agent Connolly still seemed to see himself as a hero. He continued working on a
screenplay about his role in bringing down the Mafia, hoping to sell it to
Hollywood. In 2002, after his conviction on a racketeering charge, Connolly was sentenced to ten years in prison. As of 2006 he is awaiting trial in
Florida on charges of conspiracy to murder, based on the killing of one of

the witnesses in the jai alai case. Another agent indicted in connection with the murder of the Oklahoma jai alai owner died of a heart attack before he could be brought to trial.

The greatest harm came to the reputation of the FBI. There would be a series of official investigations examining the operations of the Boston office over the previous four decades. A 2004 congressional report declared, "Beginning in the mid-1960s, the Federal Bureau of Investigation began a course of conduct in New England that must be considered one of the greatest failures in the history of federal law enforcement." In their zeal to bring down the Mafia, a few agents had made a deal with the devil. Perhaps J. Edgar Hoover had been right all along, and some corruption was inevitable when the FBI took on organized crime.

While G-men went to jail or were forced into early retirement, Whitey Bulger remained free. Bulger's last confirmed sighting was in London in 2002. Twice in 1995, suspicious police officers in Mississippi and Wyoming ran a check on his parked car, but it was registered in the name of Thomas Baxter, Whitey's alias of the moment, and there were no wanted notices on the vehicle or its owner. Whitey is thought to have plenty of money stashed both in the United States and abroad. In addition to his organized crime earnings, which may be as high as $50 million, in 1991 he was one of four people who shared winnings of $14 million in the Massachusetts lottery. At the time it was suspected that he simply muscled his way in on the real winner to provide himself with a source of legitimate income.

While some observers have expressed skepticism that the FBI will ever catch Bulger, there is little doubt that it wants him. His capture would offset some of the criticism of the agency. It would also be a huge career boost for the agents who bring him in. According to the FBI, Bulger has been known to alter his appearance with the use of disguises. He is an avid reader with a strong interest in history, and has frequented libraries and historic sites. He is also on heart medication and seeks to maintain physical fitness by walking on beaches and in parks with his female companion, Catherine Greig. The couple love pets, and it is suspected they may be found around animal facilities. Bulger has been featured twelve times on *America's Most Wanted,* and tips continue to flow in about his whereabouts.

On September 3, 2006, he turns seventy-seven. As the old saying has it, his case might be moved to a much higher court. Until that happens, however, the Bureau will keep up its search, and he may yet make his appearance in a Boston one. Whatever the outcome, his story will remain a cautionary tale for law enforcement organizations.

CHAPTER 14

STINGING THE MOBS:
DIGGING OUT THE MAFIA ROOT AND BRANCH

By the 1980s the government was employing its full range of weapons against the Mafia. One was sting operations, a type of con game run against the bad guys. It proved to be particularly effective against the twin pillars of the mob universe, Chicago and New York. Law enforcement struck hard at their core strengths: In Chicago, that meant the Outfit's political ties, and in New York, it was the five families' deep entrenchment in a diverse array of business enterprises.

The Chicago Outfit's chief executioner was Harry Aleman, dubbed by the press "the mob's killing machine." A fairly talented amateur artist whose tastes ran to outdoor scenes, he did not look like a killer. He was raised in one of the Chicago mob's traditional recruiting grounds, the Taylor Street district of the West Side, and benefited from the support of his uncle, Joe Ferriola, who would eventually become a top figure in the Outfit. Aleman and his partner, Butch Petrocelli, headed a crew that was assigned to collect the street tax from independent bookies. Some indies had the nerve to say no, and one recalcitrant even used a few four-letter words in referring to Mr. Aleman. Soon afterward he was gunned down in a restaurant by two masked men. Aleman's thumbprint was found in the getaway car. Not content with his earnings from the shakedowns, Aleman also moonlighted in home invasion robberies. In 1978 the latter activity netted him an eleven-year sentence.

Some of Aleman's criminal activity was conducted outside mob auspices. A 1972 murder was just a favor for a relative. The victim, Billy Logan, had been involved in a dispute with his ex-wife over visiting rights to his two children. On one of Billy's unwelcome surprise visits to his kids, he got into a fight with his ex's boyfriend, who turned out to be Butch Petrocelli. The ex was also Aleman's cousin, and she threatened to "call Harry." On a night in September, Billy Logan was leaving his house to go to work when he was hit by a shotgun blast and finished off with a pistol shot.

It took until 1977 to bring the case against Aleman, but it was a strong one, including an eyewitness identification. The judge was known for being tough on defendants. Nevertheless, he declared he did not believe the witness, and Aleman was acquitted. The media and public were outraged, and suspected that a bribe had been paid. They were correct. The mob had arranged a payoff to the supposedly tough judge through its political protectors. Such fixes were not uncommon in Chicago. It was one reason that organized crime experts questioned whether the power of the American Mafia would ever be significantly reduced in that city. The Hollywood extortion case that had sent the Chicago mob leadership to prison in 1944 had been tried in New York because federal prosecutors doubted they could get a guilty verdict in the Windy City. Now, though, times appeared to be changing. In the next election, voters removed from the bench the judge who had acquitted Aleman. Worse for the fixers, the case prompted federal officials to give the political and legal system a cleansing. In retrospect, the Chicago Outfit would come to dearly regret the fix that spared Harry Aleman.

The 1980s would be a time of great trouble for the Outfit. Chicago lost control of the Teamsters pension fund and its Vegas casinos. The imprisonment of leaders like Joe Aiuppa, Jackie Cerone, and Joe Lombardo upset the hierarchy. Now the federal government with undercover operatives and informers launched sting operations against the corrupt judicial and political arrangements that had enabled the Outfit to protect men like Aleman from state criminal sanctions.

Initiated in 1980, "Operation Greylord"[1] would lead to the wholesale jailing of judges, lawyers, and law enforcement officers. It featured the first

1 The name was derived from the grey wigs worn by English judges who are commonly addressed as "my Lord."

legal bug ever to be placed in the judge's chambers of an American courtroom, installed by the FBI in the Criminal Court Building on Chicago's West Side. The Cook County Circuit Court would be cited in a federal indictment as a "criminal enterprise."

Greylord began in traffic court, where the bribes were penny-ante sums, and moved to the more prestigious divisions that dealt with felonies and major civil matters. A frequent tactic used in the investigation was the creation of fake cases that could be presented to the courts. In one instance, a man whose briefcase was snatched pursued the thief through the streets, tackled him, and held him until police arrived. To the cops' surprise, witnesses were eager to come forward and tell what they had seen—so eager that they made the police suspicious, and after a few inquiries it was determined that everyone involved, including the "thief," was an FBI agent.

In addition to G-men, other undercovers used in the sting included a judge and a prosecutor. Brocton Lockwood, a downstater who was temporarily sitting in the Cook County court system, would be dubbed the "hillbilly judge." He prepared for his role by reading the spy novels of Robert Ludlum and Ken Follett. As it turned out, the equipment provided to him by the FBI was well below the technical standards of fictional spies, though a microphone concealed in his cowboy boots did manage to pick up conversations. To gain the trust of the corrupt officials around him, Judge Lockwood posed as a playboy who liked to socialize with fast women in Rush Street nightspots. In reality he was a professor's son with a strong moral compass. Terry Hake, the prosecutor, was known by his handlers as "the White Knight" and described by his associates as someone who "had the face of an altar boy and the demeanor of an Eagle Scout." Hake began his undercover work while he was still an assistant Cook County state's attorney and then quit to assume the guise of a crooked defense lawyer.

It did not take long for Hake to begin gathering evidence. He was asked by a former colleague at the state's attorney's office to deliver $100 to a judge whose criminal court chambers were bugged. After making a payment to a corrupt court official, Hake would sometimes phone his report in to the local FBI office using his cover identity. Typically the reports were short, precise, and polite:

This is Project Development Specialist Leo Murphy. The time is now 3:08 P.M., approximately eight minutes after I paid [the name of a court official] in the back of the jury room. The day is July 7, 1981. Thank you.

During the course of the investigation Hake succeeded in taping one judge as he explained to him how to present a case so that the defendant was sure to be acquitted. The undercover operation became so extensive that in one case heard before Judge Lockwood, all of the parties except the prosecuting assistant state's attorney were wearing wires. As a reward for his services, Hake would realize his life's ambition: an appointment as an FBI agent.

Greylord brought down well-connected jurists like Chancery Judge Reginald Holzer, who had worked for reform sheriff Richard Ogilvie. He and Ogilvie's chief investigator, Richard Cain, became partners in a record company that the cop set up to promote his girlfriend's musical aspirations. Cain's own career spiraled downward into prison, exile with Sam Giancana in Mexico, and death at the hands of hired killers, but Holzer was elected to the bench. Once installed, he regularly took money from lawyers who practiced before him, typically in the form of a ten- or twenty-thousand-dollar "loan" that he had no intention of repaying. In 1985, as part of Greylord, he was indicted under the RICO statute for mail fraud and extortion. Holzer's attorney argued that the judge had intended to repay the loans, but was prevented by heavy debts. The lawyers who had turned government witness, on the other hand, testified that they paid off the judge because they felt that failure to do so would jeopardize their cases. None testified that Holzer had threatened them in any way, but the lead prosecutor, Assistant U.S. Attorney (and later bestselling novelist) Scott Turow, argued that there was an implied threat constituting extortion and bribery. During a vigorous cross-examination, Turow was able to link the loans to the receiverships the judge handed out to lawyers. Holzer was convicted and sentenced to thirteen years in prison. Ultimately, Greylord led to the conviction of twenty judges, fifty-seven lawyers, and sixteen police officers or deputy sheriffs.

While Greylord weakened the Outfit's indirect hold on the courts by weeding out corrupt officials, a joint FBI-IRS sting inflicted major damage on the Outfit itself as well as toppling public functionaries. In 1986, Robert

Cooley, a mob-connected defense lawyer with heavy gambling debts, volunteered to be an informer for the local federal strike force. During the investigation—code-named Gambat, for "gambling attorney"—Cooley taped politicians, judges, and mob figures, resulting in the fall of a long-time Chicago institution. Since the nineteenth century, the First Ward Democratic organization had been a vital link between Chicago gangsters and politicians. While it was only one of the city's fifty wards, the First included "the Loop," the center of Chicago's economic and professional life.

The First's leadership did not hide its light under a bushel. Its secretary, Pat Marcy, the principal contact for the Outfit, ate lunch every day with other members of the hierarchy at a reserved booth in a restaurant across from City Hall. It was an ideal place for favor seekers to approach politicians without risk. A brief conversation in a restaurant could be explained as idle chit-chat, unlike a meeting in the nearby ward offices, which would clearly be seen as business. Inevitably the Feds took an interest in the "harmless" restaurant conversations, and a busboy discovered a microphone planted in the First Ward booth. Further searching revealed a hidden camera aimed at their table. Not long afterward, Marcy and some of the other leaders were charged with crimes under the RICO statute. Marcy died of a heart attack during his trial, but other First Warders, including an alderman and a state senator, were sent to prison. In 1992, Mayor Richard M. Daley (son of the late mayor Richard J.) took advantage of the case to re-draw the ward boundaries, excluding the valuable Loop business district.

It was Gambat that led to the indictment of Harry Aleman. Back in 1977, Pat Marcy had worked with mob lawyer Cooley to deliver a bribe of $10,000 to acquit Aleman, "the mob's killing machine." This story came out when Cooley turned informer and a Cook County grand jury handed down an indictment for the murder that had occurred twenty-one years earlier. The public was not surprised to hear Aleman named again as the killer, but the city's legal community was shocked. It is a fundamental principle of American law that an individual cannot be tried twice for the same crime.[2]

---

2 Though because certain crimes are violations of both state and federal law, an offender can be tried by both sovereignties. For example, a defendant who is acquitted in state court for holding up a bank that is federally insured could be prosecuted again in federal court. The reverse is also true, though some states, including New York, have statutorily waived their right to do so.

Because the 1977 case had been fixed, however, the state's attorney claimed that Aleman had never really been in jeopardy. The crooked judge, then living in Arizona, killed himself. Despite the head-shaking of the legal community, the indictments were not thrown out. Appeals all the way up to the U.S. Supreme Court were unsuccessful, and Aleman, who was already serving time in a federal prison, was sentenced to a minimum of one hundred years in a state one.

In a book on Greylord, veteran Chicago newsmen James Tuohy and Rob Warden noted, "Most of the men [involved] were shaped to believe that if one did not grab some graft, while others all around were grabbing, one was a sucker." With judges and politicians falling like tenpins, the mayor wiping out the First Ward, the courts setting aside the double jeopardy rule, and informers wearing wires, it was beginning to appear that the real suckers were those who took bribes.

The Outfit itself reacted to the new climate. Tony Accardo had a belated conversion. While not one to employ violence recklessly, he had always been a bad man to cross and had ordered more than a few spectacularly gruesome hits in his time.[3] Now, Big Tuna persuaded his members to stop killing people: More than ever, murders were bad for the mobs' image. When defense lawyers argued that their Mafia clients were just businessmen or simple gamblers, it was a tough sell for jurors who had become accustomed to seeing pictures of victims' bodies in newspapers and on television. Since 1990, only a handful of Chicago killings have been mob hits.

By the end of the twentieth century, the federal pressure was so intense that being identified as the leader of the Chicago mob was tantamount to having a target pasted on a man's back. When Joe Lombardo finished doing time on his Pendorf conviction in 1992, he ran a series of classified ads in the newspapers declaring that he was not a "made man" and urging, "If anyone hears my name used in connection with criminal activity, please notify the FBI, the local police, and my parole officer." After Joe Aiuppa was

3 In 1978, some thieves had broken into his suburban home while he was on vacation in California, seeking stolen jewelry that Accardo had recovered for a friend. Over the next few months, seven top Chicago burglars were found dead in various locations. Not only had they been shot, but in some instances their throats had been slit, their faces had been burned with acetylene torches, or they had been castrated. A federal grand jury was convened to look into the killings. Accardo appeared before it and took the Fifth Amendment. Later, the two hit men suspected of carrying out the murders of the burglars were themselves killed.

jailed, Sam "Wings" Carlisi, who had earned his nickname as a messenger for Aiuppa, became the top leader with Jimmy Marcello and Anthony Zizzo not far below. In December 1992, as a result of a four-year investigation by IRS agents and the FBI, Carlisi, Marcello, and Zizzo were indicted for their roles in illegal gambling and loan-sharking operations. The indictment contended that Marcello ordered a longtime Outfit figure, Lenny Patrick, to "scare off" the owner of a suburban theater. Patrick's crew made three unsuccessful attempts to burn down the theater using phosphorus grenades, gasoline-filled jugs, Molotov cocktails, and military fragmentation hand grenades.

During the investigation Patrick agreed to wear a microphone. Among those he brought down was Gus Alex, who ranked higher in the mob. While wearing his mike, Patrick handed Alex $11,000 that he had obtained in an extortion scheme. By the standards of the past it was an incredible betrayal—the two men had been close allies for nearly half a century. The news broke in April 1992, and Tony Accardo died the following month. Some mob watchers mused that the shock must have killed him. After Carlisi, Marcello, and Zizzo were sent to prison, it was John "No Nose" DiFronzo's turn to be boss.[4] In 1994, he was convicted of extortion in a California federal court, and he served four years in prison. Some longtime mob watchers had predicted that the passing of Accardo would be followed by the rapid demise of the Outfit. Two years after his death, that seemed to be coming true.

The Mafia's political power had long ago eroded in New York City. After the commission and family trials, and the takedown of John Gotti, major law enforcement assaults were conducted against the mob's economic base. Mafia-dominated areas such as the garment center, Kennedy Airport, the Fulton Fish Market, waste hauling, and construction had not only made the New York families rich, but enhanced their influence by linking them

---

4 According to DiFronzo, he earned his nickname during his burglar days when a piece of his nose was shot off in a gun battle with cops. A more likely account is that one night he broke the plate glass window of a fur store and entered to steal merchandise. While he was carrying a coat out, a portion of his nose was sliced off by a jagged piece of glass.

to the world of legitimate business. The government might send bosses and even whole hierarchies to jail, but as long as the families retained their pull in the economic sector, they remained powerful. In the New York investigations too, stings were extensively employed as a law enforcement tactic.

John Gotti was still the Gambino family boss in 1988, when New York County district attorney Morgenthau assigned a young assistant D.A. named Eliot Spitzer to investigate the family's activities in the garment center.[5] The alleged family capo there was Tommy Gambino. Tommy was the classic Mafia insider: The son of Carlo, he was also nephew by marriage of Paul Castellano and son-in-law of Tommy Lucchese. With his brother Joseph, he operated garment center enterprises including several trucking companies that had exclusive rights to service manufacturers. Tommy's personal wealth was estimated at over $100 million. Two sting operations were at the center of Spitzer's probe. First, a New York state trooper named Ron Rivera, on temporary assignment to Morgenthau's office, set up a sewing shop in Chinatown under the name "Chrystie Street Fashions." Twenty-five seamstresses turned out blouses and jeans for Rivera, unaware of who their actual employer was. At the same time, an NYC cop named Kim Lee posed as head of the small Lok-Key Trucking Company. Under the alias David Chan, he solicited business in the garment center. When Lee's trucking company pretended to offer its services to Rivera's dressmaking shop, "salesmen" from Tommy Gambino's Consolidated Carriers informed him that Chrystie's was their exclusive customer and that Lee had better work outside the garment district. Spitzer's investigators began recording such conversations and planted bugs in Gambino's offices.

In 1990, Gambino, his brother, two of their employees, and four of their trucking companies were charged with racketeering under New York's "Little RICO" law and with restraint of trade in violation of the state antitrust law. The racketeering charge presented problems for the prosecution. Tommy Gambino was college educated, gentlemanly, and a large contributor to hospitals and other charities; it was not his style to threaten people. In fact, his businesslike persona had reportedly caused the gangster wing

---

5 Later, as New York attorney general, Spitzer would become nationally famous as "the Sheriff of Wall Street." At this writing he is favored to become the state's next governor.

of the Gambino family to deride him as "a dressmaker" and had cost him the chance to succeed Castellano. His lawyer declared, "You will not find any baseball bats. You won't find any broken bodies. This is simply a business case, no matter the names and nasty things [the prosecutors] call Tommy Gambino." On one occasion, though, a Gambino employee discussing the activities of Chan in running Lok-Key declared, "I don't want to say he's going to get his ass kicked, but he will sooner or later. One of the f—ing truckers will take him apart, he will be spending the next six months in the f—ing hospital." It was undeniable that the Gambino name inspired respect in the garment district. Spitzer told the jury the defendants had "used their reputations as the Gambino crime family as a tool of fear—and they took it to the bank . . . and when someone stepped out of line the velvet gloves came off, somebody was sent to the hospital for six months."

The extortion charges may have been difficult for the prosecution to prove, but the antitrust case was a strong one. In 1992 Gambino, his brother, and five other defendants agreed to plead guilty to a single felony antitrust count, sell their trucking companies, and pay a twelve-million-dollar fine. In exchange for those concessions, the prosecutors dropped the remaining charges. After Gambino's departure, a former New York City police commissioner was appointed to monitor the settlement.[6]

Another man who fell on the wrong side of RICO also bore a famous Mafia name. When John J. Gotti went to prison, he named his son John A. (whom the press nevertheless referred to as "Junior") acting boss. In practice, a committee, including Junior's uncle Peter, ran the family. At twenty-eight, Junior was considered too young for a leadership role and did not get the respect of his troops or his fellow bosses. His 1998 RICO indictment included a charge that the Gambinos had extorted $1 million in protection money over a six-year period from Scores, an upscale East Side topless club. Stories about Scores always drew attention, especially when the tabloids ran them alongside pictures of the club's beautiful lap dancers. The Scores charges were dropped, but in 1998 Junior pleaded guilty to loan sharking, illegal gambling, and tax evasion and was sentenced to seven years and three months in prison. His father, who had stood up to a far

6 Tommy Gambino was later sentenced to five years on federal racketeering and gambling charges in a case unrelated to the garment center.

greater pressure from law enforcement, was reported to be greatly displeased by his son's guilty plea. Most distressing to the other mob bosses was the Feds' discovery, during a search of Junior's office, of a list of newly made five-families members for the years 1991 and 1992.

The government takeover of the International Brotherhood of Teamsters in 1988 provided an opportunity to attack another segment of the New York City mob's economic base. In 1992, former Abscam prosecutor Thomas Puccio was appointed monitor of Teamsters Local 295, the entity that had given the Lucchese bosses Ducks Corallo and Johnny Dio their foothold at JFK Airport. Another Teamsters airport local was put under a de facto receivership. As a result, some union officers were removed for alleged mob ties, and others were prosecuted criminally. In 1997, an FBI sting at JFK resulted in the arrest of eighty-three people for cargo theft. The following year, fifty-six more individuals were arrested for theft. In both cases, most of the defendants had no organized crime affiliation, which was seen as a sign that the Mafia no longer controlled hijacking at the terminal. Thus, while thieves continued to operate, the stealing was not facilitated by mob ties.

It had taken forty years to clean up JFK. Now, it took law enforcement only five years to cleanse a new Mafia playground. After the Javits Convention Center opened in 1986, it had quickly fallen under mob control. There, however, civil RICO suits against the Teamsters and the carpenters union enabled the government to appoint monitors over convention center locals. In the 1990s, a management team installed by the State of New York and law enforcement pressure, made significant inroads into extortion and theft at the Javits.

The election of Rudy Giuliani as mayor in 1993 also spelled trouble for the mob. In 1996 a federal grand jury indicted nineteen members of the Genovese crime family for receiving payoffs to allow concessionaires to operate at the San Gennaro festival. Honoring the patron saint of Naples, the feast of San Gennaro was the city's largest and best-known street fair. The Mayor followed up by removing the previous managers of the event and requesting that the Roman Catholic archdiocese oversee San Gennaro's finances to ensure that the profits were donated to legitimate charities.

Another Mafia profit center that caught Giuliani's attention was the

Fulton Fish Market on the Lower Manhattan waterfront. For decades it had been a Genovese stronghold. In 1995, the mayor proposed that city agencies take over rent collection at the market, conduct background investigations of companies and workers, and issue licenses and registrations only to businesses deemed of good character and integrity. The companies that were already entrenched in the fish market objected to the plan, and a few days later a fire swept through the terminal, destroying the old market building. The fire department determined that the blaze had been purposely set. If the mob had done it to send a warning message, they should have remembered that Rudy Giuliani could not be driven off by that sort of threat.[7] Shortly afterward, Giuliani's program was enacted into law by the City Council, and within a couple of years most of the firms that had functioned at the fish market for half a century were no longer there. Later the market itself was moved to a city facility in the Bronx.

Waste hauling was another New York industry with strong Mafia ties. In 1991 the national carting firm of Browning Ferris Industries (BFI) entered the local market, marking its arrival with a public announcement that it would not be driven out by organized crime. Not long afterward, a company manager found the severed head of a German shepherd dog on his doorstep, along with a note that read, "Welcome to New York." BFI was offering rates that were 40 percent lower than what the mob firms were charging, but they found few customers. In 1992, Morgenthau's office launched another sting operation, with New York City detective Richard Cowan posing as a carting company executive. During three years of operation he paid nearly $1 million (provided by the NYPD and Morgenthau) to mob-controlled carters for the right to service specific stops.

In the meantime, the established carters and BFI were conducting a public relations war in typical New York style. In some TV commercials, an out-of-towner in a cowboy hat sitting in a BFI truck pored over a map, struggling to find a New York street address. The other side complained that BFI's commercials were anti-Italian stereotypes. Less humorous were the death threats that Cowan and other legitimate carters who cooperated with them received. In one instance, one of their drivers was beaten so

7 Some detectives believe the fire was actually meant to destroy records that investigators were seeking.

badly that he was permanently incapacitated. In 1995, Morgenthau brought indictments against seventeen individuals, twenty-three companies, and four trade associations. Confronted with the testimony of Detective Cowan and their own voices on tape, most defendants chose to plead guilty. The price of hauling refuse dropped significantly with the end of mob control. The loss of carting was thought to cost the mob half a billion dollars annually—ten times the amount it lost when it was driven out of the Fulton Fish Market.

None of the five families completely escaped the onslaught of federal and state pressure. Even the man that no one thought would ever stand trial, Chin Gigante of the Genoveses, would be convicted. In 1978, the U.S. Department of Housing and Urban Development had instituted a program to install one million double-glazed thermal windows in New York City housing projects. It was a bonanza for Mafia-controlled construction businesses, which quickly snapped up $150 million in contracts. Non-mob companies were warned not to bid on jobs, or forced to pay a kick-back of two dollars on each window they installed. Under the direction of Greg O'Connell of the Eastern District U.S. attorney's office, a federal investigation known as "the Windows case" led to Gigante's downfall.

The FBI never bought Gigante's pose of being mentally unstable. When agents would follow him as he walked with a handler, appearing infirmed or befuddled, it was obvious he was acting. Once when a traffic light changed unexpectedly he sprinted to the sidewalk ahead of his protector. Another time, while walking by a church, after spotting an FBI agent, he promptly dropped to his knees and began praying. But when Gigante was indicted in 1990, he was able to obtain testimony from psychiatrists that his ailments made it impossible for him to take the stand. The press had a field day, describing the defendant as "the Odd Father." While the legal maneuverings went on in the Windows case, in 1993 the government hit Gigante with another indictment, charging him with conspiring to kill John and Gene Gotti. After six years of hearings, a judge finally ruled that he was competent to be tried, and in 1997 he was convicted on RICO charges including extortion, labor payoffs, and conspiracy to commit murder. The judge in the case declared, "He is a shadow of his former self" and sentenced Chin to only twelve years in prison. He was also required to pay a $1.25 million fine. Even then Gigante was not completely finished; he would continue to run his family from a prison cell until his death in 2005.

Despite the blows received by the Gambinos and the Genoveses, they still remained viable organizations with two hundred or more made members. Other families fared less well. In 1985, Brooklynites Vic Amuso and Anthony "Gas Pipe" Casso took over the Luccheses. Though ostensibly underboss, Casso was the driving force in the family. A product of Brooklyn's tough Red Hook section, Casso's nickname was apparently a legacy from his father, a mob slugger who was also known as "Gas Pipe"—perhaps from his practice of wielding lead pipes on union dissidents. Young Casso hated the nickname, and anyone who dared use it incurred his extreme displeasure, although friends were sometimes permitted to call him "Gas." As a boy young Gas Pipe became a crack shot, firing pistols at targets on a rooftop he and his friends used as a shooting range. Brooklyn rooftops abounded in pigeon coops, and the owners would sometimes call upon young Gas to kill predatory hawks. He once told an interviewer, "I was like a doctor on call." As a protégé of Ticks Furnari, Casso was involved in gambling, loan sharking, and drug dealing. His mob activities permitted him to acquire luxuries like a $500,000 ring and dozens of expensive suits. The downside was that in 1986 he sustained four bullet wounds in an ambush ordered by John Gotti.

The Luccheses had never been a large mob family, usually numbering only a hundred or so members, but they controlled some choice areas and maintained very tight organizational bonds. They had no history of internal warfare. However, Amuso and Casso were the first leaders of the Luccheses who did not come from its Manhattan-Bronx stronghold, and soon they faced revolts from disgruntled Manhattanites and a powerful New Jersey faction of the family. After some forty murders, their succession was confirmed. During the warfare, Gas Pipe broke some long-standing mob rules, including ordering a hit on a woman whose only link with the mob was that she was the sister of one Peter Chiodo, who was on a Casso extermination list. While she survived, Casso caused a further stir by having Chiodo's non-mob brother killed. In 1994, Amuso and Casso were indicted in the Windows case. After several years as fugitives they were caught, convicted, and imprisoned. By the end of the century the Lucchese family was still estimated to have a hundred made members, but its leadership was in flux.

Unlike the Luccheses, the Colombo family had a long history of internal warfare: Gallo versus Profaci, Colombo versus Gallo, etc. After boss Carmine "The Snake" Persico received a life sentence in the commission case, he wanted his son Alphonse—known as "Allie Boy"—to succeed him. When Allie Boy was sent to prison in 1988, Persico named Vic Orena acting boss, assuming that Alphonse would resume control after he emerged from prison. By 1991 Orena had different ideas, and war broke out within the family. Despite attempts by other families to broker a settlement, the violence led to at least a dozen murders. Orena ended up in jail, and by 2000 the Colombos were down to fifty members and thought to be in disarray.

Surprisingly, the success story of New York mobdom in the late twentieth century was the resurgence of the Bonannos. After the imprisonment of Gotti, Gigante, and Casso, the most important mob boss still at large in New York was Joe Massino. "Big Joe" was a strong leader in the mold of his good friend and Howard Beach neighbor, John Gotti. Three years Gotti's junior, Massino had become friends with "Johnny Boy" when they were both hijackers. Massino's skill at finding places to stash the stolen cargoes and receivers to dispose of them won the respect of his fellow cartage thieves. Like Gotti, Massino did time in prison for such activities. But unlike Gotti, Big Joe invariably behaved politely in his encounters with law enforcement officers and sought to keep a low profile. One time he apologized to an FBI agent for slipping his tail, explaining that he had made a quick turn after realizing he was going to be late picking up his wife. When Massino's brother-in-law "Good-Looking Sal" Vitale discovered and dismantled a hidden FBI bug, an agent knocked on the door and asked for his microphone back. Vitale stonewalled until Massino ordered him to give the G-man back his property. In similar circumstances John Gotti would have summoned TV cameras and displayed the microphone at a press conference.

Massino's restrained behavior could not mask the fact that the Mafia still contained vicious killers, including some in his own family. In 1987, New York DEA agents learned of an individual looking for someone to kill a

Bonanno capo named Thomas Pitera, a.k.a. "Tommy Karate." The reason was that he was being pressured by Pitera to pay up on a drug deal, and he was terrified by Tommy's reputation. As his nickname suggested, Pitera was skilled at martial arts (he had spent three years training in Japan). However, he preferred to do his killing with a gun and then scientifically dismember and dispose of the body parts. The DEA arranged for the man to meet two tough Bronx Irish hoodlums who would carry out the hit for a price. Naturally, they were undercover agents—Jim Hunt had spent a few years with the NYPD before joining the DEA, and his partner, Tom Giesel, had played football for the University of Tennessee. They explained that while they would be willing to kill Tommy Karate, they would prefer to obtain drugs from him so that they could all make a lot of money. And to get the ball rolling, they would pay off the man's debt. With Uncle Sam's money, arrangements were made to become part of Tommy Karate's drug operation, and over the next three years the agents received a flood of heroin and cocaine, as well as information from electronic devices and informers.

As Hunt and Giesel learned more about Tommy Karate, they realized that this was no ordinary killer. He was suspected of numerous murders; some of them had been carried out for the mob, while others were on his own initiative (after his second wife overdosed, Pitera personally murdered a girlfriend who had been partying with her). According to the agents, Pitera's voice and manner resembled the Tommy Udo character played by Richard Widmark in *Kiss of Death*—except Pitera was scarier. His approach to murder was thoroughly clinical; he studied books on dissection and carried a special tool kit for the purpose. He disposed of bodies in a marsh area of Staten Island because he believed that the damp soil would accelerate decomposition, and he insisted that they be buried deep enough so dogs could not smell them. A hardened drug dealer broke down when he described to Hunt and Giesel how Tommy had casually killed one of the drug gang, then stripped naked, took the body into a bathtub, and began the dissection by cutting off the head. Pitera also liked to keep souvenirs of his work, including a victim's ears that he had laminated and carried around with him. Sometimes he would throw them on a table and say "Talk to him." The gesture usually quickly persuaded listeners to come around to Tommy's way of thinking. According to law enforcement sources, it was Pitera who was believed to have killed Willie Boy Johnson for the Gambinos—something he didn't bother to tell his Bonanno family superiors until after the deed was done. In 1990, Pitera was arrested and convicted of six murders.

Massino, the man who raised Tommy Karate to a made member, had become de facto leader of the family in the 1980s. Like a dutiful old-timer, he adhered to protocol and waited until Rusty Rastelli died in prison in 1991 to take over officially. The Bonannos had long been shunned by other families, which turned out to be an advantage when they were not caught up in the taped conversations that proved to be the undoing of so many mob families. The only blot on their record was the infiltration by FBI agent Joe Pistone, a.k.a. Donnie Brasco, and after that fiasco Massino instituted rigorous security procedures. He closed family social clubs because he believed they were easy targets for surveillances and bugs. Borrowing a trick from Chin Gigante, he ordered his troops never to mention his name in conversation—instead, they tugged at their earlobes to indicate that they were referring to him. Seemingly Massino had found a way to escape the Feds and RICO. Under his leadership, the family, which had declined to 1,00 members in ten crews, rose to 150 in fifteen. By 2002, organized crime experts rated the Bonnanos as virtually on a par with the Gambinos and the Genoveses as one of the most powerful families in the country. But the success proved illusory. After the FBI had failed to bug Massino or to plant an informer in his organization, they tried a new strategy. Borrowing a page from the IRS, the Bureau assigned its accountants to follow the money. They discovered that Mr. and Mrs. Massino were apparently lucky gamblers: Over a period of four years their lotto winnings had totaled approximately half a million dollars. The laws of probability being what they are, it seemed more likely that Massino was paying legitimate winners for their tickets and claiming them as his own in order to account for his level of expenditures. Eventually the investigation led to a middleman funneling money for the mob, who became a government informer and then tipped the FBI to more informers.

In 2004, Massino was indicted on RICO charges, which included ordering Sonny Black's death in retaliation for Joe Pistone's infiltration. Like Gotti, Massino was undone by a close associate testifying against him. This time Sammy the Bull's role was played by Good-Looking Sal Vitale, who was both Massino's brother-in-law and his underboss. The media flocked to the trial, expecting that Massino, like Gotti, would either beat the rap or go down fighting with a snarl on his lips. Instead, after he was convicted, he immediately became a government informer and entered witness protection. When Joe Pistone heard the news, he declared, "I'm pretty close to speechless. He was a throwback, he believed in being a gangster. He believed in tradition and the code of the Mafia." Perhaps Massino, having witnessed so many informers testify, felt that the time for honoring traditions had passed—particularly as he was facing a possible death sentence.

Among the smaller mobs outside of Chicago and New York, the story was much the same. In 1977, a *Time* magazine cover story had characterized the Mafia as "big, bad and booming," but by the 1990s, stories about the Mafia were more likely to describe it as dying or in disarray. The estimated number of nationwide made members, which was once as high as five thousand, was now put between one thousand and twelve hundred. In some cities the mob was barely functioning. Philadelphia was a good example. The murder of Angelo Bruno in 1980 had ended twenty years of stability, and it was followed by two decades of internecine warfare that did as much to destroy the family as attacks by law enforcement. After Bruno's successor, Phil Testa, was blown up in 1981, Nicky Scarfo became boss. Under his rule of indiscriminate violence, the Philadelphia mob began to revert to a street gang. After Scarfo was imprisoned in 1988, he tried to run the family from prison through his son Nicky Junior, but was unable to do so.

In the late 1980s the New Jersey state police developed a sophisticated anti-organized-crime operation complete with their own witness protection program. During the course of "Operation Broadsword" they were able to recruit a Scarfo family associate as an informer. He not only collected information on a number of New Jersey mob figures but was able to get himself inducted into the Philadelphia family in a ceremony monitored by the troopers. As a result, in 1990 the New Jersey authorities arrested a number of mob figures including Nicky Scarfo, Jr.

John Stanfa, who had been driving Bruno the night he was assassinated, made his bid for leadership; by 1991 he was in control of a large portion of the family, though his rule was constantly disputed by Scarfo loyalists. After Stanfa was convicted in 1995 on RICO charges, Ralph Natale—who had himself done time for blowing up a building—became the next boss. In the '90s, Natale and Joseph Merlino contended for power, with Merlino going outside the Mafia and enlisting the support of a Philadelphia biker gang at one point. After Merlino and some of his associates were indicted in 2000, Natale became the first boss of an American Mafia family to testify for the prosecution. With Merlino in jail, by 2006 the family was reported to be down to fewer than ten made members.

For many years the DeCavalcante family of New Jersey had pretty much flown under law enforcement's radar. After Sam DeCavalcante retired, John Riggi quietly ran the family for the next twenty years. In the late '90s, the DeCavalcantes too got snared. After the 1993 attack on the World Trade Center, the Port Authority of New York and New Jersey installed a tight new security system. Unfortunately, it was not tight enough to keep out a De-Cavalcante associate named Ralph Guarino. A maintenance supervisor of a firm employed by the Port Authority gave Guarino a pass that enabled him to move about the building freely, allowing him to plan a multi-million-dollar holdup. In 1998, Guarino arranged for a three-man team to ambush a Brink's crew delivering over $2 million in foreign and American currency to a bank on the eleventh floor of the World Trade Center. The three crooks, whom the media would soon dub "Larry, Curly, and Moe," doffed their ski masks when they exited the bank, walking barefaced past a number of security cameras in the building. The film appeared on local television, and they were soon visited by the FBI. They in turn led the agents to Guarino, but the FBI kept his apprehension secret and put him to work with a wire collecting information on the DeCavalcante family. Based on conversations he recorded, Riggi and other members of the family were indicted on RICO charges in 2001. Riggi received a ten-year sentence.

The experience of Philadelphia and New Jersey was repeated across the country. In 1999 an analyst for the U.S. Department of Justice wrote that in some of its previous strongholds such as Cleveland, Detroit, Kansas City, Las Vegas, Los Angeles, and New Orleans, the Mafia was "weak or nonexistent." In Cleveland there were reported to be no more than five made members still around; former underboss and government informer Angelo Lonardo felt comfortable enough to leave the witness protection program and move back home. Detroit, which had maintained stable leadership since the prewar era, never recovered from the investigation of Hoffa's disappearance. In 1996, longtime boss Jack Tocco was convicted on RICO charges. By then the Motor City mob was reputed to be down to about twenty-five members. According to the Kansas City Crime Commission, the local mob had nearly died out. Las Vegas had ceased to be run by the Mafia. Los Angeles had never been a strong Mafia town (among lawmen, the local family was known as "the Mickey Mouse mob") and by 2000 it had only an estimated dozen members. Outsiders as big as Frank Costello once had to secure local permission to operate in New Orleans, but (pre-Katrina) it was routinely invaded by small-time punks. In New England, the FBI, capably assisted by Whitey Bulger and his Irish mob, had left Raymond Patriarca's once strong organization in tatters.

The key problem everywhere was the constant turnover in leadership. Men moved into leadership roles who were not ready to assume the responsibility or were not qualified in the first place. Under the sway of incompetent chiefs, many bad decisions were made. One need only compare the rule of Angelo Bruno to the regime of Nicky Scarfo, Tony Accardo to Joey Aiuppa, or Tommy Lucchese to Gas Pipe Casso to gauge the state of the Mafia nationally in the late twentieth century.

The government continued to rain heavy blows on the mobs. Striking at their livelihoods and their political and judicial allies, law enforcement made unrelenting use of bugs, stings, and informers. Bosses were going to jail and top figures were defecting. With its base eroding, its political clout greatly diminished, and its leaders in prison, the prospects for the traditional Mafia to continue in the twenty-first century appeared dim. If the pattern continued, the mobs would likely disappear completely from many cities, and in others would be little more than robbery gangs or guns for hire. Or so it seemed, circa 2000.

CHAPTER 15

THE FUTURE OF THE OLD MAFIA:
THE EMERGENCE OF THE NEW

As the twentieth century gave way to the twenty-first, conventional wisdom held that the traditional American Mafia was at death's door. A 1999 article in *USA Today* characterized mob families as "melting icebergs" that were regressing from sophisticated criminal enterprises to crude street gangs. Among the mourners were a significant segment of the news media and the entertainment world—whatever might be said against the Mafia, it had been an absorbing topic. From tabloid journalism and Hollywood B movies to prize-winning investigative pieces and critically acclaimed blockbusters, mob stories boosted circulation and ticket sales. In 2005, veteran chronicler of New York life Jimmy Breslin said of the Mafia, "I don't know if I can say the end of it is a good or bad thing, but if I were still working a daily beat I'd probably kill myself." It was too early for obituaries, though: Shortly thereafter, the New York media got to cover a succession of high-profile mob trials.

The first featured the return of a Gotti, albeit Junior. Journalists looking for a chip off the old block in Junior had been disappointed. In a 1999 article in *The New York Times Sunday Magazine,* Jeffrey Goldberg poked fun at him:

When he visits his father in prison he gets yelled at. His mother had to tell him to stiffen his spine and reject a plea deal he was jumping to take. His sister had to help bail him out of jail. . . . Every legitimate business he has opened has tanked. He has a weight problem. He dresses badly. He drives a minivan. The tabloids say he is stupid. And no one in the Mafia likes him.

Now he was given a chance to redeem himself, at least in terms of headline potential. As he was about to be released from prison in 2004, young Gotti was indicted on new RICO charges. One of the allegations was that he was behind the 1992 kidnapping and shooting of Curtis Sliwa, a local radio talk show host who had criticized Junior's father. The leader of a citizen patrol group called the Guardian Angels, Sliwa was as well-known a figure in New York as Gotti Senior. For years he had led his youthful followers on well-publicized patrols of the city's high-crime areas, outfitted in the Angels' distinctive red beret and white jersey.[1] On paper the 2005 trial shaped up as a clash of titans—Sliwa versus Gotti, with neither man backing down an inch. Sliwa played his part, appearing in uniform and giving bellicose statements to the press. In contrast, Gotti adopted the humble pose of a small businessman charged with a minor civil violation. His defense lawyer maintained that he had renounced mob life upon incarceration, and he was no longer a member of a racketeering organization. The jury was unable to agree on a verdict; Sliwa expressed outrage, and the government vowed to retry the case. Gotti Senior would have thrown a party to celebrate his dodging the bullet; Junior was photographed in church, praying. Meanwhile his sister Victoria and her sons were appearing on *Growing Up Gotti*, a reality TV series about the problems of an affluent single parent raising her family in suburbia. While Sliwa was still projecting the image of a caped crusader, the Gottis were morphing into a sitcom family.

The 2006 retrial was even more of a circus. A prosecution witness testified that Gotti Senior was the father of two illegitimate daughters by two different women. That did not sit well with the Gotti clan in attendance, and even observers sympathetic to law enforcement wondered what it had to do with Sliwa's shooting. To bolster the claim that Gotti Junior had re-

---

1 During his early days with the Angels, the colorful and outspoken Sliwa had occasionally reported being shot at or kidnapped, though there were never any witnesses. Later he admitted that he made the incidents up. Sliwa maintained from the start it was the Gambinos who had lured him into a taxicab where a gunman was hiding in the front seat. But because of his previous fabrications, the media were slow to believe him.

nounced mob life, his lawyers called to the stand civil rights attorney Ron Kuby, who testified that in 1998 Gotti informed him he was leaving the Mafia. Kuby also happened to be Sliwa's current radio partner. Their on-air schtick was to disagree about everything, but when the mikes were off they had always gotten along. Now Sliwa proclaimed Kuby a "Judas." Again the jury deadlocked, again Sliwa was furious, and again the government promised a new trial. After the second trial it looked as though public and media opinion was beginning to shift toward sympathy for Gotti Junior. *New York Times* columnist Clyde Haberman, in seeking to explain the deadlocked jury, wrote, "It may even be that some New Yorkers don't think that shooting the publicity-adoring Mr. Sliwa constitutes a punishable offense." A third trial was scheduled to commence in August 2006.

The biggest media attractions of all were cases that evoked memories of the Lucchese and Colombo family wars more than a decade earlier. This time, though, the accused were cops and G-men. Former NYPD detectives Louis Eppolito and Steven Caracappa were charged by the government with assisting in or carrying out eight killings on behalf of the Lucchese family.[2]

According to the prosecution the saga of "the Mafia Cops" began in 1986, after Gas Pipe Casso was shot on orders of John Gotti in retaliation for the murder of a Gambino family underboss. One of Casso's allies, a drug dealer named Burt Kaplan, engaged the detectives to hunt down the hit squad. Louie Eppolito was the son and nephew of Gambino family members. An avid bodybuilder with a weight lifter's physique, in 1980 he was assigned to the Brooklyn robbery squad, where he teamed up with Caracappa, a short, slightly built Vietnam veteran. In some cases Eppolito and Caracappa did more than provide information. On one occasion they allegedly picked up a Gambino associate, Jimmy Hydell, who had been part of the shooting crew and turned him over to Casso. At a house in Brooklyn, he used Hydell for target practice, firing bullets into his legs, arm, and body until he identified the other members of the hit team— after which Casso shot him in the head. According to Casso he paid each

---

2 In the 160-year history of the NYPD no police officer had ever been accused of being a hit man for gangsters. The closest precedent had happened 90 years earlier, when a lieutenant assigned to the police commissioner's office employed mob gunmen to silence a gambler who was squealing to the DA about payoffs to the cops. He was sent to the electric chair.

detective a $25,000 bonus. Another time the detectives allegedly pulled alongside a man named Eddie Lino, who had also been part of the team, and shot him to death. The two cops were not as efficient in tracking down another suspected shooter, Nick Guido. Using a police computer, Caracappa supposedly located his residence—but the Nick Guido whose address he furnished to Casso was a twenty-six-year-old telephone installer, not a mob guy. He was gunned down outside his home on Christmas Day.

Prior to his work on behalf of Casso, Eppolito had been brought up on departmental charges for leaking information to the mob. He managed to win an acquittal at an administrative hearing and in 1989 he retired. In 1992, with a professional writer, he coauthored a book, *Mafia Cop,* in which he presented himself as a deeply wronged man. Later he and Caracappa moved to Las Vegas, where Eppolito obtained bit parts playing mobsters in movies such as *Goodfellas* while Caracappa worked as a private investigator.

In 1994, after Casso began serving thirteen life sentences in a super-maximum-security federal prison in the Colorado Rockies, he told federal investigators of his payoffs to Eppolito and Caracappa. At the time, Casso's attempt to cut a deal with the prosecutors did not work out. A man with nearly forty murders to his credit was likely to be torn apart by defense lawyers. Casso himself admitted that he had once plotted a murder of the judge who was trying his case. Prosecutors privately referred to him as "Lucifer," and deemed him such a bad character that he could never be put on the witness stand.

In 2003, NYPD intelligence detective Tommy Dades received a tip about Eppolito and Caracappa's involvement in the Hydell murder. Burt Kaplan was in the sixth year of a twenty-seven-year sentence for drug dealing. When contacted by investigators, he too began to supply information. The local detectives joined forces with the Feds, and DEA agents in Nevada began surveilling Eppolito and Caracappa. In March 2005 the two were arrested for the sale of drugs to an informer. They were extradited to New York and held under house arrest.

The case was a boon to the entertainment world. According to press accounts, half a dozen books on the case were being written and some law enforcement figures had already sold their stories to Hollywood. The cops retained two of New York's most colorful lawyers. Eppolito's attorney, Bruce Cutler, had represented John Gotti in three trials, and Eddie Hayes, the lawyer for Caracappa, had served as the model for Tommy Killian, the defense attorney in *The Bonfire of the Vanities*. The trial turned out to be an anticlimax. The government prosecutors presented an overwhelming case. The judge, eighty-five-year-old Jack Weinstein, was a no-nonsense type, and in contrast to Judge Nickerson, he kept a tight rein on the proceedings. Under cross-examination, Burt Kaplan stood up very well. The detectives did not take the stand, and after brief deliberations the jury found both defendants guilty on all counts. The judge announced that he would give them life sentences. However, three months later he threw out the murder convictions, explaining that, although he believed they were guilty, the statute of limitations had expired.[3]

At the same time that the New York public was absorbing the charges against the NYPD detectives, there was a revival of old allegations against an FBI supervisor. Back in the early '90s, two FBI agents on the Bonanno/Colombo squad had complained that their superior, R. Lindley De-Vecchio, was giving confidential information to a Colombo captain named Greg Scarpa. Scarpa, known as "the Grim Reaper," was one of the Mafia's most feared killers. He so enjoyed his work that after committing a murder, he had been known to tell his accomplices how much he would like to dig up the corpse and kill the victim again. In the 1960s Scarpa had become an FBI informer. During the Colombo civil war between the Persico and Orena factions, he was the leader of the Persico loyalists. According to the two agents, Scarpa's handler, DeVecchio, provided him with information that enabled him to murder some of Orena's followers.

One of the strangest stories about Scarpa's relationship with the FBI involved the Ku Klux Klan in Mississippi. It was alleged that in 1964, after the disappearance of three civil rights workers in that state, the Bureau had sent Scarpa down to kidnap and assault a Klansman until he revealed where the boys' bodies were buried. Whatever Scarpa's relationship with the FBI, it was not able to make a case against him until 1993, when he

---

3 The government is appealing the decision, and there is also a possibility they could face state murder charges or be tried for other federal offenses.

pleaded guilty to murder as part of a RICO prosecution.[4] After two years of investigation, the Department of Justice decided there was no basis to charge DeVecchio, who then resigned from the Bureau.

In 2006, the old charges resurfaced. In March, Brooklyn district attorney Joe Hynes indicted DeVecchio for his role in the murder of four informants. The media immediately labeled it "the Mafia mole case." It was supposedly broken by a forty-year-old New Jersey woman, Angela Clemente, a self-styled "forensic intelligence analyst." Assisted by a former economics professor with a reputation as a whistleblower, she took her findings to Massachusetts congressman William Delahunt, who had been involved in the investigation of the Whitey Bulger affair. He referred them to the district attorney's office. A number of former FBI officials voiced their support for DeVecchio, and five of them personally guaranteed the one-million-dollar bail bond that secured his release pending trial.

The Gotti Junior and Mafia Cops trials and the FBI Mafia mole case could be read in different ways. One was to see them as an indication that the Mafia was no longer a threat. Though the cases were a boon to the media, bringing forth familiar names, dramatic happenings, and sensational charges, they revolved around ghosts of the past. Gotti Junior was no longer much of a force in the New York mob world, and Casso was doing life in prison. The great New York police scandals of yesteryear uncovered well-established relationships between the NYPD and organized crime, but the Mafia Cops appeared to be simply a pair of isolated rogues. DeVecchio's alleged actions took place more than a decade earlier.

Another perspective is that the cases reveal how the leadership of the Mafia had become so inept. Shooting Sliwa, a talk show host, violated its traditional rules. In the 1950s, when Johnny Dio ordered a journalist blinded, he came close to receiving a death sentence from his superiors. The fact that Gas Pipe Casso had to reach into the NYPD to obtain killers was also a departure. Old-time bosses had plenty of trustworthy gunmen in their family to do the dirty work. They did not have to use outsiders like cops who, when pressured, might talk. Both cases indicated how the mob fami-

---

4 In 1988, Scarpa contracted HIV from a blood transfusion. In 1992 he was shot in the eye during a drug dispute, and in 1994 he died at the age of sixty-six.

lies were now operating more like street gangs than sophisticated criminal syndicates.

The mob's co-capital, Chicago, had its own sensational case. In 2005, the local U.S. attorney, Pat Fitzgerald, brought a RICO case against mob members and associates, charging them with eighteen murders. Two of the deaths were familiar to a large portion of the American public, having been reenacted in the 1995 movie *Casino*. In the film, "Tony the Ant" Spilotro and his brother are beaten to death in an Indiana cornfield, but according to the indictment, they had been stomped to death in Illinois and transported to Indiana for burial.[5] Those indicted included James Marcello, reputed to be the current head of the mob, and the supposedly retired Joe Lombardo. When asked about Lombardo's previous public renunciation of mob membership, Fitzgerald told journalists, "You can take an ad out in the paper; it doesn't stop an indictment if we have sufficient evidence. Otherwise you guys would have lots of ads in about a week." While Fitzgerald is known as a tough prosecutor who will take a case as far as it can go,[6] it does not appear that the Chicago probe will lead to a significant political or judicial housecleaning along the lines of Greylord or Gambat.

At the beginning of the twenty-first century all the New York families, frozen in their forty-to-fifty-year-old names, remain in being. But there are no strong figures to lead them. The dearth of talent is so great that reporters cannot identify someone who could possibly be given the mythical title of Boss of Bosses. Indeed, it is hard to find anyone who can be considered a real boss. When John Gotti was strutting for the public eye, he looked the part. But when the federal government indicted Matty "The Horse" Ianniello in 2005, the discrepancy was striking. Ianniello was identified as head of the Genovese family, a title that had been borne by some of the royalty of the American Mafia. Yet at eighty-five years of age, Matty did not seem a likely prospect for media stardom. The story is much the same in Chicago. Back in the 1950s, when the FBI was drawing up its list of the top ten local figures, the Outfit had so many powerful sub-bosses that twenty or more of them would have been legitimate

---

5 This would jibe with the account in the 1993 news story cited in Chapter 8.
6 It was Fitzgerald's investigation of the Valerie Plame case that led to the jailing of a *New York Times* reporter and the indictment of Vice President Cheney's chief of staff.

choices. Now it would be difficult to name even one individual with the prestige of the old-timers. Once the Outfit had more than three hundred made members. Today the FBI estimates that it is down to no more than one hundred made men.

The reduced state of the Mafia in its two marquee cities, New York and Chicago, and the fact that it has been greatly weakened in previous strongholds like Philadelphia, Boston, Cleveland, and Kansas City, raises the question of how long it can continue to survive at all. Developing out of Prohibition, the American Mafia was a product of twentieth-century urban life. To a large extent, the environment that nourished it no longer exists. The traditional industrial city, with its distinctive European immigrant neighborhoods that retained old-world cultural values, and its politics dominated by a powerful local political machine, is no more. The Mafia has also lost many of its ties to business and labor, which provided not only a source of wealth, but a veneer of legitimacy.

In the final analysis, the Mafia's decline may have been due less to social and economic factors than to law enforcement pressure. Until the second half of the century, the American system of government generally left law enforcement to state and local agencies, which meant the mob families had little to fear. With their wealth and political influence, it was relatively easy to buy protection from local police and prosecutors and to fix criminal cases. But with a few exceptions, such as the infamous Prohibition Bureau, the federal government was not for sale. Post-Apalachin, its attacks on the mobs struck at the foundation of the Mafia. One example was the vaunted code of *omerta:* In the past, it was not hard for a mob member charged with a state crime to keep his mouth shut. He would know from experience that witnesses against him might be bought off or intimidated. If he did stand trial, the judge or jury might be fixed. And even if he were convicted, the decision might be reversed on appeal. Prison sentences tended to be relatively short, and there was always the possibility of an early parole or pardon.

When federal law enforcement moved against the mobs, the situation changed, and old loyalties were no longer expedient. In the federal system, threats to witnesses or attempts to bribe judges or juries often resulted in additional charges against the defendants. Convictions were much more likely, and under tough RICO-type laws, sentences could be very severe. Faced with forty years or more in prison, even traditionalist mob bosses are tempted to cut a deal. In retrospect, it was not *omerta* that kept mafiosi silent, but the fact that they had little to fear from the American criminal justice system. The federal witness protection program further undermined *omerta*. Today a mafioso who talks can be reasonably assured of safety from mob vengeance. He may even be able to strike it rich by selling his story for a book or movie.

A popular notion is that the newer ethnic groups will replace "traditional organized crime." This idea has been bruited about in the past: In the 1970s and '80s, the black and Latino drug gangs were predicted to push the Italians out. Instead, most of the minority gang leaders ended up in prison. In the late twentieth century, Latino gangs, such as the Colombian cartels, appeared to be strong candidates to emulate the rise of the American Mafia. In their own countries, the profits they earned from drugs enabled them to maintain large private armies and openly defy the government. But the Latino cartels have not attempted to become the top figures in American organized crime. Rather, they have been content to run their operations from secure offshore enclaves, leaving to others tasks such as distributing drugs in the United States.

Other experts favor Russian gangsters to succeed the Mafia.[7] In contrast to most immigrant criminals, the Russians are drawn not from the disadvantaged segments of society but from the educated middle class, with the skills to find well-paid employment. In some respects Russian organized crime bears a resemblance to southern Italian criminal groups. In both countries, large segments of the population have traditionally been hostile to the government, and many regard joining a criminal gang as an honorable choice. As the Sicilians were referred to as "the honored society," the Russian criminal bands were known as "Thieves with Honor" (*Vory z Zakore,* or Vory). In Russia, as in Italy, it was not uncommon for respectable citizens and government officials to be secret members of criminal organizations.

7 "Russian" being a term that refers to anyone from the former Soviet Union.

Following the classic pattern, Russian immigrants in the United States prey on individuals in their own community. In a few instances they have teamed up with the American Mafia. In Brooklyn, Michael Franzese, son of a Colombo underboss, was asked by Russian gasoline dealers involved in massive tax evasion to help them collect debts. Later he expanded his Russian business connections to include financial frauds. In another instance, when two Russian mob bosses got into a dispute, one arranged for Lucchese gunmen to kill his rival.

Another group heavily touted to succeed the American Mafia are the Asians. Organized crime is not a new phenomenon in America's Chinatowns. Early in the twentieth century, tongs (fraternal and merchant associations) hired Chinese criminals to attack rivals. In contemporary times, Chinese gangs such as the Ghost Shadows and the Flying Dragons have carried out extortions and murders in major Chinatowns from San Francisco to New York. Some Chinese gangsters have been willing to play ball with the Mafia. It has been reported that in Chicago, instead of asserting their independence, they have been paying street tax to the Outfit. In previous generations, Chinese were known for adhering to a code of silence and never talking to law enforcement. In the 1990s, though, a Chinese crew in New York turned government witness, an example of rapid assimilation into the dominant culture.

To date, none of the newcomers have been capable of supplanting traditional organized crime. In most instances they have been content to take over areas that the local Mafia was abandoning. Ethnic gangs have the skills and ruthlessness to become significant players in the world of American organized crime. But it will take more than determination for them to reach the top. They all face the same problem as the American Mafia: sustained assaults by federal law enforcement. Nor can they rely on tight ethnic bonds to insulate them from government penetration. Immigrants today quickly become immersed in American ways, and blood ties and traditional cultures no longer have the same hold over them. They will also find it difficult to create an infrastructure of business and labor unions similar to ones the Mafia has maintained. Sammy "The Bull" Gravano, a combination killer and businessman and one of the shrewdest of the mob leaders, has been reported to have said, "I hear the Chinese, the Russians are going to move in. Believe me, they can't put together what took us fifty, sixty, whatever years to do."

Can the Mafia return to its old form? A number of experts interviewed for this book believe it can, at least in places like New York, New Jersey, and Chicago. One scenario is that some individual mobs will maintain a low profile until the time is right for them to make a comeback. In such a posture, members would not be permitted to congregate at easily identified hangouts, and all conversations would have to be conducted as though someone were listening. Even crew chiefs would be told no more than was absolutely necessary for them to know; operations would be strictly compartmentalized so that if one crew was taken down by law enforcement it would not implicate the larger operation. It would probably also be necessary to maintain a much looser hierarchical structure, so that the key figures could not be included in RICO prosecutions. In New York there are already signs this is happening. Some families are declining to name an official boss in order to avoid providing the FBI with a clear target. Instead their affairs are conducted by an informal committee. There is also much less communication among and within the families.

Despite problems in recruiting members there are still mob wannabes even in suburbia. As one FBI official put it, some young gangsters "have not been through the wars [with law enforcement] and feel they can become big shots." The New York mobs and their New Jersey affiliates are still able to muster 700-800 made members.

Even before 9/11, the FBI was cutting back on organized crime investigations; in the wake of the attack, terrorist threats caused further reassignments. In New York City the number of agents working OC cases (including non-Mafia targets) has dropped from as many as 350 in the 1990s to an estimated 100 in 2005. The NYPD has also reduced the number of detectives working on organized crime. With fewer investigators pursuing the mobs, fewer cases are likely to be made against them.

While not as strong in such areas as construction, waste hauling, and other lucrative operations, the mobs have not been driven out of those areas completely. And they remain active in traditional fields such as gambling, drugs, and loan sharking. Early in the twenty-first century, the New York mobs were still making money the old-fashioned way—stealing it. For example, they found a means to turn the 9/11 attack on the World Trade Center into a cash cow. Within an hour of the second tower collapsing, a Lucchese associate was working the phones arranging to divvy up the contracts for cleaning debris from the sites. Unbeknownst to this associate, District Attorney Morgenthau's investigators were listening as he spoke to a Port Authority official suspected of steering jobs to the mob in return for payoffs. While the DA's investigators listened in, one mob associate explained how they would take advantage of a stricken city by submitting phony bills. As he put it, "We're going to bang the shit out of these guys on extras." Within the next few months, $63 million in contracts were obtained by companies with ties to the Lucchese, Gambino, Colombo, and DeCavalcante families.

Across the country, while the Mafia does not have the hold on unions that it once had, its grasp may not be entirely loosened everywhere. In 2004, former New Jersey prosecutor Ed Stier and a team of organized crime experts examined the relationship between the Teamsters union and organized crime. They reported that "the racketeer threat to the IBT emanating from Chicago persists largely because of the continued vitality of the Outfit." Thereupon Stier and twenty lawyers and investigators working for him resigned in protest, alleging that union president James A. Hoffa was stifling their efforts to uproot mob influence. Hoffa dismissed their allegations as "reckless and false."

Another scenario is that the Mafia will move into the financial world, essentially becoming a corrupt business cartel. In theory, possessed of considerable wealth with no scruples about bribing regulators or threatening competitors, they are more than capable of engaging in the kind of sharp dealing that even legitimate firms sometimes do. In 2000, nineteen defendants, including some from the Gambino, Genovese, and Colombo families, were charged with running a "pump and dump" operation. Under the name of State Street Capital Markets they fraudulently drove up the price of stock and then sold it to the public before the artificial price collapsed. In Operation Uptick, eleven members from all five families were included among 125 defendants charged with stock and pension fund frauds.

In the 1990s the Mafia went into Wall Street for the same reason many other Americans did—the market was booming. None of the various mob scams rose above the bucket shop operations that always existed, though the gangsters contributed their own unique style of operation. Journalist Greg Smith has described one mob financial firm—featuring a decor of fake masterpieces, gold block letters on polished oak doors, blond wood furniture and green carpeting—where some unusual events took place. One day a Colombo associate who believed that the firm owed him $40,000 stormed into the office, pulled out a .38, and shot up a computer. In another firm, when clients tried to get rid of their shares, they were threatened and mob-affiliated brokers refused to execute their sell orders. Such establishments are hardly likely to develop a steady customer base.

In an alternate financial scenario, the mobs will pull back from operating enterprises such as drug rings or business scams in favor of franchising these tasks to other groups, while they themselves concentrate on providing financing and services such as money laundering. In Chicago, some mob watchers believe that the Outfit is using business and professional associates to operate enterprises backed by Mafia money. For example, it will set up legitimate businesses run by "nominees" who may be trusted associates or relatives with no criminal records. The legitimate businesses will then pay invoices to phony firms as the means of funneling money back to the mob. It is doubtful, though, that the Mafia possesses the talents to become big players in the financial world.

The consensus of mob watchers in New York, New Jersey, and Chicago is that the American Mafia, while not what it once was, is not history. If the government ignores them they could become powerful once again, expanding into other cities and even re-creating some type of national syndicate. However, the kinds of crimes the Mafia engages in are all federal offenses and it is unlikely that the laws will be repealed. Thus the U.S. government will continue to pursue them. Even if its resources are cut back, the Feds have learned how to attack the Mafia in the most efficient ways. As long as the government has the will to attack the mobs, they will be able to control them, if not completely eradicate them.

In the first half of the twentieth century, journalist Herbert Asbury was regarded as a top expert on criminal organizations. His 1928 *Gangs of New York* is still considered a classic.[8] In it he wrote:

> there are now no gangs in New York, and no gangsters in the sense that the word has come into common use. In his day the gangster flourished under the protection and the manipulation of the crooked politician to whom he was an invaluable ally at election time, but his day has simply passed. Improved social, economic and educational conditions have lessened the number of recruits, and the organized gangs have been clubbed out of existence by the police. . . .

In one respect he was right. By 1928 the old-style gangs were beginning to fade away. What Asbury failed to anticipate was the emergence of a new, more powerful type of organized crime group. Just three years after Asbury made his pronouncement, Lucky Luciano laid the foundation for the national syndicate that I have labeled the American Mafia. Today, we may be too busy writing its obituary, or handicapping the odds on its ethnic successors, to notice the development of new and more powerful international criminal networks. It is more likely that the principal threat from organized crime in the twenty-first century will come not from the old Mafia or the new ethnic gangs, but from international groups including transnational corporations allied with state security services, which can function as semisovereign entities. As such, they will be in a position to withstand national law enforcement both in the USA and abroad.

In the 1990s a prototype of an international type of Mafia was exposed by Manhattan district attorney Robert Morgenthau. It was the Bank of Credit and Commerce International (BCCI). Sponsored by Arab sheiks, it

---

8 Though it is perhaps best regarded as a classic of literature rather than history: In some instances, Asbury not only embellished the facts but invented them.

was no penny-ante backstreet operation. At its peak it had $23 billion in assets, 14,000 employees, and 400 branches in 73 countries. In addition to drug dealers, its clients included dictators, international arms traffickers, and those with flight capital such as politicians with bribe money to conceal, and other assorted crooks and chiselers, as well as thousands of legitimate businesses and individuals. BCCI was a well-connected corporation. Its founder was close to former president Jimmy Carter. A paid adviser was former British prime minister James Callaghan. Its friends included the socialist presidents of Germany, France, Peru, and other countries, as well as individuals in the Reagan and Bush administrations.

The bank was the creation of a fifty-year-old Pakistani bank official named Agha Hasan Abedi. In 1972, when his country began to nationalize its banks, he conceived the idea of opening up a private bank in some other Muslim country. With the financial and political support of Sheik Zayed, ruler of the Persian Gulf state of Abu Dhabi, Abedi was able to achieve his ambition. Wealthy Arab businessmen and members of half a dozen ruling families of the Gulf city-states became shareholders, while Abedi recruited staff from Pakistan. It was a propitious time and place to start a new bank. The Arab oil embargo of 1973 led to the quadrupling of oil prices, and billions began flowing into the Middle East. Sheik Zayed's long-term stable deposits of funds with Abedi concealed the fact that BCCI had no real capital.

By the 1980s, BCCI appeared to be a fabulous success story. A close examination of its operations would have revealed a number of problems, but it had been cleverly set up to make such scrutiny impossible. It maintained an imposing corporate headquarters in London's financial district but was chartered in Luxembourg and the Cayman Islands, both countries known for their very loose banking regulations. Even if those country's bank regulators had wanted to monitor BCCI closely, the fact that its transactions could be moved from one supervisory jurisdiction to the other meant neither country's regulators could obtain a full picture of its operations. BCCI was a giant Ponzi scheme. It paid high returns to investors by using money from depositors that then had to be replaced by funds from new depositors. While many officials around the world were suspicious of BCCI—some referred to it as "the Bank of Crooks and Criminals"—no one of them was in a position to ferret out its secrets.

BCCI's ability to move dollars across international borders quickly and invisibly made it an ideal depository for dirty money as did its policy of accepting deposits without asking too many questions. The way the bank facilitated the relationship between Panamanian dictator Manuel Noriega and the Colombian Medellín cartel is a typical example. In return for large bribes from Medellín, Noriega allowed drug traffickers to ship American-bound cocaine through Panamanian airports and harbors, and helped launder their money through local banks including BCCI. Much of Noriega's own money was deposited in the bank's Panamanian branch.

Another BCCI customer was the world's most wanted terrorist, a Palestinian named Abu Nidal, who used the bank's Sloane Street branch in London to carry out his activities. Funds from BCCI financed a plot to blow up an airliner at Heathrow Airport. When a bank employee recognized Nidal from pictures and informed his superiors, he was told to forget about it. Working both sides of the street, BCCI also supplied helpful information to various Western intelligence agencies including another one of its clients, the CIA. And it reportedly rendered assistance to U.S. efforts to undermine the Soviet occupation of Afghanistan. The bank also maintained additional leverage by its power to withdraw a significant amount of petrodollars from Western economies.

After several unsuccessful attempts to do so, BCCI was able to open United States subsidiaries. The new entity was called "First American," and its chairman was Clark Clifford, who was also BCCI's American lawyer. He assured regulators that First American would operate independently; in practice, BCCI maintained control through a chain of holding companies. Clifford was the perfect front man for the bank. His ability to maneuver in the nation's capital brought him the title "King of the Washington Permanent Government." He served as personal attorney for John Kennedy and as secretary of defense for Lyndon Johnson. When President Carter's budget director, Bert Lance, was being investigated by the U.S. Senate in 1977 for banking irregularities in Georgia, the president prevailed upon Clifford to represent him. Though Lance was in too deep to be saved, Carter was grateful for Clifford's assistance. Tall, handsome, and white-haired, with a deep voice and a pontifical manner, Clifford fit the image of a statesman (though as James Ring Adams and Douglas Frantz, authors of a penetrating book on BCCI, have observed, "Washington's unique brand of self-importance transforms all its fixers into statesmen").

When President Carter left office, he was afforded the use of a BCCI corporate jet. After Abedi accompanied him on a trip to China in 1987, that country deposited $400 million with BCCI. Abedi, in turn, donated half a million dollars to Carter's presidential library. Though Bert Lance lost his job in Washington, he did not suffer financially. He was able to sell his shares in a Georgia bank at twice their market value and received a $3.4 million no-interest loan from BCCI without collateral or a repayment schedule. Former U.S. senators Stuart Symington of Missouri and Charles Mathias of Maryland served on the boards of BCCI's subsidiaries.

The year 1988 marked the beginning of a change in the fortunes of BCCI. Abedi had a major heart attack and could no longer personally direct operations. His right-hand man, Swaleh Naqvi, filled in for him. The bank was also experiencing money problems as a result of bad investments in the commodities market. And it was being investigated by the U.S. Senate Subcommittee on Terrorism, Narcotics and Government Operations, chaired by John Kerry of Massachusetts. In 1987 Kerry appointed a New York lawyer named Jack Blum to investigate the link between drug traffickers and foreign governments. Blum became convinced that BCCI was a gigantic criminal operation, but Kerry's attempt to interest federal officials and his Senate colleagues in a wider investigation went nowhere. According to a congressional report, more than seven hundred tips to U.S. law enforcement about BCCI criminal activities were ignored. The bank's friends were able to persuade key officials that BCCI was basically a respectable institution. Convinced that the United States government would never undertake a larger investigation, in April 1989 Blum decided to take his information outside the federal establishment, to New York County district attorney Robert Morgenthau.

The district attorney's office was already stretched thin. The investigation of an international banking fraud was basically the responsibility of the federal government. From a broader perspective, however, prosecuting BCCI offered an opportunity to strike a more significant blow at organized crime than any other case that the D.A. confronted. The drug wars were going full blast, and New York City was about to record more than two thousand murders in a single year for the first time in its history, 40 percent of them at-tributable to drugs. For all his media fame, John Gotti did not have a fraction of the money and power possessed by the combination of BCCI and the Medellín cartel. As long as organizations like BCCI existed to service them, the drug traffickers would continue to pour their product into American cities, employing the kind of ruthless violence that had become their hall-mark. The Medellín was far more dangerous to public safety than New York's five Mafia families. BCCI operated branches in New York state, so the D.A. had jurisdiction, and the prospect of a difficult and contentious investiga-tion did not deter him. As Blum would later tell interviewers, when he left Morgenthau's office he felt a sense of relief: "This isn't a guy who's going to be shut down by two or three fixers sliding in and saying [their] client didn't do anything."

The D.A. assigned the BCCI investigation to John Moscow, deputy chief of his investigation bureau. A Harvard Law graduate, Moscow could have gone on to a big firm and a big income, but he decided to prosecute crooks instead. His specialty was Wall Street frauds, which meant he was always up against top legal talent. But Moscow was not one to be intimidated. His rugged physique and aggressive manner conveyed to adversaries that they were in for a tough fight. However, Moscow did not have much to start with other than a money laundering case that customs agents in Florida had developed against BCCI employees. BCCI records and audits were pro-tected from discovery by the laws of other countries. Within the United States government, some officials were aware of a 1984 CIA report that re-vealed that BCCI owned First American. But no one had told Moscow or the U.S. Federal Reserve Bank of the report's existence, so initially he fo-cused on whether the bank had made false filings with New York regula-tors. He cast his net widely. Bert Lance was handed a subpoena by a D.A.'s investigator when he arrived in New York to participate in an academic seminar. When Moscow began seeking New York BCCI records, they would be thrown into the trash. So he also served subpoenas on managers of buildings in which the bank had locations in order to obtain access to their trash bins. As he expected, they contained some hastily discarded records.

In January 1990, the BCCI defendants pleaded guilty to the Florida in-dictments, with some of them sentenced to as much as twelve years. The

THE FUTURE OF THE OLD MAFIA ··· 299

bank itself pleaded guilty to laundering drug money and agreed to pay a $14.8 million fine. In return, the Department of Justice stipulated that the bank would not be prosecuted for further offenses. Senator Kerry denounced the settlement, demanding that BCCI be closed down.

By the summer of 1990 BCCI's financial difficulties had led to layoffs, and some of the former employees, when laid off, became willing to talk. Moscow shared the information he obtained with the Federal Reserve, which shared it with the Bank of England, which, in turn, began in 1991 to share information with Morgenthau and Moscow. In July 1991, bank regulators in a number of western countries descended on BCCI and closed down all of its branches outside the Middle East. Three weeks later, Morgenthau announced an indictment charging that the bank and its related entities had engaged in a multi-million-dollar scheme to defraud its depositors, falsified bank records to hide illegal money laundering, and committed thefts totaling more than $30 million. Abedi and Naqvi were accused of grand larceny in defrauding customers by misrepresenting the bank's ownership and financial condition. According to Morgenthau, it was the biggest bank fraud in world financial history.

A year later new indictments were voted in New York against BCCI nominees and Clifford. A federal grand jury in Washington also returned an indictment against Clifford for conspiring to defraud the Federal Reserve Board by misleading it about BCCI's relationship with First American and obstructing the Feds' inquiry. The charges against the eighty-five-year-old Clifford would later be dismissed on the grounds that he was too infirm to stand trial.[9]

While corporate crime is not the same thing as Mafia crime, as a criminal cartel BCCI sometimes emulated or even exceeded the operations of the Mafia. Jonathan Beaty and S. C. Gwynne, authors of *The Outlaw Bank*, have characterized it as "an armed sovereign state." The bank operated a Mafia-

---

9 The House Banking Committee held hearings during which Clark Clifford was required to testify. His appearance coincided with the publication of his autobiography, which recounted his career as a great statesman. But now every review of the book contained a discussion of the BCCI scandal. Before the committee, he claimed that he had never known that BCCI owned First American Bank, and that the contrary statements he had made to U.S. regulators were based on misinformation he had received. After listening to Clifford's testimony, Democratic congressman Charles Schumer of New York told him, "My heart wants to believe you. My head says no. There is just too much of a nexus between BCCI and First American to believe that the two are not inexorably linked."

like "black network" composed of intelligence operatives and squads of thugs to carry out missions, such as scaring off competitors and keeping employees in line by use of violence, including murder. While the Mafia had certain international ties and, for a time, a base in Cuba, BCCI had many secure enclaves that permitted it to conceal its operations behind national boundaries and to employ the influence of sovereign states on its behalf.

In the end, as with the American Mafia, BCCI's money and political connections were insufficient to save it from an assault by United States law enforcement. Had it been able to perform a significant service for the United States on a regular basis, it might have survived. For example, if it could have achieved a settlement of the Arab-Israeli conflict, or ensured that the West received a steady supply of oil at a reasonable price, it is quite possible that the bank would have been deemed too important to shut down.[10]

To survive over the long haul, an international Mafia must provide a product or service that the United States and other major powers need. In the last years of the nineteenth century, one man created an international organization offering something the nations of Europe valued so highly that his criminal operations were not only overlooked, but facilitated by governments. In a time when the Continent was a powder keg, he supplied them with arms. Basil Zaharoff (né Basileios Zacharias) was one of the best known men of his time. The character of Andrew Undershaft in George Bernard Shaw's *Major Barbara* was generally thought to have been modeled on him. Audiences also recognized him as Achille Weber in Robert Sherwood's *Idiot's Delight,* and he turned up regularly in Upton Sinclair's Lanny Budd novels of international intrigue. In real life, though, no one was sure who he really was, and the press usually referred to him as "the mystery man of Europe." Zaharoff's organization, and what was known as "the Zaharoff System," provide a model of how a twenty-first-century international criminal cartel could achieve power greater than that of the American Mafia.

During his life, Zaharoff claimed several different birthplaces and na-

10 In fact, in 1978 a Saudi intelligence chief who was heavily involved in BCCI was credited with persuading Egyptian president Anwar Sadat to attend the summit conference at Camp David that led to an accord between Egypt and Israel. But it was an isolated incident.

tionalities.[11] One element of his system was his ability to identify himself and his organization with diverse interests. He always insisted that his actions were motivated by the deepest patriotic feelings for his homeland, though he never provided a consistent story of where that might be. As he declared, "I was a Russian when in Russia, a Greek in Greece, a Frenchman in France." But it was in England that Zaharoff gained the most acceptance. He told English writers, "I am a Rugby boy," despite never having attended that training ground of the British upper classes.

Along with professing patriotism of many stripes, Zaharoff sought to ingratiate himself with the elites of various nations. In Paris, he maintained a lavish home, bought a newspaper, founded a bank, and cultivated the French establishment so successfully that he received the Legion of Honor. In Spain he socialized with the aristocracy and married a Spanish duchess. One of his subsidiary companies, a torpedo manufacturing concern, featured a parnership with a British cabinet minister, the wife of a German minister, a French admiral, and the daughter-in-law of former chancellor Bismarck.

In 1877 he began his career operating out of Athens, selling arms for a Swedish firm. There he perfected a key aspect of his System: playing one country against another. He sold submarines to Greece, then alerted Turkey to the danger the subs posed to their navy in case of war. He employed sophisticated propaganda to advertise his interests. He made it appear that a Greco-Turkish war was inevitable, so Turkey too had to buy submarines. Zaharoff understood that if European nations believed that war was always imminent, arms were a constant necessity.

In 1895, Zaharoff became the star salesman for the giant British firm of Vickers, which gave him entree into the heart of the British imperial establishment and permitted him to operate worldwide. Zaharoff sold everything from machine guns to battleships in a number of countries across the world. He supplied both sides in the Russo-Japanese War. His annual commissions reached fabulous sums: In 1905 he earned over eighty thousand pounds, the equivalent of ten million in today's dollars.

---

11 He was probably born around 1850 in a Greek district of Constantinople, though no one knows for sure, and he most likely obtained his education there, while working as a tout for bordellos.

A man whose business was death on a massive scale did not shrink from a little violence. In an attempted coup against the King of Greece, Zaharoff employed 160 agents to stir up riots and set fire to the royal palace. Later, a prince and two scientists who opposed him met with mysterious deaths. Even more than bloodshed, an essential ingredient of Zaharoff's system was intelligence. From his base in Paris, his "Bureau Zaharoff" established spy networks in various countries. Prior to World War I, no European nation possessed greater information than he did. His intelligence methods were vastly superior to anything employed by the Mafia or BCCI. The American mobs could occasionally obtain leaks from governmental sources, and BCCI had relationships with Arab intelligence and furnished information to the CIA. But neither was embedded in a major power's governmental establishment, as Zaharoff was. He also made it his business to acquire great technical expertise, not simply about arms but on such neglected subjects as logistics. In 1914 all the European generals expected a short war and an easy victory. Zaharoff knew differently and planned accordingly. When the British War Office failed to provide enough munitions for its expeditionary force in France, it was the civilian minister of munitions, Lloyd George, and his close confidant Basil Zaharoff who were able to make up the shortfall.

One element of Zaharoff's system would have been familiar to both the Mafia and BCCI: bribery. Lloyd George, who was frequently accused during his career of accepting large sums from various individuals, strangely went from being a critic of Zaharoff to being a strong supporter. During World War I, he even put a destroyer at Zaharoff's disposal so that he did not have to travel on passenger ships and risk being captured by the Germans.

For his services to the Empire, King George made Zaharoff a Knight of the Bath, and henceforth he was known as Sir Basil. In the postwar period, Zaharoff continued to draw criticism, but he could not be brought down. Sir Basil Thomson, Scotland Yard's director of intelligence, found evidence that British officials were acting as Zaharoff's secret agents. It was a time of red scares, and as always, Zaharoff was working both sides of the street, warning of the Bolshevik menace while establishing contacts with the Soviet government. Though Thomson was a son of the Archbishop of York and an old boy of Eton and Oxford, the Sir Basil who was dismissed by Lloyd George was the Scotland Yard chief.

A twenty-first-century Mafia organization might learn from BCCI and Zaharoff. It would of course have to possess a sophisticated financial network able to move vast sums swiftly. It would need to engage in a wide range of activities and be multinational in composition, with its entities so geographically dispersed that it could not be policed by any single country. In order to obtain protection from government regulation, it would dispense bribes and use respectable fronts to acquire political influence. To advance its interests, it would have to establish a sophisticated intelligence network and propaganda machine. Most important, it would need a mission that would make it of such great value to important interests that it would be protected from law enforcement. The twenty-first-century equivalent to weapons for national defense is security against terrorism.

Arms merchants like Zaharoff prided themselves on selling to both sides; such double-dealing permitted him to betray one of his clients to another. Today, men who supply terrorists are ideally situated to help a more favored client defend against terrorist attacks. If the people with these connections could set up their organizations along Zaharoff's lines, it is entirely possible that they might end up with wealth and honors rather than prison sentences.

There will, of course, be a place in the world of international organized crime for the more traditional type of group, as currently maintained by the American Mafia. Criminal gangs have always been useful in carrying out messy tasks, like murder and kidnapping, and in providing clandestine channels of operation. While an international Mafia organization would be able to employ mercenaries and terrorists in many parts of the world, in the United States it would need criminals already capable of operating within the domestic environment. In the twenty-first century the American Mafia, like other U.S. corporations, may become a subsidiary of an international conglomerate.

NOTES

• • •

In addition to the research, I have brought to the narrative my own personal experiences. I was born and raised in Chicago during a time when memories of the Prohibition era were fresh in most people's minds and gangsters roamed about freely. In my immediate environment, organized crime was a fact of everyday life. As an adult I spent a number of years with the Chicago Police Department, rising through the ranks to commander of detectives, an experience that provided me with considerable understanding of the mob world. During a few years' sojourn as a Harvard fellow, I managed to obtain some firsthand knowledge of organized crime in the Boston area. Later, as the long-serving head of the Citizens Crime Commission of New York City, I acquired a great deal of information about the American Mafia in the city that has always been its strongest base. In describing events in New York over the past thirty years, while I have endeavored to avoid taking sides in the bureaucratic conflicts, it would be disingenuous of me to pretend to have been a totally neutral observer. As a principal member of the State Law Enforcement Council and an adviser to the governor on an investigation of racketeering in the construction industry, I was involved in some aspects of the fight against organized crime.

INTRODUCTION: THE AMERICAN MAFIA
Allen Dorfman

On his murder see Malcolm, *New York Times*. A description of his life is contained in Brill, *The Teamsters*. In respect to both his life and death the Wagner interview was particularly helpful.

The pre-1950s Mafia

Nelli, *The Business of Crime*, and Reppetto, *American Mafia*, provide general descriptions. Peterson's books, *The Mob* and *Barbarians in Our Midst*, are detailed accounts of New York and Chicago, respectively, the two strongholds of the American Mafia.

CHAPTER 1. THE ROAD TO APALACHIN: WAR IS DECLARED ON THE AMERICAN MAFIA

The raid at Apalachin

Details of the event differ considerably. I have followed the account presented in the federal case that arose from it, United States v. Bufalino, 285 F2d. 408 (2nd Cir., 1960). See also Croswell, *New York Mirror*, Shearer, *Parade*, and Sondern, *Brotherhood of Evil*. Additional information on his father was provided by New York State Police Lt. Robert Croswell.

The American Mafia in the early 1950s

An overview is contained in U.S. Senate Special Committee to Investigate Organized Crime, *Kefauver Committee Report*. See also Kefauver, *Crime in America*.

Accounts of mob life

There is a vast literature on the subject. Among the most useful are (New York) Maas, *The Valachi Papers*, Pileggi, *Wiseguy*, Pistone, *Donnie Brasco*, and Raab, *Five Families;* (New England) Teresa and Renner, *My Life in the Mafia;* (Philadelphia) Anastasia, *Blood and Honor;* (Chicago) Brashler, *The Don;* and (West Coast and Cleveland) Demaris, *The Last Mafioso*.

CHAPTER 2. TOP HOODLUMS: THE FBI PLAYS CATCH-UP

Accounts of Hoover and the FBI

There are numerous books on the subject, most with a very definite point of view. The authorized history is Whitehead, *The FBI Story*, which ends in the mid-1950s. Critical accounts by former top FBI officials are Sullivan, *The Bureau*, and Welch, *Inside Hoover's FBI*. Leading popular works include Gentry, *J. Edgar Hoover*, Kessler, *The FBI*, and Powers, *Secrecy and Power*.

Law enforcement's efforts against organized crime during the 1950s

On the planting of "Little Al" and the Chicago FBI's efforts against the mob, Roemer's *Accardo* and *Man Against the Mob* are the colorful recollections of an FBI field agent who was at the center of events. For New York see Franceschini, *A Matter of Honor*. On the Genovese takedown see Salerno and Tompkins, *The Crime Confederation*, and Buse, *The Deadly Silence*. For an account of the Genovese role in the assassination of Tresca see Gallagher, *All the Right Enemies*. On the LAPD's arrest of Fratianno see Demaris, *The Last Mafioso*. Scholarly studies of law enforcement investigative operations are contained in Marx, *Undercover*, and Wilson, *The Investigators*.

CHAPTER 3. WHEELING AND DEALING WITH MOBSTERS: THE FRIENDS OF JIMMY HOFFA

On Jimmy Hoffa and the Teamsters

Sloane, *Hoffa*, Brill, *The Teamsters*, and Stier, *The Teamsters: Perception and Reality*.

Background of labor activities in Detroit

Liechtenstein, *The Most Dangerous Man in Detroit* (biography of Walter Reuther).

Robert F. Kennedy and the McClellan investigation

Kennedy, *The Enemy Within*, Schlesinger, *Robert Kennedy*, and Thomas, *Robert Kennedy: His Life*. See also U.S. Senate Special Committee on Improper Activities in the Labor or Management Field, *Final Report*.

CHAPTER 4. "DO SOMETHING ABOUT IT": BOBBY KENNEDY'S ATTACK ON THE MOBS

Robert Kennedy at the Department of Justice

Generally favorable accounts are contained in Goldfarb, *Perfect Villains*, Schlesinger, *Robert Kennedy*, and Sheridan, *The Fall and Rise of Jimmy Hoffa*. A critical account is Navasky, *Kennedy Justice*. Interviews: Blakey, Morgenthau, Ruth.

On Sam Giancana

Brashler, *The Don*, Roemer, *Accardo* and *Man Against the Mob*, and Chicago law enforcement sources.

Valachi's testimony

Maas, *The Valachi Papers*, *Newsweek*, "The kiss of death," *Time*, "The small of it."

The plot to assassinate Castro

See references for chapter 6.

CHAPTER 5. HAIL COLOMBO: THE MAFIA MAKES A COMEBACK
The Gallo-Profaci-Colombo wars

Bill Bonanno, *Bound by Honor,* Joseph Bonanno, *A Man of Honor,* Martin, *Revolt in the Mafia,* and Talese, *Honor Thy Father.* On the murder of Gallo: Hamill, *New York Times.*

President's Commission on Law Enforcement and Administration of Justice

See President's Commission, *Task Force Report: Organized Crime, The 1967 President's Crime Commission Report,* Cressey, *Theft of the Nation,* and Morris and Hawkins, *Honest Politician's Guide.* Interviews: Blakey, Rogovin, Ruth.

DeSapio, Marcus, and Corallo cases

Peterson, *The Mob,* Kandell, *New York Times* (DeSapio obit), Koch, *Politics.* Interview: Morgenthau.

CHAPTER 6. FROM HAVANA TO DALLAS: THE SUNBELT MAFIA AND THE KILLING OF JFK
On Trafficante

Deitche, *Cigar City Mafia,* Ragano and Raab, *Mob Lawyer.*

On Marcello

Davis, *Mafia Kingfish.*

Investigation of the assassination

There is a forest of literature on the subject. Among those that posit Mafia involvement are Blakey and Billings, *Fatal Hour,* the House Select Committee on Assassinations, *Findings and Recommendations,* and Ragano and Raab, *Mob Lawyer.* Posner, *Case Closed,* is a well-reasoned study that rejects organized crime involvement and generally supports the Warren commission findings. See also U.S. Senate Select Committee to Study Governmental Operations, *Alleged Assassination Plots Involving Foreign Leaders* (1975) and *Performance of the Intelligence Agencies* (1976), and Andrew, *For the President's Eyes Only.* Interview: Blakey.

CHAPTER 7. ACTORS ON THE SAME STAGE: ORGANIZED CRIME AND CORRUPT POLITICIANS

On Abscam

Demaris, *The Boardwalk Jungle*, Greene, *The Sting Man*, Puccio, *In the Name of the Law.* Interviews: McDonald, Welch.

Organized crime strike forces

U.S. House Committee on the Judiciary, Subcommittee on Criminal Justice, *Oversight Hearings on Organized Crime Strike Forces.*

Conditions in New Jersey

Barry, *New York Times*, Cook, *New York Times Magazine*, Grutzner, *New York Times*, Hoffman, *Tiger in the Court*, Sackett, *Life*. Interviews: Blakey, Ruth, Rogovin, Stier.

CHAPTER 8. STRAWMEN: SKIMMING VEGAS

The Vegas scene

Pileggi, *Casino*, Roemer, *The Enforcer*, Rappleye and Becker, *All-American Mafioso*, Denton and Morris, *The Money and the Power.* Interviews: Parsons, Yablonsky.

Background on Spilotro and organized crime in Chicago

Roemer, *The Enforcer*, and Chicago law enforcement sources. Interviews: Fuesel, Wagner.

CHAPTER 9. THE MOB AND THE TEAMSTERS: JIMMY'S FATE, JACKIE'S DILEMMA

On Hoffa's disappearance

Brill, *The Teamsters*, Brandt, *I Hear You Paint Houses*, Maynard, *New York Times*, Moldea, *The Hoffa Wars*, Stier, *The Teamsters*, Sloane, *Hoffa*. Interview: Esposito.

Presser and Cleveland

Griffin, *Mob Nemesis*, Neff, *Mobbed Up*, U.S. Senate Committee on Governmental Affairs, *Handling of the Jackie Presser Ghost Workers Case.*

CHAPTER 10. FROM THE FRENCH CONNECTION TO THE PIZZA CONNECTION: DRUGS, THE MAFIA, AND ITS WOULD-BE SUCCESSORS
On the Pizza Connection

Alexander, *The Pizza Connection*, Blumenthal, *The Last Days of the Sicilians*, Freeh, *My FBI*.

On minority gangs' ascension

Bell, *The End of Ideology*, Gibeaut, *ABA Journal*, Ianni, *The Black Mafia*, Kleinknecht, *The New Ethnic Mobs*.

CHAPTER 11. RICO: DECOMMISSIONING THE COMMISSION
On the state of the Mafia circa 1980s

Time, "The Mafia: big, bad and booming," U.S. Senate Permanent Subcommittee on Investigations, *Organized Crime: 25 Years After Valachi*, President's Commission on Organized Crime, *The Impact* and *The Edge*, New York State Organized Crime Task Force, *Final Report*.

On Lufthansa

Pileggi, *Wiseguy*. Interview: McDonald.

On RICO

Blakey and Perry, *Vanderbilt Law Review*. Interviews: Blakey, Goldstock.

Commission and Pizza Cases

Jacobs, *Busting the Mob*, Giuliani, *Leadership*, Freeh, *My FBI*, Bonavolonta, *The Good Guys*.

CHAPTER 12. THE DEFECTOR AND THE DON: TAKING DOWN JOHN GOTTI
On Gotti and the Gambinos

Capeci and Mustain, *Gotti: Rise and Fall*, Davis, *Mafia Dynasty*, Cummings and Volkman, *Goombata*.

Cases v. Gotti

Blum, *Gangland*, Maas, *Underboss*, Dannen, *Vanity Fair*, Weiser, *New York Times* (Fox obit). Interviews: Goldstock, Mack, Maloney, Morgenthau, Nicastro, Pritchard.

CHAPTER 13. DEALING WITH THE DEVIL: THE HUNT FOR "WHITEY"
Accounts of organized crime in Boston generally

O'Neill and Lehr, *The Underboss*, Teresa and Renner, *My Life in the Mafia*, local law enforcement sources.

The Bulger case

Carr, *The Brothers Bulger*, Lehr and O'Neill, *Black Mass*, Weeks, *The Untold Story of My Life Inside Whitey Bulger's Irish Mob*, U.S. House Committee on Government Reform, *Everything Secret Degenerates*. Interviews: Wyshak, Herron.

CHAPTER 14. STINGING THE MOBS: DIGGING OUT THE MAFIA ROOT
   AND BRANCH
Cases against the mob:

Chicago

Tuohy and Warden, *Greylord*, Cooley, *When Corruption Was King* (Gambat), Possley and Kogan, *Everybody Pays* (Aleman), Kurson, *Esquire*. Interviews: Fuesel, Wagner.

New York

Buetner, *Daily News*, Cowan and Century, *Takedown*, Jacobs, *Gotham Unbound*, Lubasch (Pitera case), *New York Times*, Raab, *Five Families*, Raab, *New York Times* (Gigante obit), Volkman, *Gangbusters*, local law enforcement sources. Interviews: Herron, Hunt, O'Connell, O'Neill.

New Jersey

Smith, *Made Men*. Interview: Stier.

Philadelphia

Anastasia, *Blood and Honor*, Friel and Gunther, *Breaking the Mob*, Fresolone and Wagman, *Blood Oath*. Interview: Coughlin.

CHAPTER 15: THE FUTURE OF THE OLD MAFIA: THE EMERGENCE OF
   THE NEW
On the Mafia cops

Breslin, *Playboy*, Eppolito and Drury, *Mafia Cop*, Feuer, "Judge acquits 2 ex-detectives," *New York Times*, and "You can't tell the players," *New York Times*, Marzulli, *Daily News*.

FBI mole

Dannen, *New Yorker,* Katz, *Daily News,* Ramirez, *New York Times,* Rashbaum, *New York Times,* Sherman, *Daily News,* Villano, *Brick Agent.*

On Gotti Junior cases

Goldberg, *New York Times Magazine,* Haberman, *New York Times,* Hartocollis, *New York Times.*

Chicago takedown

O'Connor and Lightly, *Chicago Tribune.*

Mob successors

Abadinsky, *Organized Crime,* Kerry, *The New War,* Kleinknecht, *The New Ethnic Mobs.*

Current state and future of the mobs

Finckenauer, "La Cosa Nostra in the United States," Hampson, *USA Today.* Interviews: Blakey, Castleman, Cunningham, Easley, Fuesel, Goldstock, Goyeneche, Herron, McDonald, O'Neill, Stier, Wagner.

On BCCI

Adams and Frantz, *A Full-Service Bank,* Beaty and Gwynne, *The Outlaw Bank,* Truell and Gurwin, *False Profits.* U.S. Senate Committee on Foreign Relations, report of Senator John Kerry et al., Interview: Moscow.

On Zaharoff

McCormick, *Peddler of Death,* Sampson, *The Arms Bazaar.*

BIBLIOGRAPHY

* * *

Abadinsky, Howard. *Organized Crime,* 7th ed. Belmont, Calif.: Wadsworth, 2003.

Adams, James Ring, and Douglas Frantz, *A Full-Service Bank: How BCCI Stole Billions Around the World.* New York: Pocket Books, 1992.

Alexander, Shana. *The Pizza Connection: The Lawyers, Money, Drugs, Mafia.* New York: Weidenfeld and Nicolson, 1988.

Anastasia, George. *Blood and Honor: Inside the Scarfo Mob—The Mafia's Most Violent Family.* New York: William Morrow, 1991.

Andrew, Christopher. *For the President's Eyes Only: Secret Intelligence and the American Presidency from Washington to Bush.* New York: HarperCollins, 1995.

Barry, Dan. "From Bergen to Camden, corruption is more than a memory." *New York Times* (March 25, 2001), pp. 1, 25.

Beaty, Jonathan, and S.C. Gwynne. *The Outlaw Bank: A Wild Ride into the Secret Heart of BCCI.* New York: Random House, 1993.

Bell, Daniel. *The End of Ideology.* Cambridge, Mass: Harvard University Press, 1988 (original 1962).

Blakey, G. Robert, and Richard N. Billings. *Fatal Hour: The Assassination of President Kennedy by Organized Crime.* New York: Berkley Books, 1992.

Blakey, G. Robert, and Thomas Perry. "An analysis of the myths that bolster efforts to rewrite RICO and the various proposals for reform: 'Mother of God— is this the end of RICO?' " *Vanderbilt Law Review* (April 1990), pp. 982–87.

Blum, Howard. *Gangland: How the FBI Broke the Mob.* New York: Pocket Books, 1993.

Blumenthal, Ralph. *The Last Days of the Sicilians: At War with the Mafia: The FBI Assault on the Pizza Connection*. New York: Times Books, 1988.

Bonanno, Bill. *Bound by Honor: A Mafioso's Story*. New York: St. Martin's Press, 1999.

Bonanno, Joseph. *A Man of Honor: The Autobiography of Joseph Bonanno*. New York: Simon & Schuster, 1983.

Bonavolonta, Jules, and Brian Duffy. *The Good Guys: How We Turned the FBI 'Round—and Finally Broke the Mob*. New York: Simon & Schuster, 1996.

Brandt, Charles. *I Hear You Paint Houses: Frank "The Irishman" Sheerin and the Inside Story of the Mafia, The Teamsters and the Last Ride of Jimmy Hoffa*. Hanover, N.H.: Steerforth Press, 2004.

Brashler, William. *The Don: The Life and Death of Sam Giancana*. New York: Harper & Row, 1977.

Breslin, Jimmy. "The end of the mob." *Playboy* (August 2005), pp. 67–68, 140–44.

Brill, Steven. *The Teamsters*. New York: Simon & Schuster, 1978.

Buetner, Russ, et al. "Towers fell and the mob scheme began: How organized crime delivered up ground zero work." *Daily News* (December 5, 2005), pp. 6–7, 22–25.

Buse, René. *The Deadly Silence*. Garden City, New York: Doubleday, 1965.

Capeci, Jerry, and Gene Mustain. *Gotti: Rise and Fall*. New York: Onyx, 1996.

Carr, Howie. *The Brothers Bulger: How They Terrorized and Corrupted Boston for a Quarter Century*. New York: Warner Books, 2006.

Chicago Crime Commission. *Organized Crime in Chicago: 1990*. Chicago: CCC, 1990.

Cook, Fred J. *The Secret Rulers: Criminal Syndicates and How They Control the U.S. Underworld*. New York: Duell, Sloan & Pearce, 1966.

———. "The people versus the mob; or who rules New Jersey." *New York Times Magazine* (February 1, 1970).

Cooley, Robert, with Hillel Levin. *When Corruption Was King: How I Helped the Mob Rule Chicago, Then Brought the Outfit Down*. New York: Carroll and Graf, 2004.

Cowan, Rick, and Douglas Century. *Takedown: The Fall of the Last Mafia Empire*. New York City: Putnam's, 2002.

Cressey, Donald A. *Theft of the Nation: The Structure and Operations of Organized Crime*. New York: Harper & Row, 1969.

Croswell, Edgar. "Trooper's own story." *New York Mirror* (November 24, 1957), p. 3.

Cummings, John, and Ernest Volkman. *Goombata: The Improbable Rise and Fall of John Gotti*. New York: Avon Books, 1992.

Dannen, Frederic. "The G-Man and the hit man." *New Yorker* (December 16, 1996), pp. 68–81.

———. "The Untouchables? How the FBI sabotaged competing prosecution teams in the race to nail alleged mob king John Gotti." *Vanity Fair* (January 1992), pp. 27–44.

Davis, John H. *Mafia Dynasty: The Rise and Fall of the Gambino Crime Family.* New York: HarperCollins, 1993.

———. *Mafia Kingfish: Carlos Marcello and the Assassination of John F. Kennedy.* New York: McGraw-Hill, 1989.

Deitche, Scott M. *Cigar City Mafia: A Complete History of the Tampa Underworld.* Fort Lee, N.J.: Barricade Books, 2004.

Demaris, Ovid. *The Boardwalk Jungle.* New York: Bantam Books, 1986.

———. *The Last Mafioso: The Treacherous World of Jimmy Fratianno.* New York: Bantam Books, 1981.

Denton, Sally, and Roger Morris. *The Money and the Power: The Making of Las Vegas and Its Hold on America, 1947 to 2000.* New York: Alfred A. Knopf, 2001.

Eppolito, Lou, and Bob Drury. *Mafia Cop: The Story of an Honest Cop Whose Family Was the Mob.* New York: Pocket Books, 1992.

Feuer, Alan. "Judge acquits 2 ex-detectives in mob killings." *New York Times* (July 1, 2006), pp. A-1, B-1.

———. "You can't tell the players without a bookmark: Mafia-Police case inspires many authors." *New York Times* (March 11, 2006), p. B-6.

Finckenauer, James O. "La Cosa Nostra in the United States." National Institute of Justice. Available at www.ojp.usdoj.gov/nij/international/lcn.html.

Fox, Stephen. *Blood and Power: Organized Crime in Twentieth-Century America.* New York: William Morrow, 1989.

Franceschini, Remo. *A Matter of Honor: One Cop's Lifetime Pursuit of John Gotti and the Mob.* New York: Simon & Schuster, 1997.

Franzese, Michael, and Dary Matera. *Quitting the Mob.* New York: Harper Paperbacks, 1992.

Freeh, Louis J. *My FBI: Bringing Down the Mafia, Investigating Bill Clinton and Fighting the War on Terror.* New York: St. Martin's Press, 2005.

Fresolone, George, and Robert Wagman. *Blood Oath: The Heroic Story of a Gangster Turned Government Agent Who Brought Down One of America's Most Powerful Mob Families.* New York: Simon & Schuster, 1994.

Friel, Frank, and John Gunther. *Breaking the Mob.* New York: Warner Books, 1990.

Gage, Nicholas, ed. *Mafia, U.S.A.* New York: Dell, 1972.

Gallagher, Dorothy. *All the Right Enemies: The Life and Murder of Carlo Tresca.* New York: Penguin Books, 1988.

Gentry, Curt. *J. Edgar Hoover: The Man and His Secrets.* New York: W.W. Norton, 1991.

Gibeaut, John. "Gangbusters." *ABA Journal* (January 1998), pp. 64–67.

Giuliani, Rudolph, with Ken Kurson. *Leadership.* New York: Hyperion, 2002.

Goldberg, Jeffrey. "The Don is done." *New York Times Magazine* (January 31, 1999), pp. 24–31, 62–66, 71.

Goldfarb, Ronald. *Perfect Villains, Imperfect Heroes: Robert F. Kennedy's War Against Organized Crime.* New York: Random House, 1995.

Greene, Robert W. *The Sting Man: Inside Abscam.* New York: EP Dutton, 1981.

Griffin, Joe, with Don Denovi. *Mob Nemesis: How the FBI Crippled Organized Crime.* Amherst, NY: Prometheus Books, 2002.

Grutzner, Charles. "Addonizio, Boiardo and 12 enter pleas of not guilty." *New York Times* (December 20, 1969), p. 1.

Haberman, Clyde. "This Column, by the Way, Is a Second Draft," *New York Times,* March 17, 2006, p. 1.

Hamill, Pete. "Bright lives, big city," *New York Times* (January 2, 2005), section 4, p. 9.

Hampson, Rick. "Death of the mob, once grand criminal society a shadow of its storied past." *USA Today* (July 28, 1999) p. 1A.

Hartocollis, Anemona. "A second mistrial for Gotti as the jury deadlocks." *New York Times* (March 11, 2006), pp. A-1, B-6.

Hoffman, Dave. *Tiger in the Court.* Chicago: Playboy Press, 1973.

Ianni, Francis A.J. *The Black Mafia: Ethnic Succession in Organized Crime.* New York: Simon & Schuster, 1974.

Jacobs, James B. *Mobsters, Unions and Feds: The Mafia and the American Labor Movement.* New York: New York University Press, 2006.

Jacobs, James B., with Coleen Friel and Robert Radick. *Gotham Unbound: How New York City Was Liberated from the Grip of Organized Crime.* New York: New York University Press, 1999.

Jacobs, James B., with Christopher Panarella and Jay Worthington. *Busting the Mob: United States v. Cosa Nostra.* New York: New York University Press, 1994.

Kandell, Jonathan. "Carmine DeSapio, political kingmaker and last Tammany boss, dies at 95." *New York Times* (July 28, 2004), p. C-12.

Katz, Nancy L. "Their probe of G-man pays off big." *Daily News* (April 2, 2006), p. 6.

Kefauver, Estes. *Crime in America.* Garden City, N.Y.: Doubleday, 1951.

Kennedy, Robert F. *The Enemy Within.* Harper Brothers, 1960.

Kerry, John. *The New War: The Web of Crimes That Threatens American Security.* New York: Simon & Schuster, 1997.

Kessler, Ronald. *The FBI.* New York: Pocket Books, 1993.

Kleinknecht, William. *The New Ethnic Mobs: The Changing Face of Organized Crime in America.* New York: Free Press, 1996.

Koch, Edward I., with William Rauch. *Politics.* New York: Simon & Schuster, 1985.

Kurson, Robert. "The Chicago crime commission." *Esquire* (July 2001), pp. 107–13, 134–35.

Lacey, Robert. *Little Man: Meyer Lansky and the Gangster Life.* Boston: Little, Brown, 1991.

Lait, Jack, with Lee Mortimer. *Chicago Confidential.* New York: Crown, 1950.

Lardner, James, and Thomas Reppetto. *NYPD: A City and Its Police.* New York: Henry Holt, 2000.

Lehr, Dick, and Gerard O'Neill. *Black Mass: The True Story of the Unholy Alliance Between the FBI and the Irish Mob.* New York: HarperCollins, 2000.

Liechtenstein, Nelson. *The Most Dangerous Man in Detroit: Walter Reuther and the Fate of American Labor.* New York: Basic Books, 1995.

Lubasch, Arnold H. "Federal Jurors Considering Death Penalty for Mobsters." *New York Times,* July 2, 1992, p. B3.

Maas, Peter. *Underboss: Sammy the Bull Gravano's Story of Life in the Mafia.* New York: HarperCollins, 1997.

———. *The Valachi Papers.* New York: Putnam's, 1968.

Malcolm, Andrew H. "Dorfman, Teamster adviser, slain; faced a long term in bribery case." *New York Times* (January 21, 1983), pp. A-1, D-15.

Martin, Raymond. *Revolt in the Mafia.* New York: Duell, Sloan & Pearce, 1963.

Marx, Gary T. *Undercover: Police Surveillance in America.* Berkeley: University of California Press, 1988.

Marzulli, John. "Unsung mob cop heroes." *Daily News* (April 2, 2006), p. 10.

Maynard, Micheline. "FBI calls off its latest search for Hoffa." *New York Times* (May 31, 2006), p. A-14.

McCormick, Donald. *Peddler of Death: The Life and Times of Sir Basil Zaharoff.* New York: Holt Rinehart and Winston, 1965.

Moldea, Dan E. *The Hoffa Wars.* New York: Charter Books, 1978.

Morris, Norval, and Gordon Hawkins. *The Honest Politician's Guide to Crime Control.* Chicago: University of Chicago Press, 1970.

Navasky, Victor S. *Kennedy Justice.* New York: Atheneum, 1977.

Neff, James. *Mobbed Up: Jackie Presser's High Wire Life in the Teamsters, the Mafia, and the FBI.* New York: Atlantic Monthly Press, 1989.

Nelli, Humbert. *The Business of Crime: Italians and Syndicate Crime in the United States.* New York: Oxford University Press, 1976.

Newsweek. "The kiss of death" (October 7, 1963), pp. 34, 39.

New York State Organized Crime Task Force. *Corruption and Racketeering in the New York City Construction Industry: Final Report.* 1989.

O'Connor, Matt, and Todd Lightly. "U.S. drops hammer on Who's Who of mob." *Chicago Tribune* (April 26, 2005), p. 1.

O'Neill, Gerard, and Dick Lehr. *The Underboss: The Rise and Fall of a Mafia Family.* New York: St. Martin's Press, 1989.

Peterson, Virgil. *Barbarians in Our Midst: A History of Chicago Crime and Politics.* Boston: Little, Brown, 1952.

———. *The Mob: 200 Years of Organized Crime in New York.* Ottawa, Ill.: Green Hill Publishers, 1983.

Pileggi, Nicholas. *Casino.* New York: Pocket Books, 1995.

———. *Wiseguy: Life in a Mafia Family.* New York: Pocket Books, 1990.

Pistone, Joseph D. *Donnie Brasco: My Undercover Life in the Mafia.* New York: New American Library, 1987.

Posner, Gerald. *Case Closed: Lee Harvey Oswald and the Assassination of JFK.* New York: Random House, 1993.

Possley, Maurice, and Rick Kogan. *Everybody Pays: Two Men, One Murder, and the Price of Truth.* New York: Putnam, 2001.

Powers, Richard Gid. *Secrecy and Power: The Life of J. Edgar Hoover.* New York: Free Press, 1987.

President's Commission on Law Enforcement and Administration of Justice. *The Challenge of Crime in a Free Society.* Washington, D.C.: GPO, 1967.

———. *Task Force Report: Organized Crime.* Washington, D.C.: GPO, 1967.

President's Commission on Organized Crime. *The Impact: Organized Crime Today.* Washington, D.C.: GPO, 1986.

———. *The Edge: Organized Crime, Business and Labor Unions.* Washington, D.C.: GPO, 1986.

The 1967 President's Crime Commission Report: Its Impact 25 Years Later. Ed. John A. Conley. Cincinnati, Ohio: Anderson Publishing, 1994.

Puccio, Thomas, with Dan Collins. *In the Name of the Law: Confessions of a Trial Lawyer.* New York: W.W. Norton, 1995.

Raab, Selwyn. "Vincent Gigante, mob boss who feigned insanity to avoid jail, dies at 77." *New York Times* (December 20, 2005), p. A-29.

———. *Five Families: The Rise, Decline and Resurgence of America's Most Powerful Mafia Empire.* New York: St. Martin's Press, 2005.

Ragano, Frank, and Selwyn Raab. *Mob Lawyer.* New York: Scribner's, 1994.

Ramirez, Anthony. "Retired FBI agent accused of helping in Mafia murders." *New York Times* (March 26, 2006), p. 32.

Rappleye, Charles, and Ed Becker. *All-American Mafioso: The Johnny Roselli Story.* New York: Doubleday, 1991.

Rashbaum, William K. "FBI colleagues help Ex-Agent post bail." *New York Times* (March 31, 2006), pp. B1–B6.

Reppetto, Thomas. *American Mafia: A History of Its Rise to Power.* New York: Henry Holt, 2004.

Roemer, William F., Jr. *Accardo: The Genuine Godfather.* New York: Donald I. Fine, 1995.

———. *The Enforcer, Spilotro: The Chicago Mob's Man over Las Vegas.* New York: Ivy Books, 1994.

———. *Man Against the Mob.* New York: Donald I. Fine, 1989.

Rudolph, Robert. *The Boys from New Jersey.* New York: William Morrow, 1992.

Russo, Gus. *The Outfit: The Role of Chicago's Underworld in the Shaping of Modern America.* New York: Bloomsbury, 2001.

Sackett, Russell, et al. "The Congressman and the hoodlum." *Life* (August 9, 1968).

Salerno, Ralph, and John S. Tompkins. *The Crime Confederation.* Garden City, N.Y.: Doubleday, 1969.

Sampson, Anthony. *The Arms Bazaar: From Lebanon to Lockheed.* New York: Viking Press, 1977.

Schlesinger, Arthur M., Jr. *Robert Kennedy and His Times.* Boston: Houghton Mifflin, 1978.

Shearer, Lloyd. "How a country cop crippled the Mafia." *Parade* (June 14, 1959), pp. 3–13.

Sheridan, Walter. *The Fall and Rise of Jimmy Hoffa.* New York: Saturday Review Press, 1972.

Sherman, William. "Mob G-man has A-List of pals, FBI Bigs backed him against slay raps." *Daily News* (March 28, 2006), p. 8.

Sloane, Arthur D. *Hoffa.* Cambridge, Mass.: MIT Press, 1991.

Smith, Greg B. *Made Men: The True Rise-and-Fall Story of a New Jersey Mob Family.* New York: Berkley Books, 2003.

Sondern, Frederick, Jr. *Brotherhood of Evil: The Mafia.* New York: Farrar, Straus and Cudahy, 1959.

Stier, Anderson & Malone, LLC. *The Teamsters: Perception and Reality. An Investigative Study of Organized Crime Influence in the Union.* Prepared for the International Brotherhood of Teamsters, 2002.

Sullivan, William C., with Bill Brown. *The Bureau: My Thirty Years in Hoover's FBI.* New York: W.W. Norton, 1984.

Talese, Gay. *Honor Thy Father.* New York: World Publishing, 1971.

Teresa, Vincent, and Thomas C. Renner. *My Life in the Mafia.* Greenwich, Conn.: Fawcett, 1973.

Thomas, Evan. *Robert Kennedy: His Life.* New York: Simon and Schuster, 2000.

Time. "The Mafia: big bad and booming." (Cover story, May 16, 1977).

Time. "The small of it." (October 11, 1963) p. 28.

Truell, Peter, and Larry Gurwin. *False Profits: The Inside Story of BCCI, the World's Most Corrupt Financial Empire.* New York: Houghton Mifflin, 1992.

Tuohy, James, and Rob Warden. *Greylord: Justice Chicago Style.* New York: G.P. Putnam's Sons, 1989.

U.S. House Committee on Government Reform. *Third Report: Everything Secret Degenerates: The FBI's Use of Murderers as Informants.* Washington, D.C.: GPO, 2004.

U.S. House Committee on the Judiciary, Subcommittee on Criminal Justice. *Oversight Hearings on Organized Crime Strike Forces.* June 29, 1989. Washington, D.C.: GPO, 1989.

U.S. House Select Committee on Assassinations. *Findings and Recommendations.* Washington, D.C.: GPO, 1979.

U.S. Senate Committee on Governmental Affairs, Permanent Subcommittee on Investigations. *The Department of Justice's Handling of the Jackie Presser Ghost Workers Case.* Washington, D.C.: GPO, May 9, 1986.

U.S. Senate Permanent Subcommittee on Investigations of the Committee on Governmental Affairs. *Organized Crime: 25 Years After Valachi.* Washington, D.C.: GPO, 1988.

U.S. Senate Select Committee to Study Governmental Operations with Respect to Intelligence Activities. *Alleged Assassination Plots Involving Foreign Leaders.* Washington, D.C.: GPO, 1975.

————. *The Investigation of the Assassination of President Kennedy: Performance of the Intelligence Agencies.* Washington, D.C.: GPO, 1976.

U.S. Senate Committee on Foreign Relations. Report of Senator John Kerry et al., December 1982.

U.S. Senate Special Committee on Improper Activities in the Labor or Management Field. *Final Report.* Washington, D.C.: GPO, 1960.

U.S. Senate Special Committee to Investigate Organized Crime in Interstate Commerce. *The Kefauver Committee Report on Organized Crime.* New York: Didier, 1951.

Villano, Anthony. *Brick Agent.* New York: Ballantine, 1978.

Volkman, Ernest. *Gangbusters: The Destruction of America's Last Mafia Dynasty.* Boston: Farber & Farber, 1998.

Von Hoffman, Nicholas. *Citizen Cohn: The Life and Times of Roy Cohn.* New York: Doubleday, 1988.

Weeks, Kevin, and Phyllis Karas. *The Untold Story of My Life Inside Whitey Bulger's Irish Mob.* New York: Regan Books, 2006.

Weiser, Benjamin. "James M. Fox 59 is dead, led the FBI in bomb case." *New York Times* (May 17, 1997), p. 1.

Welch, Neil J., with David W. Marston. *Inside Hoover's FBI: The Top Field Chief Reports.* Garden City, N.Y.: Doubleday & Co., 1984.

Whitehead, Don. *The FBI Story.* New York: Random House, 1956.

Wilson, James Q. *The Investigators: Managing FBI and Narcotics Agents.* New York: Basic Books, 1978.

ACKNOWLEDGMENTS

Throughout the preparation of the present work, I have benefited greatly from the counsel of my editor at Henry Holt, Jack Macrae, and his assistant, Supurna Banerjee. In addition, I received considerable editorial advice from Katy Hope. I would also like to express thanks to my agent, Andrew Wylie, and his assistants, Sarah Chalfant and Ed Orloff.

During the course of the research, many people generously consented to be interviewed or assisted me in other ways. I would particularly like to acknowledge John Appeldorn, Jeanette Callaway, Dan Castleman, Walter Coughlin, Robert Croswell, Charles Cunningham, Richard Easley, James Esposito, Robert Fuesel, Rafael Goyeneche, Matthew Herron, James Hunt, John Jemilo, Walter Mack, Andrew Maloney, Edward McDonald, Mark Mershon, Celeste Morello, Robert Morgenthau, John Moscow, Richard Nicastro, Gregory O'Connell, Brian O'Neill, Charles Parsons, John Pritchard, Charles Rogovin, Henry Ruth, Edwin Stier, James Wagner, Neil Welch, Fred Wyshak, and Joseph Yablonsky.

Two people who provided inestimable assistance by sharing their voluminous knowledge of organized crime and law enforcement were the "inventor" of the RICO law, G. Robert Blakey, professor at Notre Dame Law School, and Ronald Goldstock, former director of the New York State Organized Crime Task Force.

I am also grateful to a number of people who helped me but for various reasons do not wish to be acknowledged. Over the years, individuals no longer alive have also shared information and insights that have proved invaluable in the writing of the present work. To list them would require several pages and still be incomplete. However, I would like to record a debt of gratitude to the late Jim Fox, who, over six critical years, headed the New York FBI office.

During my research, I drew upon the services of several research organizations including the Crime Commissions of Chicago, Kansas City, New Orleans, and Philadelphia. I would also like to thank the staffs of the Lloyd G. Sealey Library at the John Jay College of Criminal Justice in New York City, the New York Public Library, and the Westchester County library system.

INDEX

ABOUT THE AUTHOR

THOMAS REPPETTO is a former Chicago commander of detectives and was president of New York City's Citizens Crime Commission for more than twenty years. He is the author of *NYPD: A City and Its Police,* a New York Times Notable Book, and of *American Mafia: A History of Its Rise to Power.* He lives in Westchester, New York.